Joint Ventures of Labor and Capital

Joint Ventures of Labor and Capital

Lester G. Telser

Ann Arbor
THE UNIVERSITY OF MICHIGAN PRESS

658.04
T27j

A CIP catalog record for this book is available from the British Library.

Library of Congress Cataloging-in-Publication Data

Telser, Lester G., 1931–
    Joint ventures of labor and capital / Lester G. Telser.
        p.   cm.
    Includes bibliographical references and index.
    ISBN 0-472-10866-2 (alk. paper)
    1. Joint ventures.   I. Title.
    HD62.47.T45   1997
    658'.044—dc21   97-41423
    JK   CIP

Contents

Preface

This book focuses on how competition among coalitions for members explains which profit-seeking joint ventures of labor and capital form and can survive. The nature, direction, and control of investments by joint ventures, the division of labor, and the determinants of wages are among the main topics. Core theory is the principal tool for studying them. It is used to explain under what conditions a corporation is a stable entity. It can also describe in terms of the nature and diversity of the projects the types of investors in these projects consistent with stable joint ventures. Core theory can answer several important questions about wages that are often ignored and much harder to answer without it. Among these are the relation between ability and wages as well as the relation between the size of a venture and the wage formula conducive to its stability.

The introduction provides a general description of the usefulness of core theory in economics in elementary terms. The first chapter uses core theory to study pure exchange, a situation in which there is trading but no production. The problem is to see when a competitive market has a core. This theory is applied to the market for shares of stock in chapters 2 and 3. Chapter 2 offers a theory of joint ventures using core theory. It describes the conditions for stability of these ventures in terms of the specialization of projects and the heterogeneity of the investors. These have implications about the holders of mutual funds as well as the owners of corporations. The internal stability of joint ventures is the subject of chapters 4 and 5. Chapter 4 describes when self-enforcing agreements can induce loyalty from the participants in a joint venture. Chapter 5 describes how superiors can remunerate their subordinates in order to bring about a harmony between their own interests and the self-interest of their subordinates. Chapter 6 applies core theory to determine wages. The last chapter analyzes the special problems of multiproduct firms. It finds optimal coalitions between the firms and their customers that can resolve empty core problems. Such optimal coalitions can explain some puzzling practices of the old motion picture industry. The key is how motion picture producers used these practices to cope with risk and uncertainty.

With the help of simple numerical examples the introduction shows how core theory is useful in economics and especially in industrial organization. It presents the elements of core theory and describes many economic applications. Unrestricted contracting among individuals who are free to band together in groups lies at the heart of the competitive process. Depending on the particular application this theory can say what conditions are conducive to efficient outcomes. Sometimes, however, unrestricted freedom of contracting does not lead to efficient outcomes. When this happens the core is empty. Many of the most important challenges to core theory arise from empty cores. People facing empty cores try to devise suitable restrictions and rules in order to obtain efficient outcomes. Efficiency is when it is not possible for anyone to become better off without making somebody else worse off. Inefficiency entails deadweight losses. This means it would be possible to make somebody better off without making anybody else worse off. Core theory assumes that people arrange their affairs to avoid deadweight losses. These themes occur repeatedly in the various applications of core theory to joint ventures in this book.

Chapter 1 presents an application of core theory to pure exchange. Pure exchange is a situation in which traders exchange their initial holdings of things for what they prefer. There is no production in models of pure exchange. The first section describes a market with a finite number of traders, each with a concave valuation function of commodities. It gives two sufficient conditions for a nonempty core: first, the valuation functions of the traders are nondecreasing, and, second, the final allocations are strictly positive for all traders. The next section studies markets with infinitesimally small traders. This means individual traders have a negligibly small effect on the outcome. It shows that such markets have a core if the budget constraint for each trader is satisfied with equality. Consequently, under very general conditions a Walrasian equilibrium belongs to the core. A Walrasian equilibrium is what economic theory means by a competitive equilibrium. A Walrasian equilibrium has prices that can guide traders to the best final allocation of their initial resources. The third section offers various numerical examples that illustrate the uses and limits of the models. One of these is especially pertinent because it describes a market with a core but without a Walrasian equilibrium. This means there are cases in which a competitive equilibrium in the sense of a nonempty core can exist but cannot be attained using prices of a Walrasian equilibrium. The more general kind of competition in the sense of core theory describes terms of trade that can attain the best allocation of resources without prices to guide the traders. The last section explains why money is the yardstick. It derives the properties of a commodity that enable it to become the most widely used medium of exchange.

Chapter 2 begins with a discussion of a theory of joint ventures. A joint venture is a coalition of investors at an early stage in the life of a corporation before its shares can be traded on an organized public stock market. These early investors determine the size and direction of the projects of the joint venture. Coalitions of investors compete for new members, a process that determines the cost of membership in a coalition. The theory implies that limited liability is necessary for a stable joint venture. Limited liability means that an investor cannot lose more than his initial stake in the joint venture. He is not liable for the debts of the joint venture. This differs from a partnership that requires all partners to be liable for its debts. The assets of a corporation are semiprivate. A semiprivate good is in contrast to a private good—an individual acting on his own can decide how much of a private good he wants. A semiprivate good is owned jointly by all the members of the coalition, who must agree on how much of it to have. For instance, a blast furnace is a semiprivate good to a corporation because all the owners (or their representatives), who may each own a different fraction of the total assets of the corporation, must agree on the total investment in blast furnaces. The return to an investor depends on his share of the total equity in the corporation. Usually, economists speak of a firm run by an entrepreneur. This ignores the nature of the organization that obtains the funds for carrying on its activities. In the conventional story corporations enter the scene only as a source of the different kinds of financial assets that are traded in the financial markets. These markets are divorced from the markets for actual goods and services. By using core theory and treating the investor as the basic entity, we can ask and answer questions about who owns corporations and mutual funds. For example, core theory solves puzzles about takeover bids out of reach of the standard theories.

In the second stage of its life, the shares of a joint venture can be traded publicly. The theory of pure exchange in chapter 1 applies to the market for shares of stock. When the corporation goes public, its original owners may sell their shares to anyone they please at mutually agreed-upon prices on an organized public stock market such as the New York Stock Exchange. Owing to limited liability, the owners of a corporation can sell their shares without the consent of the other owners. This is not true in a partnership. A partner cannot sell his share to an outsider without the consent of the other partners. A corporation is not like a private club. Private clubs usually do not allow members to sell their memberships to nonmembers without the approval of the present members.

A central feature of the theory is its emphasis on uncertainty. It treats the return to a joint venture as a random draw from a probability distribution. The size of the capital stock is a parameter of the probability distribution. Potential investors may differ in their views about the probability distribution, and their willingness to put funds at the disposal of the joint venture depends on these opinions.

The last section of this chapter describes empirical studies of investors' holdings. These include some material on the concentration of ownership in publicly traded corporations. This section also considers the major differences among investor types. Owing to current fashions in finance, there is little interest in who owns corporations and, therefore, few studies of this subject. These few, lacking guidance from any theory, seldom contain material pertinent to the theory here. For instance, it is worth noting that the distribution of ownership of common stock is more concentrated than that of preferred stock. This is significant in view of the material given in chapter 2 but seems to be of no interest in the standard theory. The chapter concludes with an appendix containing some technical material on core theory relevant for the theory of joint ventures.

A key element in the theory of corporations as developed in chapter 2 is the individual investors' valuations of the prospects for a joint venture. Chapter 3 presents models of these valuations. The first section begins with the simplest case in which there is certainty. The next section treats the more difficult problem of how to value joint ventures when there is uncertainty about their prospects. Chapter 2 describes studies that imply that the valuation of a firm to its present owners is generally above its market value as determined in the stock market. This raises a question that a theory of valuation must answer—how to explain the difference between the market value of a firm as determined by the price of its shares of stock and the value of the firm as perceived by its present owners. Chapter 4 answers this question.

Chapter 4 opens with a description of the neoclassical theory of the optimal stock of capital for a profit-making firm in a perfectly competitive industry with certainty. It begins with a discussion of the effects of inflation on the value of a firm. It goes on to show when it is correct to say that the market value of a firm equals the price per share of its stock multiplied by the number of its shares outstanding. Sometimes this measure of the market value of a firm understates the value of the firm to its owners. The accuracy of the market value as a measure of the firm's prospects depends on the nature of the returns to scale of the firm. For constant returns to scale this measure of market value is correct. However, the value of the firm as measured by the price per share as determined in the stock market is downward biased for decreasing returns to scale.

The theory of corporations in chapter 2 says that the willingness of an investor to back a firm depends on how much value he attaches to it. Chapter 4 describes in detail the valuation of uncertain prospects. A novel aspect of this analysis is its emphasis on the uncertain duration of the firm's prospects. This leads to a theory of when a joint venture stops as a result of an autonomous voluntary decision of its owners even if the joint venture has no debt and no creditors who can force it into bankruptcy. The laws of bankruptcy need not be invoked to explain the demise of a firm.

The last section in this chapter presents evidence to test the validity of the preceding theory of the valuation of joint ventures. It begins with a derivation of an equation for stock prices using the theory in sections 1 and 2. Next it presents estimates of regressions to estimate this equation. The estimates use monthly data for two periods: January 1920 to December 1940 and January 1947 to December 1991. The first includes the October 1929 stock market crash and the second the October 1987 stock market crash. The regressions for the first sample up to October 1929 and for the entire post–World War II period including the October 1987 crash all strongly support the predictions of the theory. Except for the period from October 1929 to March 1933, the Great Depression itself, the results for the period from April 1933 to December 1940 also support the theory.

Core theory given in chapter 2 as applied to joint ventures emphasizes the external forces acting on a coalition that threaten to disrupt it. The coalition can survive only if it can offer its members enough inducements to remain as members. It also faces internal problems that may threaten its survival. Chapter 4 tackles the problems facing a group of like-minded peers with a common interest who must rely on self-enforcement to maintain the group. Self-enforcement means no outsiders intervene to carry out the provisions of the agreement among the parties. In the economic situations to which this book applies core theory, conflict often arises between the group interest and the individual interest. While adherence to the agreement advances the long-term interest of the group, one who violates the agreement without giving notice of this may gain enough to break his promise even after subtracting the loss from the punishment that such treachery provokes. When punishment cannot deter treachery, an alliance cannot survive. We want to see when suitable punishment of violations of a self-enforcing agreement among the individuals can instill enough harmony between the group and an individual so that the alliance can survive internal disruptive forces.

Chapter 2 recognizes at the outset that investors in a joint venture hire people to act in the best interest of the owners. Chapter 4 deals with the problems that arise among peers in a joint venture. Chapter 5 takes up the problems that arise in a hierarchy. Those at the higher levels in a hierarchy must devise ways that will inspire those at the lower levels to advance the interests of their superiors. Delegation of power is pervasive and necessary in all large organizations. Since it is prohibitively costly for a principal to watch closely everything an agent does, the principal needs ways to pay the agent that will reduce these costs and will induce a self-seeking agent to act so as to move toward the principal's goals.

In the simplest case there is one principal and one agent, and even so most of the major issues are present. Analysis of this case is the topic of the second section of chapter 5. The next section assumes the principal has many agents. It suitably modifies the theory to reckon with the complications that ensue.

A major implication of this model applies to the type of remuneration for top corporate executives. In many corporations the managers own a very small fraction of the shares. Hence their return from these shares cannot induce them to act in the interest of the shareowners. This is to say that a manager's action may have a big effect on the corporation but a small effect on his return as a shareowner. What does motivate managers is a method of remuneration in the form of rewards contingent on the results of their actions. The models in this chapter explain how these promises can align the interests of the managers and the owners.

Chapter 6 applies core theory to the determination of wages among competing firms. It is noteworthy that Frank Knight in his *Risk, Uncertainty and Profit* (1921) presents a theory of wages, stemming from Edgeworth, much like one based on core theory. Competition for workers among the firms that are regarded as coalitions of workers raises the question of whether a worker's wage will equal his incremental contribution to the coalition that he joins. It is shown, contrary to the standard theory, that wages may be less than the worker's incremental contribution even with vigorous competition among firms for workers. Core theory also facilitates study of the relation between wages and ability. While the normal distribution seems to give a good fit to some measures of ability, it poorly fits wage distributions. The distribution of wages is often found to be highly skewed to the right, suggesting either that a normal distribution of ability is wrong or that the wage distribution reflects more than just the abilities of the workers. Core theory shows precisely how abilities and competition interact so as to determine the wage distribution as a function of workers' abilities. Core theory also illuminates an important relation between the size and stability of a firm depending on the nature of the wage formula. The last section of this chapter uses a more general production function than the preceding sections. It allows the productivity of a worker to depend on the identity and specific skills of the fellow workers. In this more general setting, core theory can derive many important new properties of wages determined in a competitive labor market.

Chapter 7 presents a theory of the best coalition for an industry for which the core would be empty. It extends the results for single-product Viner industries to multiproduct Viner industries. In a single-product Viner industry each firm has a U-shaped unit cost curve. When more than one firm is optimal, a Viner industry has no core. The situation is more complicated when firms make several products. Yet, it remains true that the core is empty for almost all rates of demand. This raises an important question. Given an empty core, what arrangements do firms and their customers contrive in order to secure an efficient outcome? The answer is a coalition that is best for all its members, both the firms and their customers. Such a coalition restricts entry and exit of both buyers and sellers. In practice this often means distinguishing between regular and transient buyers and sellers. People in an optimal coalition are the regular buyers and those sellers who make long-term arrangements with them like a *keiretsu* among Japanese firms. The people outside the optimal coalition are the transients who buy and sell in spot markets usually on less favorable terms than the regulars who are inside the best coalition. Study of the motion picture industry in the period preceding World War II suggests that the theory of optimal coalitions can explain many of its practices, especially in view of the uncertainty about the success of individual motion pictures.

Core theory, the basic tool used in this book, focuses on many often ignored yet important problems in the theory of the firm. Now with the help of core theory we can see a relation between those who invest and the sorts of investments that they make. A gap between wages and marginal productivity is consistent with a competitive labor market. The nature of the wage agreement depends on the size of the enterprise. These are a sample of the problems that this book addresses with the help of core theory.

Finally, it will be helpful to describe the conventions in this book. The chapters in this book are divided into numbered sections and, sometimes, numbered subsections. Equations, theorems, and lemmas are numbered from (1) in each section. Reference to an equation or theorem in the same section has the equation, theorem, or lemma number. Reference to an equation, theorem, or lemma in another section of the same chapter has the section number, followed by a period and then the equation number. Thus, (2.11) means equation (11) in section 2. An equation in another chapter has three numbers: chapter number, period, section number, period, and equation number. Thus, (3.2.11) means chapter 3, section 2, equation (11). In this fashion the search necessary to find an equation or a theorem is minimized.

Some particular mathematical conventions in this book are as follows. The two notations for greater than or equal to are:

$x \geqq y$ for two vectors x and y means corresponding coordinates have the relation greater than or equal to, $\geq$, and equality is possible for each coordinate;

$x \geq y$ for two vectors means there is greater than for at least one pair of corresponding coordinates and equality for every pair of corresponding coordinates is not possible. The usage $\geq$ for two scalars is obvious.

The notation $x \circ y$ denotes the scalar product of the two vectors x and y. That is, $x \circ y = \Sigma x_i y_i$. The notation a^- means approach the scalar a from the left and a^+ means approach the scalar a from the right.

Several readers and listeners have given me helpful comments, criticism, and encouragement on the material in this book. George Bittlingmayer, Sheldon Kimmel, and John Matsusaka are at the forefront of this group together with many of the students in my classes. Alan Krueger, Carl Shapiro, Joseph Stiglitz, and Timothy Tyler were of great help to me in the article "Usefulness of Core Theory" that is the introduction to this book. The comments of James Coleman helped improve the chapter "When an Alliance Can Survive." Louis Chan and Thomas Philipson's comments on multiproduct Viner industries made chapter 7 better. None of these should be held responsible for any errors or shortcomings of this book.

Introduction: The Usefulness of Core Theory in Economics

Core theory furnishes a useful framework for studying a wide variety of economic problems. It has an undeserved reputation of being too abstract, owing mainly to the manner in which it is employed in the theory of general equilibrium. In fact, core theory is a highly flexible way of looking at practical economic problems, especially problems in industrial organization. This introduction seeks to show how simple numerical examples can illustrate the idea of the core and, in turn, how the core can illustrate basic principles of economics.

Principles of the Core

The theory of the core begins with the assumption that there are n individuals who can do something either all together, individually, or in small groups. For economic applications, a typical example is trade in a market, where all individuals may trade with each other in a single market or in submarkets or some may decide not to trade at all. The theory assumes that the individuals can measure the results of their actions. For the example of trade in a market, it is traditional to assume that an individual measures the outcome by the utility from the bundle of commodities. Alternatively, an individual can measure the gains from trade in terms of money. For a buyer, this is the maximum amount the buyer would have been willing to pay for the quantities purchased minus the amount actually paid. For a seller, it is the actual receipts minus the amount the seller would have been willing to accept for what was sold. Thus the theory of the core has three elements: n individuals; the various groups they can form, called coalitions; and functions that measure the results of the actions taken by the individuals and coalitions.

There are some outcomes that the whole group of individuals cannot improve. These are the outcomes such that it is not possible to make one person better off without making at least one other person worse off. Such outcomes are called Pareto optimal. They involve no deadweight loss. The originator of this theory, F. Y. Edgeworth (1881), went on to obtain remarkable results showing how competition among many traders and coalitions leads toward a Pareto-efficient outcome.[1] Edgeworth called the mechanism that produces this result "recontracting." The approach is to consider all possible coalitions of traders, recognizing that any coalition of traders will only participate in the market as a whole if and only if they can do at least as well as they could by themselves in their own coalition. To put it another way, the best outcomes available to a coalition set lower bounds on what its members would be willing to accept as participants in the whole market. For example, the complete set of 1-person coalitions implies the constraint that each individual will not trade in the market unless the trade makes that person better off. Next consider all 2-person coalitions. In this case, any trades must make the individuals at least as well off as they would be in choosing any possible 2-person partnership. When this logic is extended from 3-person on up to the n-person coalition, there is a total of $2^n - 1$ possible coalitions, with each coalition placing a constraint on the outcome of trade. The larger the number of traders, the smaller is the range of outcomes without deadweight losses. Under certain conditions the terms of trade that can satisfy all these constraints constitute a competitive equilibrium.

Core theory examines this process systematically. Outcomes that are unacceptable to some coalition because it can do better for its members are said to be *dominated*. The set of undominated outcomes constitutes the core. Depending on the number of individuals and the process of recontracting, the core will sometimes consist of a range of outcomes, sometimes a single outcome, and sometimes the core will not exist at all.

An Example of Pure Exchange with a Nonempty Core

A simple example can illustrate these concepts. Say there are three individuals and the first two are potential buyers of a house from the third. The potential seller will not sell the house for less than $100,000. Buyer 1 will not pay more than $120,000 and buyer 2 not more than $150,000. (From now on units are understood to be in $1,000.) Let x denote the return to the seller, y_1 the gain to buyer 1, and y_2 the gain to buyer 2. In case it turns out the owner of the house sells it, x is the price of the house. The owner can ensure $x \geq 100$ because retaining the house is an option worth at least 100. For the potential buyers, $y_1 \geq 0$ and $y_2 \geq 0$, because each buyer can refuse to make a purchase and thereby can ensure a net gain of zero, no matter what anyone else does. These three inequalities are the constraints for the three 1-person coalitions.

A coalition of both buyers can do the same as either one of them separately, and the coalition of this pair will have the same lower bound on the sum of their gains. As a result, the relevant constraint for the coalition of both buyers is that $y_1 + y_2 \geq 0$.

---

1. Carl Menger (1871, chaps. 4 and 5) gives perhaps the first rigorous account of a competitive market. There is a direct line from Menger to Böhm-Bawerk ([1891] 1930) to the game theory of von Neumann and Morgenstern (1947).

There are two more coalitions involving pairs of traders. Each is a coalition between the seller and either one of the buyers. A trade between the seller and buyer 1 must ensure them a return equal to the larger of the two values {100, 120}. The first value comes from the fact that the seller will only participate if the gain is at least 100; thus the gain to the coalition of the two must also be at least 100. But what determines the minimum gain is the willingness of buyer 1 to pay 120. Given the existence of an outside, higher offer for the house, with the possibility of reselling it to buyer 1 afterward, the coalition between the seller and buyer 1 would reject any offer below the valuation either places on the house because each member of this coalition can bid for the house in competition with an outside offer. Similarly, the coalition between the seller and buyer 2 will demand a return of at least 150 because this is the larger of the two values {100, 150} applicable to this coalition. These conditions set two additional constraints on the outcome: $x + y_1 \geq 120$ and $x + y_2 \geq 150$.

Lastly, the valuation for the coalition of all three traders equals the maximum of {100, 120, 150}. To put it another way, the cumulative return for the coalition of the whole must be at least as much as the most generous buyer is willing to pay. This condition puts an upper bound on the sum of the returns, given by $x + y_1 + y_2 \leq 150$.

Any triplet $\{x, y_1, y_2\}$ that can satisfy all these inequalities is undominated and is said to be in the core of the market. As an example, consider the triplet {115, 0, 35}, where buyer 2 purchases the house at a price of 115. This triplet is not in the core; it does not satisfy the inequality that the gains to the coalition of the seller and buyer 1 must sum to at least 120. Thus, the seller and buyer 1 can form a coalition leading to the triplet {118, 2, 30} in which buyer 1 buys the house from the seller for 118 and resells it to buyer 2 for 120 so that buyer 2 gains 30.

But this set of trades is not in the core either, because it does not fulfill the inequality that the gains to the coalition of the seller and buyer 2 must be at least 150. The imputation {120, 0, 30}, in which the seller deals directly with buyer 2, *is* in the core. It is undominated and satisfies all the constraints. More generally, all imputations in which $y_1 = 0$, $x + y_2 = 150$, $x \geq 120$, and $y_2 \geq 0$ are undominated and form the core of the market. Thus, any outcome where buyer 2 buys the house for at least 120, but no more than 150, is in the core, and nothing else is in the core.

When a nonempty core exists, it means that any trader or group of traders prefers the outcome determined by the whole market to those they could get in any possible submarket involving a subset of traders. These submarkets present feasible alternatives that place limits on the prices that can emerge from the market as a whole. When the market has a nonempty core, it can survive all possible competing alternatives. In core theory, coalitions compete for members by making offers to individuals to induce them to join the coalition. The grand coalition, which includes all the members, can survive only by offering terms that are at least as good as any feasible offer coming from a sub-coalition.

Although the example presented here illustrates only the simplest case of pure exchange, it can be extended into a comprehensive analysis of nearly everything there is to say on this topic. Because there is only one seller in the example, competition is present only between the two buyers. More complicated examples would have many sellers and buyers. The core is not empty for the more general case in which there are m sellers and n buyers each of whom seeks or offers at most one unit of the commodity. It can be shown that all those who sell the commodity must get the same price. This common price is determined by the constraints that emerge as a result of the terms that various coalitions could arrange by dealing among themselves. A still more general model allows the buyers and the sellers to seek or offer more than one unit of the commodity. If the demand schedules of the buyer are downward sloping and the supply schedules of the sellers are upward sloping then there is a nonempty core. Therefore, it remains true that each individual prefers the terms determined in the whole market to those that subsets of traders could agree upon by confining trade among themselves.

However, with multiunit traders, a wider range of alternatives is consistent with the core constraints than if each trader were replaced by an equivalent set of single-unit traders. This is true because multiunit traders do not make or tender offers for their commodities one unit at a time unless the forces of competition compel them to. In particular, it need no longer be true that a single price must prevail for the commodity throughout the market in this case. Different sellers could get different receipts per unit, and different buyers could pay different prices per unit. In these cases core theory shows how the sizes of the traders could affect the outcome.

A still more general model allows the traders to deal in bundles of continuously divisible commodities. There is a nonempty core in this case if the valuation functions of the traders are continuously increasing concave functions of quantities. Chapter 1 on pure exchange derives this result. The most general analysis assumes a continuum of traders. Think of each trader as indexed by a real number and suppose there are as many traders as there are real numbers in the unit interval. An individual trader is infinitesimally small and has a correspondingly small effect on the outcome of trade. A nonempty core exists for this market under very general conditions on the preferences of the traders. Even with many "crazy" traders, who violate assumptions of rational choice such as transitivity or revealed preference, there is a nonempty core if the "sane" traders are sufficiently more numerous than the crazy ones.[2]

2. Models of pure exchange using core theory are in Scarf and Debreu 1963. For a continuum of traders, see Aumann 1964, 1966 and Hildenbrand 1974. Simpler versions are in Telser 1972 and 1988.

Examples of an Empty Core

Sometimes it is not possible to satisfy the conditions for a nonempty core. This happens when the lower bounds on the terms that the coalitions would be willing to accept cannot all be met by the grand coalition. In this event, the core is empty. It means a fully competitive market fails to bring about a Pareto-optimal result.

Consider an example that is most easily visualized as applying to the cost conditions of the airline industry. Two sellers each operate an airline; they have one airplane apiece. The first airline, A_1, has a small airplane that can carry only two passengers at a total cost of 85. Or, to put it another way, not making the trip will save a cost of 85. (In the preceding example, this condition corresponds to the seller of the house retaining it, as if selling it to himself at the minimal price he would be willing to take for it, which is 100 in that example.) The second airline, A_2, has a bigger airplane that can carry up to 3 passengers at a total cost of 150. It can avoid this cost entirely by not making the trip. Note that the costs of the airlines are not dependent on whether they fly partly or entirely full but only on whether they make the trip at all. In this example, let us agree to ignore both fixed and variable costs. This does not affect the validity of the results, and it simplifies the arithmetic.

Let there be three potential travelers: B_1, who is willing to pay at most 55 for the trip; B_2, who is willing to pay at most 60 for the trip; and B_3, who is willing to pay up to 70. The total number of coalitions in this example is $2^{2+3} - 1 = 31$. Let us again adopt the terminology that x represents the returns to the sellers while y represents the gains to the buyers. For starters, consider the 1-person coalitions; these have a buyer or a seller acting alone. To make a deal the sellers must receive enough to cover the costs of a trip: that is, $x_1 \geq 85$ and $x_2 \geq 150$. The buyers must all perceive themselves as better off by making a purchase; therefore, y_1, y_2, and $y_3 \geq 0$.

Plainly, no coalition of a seller with only one buyer can cover the cost of a trip. Also, a coalition of either two or three buyers cannot gain more than zero. The remaining 2-person coalition, the two airlines without any passengers, cannot get more than the sum of what they could each get by themselves. Therefore, the interesting possibilities involve a seller with at least two buyers.

Consider the alternatives for the small airline A_1 with the three possible pairs of buyers. Again the return for each possible coalition is determined by the maximum of what the various purchasers might pay. For example, the potential gains for the coalition A_1, B_1, B_2 would be determined by the maximum of what the two buyers would pay and the seller would demand, that is, the maximum of $\{55 + 60, 85\}$, which equals 115. Similarly, the gains for the coalition A_1, B_1, B_3 would be the maximum of $\{55 + 70, 85\}$, or 125, and the gains for the coalition A_1, B_2, B_3 would be the maximum of $\{60 + 70, 85\}$, or 130.

These conditions lead to the following three constraints:

$$x_1 + y_1 + y_2 \geq 115,$$
$$x_1 + y_1 + y_3 \geq 125,$$
$$x_1 + y_2 + y_3 \geq 130.$$

Of course, seller 2 can also make a potential deal with all three buyers. Hence this coalition $\{A_1, B_1, B_2, B_3\}$ can guarantee itself a return of 185 = max $\{150, \ 55 + 60 + 70\}$. The constraint on the gains of this potential deal is $x_2 + y_1 + y_2 + y_3 \geq 185$.

Last, there is the maximum return available to the coalition of all 5 individuals, the 3 buyers and the 2 sellers. This coalition of everybody has two especially relevant alternatives: one where the first airplane flies full and the second does not fly at all; and the other where the second airplane flies full and the first does not fly at all. In the first, the two travelers who value the trip the most fly with the smaller airline; that is, B_2 and B_3 fly with A_1, B_1 does not make the trip, and A_2 saves the avoidable cost of its service. For this alternative, the coalition of all five would get $60 + 70 + 150 = 280$. In the second alternative, A_1 does not fly, thereby avoiding the cost of 85, and A_2 carries all three passengers, generating a value of 185. For the second alternative, the return would be $185 + 85 = 270$. The value for the coalition of 5 is the larger of the returns under these two alternatives. This is given by max $\{280, 270\}$. Therefore, the most efficient arrangement does not satisfy the demand of buyer 1; buyer 2 and buyer 3 make the trip on the airplane of seller 1; and seller 2 saves the cost of 150. Consequently, the upper bound on the x's and y's is given by

$$x_1 + x_2 + y_1 + y_2 + y_3 \leq 280.$$

There is no core solution to this market; it is impossible to describe an outcome acceptable to every possible coalition. This is so because the set of inequalities given here has no solution. An outcome in the core must be Pareto optimal so that it gives the most efficient arrangement. Pareto optimality requires that

$$x_1 + y_2 + y_3 = 130, \qquad x_2 = 150, \qquad y_1 = 0, \qquad \text{and}$$
$$x_1 + x_2 + y_1 + y_2 + y_3 = 280.$$

The first equation says that airline 1 carries passengers 2 and 3. The second says that airline 2 saves its avoidable cost, and the third says that buyer 1 gains zero either because of not making the trip or because of paying his maximal valuation of the trip, which is 55. The last equation makes the sum of everybody's gains as big as possible.

There are two constraints that set upper bounds on the gains of buyers 2 and 3 necessary to have a nonempty core. The coalition involving passengers 1 and 2 going on airplane 1 can ensure themselves a gain of 115. Since $y_1 = 0$ is necessary for a nonempty core, it follows that the sum of x_1 and y_2 is bounded below by 115. But $x_1 + y_2 + y_3 = 130$ is also necessary for a nonempty core so that the gain to passenger 3 cannot exceed 15 ($= 130 - 115$). Likewise, the coalition in which passengers 1 and 3 go on airplane 1 can guarantee themselves a return of 125. Again, for a nonempty core, $y_1 = 0$ and $x_1 + y_2 + y_3 = 130$. This puts an upper bound on the gain of passenger 2 given by 5 ($= 130 - 125$). Therefore, a nonempty core requires that the sum of the gains to passengers 2 and 3 does not exceed 20, or, in symbols,

$$y_2 + y_3 \leq 20.$$

However, the second airline can also offer a deal to the three buyers. The lower bound for this deal is 185, and so the sum of the gains to the 4 participants in this coalition satisfies the inequality

$$x_2 + y_1 + y_2 + y_3 \geq 185.$$

A nonempty core requires that $y_1 = 0$ and $x_2 = 150$. Therefore, substituting in the preceding inequality, this competition from the second airline would set a lower bound on the gains to buyer 2 and buyer 3 that is

$$y_2 + y_3 \geq 35 = 185 - 150.$$

Consequently, the upper and lower bounds on the sum $y_2 + y_3$ are contradictory, which proves the core is empty.[3]

Admittedly, the cost conditions in this example are contrived in such a way as to make the core empty. It should be noted, for the record, that extending the model from pure exchange to production need not give an empty core. Also, in the example, the total capacity exceeds the total quantity demanded. Although capacity equal to demand is a sufficient condition for a nonempty core, it is not a necessary condition. The core can be empty for other reasons. The key lessons of this example is that introducing production into the model does add many complications to the theory, which in turn lead to important practical ramifications. To understand why this is so, let us look more closely at how the model treats coalitions.

The return to a coalition of n individuals stems from the activities of its members. The coalition can survive if and only if it can offer its members more than they could get by breaking away and forming their own subcoalition or joining another coalition. Each coalition must also ask whether it can make its present members better off by expanding its membership. There will be a gain if the incremental return from adding a member exceeds the current return per

3. Telser 1978, chap. 2 contains a detailed analysis of these airplane examples.

member. Or, to put it another way, at the optimal size of a coalition, the return per member is a maximum. When the coalition of everybody maximizes the return per member so that it is optimal for everybody to join the grand coalition, the core is not empty. Applied to markets, this means there is a core if the traders are better off with the terms they get in the whole market than they would be in any submarket. Therefore, a market with a nonempty core attracts all the trade.

Consider a coalition of individuals who constitute the demand for various commodities. The return to a member of such a coalition equals the valuation of the commodities minus the sum of the quantities bought at prices equal to the marginal cost of producing these commodities. An expansion of the size of the coalition corresponds to an increase in the demand for the commodities from the new members of the coalition. This does not harm the present members provided the marginal costs of the commodities they buy, which equal the prices they pay, do not increase when the demand expands. When adding more and more members to the coalition does not raise marginal costs, the optimal coalition is the coalition of everybody and the core exists. Therefore, a nonempty core requires constant or increasing returns to scale. Another way to see this is by starting with the coalition of everybody and asking whether it can survive. Survival means that it can offer its members a better deal than they could get in any subcoalition. However, with rising marginal cost, a subgroup of demanders has an incentive to break away from the grand coalition. By doing this, they can obtain their commodities at lower prices because marginal costs are lower.

A specific example of an empty core is an industry with identical firms having U-shaped average cost curves such that marginal cost rises with output and equals average cost at the positive output where average cost is a minimum. This case, presented in many textbooks on elementary economics, is familiar to readers of Jacob Viner's famous article ([1931] 1952) on cost curves.[4] In an optimal coalition it must be true that firms are producing where their unit cost is at a minimum; otherwise, a coalition would form where the firm changes its output, produces at a lower unit cost, and sells to the demanders in this coalition at a lower price than they would have to pay in the grand coalition. But the efficient equilibrium for the market as a whole must be where the price at the quantity demanded equals the marginal cost of the total quantity produced by the firms. The problem arises because the efficient equilibrium for the industry also involves the optimal number of firms that must reckon with the fact that this number is an integer. Changing from n to $n + 1$ firms affects the total cost of production in two ways: it changes both the total variable cost and the total fixed cost of the industry. Optimality requires a comparison between the increase of the fixed cost from having one more firm and the reduction of the vari-

---

4. Such industries are called Viner industries and are studied in Telser 1978, chap. 3, sec. 4.

able cost from having each of the firms producing a smaller output while the total output satisfies the total demand at a price equal to marginal cost. The efficient industry equilibrium will not in general be where the unit cost of the firm is at a minimum. The magnitude of the difficulty depends on size of the output per firm where unit cost is a minimum compared to the total equilibrium quantity. The gap between a nonempty and an empty core is smaller, the more numerous the firms in the optimal industry equilibrium. Therefore, there is a closer and closer approximation to the standard competitive equilibrium, the bigger the Pareto-optimal number of firms. Chapter 7 has a detailed analysis of multiproduct Viner industries.

Resolving an Empty Core

What happens in a market when the core is empty? The answer to this question is referred to as "resolving" an empty core. For the type of cost conditions in the second example, a general method of resolving an empty core requires imposition of suitable upper bounds on the quantities that may be sold by certain sellers. Such bounds always exist.[5]

It may seem that a proposal for restricting output must be inefficient, since it has the character of a profit-maximizing cartel. However, in the situation where no core exists, such upper bounds can be efficient, if suitably chosen, in the sense that although removing the bounds can help some economic actors, it can do so only at the expense of creating a deadweight loss for the whole group. A real example of this occurred in Hyde Park, which has a regular limo service to O'Hare Airport, 25 miles away. Going to O'Hare, this service makes scheduled stops at certain times and locations in the neighborhood where it picks up passengers. Demand is heavy at spring and Christmas breaks. Once at 7 A.M. on spring break, we were waiting with several students for the limo to O'Hare. Just before 7, a Yellow taxi pulled up, flag down, meter off, and offered to take up to 5 customers to O'Hare for $8 each, nonstop, which is below the limo price. The taxi got a full load and left for O'Hare. No one remained for the regular limo service. Although the taxi driver and those who accepted his offer were made better off, the incentive for providing the regular limo service was impaired. The limo service would not continue, thereby harming the interest of any residents of Hyde Park desiring regular limo service to the airport, unless it could stop this skimming by taxis. This example closely matches the situation facing shipping conferences. Here a group of shipping firms promises to furnish regular service and enough capacity to handle the cargo of the shippers at certain ports. The conference sets minimum rates. Cargoes accumulate

---

5. For a detailed analysis of suitable upper bounds on output that can give a nonempty core, see Telser 1987, chap. 5.

at the port between arrivals of the regular freighters and are transported on the ships of the members of the conference. However, tramps may arrive at the port just before the scheduled stop and offer to take the freight at rates below the conference rates. The shippers who take advantage of these lower rates reduce the incentive for the conference to provide regular service. The lack of regular service would harm the shippers. Both the shippers and the carriers seek arrangements that can preserve regular service. One way that the conference deals with the problem of tramps is by offering shippers a deferred rebate for loyalty. Shippers who use members of the conference exclusively for a pre-scribed period, usually a year, get a rebate proportional to their total annual shipping costs at the end of the year. This helps ensure loyalty by the shippers to the conference members and thereby preserves regular service. Studies of shipping conferences by Sjostrom (1989) and Pirrong (1992) support the view that a cooperative arrangement among shipping firms is consistent with effi-ciency and a competitive return.

To demonstrate the flexibility of core theory as a tool of analysis, the sec-ond example can also illustrate how long-term (forward) contracts or vertical integration can sometimes resolve an empty core problem. Forward contracts work better when each party may have many interests other than the commod-ity involved in the particular exchange. Vertical integration entails closer rela-tions between the two parties and usually needs agreement on many aspects of their operations, and so it works better when the two parties have a number of common interests.

Let B_1 own A_1, the smaller airline, and B_2 own A_2, the bigger airline. The third buyer, B_3, buys the service on the open or spot market. Neither B_1 nor B_2 has a big enough demand to cover the cost of using the airline for themselves exclusively. Hence each has an incentive to seek outside business. Notice that by this vertical integration, B_1 and B_2 become involved in the airline business. This would not happen if they made forward contracts for long-term service with the airlines as separate businesses. With three economic actors, there are three singleton coalitions: B_1 must receive the maximum of $\{85, 55\}$: the first for being willing to run its plane, the second for what it is willing to pay for a flight. Similarly, B_2 must receive the maximum of $\{150, 60\}$, and B_3 must not incur a loss by participating.

For the three groups, there are three coalitions of pairs. In a coalition be-tween B_1 and B_2, there are two alternatives: either both fly in the smaller plane and save the cost of using the bigger one (which is 150) or neither flies so that they save $150 + 85$. The potential for gain will be the maximum of $\{55 + 60 + 150, 150 + 85\}$, which is 265. In a coalition between B_1 and B_3, both pas-sengers must choose either to fly in the small plane owned by B_1, which has a value of $55 + 70$, or save the cost of the trip that has a value of 85. In this case, the maximum of $\{125, 85\}$ will be 125. Last, in a coalition between B_2 and B_3, the pair can either fly in the big plane, owned by B_2, where the trip has a value of $60 + 70$ or they can forgo the trip and save 150. The potential for gain is the maximum of $\{130, 150\}$, or 150.

The remaining option is the grand coalition of all three. For this coalition, the best outcome will be a choice between flying in one plane or the other or not flying at all, with the valuation as the maximum of $\{130 + 150,\ 185 + 85,\ 85 + 150\}$. The latter, $85 + 150$, is what would be gained by not flying at all. Notice that the maximum valuation of 280 is the same as in the case when the A's and B's were not vertically integrated.

Many solutions are possible that will satisfy all of these inequalities, and so the core is nonempty in this case; one of them is the triplet $y_1 = 115$, $y_2 = 150$, and $y_3 = 15$.[6] This solution is based on a particular allocation of the property rights, but with three different buyers and the two airlines, there are actually five other allocations: B_1 owns A_2 and B_2 owns A_1; B_2 owns A_1 and B_3 owns A_2; B_2 owns A_2 and B_3 owns A_1; B_1 owns A_1 and B_3 owns A_2; B_1 owns A_2 and B_3 owns A_1. Allowing one buyer to own both airlines would provide three more allocations but with less competition than the six just described. It is a general result that if any allocation of the property gives a nonempty core, then all will do so, although the imputation of the gains differs in each. Because the efficiency of the outcome does not depend on the allocation of the property, one may take this as an illustration of the Coase "theorem."[7]

Vertical integration gives a nonempty core in this example by eliminating certain potential contracts. These would confer gains on those who participate in them, but such contracts would prevent the Pareto-optimal outcome. Ownership of an airline by a particular buyer means that the pair involved always operates together in a potential contract with other participants. Therefore, all the constraints involving an x disappear owing to the vertical integration. Only those constraints involving y's remain, and there is a suitable adjustment of the lower bounds on the returns for the coalitions giving rise to these constraints.

The original situation in which the buyers and sellers are separate allows the most leeway for opportunistic behavior to the individuals. Vertical integra-

---

6. In particular, these are the relevant inequalities:

$$y_1 \geq 85; \qquad y_2 \geq 150; \qquad y_3 \geq 0; \qquad y_1 + y_2 \geq 265; \qquad y_1 + y_3 \geq 125;$$

$$y_2 + y_3 \geq 150 \qquad \text{and} \qquad y_1 + y_2 + y_3 \leq 280.$$

7. The Coase "theorem" needs much repair when there is an empty core. Aivazian and Callen (1981) give an example with three firms: two factories that pollute the third, a laundry. They show there is an empty core because there is no undominated allocation of the gains among the three. Coase's elaborate analysis in his comment (1981) fails to come to grips with the issues raised by this example. Also, the allocation of the gains that Coase proposes is dominated by every 2-person coalition. Coase's most recent and authoritative exposition of his "theorem" (1988) is silent on the challenge posed by an empty core although chapter 6 discusses several criticisms of the theorem.

tion by joining certain pairs of buyers and sellers forces them to recognize their common interest and reduces their incentive to take temporary advantage of each other. Core theory shows this formally, when there is vertical integration, by removing some of the constraints from the original situation. However, this does not answer the question of how the members of a vertically integrated pair will divide their gain between them. Since divorce is possible because of disagreement, the situation can revert to the empty core. Nor is this all. Even if the constituents in a vertical integration can reach amicable settlements, vertical integration cannot always resolve an empty core problem.

A simple change in the preceding example shows this. Say there is a third seller, A_3, with a capacity of 2 and an avoidable cost of 90. Also, let there be a fourth buyer, B_4, willing to pay at most 34. The core is empty with the addition of these two individuals. Vertical integration would not change the empty to a nonempty core, for instance, if B_4 integrates with A_3. The emptiness of the core in this new example is not affected by shuffling the property among the buyers (as the reader should be able to verify).

The original version of the airline coalition story can also illustrate how the gains to the participants change as the size of the coalition expands. To this end—and to show how the definition of the return to a coalition is malleable and therefore useful for many different purposes—now define the gain to a coalition as the total value of what they can produce, which is measured by what people are willing to pay for it, minus the cost of producing it. Assume vertical integration in the form that B_1 owns A_1 and B_2 owns A_2. Since no single passenger can cover the cost of a trip, no coalitions made up of a single member will form. Or to put it another way, the singleton coalitions can always decide to do nothing, and each guarantees a gain of zero.

There are three possible pair coalitions. The coalition between B_1 and B_2 will either choose not to fly at all, for a gain of zero, or to pay 55 + 60 to fly before subtracting 85 in costs for a gain of 30. Similarly, the coalition between B_1 and B_3 will either not fly at all, for a gain of zero, or will pay 55 + 70 to fly, minus a cost of 85, for a gain of 40. Finally, the coalition between B_2 and B_3 will either not fly for a gain of zero or will fly the large plane, only two-thirds full, paying 130 with costs of 150. Notice that as this example moves from singleton to pair coalitions, the incremental gain is indeterminate because it depends on who joins whom.

The grand coalition of the three will choose the best of several possibilities. First, it may choose not to fly at all for a gain of zero. Second, it may choose to put the two highest-paying passengers in the small plane, for a gain of 130 − 85. Or it may choose to put all three passengers in the largest plane, for a gain of 185 − 150. The second alternative offers the biggest gain of 45, and so that will be chosen.

Notice that adding B_1 to a coalition of B_2 and B_3 raises the gain from zero to 45, while adding B_2 to a coalition of B_1 and B_3 raises the gain only from 40 to 45 and adding B_3 to a coalition of B_1 and B_2 raises the gain from 30 to 45. It is a general proposition that when the core is not empty, the return to each person cannot exceed that person's incremental contribution to the grand coalition. In this case, the return to B_1 cannot exceed 45, to B_2 the upper bound is 5, and to B_3 it is 15. These upper bounds are a good starting point to see whether there is an imputation of the gains in the core. Thus, try y_2 at its upper bound, which is 5, and y_3 at its upper bound, or 15. The sum of the gains must equal 45 because it is the maximum available to the grand coalition. For $y_2 = 5$ and $y_3 = 15$, y_1 must be 25 ($= 45 - 5 - 15$). This gain for B_1 is admissible because it does not exceed the upper bound, which is 45. The triplet $\{25, 5, 15\}$ is in the core because it satisfies all the inequalities required by a nonempty core. It is an extreme imputation of the gains because it gives the largest possible amount consistent with the core to two of the three actors in this market. Another imputation in the core is at the other extreme where B_1 gets 45, the upper bound, and the other two get zero. Thus $\{45, 0, 0\}$ is also in the core and is the most favorable imputation for B_1. The theory does not determine which of these imputations or certain others in between will be chosen by the participants.

Conclusion

The existence of production introduces a number of complications into economic analysis. Setup or avoidable costs are common, as illustrated in the airplane example, and coalitions will form to break down simple marginal cost in this case. There may be lower bounds on the scale of operation, as also illustrated in the airplane example. Continuous changes in output are often more expensive than discontinuous changes in discrete amounts, as in industries like auto assembly, electricity generation, and railroad shipping. In addition, the least costly way to satisfy demand usually requires standby capacity available before the actual demand is known. This raises the problem of how to generate enough revenue to cover the cost of the standby capacity as well as the out-of-pocket costs of the demand that actually materializes. Both buyers and sellers have a definite interest in the resolution of these problems.

   Core theory offers tools for confronting these challenges explicitly. It shows how opportunistic behavior by customers can destroy an efficient equilibrium and how suitable arrangements between customers and suppliers in the form of vertical integration can sometimes restore an efficient equilibrium.

   Core theory has many other interesting uses in areas not discussed in this introduction. Chapter 2 presents new results that advance understanding of business organizations such as corporations. It explains why they have limited liability, fungible shares and how the nature of their investments relates to the preferences of their owners. Core theory also gives reasons other than the desire to pool risk for joint ventures such as mutual funds.

CHAPTER 1

Pure Exchange

1. Summary

How traders value commodities and the total resources determine an optimal distribution of the commodities together with an associated set of optimal prices that depends on the total resources but not on the initial distribution of the total. These optimal prices illuminate several different sufficient conditions for a market to have a core. This chapter treats two cases. The first assumes a finite number of traders each with a concave valuation function for the commodities. The market has a core when the valuation function of each trader is a nondecreasing function of quantities or when the valuation functions are not necessarily nondecreasing and each trader gets a positive amount of every commodity in the final allocation. The second case assumes a continuum of infinitesimally small traders. Here the market has a core if each trader has enough resources to cover the cost of the optimal allocation. The examples in section 4 show that while a market can have a core and optimal prices, these optimal prices cannot always support the imputations in the core using the proceeds of trade. Such markets have cores but do not have a Walrasian equilibrium. Section 5 explains the role of money.

2. The Finite Case

The valuation function of trader i is $f^i(x^i, w^i)$ where x^i is an n-vector representing the quantities of the n commodities that trader i can choose and w^i is an n-vector representing his initial holdings of the same n commodities. The valuation of x^i depends on the initial holdings of w^i because each commodity represented by a coordinate of one vector is a perfect substitute for the commodity given by the same coordinate of the other vector. Hence the initial allotment of a commodity affects how much trader i would value it. Alternatively we may write the argument of the valuation function as $y^i = w^i + x^i$, thereby showing that w^i and x^i are perfectly substitutable. Let each valuation function be continuous and concave in both x^i and w^i. There are m traders ($i = 1, \ldots, m$). Let M denote the set of all traders and let S denote a subset of M also called a coalition. The members of a coalition can change their initial holdings by trading among themselves in a submarket. The number of possible submarkets is

15

immense, $2^m - m - 1$, counting pairs of traders, triplets, and so on. All may form. The optimal allocation of the holdings of the members of a coalition S is the solution of the following constrained maximum problem:

$$V(S) = \max \sum_{i \in S} f^i(x^i, w^i) \tag{1}$$

with respect to $x^i \geq 0$ subject to the following resource constraint:

$$\sum_{i \in S} x^i = \sum_{i \in S} w^i.$$

Call $V(S)$ the *characteristic function* of the coalition S. It shows the maximal value of the holdings of the coalition that can be attained by an optimal allocation of its total resources. The resource constraint is an equation, not an inequality, because a coalition cannot alter the total amount of the initial quantities of the commodities owned by its members. They can reallocate their holdings only by trading among themselves because costless disposal of any commodity is not feasible.

LEMMA 1.   *If each f^i is continuous, $w^i \geq 0$, and $\Sigma_{i \in S} w^i > 0$, the maximum problem has a solution.*

PROOF.   The hypotheses imply that the constraint set is a closed bounded set, indeed a simplex, and that the objective function is continuous. Hence the Weierstrass theorem on extrema yields the desired conclusion.   QED

The Lagrangian for this maximum problem is defined as follows:

$$\sum_{i \in S} f^i(x^i, w^i) + p \circ \sum_{i \in S} (w^i - x^i), \tag{2}$$

where p is an n-vector of Lagrangian multipliers. Owing to the nature of the constraints, these multipliers are not necessarily nonnegative. Let $f^i(x^i, w^i)$ have continuous first-order partials. Since the constraint set does have an interior point, the Kuhn–Tucker theorem applies so that a solution of the maximum problem must satisfy

$$f_x^i[x^i(S), w^i] - p(S) \leq 0 \quad \text{and} \quad [f_x^i[x^i(S), w^i] - p(S)] \circ x^i(S) = 0, \tag{3}$$

where $x^i(S)$ denotes the optimal bundle of commodities for trader i as a member of the coalition S and $p(S)$ is the vector of Lagrangian multipliers given by the solution of the constrained maximum problem.

Because S ranges over all possible coalitions and these coalitions compete for members, expression (1) is a sensible definition of the characteristic function. Corollary 1, which follows, shows that each person is at least as well off by trading as by retaining his initial endowment.

In order to shorten the notation, write $f^i(S)$ instead of $f^i[x(S), w^i]$. Call $\phi(S)$ the indicator function of the coalition S. It is an m-vector whose ith coordinate is one if individual i is a member of S and whose ith coordinate is zero if individual i is not a member of S. The indicator function shows who is a member of S. The scalar product $\phi(S) \circ a = \Sigma_{i \in S} a_i$.

THEOREM 1.a.   *Let each $f^i(x^i, w^i)$ be concave in both x^i and w^i and have first-order partial derivatives. If f^i is a nondecreasing function of x^i then*

$$a_i = f^i(M) - p(M) \circ [x^i(M) - w^i] \tag{4}$$

is in the core.

PROOF.   Since f^i is concave, it is differentiable on the hypothesis that it has first-order partials so that the Kuhn–Tucker theorem applies.[1] We must show that the imputation $a = \{a_i\}$, which is an m-vector, satisfies the following two conditions.

$$\phi(M) \circ a = V(M) \quad \text{and} \quad \phi(S) \circ a \geq V(S) \quad \text{for all } S \subset M. \tag{5}$$

The first condition is immediate.

$$\phi(M) \circ a = \sum_{i \in M} a_i = \sum_{i \in M} f^i(M) - \sum_{i \in M} p(M) \circ [x^i(M) - w^i] = V(M)$$

because $\Sigma_{i \in M}[x^i(M) - w^i] = 0$.

The proof of the second part of (5) employs the hypothesis that the valuation functions are concave so that

$$f^i_x(M) \circ [x^i(M) - x^i(S)] \leq f^i(M) - f^i(S).$$

Rearranging terms, this becomes

$$f^i(S) - f^i_x(M) \circ x^i(S) \leq f^i(M) - f^i_x(M) \circ x^i(M). \tag{6}$$

Since $x^i(M)$ satisfies the first-order conditions for a maximum, inequality (3) for $S = M$ says

$$0 \leq f^i_x(M) \leq p(M) \quad \text{and} \quad f^i_x(M) \circ x^i(M) = p(M) \circ x^i(M). \tag{7}$$

Together (6) and (7) imply that

$$f^i(S) \leq f^i(M) - p(M) \circ x^i(M) + f^i_x(M) \circ x^i(S).$$

Because $f^i_x(M) \geq 0$ and $x^i(S) \geq 0$, it follows that $0 \leq f^i_x(M) \circ x^i(S) \leq p(M) \circ x^i(S)$. Hence

$$\begin{aligned} f^i(S) &\leq f^i(M) - p(M) \circ [x^i(M) - x^i(S)] \\ &= f^i(M) - p(M) \circ [x^i(M) - w^i + w^i - x^i(S)] \end{aligned}$$

---

1. Owing to concavity the functions are differentiable if they have first-order partials that are not necessarily continuous.

so that

$$f^i(S) + p(M) \circ [w^i - x^i(S)] \leq f^i(M) - p(M) \circ [x^i(M) - w^i] = a_i. \quad (8)$$

$\Sigma_{i \in S} [w^i - x^i(S)] = 0$ because coalition S can only reallocate the initial holdings of its own members. Therefore, summing (8) over the members of S yields

$$V(S) = \sum_{i \in S} f^i(S) \leq \sum_{i \in S} a_i = \phi(S) \circ a. \qquad \text{QED}$$

Theorem 1.a postulates nondecreasing valuation functions and allows $x^i(M)$ to have zero coordinates. There is also a nonempty core under somewhat different assumptions. Let $x^i(M) > 0$ for all i. This assumption can be justified for example by certain kinds of valuation functions. Even if the valuation functions are not nondecreasing, $a_i = f^i(M) - f^i_x(M) \circ [x^i(M) - w^i]$ is in the core. Theorem 1.b establishes this result.

THEOREM 1.b. *Let each f^i be concave and have first-order partials. If $x^i(M) > 0$ for every i then $a_i = f^i(M) - f^i_x(M) \circ [x^i(M) - w^i]$ is in the core.*

PROOF. Concavity implies that

$$f^i(S) \leq f^i(M) - f^i_x(M) \circ [x^i(M) - x^i(S)] = a_i + f^i_x(M) \circ [w^i - x^i(S)] \quad (9)$$

because the hypothesis $x^i(M) > 0$ allows the substitution of $p(M)$ for $f^i_x(M)$. Inequality (9) implies

$$a_i \geq f^i(S) - f^i_x(M) \circ [w^i - x^i(S)] = f^i(S) - p(M) \circ [w^i - x^i(S)] \Rightarrow$$

$$\phi(S) \circ a \geq V(S) - p(M) \circ \sum_{i \in S} [w^i - x^i(S)] = V(S)$$

because S can only reallocate its own resources so that $\Sigma_{i \in S} [w^i - x^i(S)] = 0$.
QED

Note that the proofs of both parts of Theorem 1 show $V(S) \leq V(M) \; \forall \; S \subset M$. Therefore, the total resources are most valuable if all the trades occur in the central market provided that market has a core.

Under the hypotheses of Theorem 1.b, all prices need not be nonnegative, but under the hypotheses of Theorem 1.a, all must be nonnegative. Theorem 1.a allows some coordinates of $x^i(M)$ to be zero, but Theorem 1.b assumes all components are positive. Since disposal of commodities is costly, $x^i(M) \geq 0$, not all coordinates of $x^i(M)$ must be positive, and the sum of each coordinate over all the traders must be positive. The resource constraint says that $\Sigma_{i \in M} (x^i - w^i) = 0$ so that $p(M) \circ \Sigma_{i \in M} (x^i - w^i) = 0$, but it is not necessarily true that $p(M) \circ (x^i - w^i) = 0$ for each i. Hence so far in this model a trader's money stock need not be the same before and after trade. Although the sum over all traders of these changes of the money stocks is zero, the final distribution of the money holdings can differ from the initial distribution.

COROLLARY 1.   *Under the hypotheses of Theorem 1.a or 1.b, $a_i \geq f^i(w^i, w^i)$.*

PROOF.   This inequality is a consequence of the core constraint for a single individual i.   QED

These results reveal more about the valuation of the commodities and the properties of their demand functions. The total amount of resources available to a coalition of traders is the sum of their initial endowments. For the coalition of all traders, M, this total is $w = \Sigma_{i \in M} w^i$. The characteristic function $V(S)$ gives the maximal value for the initial resources w^i owned by the members of S. It depends on the optimal allocation of the coalition's *total* resources among its members but not on the initial distribution of their resources. The maximal valuation exists for every S under the hypotheses of Lemma 1. However, the price vector $p(M)$ depends on the total resources w but not on how it is distributed among the members of M. This remarkable fact needs proof.

COROLLARY 2.   *The price vector $p(M)$ depends on the total resources of M but does not depend on the initial distribution of these resources among the traders.*

PROOF.   Let $\{y^i\}$ be another initial distribution of the resources such that $\Sigma_1^m y^i = \Sigma_1^m w^i$. Let x_0^i denote the solution of the maximum problem for trader i as a member of the all-trader coalition, M. Recall that corresponding commodities in each of the vectors w^i, y^i, and x_0^i are perfect substitutes for each other. Let Δx^i denote the difference between the initial endowment of trader i and his optimal assignment so that $x_0^i = \Delta x_0^i + w^i = \Delta x_1^i + y^i$. Therefore, the first-order necessary condition for the maximum problem has the same price vector $p(M)$ as in the preceding because the first-order condition is the same $f_x^i(x_0^i) \leqq p(M)$ (cf. footnote 1).   QED

Next we show how the price vector, $p(M)$, given by the solution of the constrained maximum problem for the coalition of all the traders, M, is related to the gradient of the valuation function for the whole coalition M with respect to w^j.

$$V_{w^j} = f_{w^j}^j + \sum_{i=1}^{m} f_x^i \frac{\partial x^i}{\partial w^j} + \sum_{i \neq j} f_w^i \frac{\partial w^i}{\partial w^j}$$

$$= f_{w^j}^j + p(M) \sum_i \frac{\partial x^i}{\partial w^j} = f_{w^j}^j + p(M) \frac{\partial w}{\partial w^j}$$

because

$$w \equiv \sum_i x^i \Rightarrow \frac{\partial w}{\partial w^j} = \sum \frac{\partial x^i}{\partial w^j}$$

$$w \equiv \sum_i w^i \Rightarrow \frac{\partial w}{\partial w^j} = \sum \frac{\partial w^i}{\partial w^j} = 1.$$

Therefore,

$$V_{w^j} = f^j_{w^j} + p(M). \tag{10}$$

Equation (10) shows how the maximal valuation for the coalition M changes when the initial amount of wealth belonging to individual j changes. It is the sum of the wealth effect on individual j and the prices of the n commodities. The next result shows how the relations among the valuation functions of different coalitions depend on the status of the core.

It follows from equation (10) that the gradient of $V(M)$ with respect to w^j is the demand function for the n commodities. This gradient is a continuous function of $\{w^i\}$ if

i. $x^i(M) > 0$ for all w so that the necessary condition for the optimal x^i is an equation;

ii. each $f^i_w(x^i, w^i)$ is a continuous function of its arguments;

iii. each $f^i_x(x^i, w^i)$ is a continuous function of x^i and w^i.

Although the third condition is more than enough to prove the existence of a maximum (cf. lem. 1), it is needed to show the existence of prices capable of clearing the market. In addition to conditions i–iii, assume that the $n \times n$ matrix

iv. $f^i_{xx}(x^i, w^i)$ exists and is invertible for all nonnegative x.

It follows from the first-order necessary condition for the optimal x, $f^i_x(x^i, w^i) = p(M)$, that

$$f^i_{xx}(x^i_0, w^i) \circ \Delta x^i + f^i_{xw}(x^i_0, w^i) \circ \Delta w^i - \sum_j p_{w^j} \circ \Delta w^j = 0. \tag{11}$$

Note that p_{w^j}, $f^i_{xx}(x^i_0, w^i)$, and $f^i_{xw}(x^i_0, w^i)$ are $n \times n$ matrices and that Δx^i and Δw^i are n-vectors. If $f^i_{xx}(x^i_0, w^i)$ is invertible, equation (11) implies that

$$\Delta x^i + f^i_{xx}(.)^{-1} \left[f^i_{xw}(x^i_0, w^i) \circ \Delta w^i - \sum_j p_{w^j} \circ \Delta w^j \right] = 0. \tag{12}$$

The resource constraint implies

$$\sum \Delta x^i = \sum \Delta w^i = \Delta w.$$

Therefore, summing equation (12) over i yields

$$\sum_i \Delta w^i + \sum_i (f^i_{xx})^{-1} \left[f^i_{xw} \circ \Delta w^i - \sum_j p_{w^j} \circ \Delta w^j \right] = 0.$$

which becomes

$$\sum_i \left[I + (f^i_{xx})^{-1} f^i_{wx} \right] \circ \Delta w^i - \sum_i (f^i_{xx})^{-1} \sum_j p_{w^j} \circ \Delta w^j = 0. \tag{13}$$

Let all $\Delta w^i = 0$ save $\Delta w^h \neq 0$. Hence equation (13) implies that

$$\left[I + (f^h_{xx})^{-1} f^h_{wx} - \sum_j (f^i_{xx})^{-1} p_{w^h} \right] \circ \Delta w^h = 0.$$

Therefore, the expression within brackets must be singular so that

$$I + (f^h_{xx})^{-1} f^h_{wx} - \sum_j (f^i_{xx})^{-1} p_{w^h} = 0 \Rightarrow$$

$$p_{w^h} = \left[\sum_j (f^j_{xx})^{-1} \right] \left[I + (f^h_{xx})^{-1} f^h_{wx} \right]. \tag{14}$$

Equation (14) completes the proof of the following theorem:

THEOREM 2. *Let x^i_0 denote the optimal commodity vector for trader i so that $x^i_0 = x^i(M)$. If $x^i(M) > 0$ for all i so that $f^i_x(x^i_0, w^i) = p(M)$ for each i, $f^i_{xx}(x^i_0, w^i)$ is invertible, and $f^i_x(x^i, w^i)$ is continuous in a neighborhood of x^i_0, then the $n \times n$ matrix p_{w^j} satisfies equation (14).*

The matrix on the right-hand side of equation (14) is neither symmetric nor negative definite owing to the presence of the wealth effect given by the matrix $f^i_{wx}(x^i_0, w^i)$.

Prices are the Lagrangian multipliers from the solution of the problem of an optimal allocation of the given commodities among the *m* traders. These prices furnish every trader with a more powerful incentive to trade in the central market than in any submarket. This is a salient feature of the core. Since imputations in the core are undominated, no trader or group of traders can do better than to trade in the central market.

It is also useful to look at this in another way as if there were an auction of more than one commodity. A leading example is different kinds of financial assets. It is usually harder for an individual to make simultaneous bids and offers for various quantities of the *n* commodities than for a single commodity, especially when the value of each commodity depends on the quantities of the others. A trader who makes simultaneous bids or offers on many commodities must be ready to reverse or revise these for some in later auctions. He may wish to sell some things that he had bought earlier or bid more for some things that he could not buy in the preceding auctions. Owing to this, traders organize a sequence of auctions in order to simplify the purchase or sale of more than one commodity at a time. Organized markets for financial assets are the leading but are not the only cases in which there is a regular sequence of auctions.[2]

---

2. Bids or offers for substitute commodities could be treated as independent while bids or offers for complementary commodities could be regarded as a single commodity with components in fixed proportions to each other. If a trader were to suppose that his bid or offer on each com-

This model also illuminates some dynamic aspects of pure exchange. Write a new valuation function of trader i

$$v_{it} = f^i(x_t^i, x_{t-1}^i)$$

so that his valuation of the n-vector of commodities in round t depends on the quantities of the commodities on hand from the preceding round of exchange, $t - 1$. Let the total remain the same from round to round so that

$$\sum_{i=1}^{m} x_t^i = \sum_{i=1}^{m} x_{t-1}^i. \tag{15}$$

If traders could form all possible submarkets and could make tentative contracts during the first round so that x_1^i is in the core, then there would be no incentive to trade after the first round and $x_t^i = x_1^i$ for all $t \geq 1$. In this setting change would occur from one round to the next only if some traders enter or leave the market or if the total amount of available commodities changes from one round to the next. Equation (15) would not hold under either of these conditions. However, if equation (15) is valid but all potential trades could not be considered simultaneously on each round so that x_t^i is not necessarily in the core, then, as shown in the preceding discussion of auctions, additional trades would occur. Consequently, even if the sequence of trades $\{x_t^i\}$ is convergent, the limit would be in the core.

The task is easier for an individual who can trade at given prices, admittedly begging the question for now about the source of these prices. At these prices, an optimizing individual could choose x as the solution of the following maximum problem:

$$\max f(x, w) - p \circ (x - w)$$

with respect to nonnegative x. The term $p \circ (x - w)$ is the net cost of x so that the objective of this maximum problem is the maximum gain obtained by going from the initial w to the optimal x. A solution must satisfy the following first-order conditions:

$$f_x - p \leq 0 \quad \text{and} \quad (f_x - p) \circ x = 0.$$

The similarity of these conditions to equation (1) is evident. If $p = p(M)$, the prices support the imputations in the core and emerge from the trading that is induced by undominated imputations. Also, the solution of this maximum problem coincides with $x^i(M)$. Although the budget constraint summed over everybody equals zero, it does not follow that $p(M) \circ [x^i(M) - w^i] = 0$ for each trader i. However, because $x^i = w^i$ is a feasible choice for each trader, it is true that

---

modity would be successful then he would trade only one commodity at a time, contrary to what typically happens.

$$f^i[x^i(M), w^i] - p(M) \circ [x^i(M) - w^i] \geq f^i(w^i, w^i) \iff$$

$$f^i[x^i(M), w^i] - f^i(w^i, w^i) \geq p(M) \circ [x^i(M) - w^i]$$

so there is an upper bound on the net outlay.[3]

A different model can show how initial wealth affects trade. Let w_j^i denote arbitrary initial holdings of trader i at time t and let x_t^i denote the outcome of trade. The valuation function is $v_{it} = f^i(x_t^i, w_t^i)$. The resource constraint under pure exchange is $\sum_{i=1}^{m_t} x_t^i = \sum_{i=1}^{m_t} w_t^i$. Even if all potential trades affect the outcome on each round so that the imputations are the market's core on every round, because the initial bundles may change from round to round so do the market-clearing prices. By elaborating this model one could construct a dynamic theory of exchange.

3. A Continuum of Traders and the Extensive Margin

The preceding analysis focuses on the intensive margin so that an individual can get different amounts of the commodities depending on which coalition he joins. It is also instructive to consider the situation in which there is a continuum of infinitesimally small individuals. Each person is regarded as a point composed of three elements, (v, x, w), such that v, a scalar, is his valuation of the n-vector x that also depends on the n-vector w, his initial holdings of the n-commodities. No one varies the coordinates of x in response to changes in the terms of sale. An individual either buys or does not buy x. All variations of the total quantities demanded are due to changes in the *number* of buyers. Therefore, in this case the aggregate demand for commodities changes only when the extensive margin changes.[4]

This approach presents complications even in a simple case. For example, many individuals may want the same n-vector x, but each may value it differently even if all have the same w. Hence there is a distribution of v for given x and w. This cumulative distribution function (cdf), $H(.)$, of the v's depends on x and w so that

$$1 - H(v, x, w) = \int_v^\infty h(\zeta, x, w)d\zeta, \tag{1}$$

where $h(.)$ denotes the probability density function (pdf) of v. The cdf $H(.)$ shows how many people in the population attach a valuation not above v to x

---

3. The problems that arise in calculating $p(M)$ are outside the scope of this analysis. See Scarf 1973 for a detailed analysis of this difficult problem.

4. Hildenbrand 1994 is a recent detailed study that emphasizes market demand instead of individual demand. This gives a prominent place to the effects of changes in the number of buyers. The extensive margin in David Ricardo's theory of rent is perhaps the first important contribution to this approach. See Telser 1978, chap. 10, sec. 8.

given w. This means the n-vectors x and w are the parameters of the density function, h. Note that

$$\frac{\partial(1 - H(v, x, w))}{\partial v} = -h(v, x, w) \leq 0$$

so that the fraction of all the individuals with valuations not below v is a decreasing function of v. Although no individual intramarginal buyer responds to a change in the terms of sale, the total demand does respond owing to the effect on the number of individuals who become buyers. The expression in equation (1) shows how many individuals place a value on x that is above v. Their total valuation is given by the following function:

$$B(v, x, w) = \int_v^\infty \zeta h(\zeta, x, w) d\zeta . \tag{2}$$

The term $B(.)$ corresponds to the objective function $\Sigma_i f^i(x^i, w^i)$ for the finite case shown in equation (1.1).

Each trader is represented by a point (v, x, w) in R^{2n+1} such that the first coordinate is the scalar v giving the valuation and the remaining $2n$ coordinates are the coordinates of the n-vectors, x and w. For the grand coalition, M, that owns the n-vector of the total resources, W, the optimal allocation to its members is a continuous functional, $x(v, w)$, that is the solution of the following constrained maximum problem:

$$\max \iiint_{v \in M} vh(v, x, w) dv \, dx \, dw \tag{3}$$

with respect to $x \geq 0$ subject to $\iiint_{v \in M} xh(v, x, w) \, dv \, dx \, dw = W$. The existence of a maximum is assured because the constraint set is compact and the objective function is continuous (cf. lem. 1). The Lagrangian for this problem is given by

$$\iiint_{v \in M} vh(v, x, w) dv \, dx \, dw + p \circ \left[W - \iiint_{v \in M} xh(v, x, w) dv \, dx \, dw \right],$$

where p denotes the n-vector of Lagrangian multipliers. The optimal x must satisfy the following first-order condition:

$$vh_x - h(v, x, w)p - (p \circ x)h_x \leq 0. \tag{4}$$

Rearranging terms in inequality (4) yields

$$(v - p \circ x) h_x (v, x, w) - p \, h(v, x, w) \leq 0. \tag{5}$$

Suppose that $v - p \circ x = 0$. For the positive coordinates of $x(v, w)$, the corresponding coordinates of condition (5) would be equalities. For these positive coordinates of x, it would follow that the corresponding coordinates of $-p \, h(v, x, w)$ equal zero. Since h is a pdf, it is nonnegative. It would follow that either $h(v, x, w) = 0$, which is impossible for these x, or that the prices of these commodities would be zero, so that there would be positive quantities of only the free commodities, another impossibility. Therefore, $x \geqq 0$ implies $v - p \circ x > 0$. The set of buyers includes the x such that $v - p \circ x > 0$. Consequently, the corresponding nonzero coordinates of the two vectors, h_x and p, have the same sign. This finishes the proof of

LEMMA 1.   *The maximum problem defined in equation (3) has a nonnegative solution in the set $B(M) = \{x \mid v - p \circ x > 0\}$. For $x \in B(M)$, the coordinates of h_x and p agree in sign.*

This lemma says that only those persons get a commodity who value it more than its cost. The buying region $B(M)$ is an open set. The boundary of the extensive margin is given by the functional $x(v, w)$ that satisfies equation (5). When a commodity has a positive price, the sign of its coordinate in h_x is positive. If a commodity has a negative price then its coordinate in h_x has a negative sign.

Complementary slackness gives a second necessary condition. Any solution must satisfy

$$[(v - p \circ x) h_x (v, x, w) - h(v, x, w) p] \circ x = 0. \tag{6}$$

Since $v - p \circ x > 0$ by Lemma 1 and $h(v, x, w) \geqq 0$, it follows from equation (6) that $h_x \circ x$ and $p(M) \circ x$ must agree in sign. This completes the proof of

LEMMA 2.   *The maximum problem defined in equation (3) has a solution only at those points in the set $B(M)$ where $h_x \circ x$ and $p(M) \circ x$ agree in sign.*

The results of Lemma 2 are weaker than those of Lemma 1. While Lemma 2 refers to the scalar products, $h_x \circ x$ and $p \circ x$, Lemma 1 refers to the signs of the coordinates of the two vectors, p and h_x.

The solution of the constrained maximum problem defined by equation (3) determines the value of the resources owned by a coalition as in the finite case. Let $V(W, M)$ denote the function giving the maximal value of the resources owned by M. The parallel to the finite case is striking. For each $x > 0$ in the buying region, the demand function satisfies the equation

$$V_w = p \tag{7}$$

like equation (1.10). To verify this, first, there is

$$V_w = \iiint v h_x \circ x_w \, dv \, dx \, dw,$$

and, second, there is the resource constraint that implies

$$\iiint (h + x \circ h_x) dv \, dx \, dw = 1.$$

Together with the first-order condition (5), these two equations imply equation (7).

The necessary condition (5) for the optimal x reveals more properties of the solution as well as a suggestion for computing it. First, x is in the buying region if $v \geq v_0$ so that there is a critical lower bound of the valuations marking the floor of the buying region. To show that the optimal prices depend on the coalition M and its total resources w, write $p(M, W)$ or, more concisely, $p(M)$. Integrating condition (5) over the buying region gives the following equation:

$$\iiint_{v_0}^{\infty} vh_x \, dv \, dx \, dw - p(M) \iiint_{v_0}^{\infty} (h + x \circ h_x) dv \, dx \, dw = 0. \tag{8}$$

Solve this for $p(M)$ and obtain

$$p(M) = \frac{\displaystyle\iiint_{v_0}^{\infty} vh_x \, dv \, dx \, dw}{\displaystyle\iiint_{v_0}^{\infty} (h + x \circ h_x) dv \, dx \, dw}.$$

Equation (8) suggests a possible way to compute $p(M)$. Begin with a very small value of v_0 and calculate the two integrals in equation (8). Next seek an n-vector $P(M)$ that can make the two sides equal. If this is not possible, raise v_0 by a small amount and repeat this procedure. Under suitable conditions, there will be convergence to a solution that will approximate equality in (8) as closely as desired.

Equation (8) also gives useful information about the gradient of $p(M)$ with respect to the lower bound v_0.

$$\frac{\partial p(M)}{\partial v_0} = \frac{\displaystyle\int vh_x(v_0, x) dx \, dw}{\displaystyle\int [h(v_0, x) + xh_x(v_0, x)] dx \, dw}.$$

By Lemma 1, p and h_x agree in sign. If $p > 0$ then $h_x > 0$ and all the coordinates of the gradient $p_v(M)$ would be positive. This is plausible. The higher is the critical lower bound of the extensive margin, the higher is the price of each commodity.

To study the status of the core for this case requires an assumption about the distribution of the initial endowment of resources among the traders. Denote an individual trader by X. The term X corresponds to a commodity bundle, the n-vector x, to which the trader attaches the value v. Let $w(X)$ denote the initial endowment of trader x. The integral over all the traders equals their total resources,

$$\iiint wh(v, x, w) dv \, dx \, dw = W.$$

Given an initial distribution of the resources among the traders, let them form any coalition they please. When will there be a nonempty core? As we shall see, the status of the core depends on the initial distribution of the resources among the traders.

Let the initial distribution of the resources w among the traders be such that any trader X in the buying set $B(M)$ can afford to buy x so that $p(M) \circ x = p(M) \circ w$. Hence trader X can exchange $w(X)$ for x at the prices $p(M)$. Consequently, X will choose x or $w(X)$ depending on which is bigger, v or $p(M) \circ x$. Since x is feasible for X, the return to X is

$$\max \{p(M) \circ w(X), v + p(M) \circ [w(X) - x]\}.$$

THEOREM 1.   *Let the distribution of the initial resources among the traders be such that $p(M) \circ x = p(M) \circ w(X)$ so that x is feasible for each trader in the buying set. Then*

$$a = v - p(M) \circ [x - w(X)]$$

satisfies all the core constraints so there is a nonempty core.

PROOF.   For $v \in M$,

$$\iiint ah \, dv \, dx \, dw = \iiint \{v - p(M) \circ [x - w(X)]\} h \, dv \, dx \, dw$$

$$= \iiint vh \, dv \, dx \, dw = V(M).$$

Next we must verify that

$$\int_S ah \, dv \, dx \, dw \geq V(S). \tag{9}$$

This is equivalent to

$$\int_S \{v - p(M) \circ [x - w(X)]\} h \, dv \, dx \, dw \geq \max \int_S vh \, dv \, dx \, dw$$

subject to

$$\int_S p(M) \circ [x - w(X)] h \, dv \, dx \, dw = 0.$$

Owing to the nature of the resource constraint, inequality (9) is true.   QED

Theorem 1 gives an implication of a nonempty core for infinitesimally small traders if the distribution of resources among the traders allow each person who places a value on x above its cost to pay for x from his initial endowment. For any trader X such that $v > p \circ x$, his initial endowment is big enough to satisfy the equation $p \circ x = p \circ w(X)$. This means there is no monetary gain or loss resulting from the exchange of $w(X)$ for x by any trader whose valuation of x exceeds its cost. The situation described in this theorem may be called a Walrasian equilibrium. Market-clearing prices are at the center of the stage in a Walrasian equilibrium. Each trader values his initial holdings at these prices. Because the value of his initial holdings at these market-clearing prices equals the value of x at these prices so that his budget constraint holds with equality, there is no monetary gain or loss from the trades themselves. Each trader can decide whether to keep w or exchange it for x solely on the basis of the comparison between v and $p \circ x$. This does not mean that a trader takes the market-clearing prices as data in the sense that he faces infinitely elastic supplies of commodities at these prices. It is true that these prices do not depend on the initial distribution of resources among the trader but only on the total amount of resources. One can say that prices are data for an individual trader but it would be misleading to say this. The prices result from vigorous competition among the traders. Core theory implies all trades occur at these prices. However, there are many equilibria in the core of a market that are not Walrasian. Example 3 in section 3 is a non-Walrasian equilibrium in the core of a market. Negishi (1985) is a forceful expositor of some consequences of a non-Walrasian equilibrium.

The market with a continuum of traders is not like the finite case where the valuation for each trader is a concave function of x. The status of the core in the present case, since it relies entirely on the extensive margin, cannot depend on the shape of the traders' valuation functions. Yet there is a common feature. In the finite case, Theorem 2.1.b assumes $x^i(M) > 0$. The corresponding assumption for a continuum of traders is that $v - p(M) \circ x > 0$ for each active trader. Hence each trader X who exchanges w for x must value x above its cost.

The hypothesis in Theorem 1 that each trader X can pay the cost of x places a restriction on the initial distribution of the resources among the traders. The market-clearing price given by the solution of the constrained maximum problem as defined in (3) depends on the *total* resources but not on how these are distributed among the individual traders. Some distributions of the total resources could stop some individuals from getting x because $p(M) \circ w(X) < p(M) \circ x$ although their values of x are above the cost of x so that $v > p(M) \circ x$. Such distributions cannot support a nonempty core by means of trade alone without payments among the individuals independent of their trades. Example 3 in the next section shows this, since $v > px^3 > pw^3$. Therefore, the conditions in Theorem 3 are sufficient but are not necessary for a nonempty core. More generally, a nonempty core cannot be supported by constant-unit prices for those distributions of the initial resources such that some traders retain $w(X)$ because x is beyond their means at the prices given by the solution of the optimization problem. Hence a market can have a core without having a Walrasian equilibrium.

4. Examples

Simple examples can illuminate the breadth of the preceding results. Each of
the following examples has three traders, two commodities, and an integer
quantity of each commodity. While the latter assumption is a departure from
the preceding theory that assumes continuously divisible commodities, it has a
considerable advantage because it makes computations easier and thereby
brings out more readily some subtle and important aspects of exchange.

EXAMPLE 1.   The valuation functions of the three traders, $T_i, i = 1, \ldots, 3,$
are as follows.

T_1			T_2			T_3		
x_{11}	x_{12}	v_1	x_{21}	x_{22}	v_2	x_{31}	x_{32}	v_3
0	1	100	0	1	90	0	1	95
1	0	80	1	0	100	1	0	85
1	1	max {100, 80}	1	1	max {90, 100}	1	1	max {85, 95}

The first two columns for each trader show the number of units of each commodity, and the third column shows the trader's valuation of that vector. Thus,
Trader 1 places a valuation of 100 on the vector $\{0, 1\}$ and a valuation of 80 on
the vector $\{1, 0\}$. In this example the nature of the valuation as shown in the
last row is such that no trader wants more than one unit of any commodity. The
vector $w = \{1, 1\}$ denotes the total resources so that one unit of each commodity
is available for distribution. The allocation of the resources to the 3 traders that
maximizes $\Sigma\, v(x^i)$ is as follows:

$$x^1 = \{0, 1\}; \qquad x^2 = \{1, 0\}; \qquad \text{and} \quad x^3 = \{0, 0\}.$$

The optimal prices satisfy the following conditions:

$$95 < p_1(M) \le 100 \quad \text{and} \quad 85 < p_2(M) \le 100.$$

Let the initial distribution of the total resources among the three individuals be
given by

$$w^1 = \{1, 0\}; \qquad w^2 = \{0, 1\}; \qquad \text{and} \quad w^3 = \{0, 0\}.$$

Plainly, $p(M) \circ x^i = p(M) \circ w^i$. Hence the cost of the optimal vector equals the
value of the initial endowment for each trader. Given the initial endowments of
its members, each coalition can be sure of getting at least the following returns:

$$v(T_1) = 80; \qquad v(T_2) = 90; \qquad v(T_3) = 0; \qquad v(T_1, T_2) = 200;$$

$$v(T_1,\, T_3) = 85; \qquad v(T_2, T_3) = 95; \quad \text{and} \quad v(T_1, T_2, T_3) = 200.$$

By Theorem 3.1, when $p(M) \circ x^i = p(M) \circ w^i$ and x^i is the optimal vector for T_i, the imputation

$$a_i = v(x^i) - p(M) \circ (x^i - w^i) \tag{1}$$

satisfies all the core constraints. Therefore in Example 1, $a_i = v(x^i)$ does satisfy all the conditions for a nonempty core.

Now change the initial w to $\{1, 2\}$. The optimal assignment becomes

$$x^1 = \{0, 1\}; \qquad x^2 = \{1, 0\}; \qquad \text{and} \quad x^3 = \{0, 1\}.$$

Let the distribution of w among the three traders be given by

$$w^1 = \{1, 0\}; \qquad w^2 = \{0, 1\}; \qquad \text{and} \quad w^3 = \{0, 1\}.$$

Save that the optimal assignment of commodities to T_3 is the same as his original endowment, the imputation $a_i = v(x^i)$ satisfies all the core constraints and, as in the preceding, $p(M) \circ (x^i - w^i) = 0$.

Changing w to $\{2, 1\}$ gives a similar result for the following initial distribution:

$$w^1 = \{1, 0\}; \qquad w^2 = \{0, 1\}; \qquad \text{and} \quad w^3 = \{1, 0\}.$$

Now, however, although Trader 3 still has the same final allocation as his initial resources so that he does not trade, his presence still affects the outcome because it narrows the bounds on the prices as compared to the previous examples.

Scarf and Shapley (1974, 104–23) give a result for a more general class of models that includes this example. They assume no trader wants more than one unit of an array of commodities and has ordinal preferences among them. They prove that in this case the market always has a nonempty core. When preferences among the indivisible commodities are more complicated, they show that the core may disappear.

EXAMPLE 2.   The next two examples are more complicated. Example 2 shows that although the core is nonempty, it cannot be supported by trades at the optimal prices. Trades at the optimal prices that satisfy each person's budget constraint constitute a Walrasian equilibrium. Therefore, there is no Walrasian equilibrium in this nonempty core. It is a well-known result that if a Walrasian equilibrium exists, it must be in the core. (For this result, due to Shapley, see Scarf 1962, 130, and also Debreu and Scarf 1963, thm. 1.) More generally, a market must have a nonempty core in order to have a Walrasian equilibrium. Hence these examples are especially important since they show that a market with a nonempty core need not have a Walrasian equilibrium. Therefore, while a nonempty core for a market is necessary, it is not sufficient for the existence of a Walrasian equilibrium.

The pertinent data for the three traders are as follows.

T_1			T_2			T_3		
x_{11}	x_{12}	v_1	x_{21}	x_{22}	v_2	x_{31}	x_{32}	v_3
0	1	100	0	1	90	0	1	95
1	0	80	1	0	100	1	0	85
1	1	170	1	1	185	1	1	175

Let the vector of resources, w, be $\{2, 2\}$. The optimal allocation of w among the three traders is

$$x^1 = \{0, 1\}; \qquad x^2 = \{1, 0\}; \qquad \text{and} \quad x^3 = \{1, 1\}.$$

Let the initial distribution of the commodities among the three traders be as follows:

$$w^1 = \{1, 0\}; \qquad w^2 = \{1, 1\}; \qquad \text{and} \quad w^3 = \{0, 1\}.$$

For this initial distribution of resources, the values of the characteristic functions are given by

$$v(T_1) = 80; \qquad v(T_2) = 185; \qquad v(T_3) = 95; \qquad v(T_1, T_2) = 270;$$

$$v(T_1, T_3) = 185; \qquad v(T_2, T_3) = 280; \qquad \text{and} \quad v(T_1, T_2, T_3) = 375.$$

It is not difficult to verify that the core is not empty. Thus, $a = \{90, 190, 95\}$ satisfies all of the core constraints. The optimal prices must satisfy the following conditions:

$$80 < p_1(M) \leq 85; \qquad 90 < p_2(M) \leq 95; \qquad \text{and}$$

$$p_1(M) + p_2(M) \leq 175.$$

Let us see whether, given prices that satisfy these inequalities, the following imputations,

$$a_i = v(x^i) - p(M) \circ (x^i - w^i),$$

are capable of meeting all the core constraints.

It is evident at the outset that a nonempty core requires a lower bound of 95 on a_3. Given $w^3 = \{0, 1\}$, it follows that $p_2(M)$ must equal 95. This would imply $80 < p_1(M) \leq 80$, giving a contradiction. This proves that the optimal prices cannot yield a_i satisfying equation (1) that would be in the core. Yet the core is nonvoid because the imputation $\{90, 195, 95\}$ does satisfy all the core constraints.

EXAMPLE 3.   Example 3 has a nonempty core, the imputations given by equation (1) satisfy all the core constraints, but it is not possible to satisfy the individual budget constraint $p(M) \circ (x^i - w^i) = 0$ for all the traders. In this example a different display of each trader's valuation is more revealing. The left-hand column of Example 3 shows the coordinates of commodity 2. The bottom row shows the coordinates of commodity 1. The entries in the body of the tableau show the trader's valuations. The tableau is like a graph such that the bottom row is the x-axis, the left-hand column is the y-axis, and the entries in the body of the tableau are the valuations for the commodity vectors. Thus for Trader 1, the entry 165 is his valuation of the vector $x = \{1, 2\}$.

Trader 1			
2	110	165	215
1	60	125	180
0	0	70	130
(0, 0)	0	1	2

Trader 2			
2	100	170	220
1	55	130	190
0	0	80	145
(0, 0)	0	1	2

Trader 3			
2	75	150	220
1	40	125	200
0	0	90	170
(0, 0)	0	1	2

For all 3 traders the valuations are increasing concave functions (cf. thm. 2.1.a). Let the total resources be $w = \{3, 3\}$. The optimal assignment of commodities giving the maximum $\Sigma\, v(x^i)$ is as follows:

$$x^1 = \{0, 2\}; \qquad x^2 = \{1, 1\}; \qquad \text{and} \quad x^3 = \{2, 0\}.$$

These three imputations have the interesting property that each one is optimal with respect to a certain set of alternatives. Thus, consider the best allocation of a bundle with two units of commodity 2. This bundle $\{0, 2\}$ is most valuable in the hands of Trader 1 because his valuation of $\{0, 2\} = \max\{110, 100, 75\}$. Similarly, a bundle $\{1, 1\}$ is most valuable to Trader 2, and a bundle $\{2, 0\}$ is most valuable to Trader 3. The maximum, $v(T_1, T_2, T_3)$, equals 410.

The optimal prices induced by this optimal assignment must satisfy the following conditions:

$$60 < p_1(M) \le 75; \qquad 40 < p_2(M) \le 50.$$

These bounds support the optimal distribution of the commodities among the three traders in the sense that no one has an incentive to trade his optimal assignment for some other bundle at prices that are within these limits. The upper bound for $p_1(M)$ comes from the condition that it must not exceed the incremental gain of the value to Trader 2 from decreasing his holdings of commodity 1 by 1 unit from $\{1, 1\}$ to $\{0, 1\}$. The incremental gain is $130 - 55 = 75$. The lower bound must be high enough to prevent Trader 2 from increasing his holdings of commodity 1 by 1 unit $(190 - 130 = 60)$. The upper bound on $p_2(M)$ equals $110 - 60 = 50$ because this is the incremental value of commodity 2 in Trader 1's optimal allocation. The lower bound of 40 is high enough to prevent Trader 2 from increasing his holdings of commodity 2 by 1 unit $(40 = 170 - 130)$.

Let the initial distribution of the resources among the traders be as follows:

$$w^1 = \{1, 1\}; \qquad w^2 = \{2, 0\}; \qquad \text{and} \quad w^3 = \{0, 2\}.$$

Next we compute the maximum valuations for each of the coalitions as determined by the distribution of the resources among the individual members of the coalitions. For the singletons, the valuations of the initial endowments are as follows:

$$v(T_1) = 125; \qquad v(T_2) = 145; \qquad \text{and} \quad v(T_3) = 75.$$

For the pairs, the values of the characteristic function are:

$$v(T_1, T_2) = 270,$$

and the optimal assignments are $x^1 = \{1, 1\}$ and $x^2 = \{2, 0\}$;

$$v(T_1, T_3) = 235,$$

and the optimal assignments are $x^1 = \{0, 2\}$ and $x^3 = \{1, 1\}$;

$$v(T_2, T_3) = 270$$

and the optimal assignments are $x^2 = \{0, 2\}$ and $x^3 = \{2, 0\}$.

The claim is that for $p_1(M) = 75$ and $p_2(M) = 50$, the imputations, a_i, given by equation (1), satisfy all the core constraints.

$$
\begin{array}{lllll}
p \circ w^1 = 125 & p \circ w^2 = 150 & p \circ w^3 = 100 & p \circ \sum w^i = 375 \\
p \circ x^1 = 100 & p \circ x^2 = 125 & p \circ x^3 = 150 & p \circ \sum x^i = 375 \\
v(x^1) = 110 & v(x^2) = 130 & v(x^3) = 170 & \sum v(x^i) = 410 \\
v(w^1) = 125 & v(w^2) = 145 & v(w^3) = 75 & \sum v(w^i) = 345 \\
a_1 = 130 & a_2 = 150 & a_3 = 130 & \sum a_i = 410 .
\end{array}
\tag{1}
$$

The imputation $\{a_1, a_2, a_3\}$ given in (1) does satisfy all the core constraints as follows:

$$a_1 + a_2 \geq 270, \qquad a_1 + a_3 \geq 235, \qquad a_2 + a_3 \geq 270,$$

$$a_1 \geq 125, \qquad a_2 \geq 145, \qquad a_3 \geq 75, \qquad a_1 + a_2 + a_3 = 410. \qquad (2)$$

However, because $p \circ x^3 > p \circ w^3$, Trader 3 cannot pay for his optimal allocation from the proceeds of the sale of his initial endowment at the optimal prices, and his deficit is 50. Also, the proceeds of traders 1 and 2 from the sale of their initial endowments at these optimal prices exceed their payments for their optimal allocations, and the surplus of each of these traders is 25.

Example 3 shows there can be a nonempty core associated with the optimal price vector and imputations given by equation (1) although the value of some individual's initial endowment at the optimal prices is too small to cover the cost of his optimal assignment. Although for each trader i, $a_i = v_i + p(M) \circ (w^i - x^i)$ is in the core, it does not follow that $p(M) \circ (w^i - x^i) = 0$ for each trader. This is clear because $\{v_1(x^1), v_2(x^2), v_3(x^3)\}$ does not satisfy the core constraints. Therefore, some trader could not obtain enough revenue from the proceeds of the sale of his initial holdings of the commodities to pay the cost of his optimal allocation. To satisfy the core constraints by means of trade among the individuals may also require that some traders receive an amount in excess of their net sales at optimal prices while others pay an amount above their initial endowment at these optimal prices. A nonempty core for pure exchange can be supported by trades at the optimal prices if the budget constraint is satisfied for *each* individual trader. When this is possible, it is a Walrasian equilibrium. However, as Example 3 shows, this is not always possible. Even so, the imputation shown in (1) is in the core. This raises the question of how this can be done.

The imputation a_i is the net gain in money from trade. It can be written more generally as follows:

$$a_i = v(x^i) + b_i, \qquad (3)$$

where b_i is the payment, if negative, or receipt, if positive, in money[5] and

$$\sum_i b_i = 0. \qquad (4)$$

Neither $b_i = p(M) \circ (w^i - x^i)$ nor $b_i = 0$ for each i is necessary for the validity of equation (4) although these conditions are sufficient for equation (4). The formula for the imputation shown in equation (3) means that a trader does not value his initial allocation w^i at the market-clearing prices $p(M)$. His valuation is $v(w^i)$ just as his valuation of his optimal allocation x^i is $v(x^i)$. The imputation $\{v(x^i) + b_i\}$ is in the core if it can satisfy the inequalities (2). The following ar-

---

5. Because the valuation is in money, b_i is commensurate with the valuation. It is not "transferable utility." See the appendix for more details on this.

ray shows three distinct imputations in the core for this example given by equation (3).

Imputation	(1)	(2)	(3)
$a_1 = b_1 + v(x^1)$	$30 + 110 = 140$	$30 + 110 = 140$	$15 + 110 = 125$
$a_2 = b_2 + v(x^2)$	$30 + 130 = 160$	$45 + 130 = 175$	$45 + 130 = 175$
$a_3 = b_3 + v(x^3)$	$-60 + 170 = 110$	$-75 + 170 = 95$	$-60 + 170 = 110$

The discrepancy between payments and receipts would vanish if Example 3 were modified so that the quantities were continuously divisible and the valuations were continuous concave functions of the quantities. There would be initial endowments of the given resources that would support a nonempty core via the imputation $a_i = v_i + p(M) \circ (w^i - x^i)$. Thus let the initial endowments be as follows:

$$w^1 = \left(\frac{2}{3}, 1 \right) \qquad w^2 = \left(\frac{4}{3}, \frac{1}{2} \right) \qquad w^3 = \left(1, \frac{3}{2} \right).$$

Hence $p(M) \circ w^i = p(M) \circ x^i$ for each i. By suitably interpolating valuations between the points in the array it can be shown that the core is supportable by trades such that expenditures equal receipts for each individual. However, the feasibility of this procedure does depend on the initial distribution of the resources. These must be on the hyperplanes containing the optimal allocations at the optimal prices for each individual.

5. Conclusions

The first main result, Theorem 1.a, shows that a market has a core if there is a finite number of traders each with a concave nondecreasing valuation function. Alternatively, by Theorem 1.b, the market has a core even if the valuation functions are not nondecreasing if every trader obtains a positive quantity of each commodity in the optimal assignment. In both cases the market has a core even if trade results in monetary gains for some traders and losses for others. The aggregate demand for the commodities depends only on the intensive margin because individual demand responds to price changes. The aggregate demand does not depend on entry or exit of traders.

The second case assumes a continuum of infinitesimally small traders. Now the total quantities demanded respond to prices although no individual changes the quantities demanded as prices change since there is no intensive margin. Each person compares the cost of the bundle of commodities at the optimal prices to his valuation of this bundle. He buys if his valuation exceeds the cost and if his resources are ample enough to pay the cost. The aggregate demand changes when price changes because of changes in the *number* of buyers. The market has a core for very general distributions of traders' valuations of commodity bundles provided no individual has a monetary gain or loss from trade at the optimal prices.

Study of these situations is inspired by some interesting results for markets with individuals who trade one commodity (Telser 1988, chap. 1). A single-unit trader wants or offers at most one unit of the commodity. Such a market always has a core. When traders want or offer more than one unit of the commodity, the market has a core if the individual trader's valuation is a concave function of the commodity. Many results for multiunit trade can be deduced from those for single-unit trade on the hypothesis that individual valuation functions are concave. However, when more than one commodity is traded, the situation is much more complicated. It is not possible to relate the status of the core for the market when the traders have concave valuations to the status of the core for a market with a continuum of infinitesimally small traders because concave valuations do not reduce unambiguously to component infinitesimally small traders.[6]

APPENDIX. HOW MONEY ENTERS[7]

Section 1 assumes each trader has a valuation function $f^i(x^i, w^i)$ showing how much he values x^i given his initial holdings of the commodities, w^i. This valuation of the commodities, call it v_i, is a number measured in money and $v_i = f^i(x^i, w^i)$. This raises several questions. First, must v_i be an amount of money that individual i could pay for x^i? Second, if money is itself one of the n commodities, how does a change in its quantity affect v_i? Third, what distinguishes the thing called money from other commodities?

Before answering these questions, it is desirable at the outset to describe several appealing aspects of valuations in terms of money. As in Section 1, let $p(M)$ denote the optimal price vector given by the solution of the constrained maximum problem. Hence $p(M) \circ x^i$ is the market value of x^i. Similarly, in more concise notation write $f^i(M) \equiv f^i[x^i(M)]$. The first-order necessary conditions for the maximum are

$$f^i_x(M) \leq p(M) \quad \text{and} \quad f^i_x(M) \circ x^i(M) = p(M) \circ x^i(M).$$

Individual i content with $x^i(M)$ must attribute a value to it at least as high as the market so that

6. They would do so if all commodities were gross substitutes.

7. For a related and more detailed analysis of the role of money, see Telser 1978, chap. 10.

$$f^i(M) \geq p(M) \circ x^i(M) = f^i_x(M) \circ x^i(M).$$

A subhomogeneous f^i satisfies this inequality.[8] The following imputation a_i,

$$a_i = f^i(M) - p(M) \circ [x^i(M) - w^i],$$

is in the core under the hypotheses of Theorem 1.a. Individual i begins with w^i and moves to $x^i(M)$. The money measure of this change at the prices $p(M)$ is $p(M) \circ [w^i - x^i(M)]$. In terms of the valuation function, the measure of the change is $f^i(x^i) - f^i(w^i)$. Since individual i regards $x^i(M)$ as more valuable than w^i, the increment of the valuation is not below the market measure of the change. In symbols,

$$f^i(M) - f^i(w^i) \geq p(M) \circ [x^i(M) - w^i].$$

This inequality shows that the imputation a_i does satisfy the core constraint for individual i.

It is superfluous to require individuals to possess an amount of money equal to their valuations of x. Any commodity in x is available for trade. To assume valuations are in terms of money does not mean traders must have enough of the particular commodity called money to pay an amount equal to their valuation for the bundle x.

Imputation a_i seems vulnerable to the objection that there is double counting of money. Thus if money is one of the n commodities included in x^i then it is an argument of the valuation function. Hence $p(M) \circ [w^i - x^i(M)]$ should not be subtracted from the valuation since it is a monetary magnitude already present as an argument in the valuation function. However, there would be no double counting if $x^i(M)$ did satisfy the budget constraint as an equation so that

$$p(M) \circ [w^i - x^i(M)] = 0.$$

If so, the exchange of w^i for $x^i(M)$ would not change the money holdings of individual i. Thanks to Corollary 2 of Theorem 1 that asserts $p(M)$ and $x^i(M)$ do not depend on the distribution of the initial holdings $\{w^i\}$ but only on the sum $\sum_i w^i$, there is no loss of generality in assuming that each individual budget constraint holds with equality. As we shall see, there are compelling reasons to measure the valuation of commodities in terms of money.

The standard approach equips trader i with a function $g^i(x^i, w^i)$ indicating the utility of the commodities. Ordinal utility means anyone can compare any two vectors of commodities and state which is better or if the two are equivalent. Ordinal utility does not allow a numerical measure of the difference be-

---

8. If ϕ is subhomogeneous then $\phi(\lambda x) \leq \lambda \phi(x) \ \forall \lambda \geq 1$. If it also has a continuous gradient then

$$\phi(x) \geq \phi_x(x) \circ x.$$

tween the utilities of two bundles unless both have the same utility so their difference is zero. Cardinal utility can measure the numerical difference between the utilities of any two bundles. Also, cardinal utility hardly strains credulity more than ordinal utility thanks to the von Neumann–Morgenstern axioms leading to their utility function (Neumann and Morgenstern 1947, chap. 1, sec. 3). To see this, consider an experiment. Let an individual rank order three n-vectors of commodities, A, B, and C, so that $A > B > C$. Let the individual choose between two alternatives: either B for sure or A with probability p and C with probability $1 - p$, $0 < p < 1$. It is reasonable to believe there is a p such that the individual is indifferent between these two alternatives. If so, there is a cardinal indicator of utility supplying a numerical measure of utility determinate up to an increasing linear transformation. Call this cardinal utility indicator $g^i(.)$. Assume also that it has continuous first-order partial derivatives so that it is differentiable.

Neither ordinal nor cardinal utility compares utility among different people. The utility of each individual is sui generis. Nevertheless one can say useful things about different individuals with the help of the concept of dominance and without interpersonal comparisons of utility.

Let $\mathbf{X} = \{x^i\}$ and $\mathbf{Y} = \{y^i\}$ be two different distributions of the commodities among the m individuals. Here $\mathbf{X}$ strongly dominates $\mathbf{Y}$ if $g^i(x^i, w^i) > g^i(y^i, w^i)$ for all i. If $\mathbf{X}$ strongly dominates $\mathbf{Y}$ then everybody prefers $\mathbf{X}$ to $\mathbf{Y}$. If these were the only two alternatives, $\mathbf{X}$ would be chosen unanimously. The terms $\mathbf{X}$ and $\mathbf{Y}$ do not strongly dominate each other if $g^i(x^i, w^i) \not> g^i(y^i, w^i)$ for all i and $g^i(y^i, w^i) \not> g^i(x^i, w^i)$ for all i. When $\mathbf{X}$ and $\mathbf{Y}$ do not strongly dominate each other there is an m-vector $\mathbf{b} = \{b_1, \ldots, b_m\} \geq 0$ such that $\sum_{i=1}^m b_i[g^i(x^i) - g^i(y^i)] = 0$. This vector $\mathbf{b}$ is determinate only up to multiplication by a positive scalar.

Let $\{w^i \mid i = 1, \ldots, m\}$ denote an initial distribution of resources. An admissible distribution is a set $\{w^i\}$ such that $w^i \geq 0$ and $\Sigma_i w^i > 0$. An optimal allocation of the total resources for the members of M is given by the solution of a constrained maximum problem. Choose a positive $\mathbf{b}$ and consider the following constrained maximum problem:

$$\max \sum_{i=1}^m b_i g^i(x^i)$$

with respect to $x^i \geq 0$ subject to

$$\sum_i x^i \leq \sum_i w^i, \qquad w^i \geq 0, \qquad \text{and} \qquad \sum_i w^i > 0.$$

Since the objective function is continuous and the constraint set is closed and bounded, the Weierstrass extremum theorem guarantees a solution exists. The Lagrangian is $\Sigma b_i g^i(x^i) + p \circ \Sigma (w^i - x^i)$. Because the functions are differentiable and the constraint set has a nonempty interior, the Kuhn–Tucker theorem asserts a solution must satisfy

$$b_i g^i_x[x^i(M)] - p(M) \leqq 0 \quad \text{and} \quad \{b_i g^i_x[x^i(M)] - p(M)\} \circ x^i(M) = 0 \quad (1)$$

as well as complementary slackness at the price vector $p(M) \geqq 0$ so that

$$\sum_{i \in M} [w^i - x^i(M)] \geqq 0 \quad \text{and} \quad p(M) \circ \sum_{i \in M} [w^i - x^i(M)] = 0. \tag{2}$$

Therefore, the price of any commodity j is zero if the jth coordinate of $\sum_i [w^i - x^i(M)]$ is positive owing to a surfeit of that commodity. Equation (2) asserts that the optimal price vector conserves the value of the resources. To put it another way, the sum of the values of the optimal allocation over all the individuals is the same as the sum of the values of the initial resources at the optimal price vector $p(M)$. However, to avoid counting money twice, an individual must obey a budget constraint as an equation so that $p(M) \circ [x^i(M) - w^i] = 0$. Therefore, the market value of an individual's optimal vector equals the market value of his initial vector so that trades among individuals do not alter the distribution of their net worths measured in money. Since neither $p(M)$ nor $x^i(M)$ depends on the distribution $\{w^i\}$, to require that the individual budget constraint holds as an equality restricts the admissible initial distributions. While it must be recognized that $p(M)$ and $\{x^i(M)\}$ do depend on $\sum_i w^i$ for given **b** but not on the distribution of w^i, changing the components of **b** *does* alter both $p(M)$ and $\{x^i(M)\}$.

Condition (1) poses two problems. First, $g^i_x(M)$ is in terms of cardinal utility and $p(M)$ seems to be in a different unit. This raises a question about how to interpret the two terms in the inequality (1). Is it meaningful to compare them? If one wishes to say that commodities have a money price then one must say that cardinal utility is commensurate with money. Second, because **b** is determinate only up to multiplication by a positive constant, it follows that the Lagrangian multiplier, $p(M)$, also is determinate only up to multiplication by a positive scalar. Consequently, it is tempting to claim that one of the n commodities can be a numeraire. However, such a commodity must have a *positive* price. Also, the numeraire commodity must *always* have a positive price for each solution as determined by an admissible distribution $\{w^i\}$. This can hold even if some individuals do not start with a positive quantity of the numeraire commodity. No condition or assumption so far implies that there is such a commodity that always has a positive price. It is not difficult to describe a condition that does imply a positive price for, say, commodity 1 in all solutions of the constrained maximum problem determined by admissible distributions $\{w^i\}$. The following is such a condition.

$$\frac{\partial g^i(x^i, w^i)}{\partial x^i_1} > 0 \qquad \forall\, x^i \tag{3.i}$$

and

$$\lim_{x_1 \to 0} \frac{\partial g^i(x^i, w^i)}{\partial x_1^i} = \infty. \tag{3.ii}$$

Before discussing the economic meaning of conditions (3.i) and (3.ii), we must clarify some technical issues. The existence of a solution of the constrained maximum problem assumes the utility indicators are continuous. This is compatible with (3.i) and (3.ii). The Kuhn–Tucker theorem assumes that each g^i is differentiable and the most straightforward sufficient condition for differentiability is continuous first-order partials. However, (3.ii) is not consistent with a continuous first-order partial on the nonnegative orthant. But if each g^i is concave and has first-order partials that are not necessarily continuous then g^i is differentiable and the Kuhn–Tucker theorem does apply.[9]

Condition (3.i) ensures that commodity 1 must always have a positive price. This follows from the first-order necessary condition $0 < b_i g_{x_1^i}^i(x^i) \le p_1$. Condition (3.ii) implies that the optimal amount of commodity 1 held by each individual is positive, though possibly very small. Commodity 1 can be the numeraire on the basis of (3.i) alone. Although condition (3.ii) means commodity 1 is indispensable, it has the drawback that it makes $\partial g^i(x^i)/\partial x_1^i$ discontinuous at zero.[10]

That x_1 is used as money and is in the valuation function asks the question of how changes in this commodity affect the valuation. The answer raises some basic issues about the theoretical role of money. It is helpful to begin with a slight redefinition of the valuation function,

$$v = F(z, Z, x), \tag{4}$$

in which z is the amount of money held by the individual, Z is the amount held by all other individuals, and x is an n-vector of the nonmonetary commodities. The function shows the maximum value of the $(n + 2)$-vector (z, Z, x) to the individual. Using the following differential,

$$dv = F_z \, dz + F_Z \, dZ + F_x \, dx, \tag{5}$$

we may rephrase the question in this shape. Does a change in the individual's stock of money cause the same change in the valuation, v?

---

9. Given a nondecreasing concave function f that has first-order partials, $0 \le f_x \circ x \le f(x) - f(0)$. Fix all coordinates save the first and consider what happens as it approaches 0. Let $\xi_2, \ldots, \xi_n > 0 \Rightarrow f(x) - f(0) > 0$. We assume that $f_{x_1} \to \infty$ as $\xi_1 \to 0$ and that $f(x)$ remains finite. Therefore, $f_{x_1} \xi_1 \to 0$ so $f_{x_1} = o(\xi_1)$. Say that $f_{x_1} \approx 1/\xi_1^\alpha$, $0 < \alpha \le 1$. Consequently, $f_{x_1} \xi_1 = \xi_1^{1-\alpha} \to 0$ as $\xi_1 \to 0$. This is consistent with a concave f. For an analysis of the step from quasi-concave to concave utility functions, see Mas-Colell 1985, prop. 2.6.4, pp. 80–81.

10. A continuous function on a closed set must be bounded. The closed set in the present case is $\{x \mid 0 \le \Sigma \, w^i\}$. Assuming condition (3.ii) implies that $\partial g^i(x^i)/\partial x_1^i$ is not continuous on this set (Graves, 1946, thm. 22, cor. 1, p. 65).

One way to answer this question introduces the classical distinction between value in exchange and value in use. The thing called money may have value in exchange but none in use. Its value in exchange depends on its widespread acceptance by the members of the community. Moreover, a proportional change in z and Z would not affect the value of money. This proposition goes back to the classical exposition of the quantity theory given by David Hume in 1752 (1955). Mathematically, F is homogeneous of degree 0 in z and Z so that

$$F(\lambda z, \lambda Z, x) \equiv F(z, Z, x), \tag{6}$$

and, assuming F has first-order partials, identity (6) is equivalent to

$$F_z(z, Z, x)z + F_Z(z, Z, x)Z \equiv 0. \tag{7}$$

Therefore, F_z and F_Z cannot have the same sign. What matters to an individual is not z but the *relative* size of z, which is z/Z. It would be better to write the valuation function using the ratio z/Z so that

$$v = F(z/Z, 1, x).$$

It is instructive to study the best allocation of this medium of exchange among the members of the community in order to learn more about it. To this end, write the valuation of individual i as follows:

$$v_i = F^i(\theta_i, x^i) \qquad \theta_i = z_i/(\mu - z_i),$$

where $\mu = \Sigma_i \, z_i$ is the total stock of money. Now the vector x^i excludes any commodity used as money. Because the share of the stock of money in the hands of individual i is $\theta_i/(1 + \theta_i)$,

$$\sum_i \frac{\theta_i}{1 + \theta_i} = 1. \tag{8}$$

The best allocation is the solution of the constrained maximum problem:

$$\max \sum_i F^i(\theta_i)$$

with respect to $\theta_i \geq 0$ subject to (8). The Lagrangian is

$$\sum_i F^i(\theta_i) + \pi \left(1 - \sum_i \frac{\theta_i}{1 + \theta_i} \right).$$

If there is a maximum, it must satisfy

$$\frac{\partial F^i}{\partial \theta_i} - \pi \frac{1}{(1 + \theta_i)^2} \leq 0.$$

Assume that F is a concave function of θ and that $\partial F(0)/\partial \theta > 0$ for all x^i. This implies there is a maximum. Because the marginal valuation of money is positive at $\theta = 0$, the optimal θ is positive for everybody, the necessary condition must hold with equality, and the shadow price of money, π, is positive. The latter result is indispensable for a commodity that derives its value from being a medium of exchange, not from its value in use.

Now reconsider equation (5). To see whether we can entertain the possibility that v can move pari passu with z, suppose $F_z = 1$. It follows from equation (7) that $F_Z = -(z/Z)$. Since Z is the amount of money held by others, any change in the amount held by an individual is necessarily offset by an equal change in the amount held by others. Formally,

$$dz + dZ = 0 \Rightarrow dv = (1 + z/Z)dz + F_x\, dx.$$

Therefore, even for this extreme case the directional derivative of the valuation v with respect to z exceeds one by the share z/Z, which may be small. Even so, as shown in the preceding, because money derives its value from exchange, F_z cannot equal one for all values of z.

In the preceding case money enters the valuation function as a real magnitude via the ratio z/Z. Alternatively it may enter as a physical commodity. If so the question of how changes in the individual's stock of the monetary commodity affect his valuation raises no problem. Gold is the leading example of a commodity that satisfies postulate (3.i). The price of every commodity can be written relative to commodity 1. The weights $\{b_i\}$ must also be expressed relative to p_1. Owing to assumption (3.i), commodity 1 is universally desired. Becoming a medium of exchange may make it universally acceptable and so a standard of value.[11] Since the physical quantity of commodity 1 is an argument of the function $g^i(.)$, there is no uncertainty about how much there is. Its price is determined by the solution of the constrained maximum problem. Because its price is always positive, all other prices can be reckoned relative to the price of gold.[12] Possibly other commodities satisfy condition (3.i). Even if only one does, there is a question about the comparability of the two terms in inequality (2). We consider this question subsequently.

It is not difficult to modify the model to make it accommodate a cardinal utility indicator in place of the valuation function and thereby obtain sufficient

---

11. Carl Menger (1994, chap. 8) gives a fascinating account of the evolution of money.

12. If commodity 1 obeys the standard law of demand then the price of commodity 1 varies inversely with the quantity. Thus an increase in the quantity of commodity 1 lowers its price relative to the prices of all other commodities. Therefore, an increase in the stock of money in the form of commodity 1 raises the price level. For pure exchange a change in the quantity of commodity 1 does not affect the quantities of the other commodities. However if there were production and the quantity of commodity 1 were an input in the production function then an increase in the quantity of this commodity could raise real output. The stock of money may have a positive marginal product because, being readily accepted in trade, it can be used as a substitute for stocks of other commodities held as a buffer for unexpected vagaries of supply or demand.

conditions for a core. First, choose positive weights **b** so that the objective for a coalition S becomes $\Sigma_{i \in S} \, b_i g^i(x^i, w^i)$. Second, let each $g^i(.)$ be a concave function of its arguments. Concavity implies that all efficient outcomes can be found by choosing different positive **b**'s.

> THEOREM 1.   *i. If $g^i(x^i, w^i)$ is an increasing, concave function of x^i that has first-order partial derivative so it is differentiable then*

$$a_i = b_i g^i(x^i, w^i) - p(M) \circ [x^i(M) - w^i] \tag{9}$$

> *is in the core.*

> *ii. If $g^i(x^i, w^i)$ is concave and has first-order partials, and $x^i(M) > 0$ then*

$$a_i = b_i g^i(M) - g^i_x(M) \circ [x^i(M) - w^i] \tag{10}$$

> *is in the core.*

Theorem 1 has the same proof as Theorem 2.1.

Several aspects of this result deserve attention. First, because both the weights **b** and prices $p(M)$ are determinate only up to multiplication by a positive scalar, the same holds for the imputations given by equations (9) and (10). Second, there is the problem that while $b_i g^i(x^i, w^i)$ is in terms of cardinal utility, the expression $p(M) \circ [x^i(M) - w^i]$ seems to be in a different unit. Once again we must conclude that cardinal utility must be measured in money if the values of commodities are measured in terms of money. However, to say that cardinal utility is commensurate with money does not mean it is actually money. It means money is the yardstick of value.

Depending on the nature of the admissible distribution $\{w^i\}$, the optimal trades do not necessarily change the net worth of the individuals as measured in money. This point needs elaborating. By Corollary 2, Theorem 2.1, the optimal price vector $p(M)$ and the optimal assignments $\{x^i(M)\}$ do not depend on the distribution $\{w^i\}$ and only depend on the total $\Sigma_i \, w^i$. Given $p(M)$, it is always possible to choose an admissible distribution $\{w^i\}$ such that the value of the optimal assignment $x^i(M)$ satisfies the equation $p(M) \circ [w^i - x^i(M)] = 0$. Give individual i the opportunity to solve the following constrained maximum problem:

$$\max b_i g^i(x^i, w^i) \tag{11}$$

with respect to $x^i \geq 0$ subject to $p(M) \circ [w^i - x^i] \geq 0$. The Lagrangian for this problem is

$$b_i g^i(x^i, w^i) + \lambda^i p(M) \circ [w^i - x^i],$$

and a solution $\bar{x}^i, \bar{\lambda}^i$ must satisfy

$$b_i\bar{g}^i_x - \bar{\lambda}^i p(M) \lesseqgtr 0, \qquad [b_i\bar{g}^i_x - \bar{\lambda}^i p(M)] \circ \bar{x}^i = 0,$$

$$\text{and} \quad \bar{\lambda}^i\, p(M) \circ [w^i - \bar{x}^i] = 0. \tag{12}$$

Therefore, $x^i(M)$ satisfies the necessary conditions (12) for a solution of the constrained maximum problem given by (11). Moreover, $x^i(M)$ requires no change in the monetary net worth of individual i and it makes the second term for a_i in equation (9) zero. Even so, this solution does not escape the need for comparing cardinal utility to a monetary value as is evident from the first inequality in (12). Moreover, equality between $x^i(M)$ and $\bar{x}^i$ cannot be assured unless the hypothesis about the shape of g^i is strengthened to strict concavity from concavity.

This reasoning justifies valuation functions measured in terms of money as the most useful and most straightforward way to express the preferences of individuals for the purpose of studying markets. To recapitulate, here are the steps in the argument. First, from ordinal to cardinal utility is a small step thanks to the von Neumann and Morgenstern axioms. Second, comparisons of commodity allocations based on the principle of dominance lead to a linear objective function such that each member of M gets a positive weight. The weight of an individual in any coalition he joins is the same as his weight in M. The optimal allocation is given by the solution of a certain constrained maximum problem. A desire to measure the value of commodities in terms of money forces one to measure cardinal utility in comparable units, money. If there is at least one universally acceptable commodity that satisfies conditions (3.i) and (3.ii), gold, for example, then the price of everything can be expressed relative to the price of gold. Therefore, gold would be the numeraire and would be money, and claims to gold would also be money.[13]

---

13. Ludwig von Mises ([1924] 1981) is a forceful advocate of this position.

CHAPTER 2

Theory of Joint Ventures

1. Introduction and Summary

The term *corporation* rarely appears in a text on microeconomic theory. The typical text describes an entity called a firm consisting of one or more plants that is owned and operated by an entrepreneur. The firm hires or buys inputs, and it sells or rents outputs. Little is said about the firm or about how it begins. Somehow the entrepreneur obtains the resources to start the firm.

In contrast, the theory of finance says little or nothing about what firms actually do. It focuses on financial markets and on those who trade in these markets the various kinds of paper that constitute direct or indirect claims on firms. Individuals or groups own portfolios of these claims, and they can issue their own financial paper. Individual investors can compose their own portfolios according to their individual preferences. Owing to this, the theory claims that firms can ignore the preferences of their individual owners and can focus exclusively on maximizing expected profit. In this fashion the standard theory of finance divorces what firms actually do as producers of goods or services from the web of paper representing these activities. An example makes this point forcefully. Let a group of investors believe there are profitable opportunities in generating electricity from nuclear reactors. Hence they propose investment in these reactors. No combination of paper investments can accomplish their purpose without actual nuclear facilities.

I shall assume that individual investors combine in stable coalitions that represent corporations. I use the theory of the core to derive necessary and sufficient conditions for the stability of these coalitions and deduce some of the implications of these conditions. The result is a closer link between microeconomic theory and the modern theory of finance. This application of core theory employs two basic entities, types of investors and investment projects. The theory defines an investor type with respect to two attributes, attitude toward risk and belief about the probability distribution describing the stream of profits from an investment project. Neither of these is outwardly visible. This raises the problem of how to relate the theoretical entity, an investor type, to observable things. One implication of this theory goes some way toward a solution of this problem. Investors of the same type have the same portfolio of assets and liabilities. If we could sort investors by the contents of their portfolios, we would have a tolerably homogeneous group of investors. A special case is sorting equity holders of a given corporation by the number of shares they own. Sometimes the available data force us to use this expedient. This special case depends on the proposition that a necessary but not a sufficient condition that investors are the same type is that they hold the same number of shares in the corporation. Admittedly, knowing the whole portfolio of an investor would furnish a better basis for classification.

An investment project is defined here in somewhat the same abstract way as in the theory of finance. A project yields a stream of profits or losses as if these were generated by random drawing from a probability distribution. The similarity to finance theory stops here. Investment projects are semiprivate goods to the members of the coalition that undertakes them. This is because the members of the coalition can decide jointly how much and in what to invest. They are the sole beneficiaries of their decisions (aside from the government, who is the tax collector or the fount of special favors and subsidies). The determination of the optimal investments by the coalition somewhat resembles the problem of finding the optimal amounts of semiprivate goods. A novel aspect of my model is that the probability distribution assumed to generate the net return depends on the size of the investment. The credibility of an investment project may differ among the investors so that they do not all agree on the chances of success or failure. A stable coalition is a group of investors in terms of the number of each type and a collection of investment projects that can maintain itself in the face of competing offers from other coalitions to its members as inducements to join them. A corporation or a mutual fund illustrates such a coalition.

The problem of how to control subordinates and to ensure that their actions advance the interest of their superiors is not peculiar to corporations. It is, therefore, not an issue that I address in this chapter, but it is the subject of chapters 4 and 5.

The theory herein assumes that all the information about an investment project is contained in the description of the probability distribution that is assumed to generate the net returns. This raises the question of how to measure the return, which is a residual, the difference between receipts and outlays. This only begins to answer the question since it raises more questions about how to measure these things. Thus if a corporation occasionally sells some of its assets or a subsidiary, the proceeds are excluded from the ordinary receipts of the corporation used in calculating its net return. The rules of accounting and corporate law are pertinent. They define a legitimate receipt and expense. They require corporations to reveal some kinds of information. They require corporations to hire outside auditors to scrutinize their records in order to determine the legitimacy of their receipts and their expenditures. The corporation must separate its ordinary from its extraordinary outlays. The latter are incurred to acquire long-lived items. Ordinary receipts must be distinguished from unusual ones that may come from the sale of tangible or intangible assets. Auditors examine the payments made to officers of the corporation to see if any are fraudulent. The law requires corporations to make a considerable effort to measure properly their net revenue. The corporation must have a board of directors who represent the owners of the corporation. A major fiduciary responsibility of the directors is to ensure that net revenue is measured reasonably accurately. These rules and the provisions for their enforcement explain the assumption that the probability distribution generating the net revenue of the corporation can adequately represent an investment project as a basic element of the theory of corporations.

The theory gives three sufficient conditions for a stable coalition. First, a coalition with a single investment project and a heterogeneous group of investors who all have a positive marginal willingness to put funds into the corporation is stable. It also follows that there may be different stable coalitions with investors of the same type. Second, a coalition with a single type of investor and a heterogeneous group of investment projects is stable. Different stable coalitions of this kind may invest in similar projects. Third, a coalition with several projects and several types of investors is stable if the maximum amount each investor type is willing to put into the coalition is an increasing concave function of the amounts invested in these projects by the coalition and if any subcoalition would also be willing to put positive amounts into these projects. In the third situation these conditions are sufficient to bring about enough affinity between the investors and the projects to maintain the coalition as a stable organization. The first condition describes a specialized corporation, the second a closed-end mutual fund, and the third a conglomerate. If the coalition is stable then the theory says there is limited liability for the owners. Limited liability is necessary but not sufficient for the stability of the coalition. Moreover, limited liability is essential for the fungibility of the equity shares in the corporation. Without limited liability every investor would need to know the financial standing of each potential shareholder in the corporation because every owner would be responsible for the debts of the corporation to the extent of his own assets and those of the other shareholders.

The credibility of the investment projects is another element of the theory. If the credibility of a project depends on how much the coalition spends disseminating information about it, then the coalition is stable only if the return of these outlays on credibility decreases rapidly enough. The stability of a coalition depends on how well outlays on credibility attract potential investors to its projects. Paradoxically, the more effective are these outlays, the less the likelihood of stability.

The theory explains why a takeover bid exceeds the current market price per share by an amount that is an increasing function of the proportion of shares that the buyer wants to acquire. In this theory every current shareholder puts a value on his shares that is not below the current market price of a share, and some place a higher value on their holdings. All the current shareholders are more optimistic about the prospects of the corporation than are any of the nonshareholders. The valuations of the current shareholders may be ranked from the lowest to the highest starting from the current share price of the stock. There is, therefore, an upward sloping supply schedule of shares. The bigger is the fraction of the shares a buyer wants to acquire, the higher the price he must bid for them.

This theory asserts that the magnitude and direction of the investment outlays of a corporation depend on the number and types of its owners. It also allows for different classes of stocks.

Before presenting the detailed theory it is helpful to give an informal summary. A group of investors who are venture capitalists considers various new joint projects. Each person can embark on a project alone or can join with others. By forming groups each individual can limit his exposure to risk, and the group can invest more than any individual. Subsets of individuals can form coalitions. Each coalition can choose its own optimal scale and direction of investment. The coalitions compete for investors to join them. An individual joins that coalition which offers him the best terms. An individual has competing offers from all the possible coalitions. A possible coalition is any combination of k out of the n individuals. For n individuals the number of possible coalitions is $2^n - 1$ (not counting the empty coalition). The theory determines

1. the stable coalition with respect to the number and types of their members and with respect to the scale and nature of its investment projects;
2. the amount each investor puts at the disposal of any stable coalition that he joins and the gain he expects from his participation in that coalition.

This theory determines the expected gain of each individual as the result of competition among coalitions for members. The expected gain is the difference between the maximal amount an individual would be willing to pay for membership in the coalition and the amount he does pay. Let $\overline{W}^j(x)$ denote the maximal willingness to pay by individual j, where x is a vector representing the amounts invested in its projects by the coalition. Let c_j denote the amount investor j pays to the coalition in return for his ownership share. The willingness of a type j investor to participate in the ventures undertaken by the coalition is a nondecreasing function of his valuation of the prospects for these ventures. Chapter 3 contains a detailed analysis of the determinants of this valuation. For m projects, x_i is the amount invested in project i by the coalition so that x is the m-vector $\{x_1, \ldots, x_m\}$. Let the coalition t have t_j members of type j, $j = 1, \ldots, n$. Hence t is an n-vector with jth coordinate t_j. Since each type j investor is willing to pay at most $\overline{W}^j(x)$ to join the coalition t, the maximum amount that all type j investors would be willing to put at the disposal of t is $t_j \overline{W^j}(x)$. Summing over all n types of investors gives the maximal total amount they would be willing to subscribe to the coalition t for its projects. This sum is $\sum_{j=1}^{n} t_j \overline{W^j}(x)$. Because investor j pays c_j for his share of the coalition, the gain that he expects is $\overline{W^j}(x) - c_j$. Let w_j denote this expected gain so that by definition $w_j \equiv \overline{W^j}(x) - c_j$. The share of a type j investor in the total capital of the coalition, call it q_j, is defined as follows:

$$q_j \equiv \frac{c_j}{\displaystyle\sum_{k=1}^{n} t_k c_k}.$$

Consequently, $\sum_{j=1}^{n} t_j q_j = 1$.

The theory determines the optimal investments made by a stable coalition t. It is an implication of this theory that

$$\sum_{j=1}^{n} t_j c_j = \sum_{i=1}^{m} x_i. \tag{1}$$

This is an important equation. It shows that the total amount subscribed by the members of the coalition t covers the total cost of its investments. No investor pays the coalition t more than this initial investment so there is an implication of limited liability. Equation (1) is necessary for the stability of the coalition t.

As time passes, the coalition t sees the results of its ventures as a random variable R. A type j investor realizes a return given by

$$q_j R - c_j. \tag{2}$$

By virtue of equation (1) and $\sum_{j=1}^{n} t_j q_j = 1$ the realized net return is as follows:

$$\sum_j t_j q_j R - \sum_j t_j c_j = R - \sum_i x_i. \tag{3}$$

Equation (3) shows that the realized net return is positive if and only if it covers the original total cost of the investments. The share of the total return going to investor j is $q_j R$, and his cost is c_j. Thus expression (2) shows his *realized* gain or loss. His *expected* gain is

$$E_j[q_j R - c_j] = \overline{W^j} - c_j = w_j.$$

The expected gain for the whole coalition is the sum of the preceding expression over all the investors in the coalition, that is

$$\sum_j t_j E_j[q_j R - c_j] = \sum_j t_j \overline{W^j} - \sum_i t_i c_i.$$

The model also describes the situation after the stable coalition has begun its existence. In the parlance of finance, the corporation can go public. This allows the venture capitalists who were the original investors in the corporation to sell their shares on an organized stock exchange to the public if they wish. The situation described in the preceding refers to corporations as joint ventures before their shares are listed in a stock market. In the next stage outsiders can buy shares in the corporation. The fungibility of these shares results from the limited liability of the owners. An owner cannot lose more than his original investment when there is limited liability. He is not liable for any debts of the enterprise in which he owns shares. Therefore, the wealth of the other shareholders is not relevant to any current or prospective shareholder. The limited liability makes the shares fungible and thereby enhances the liquidity of the market for shares. Although the investments in the coalition are semiprivate goods to the owners, their shares of stock are private goods because they can be traded by any shareholder without the consent of any other shareholder. Investors in a joint venture must somehow agree on the size and direction of their investments. Thus, if steel production is their business they must agree themselves upon or have management determine the number and sizes of the blast furnaces. In this sense blast furnaces are semiprivate goods to the owners of the business. Shares of stock in the business are private goods because each person may decide for himself how many shares he wants.

This important point is worth elaborating. When an original investor in the joint venture decides to sell his share of ownership in the coalition, he may do so to whomever he pleases at a mutually agreed-upon price without the consent of any other shareholder. This is not true for all joint ventures in the U.S. economy. Partnerships, some cooperatives, notably in real estate, teams in professional sports, seats on organized exchanges such as the New York Stock Exchange, the Chicago Board of Trade, and the Chicago Mercantile Exchange are examples of joint ventures where a transfer of ownership needs the consent of all the current owners of the joint venture. The theory given subsequently does *not* apply to such joint ventures. Theories about joint ventures that prevent a member from selling his membership to an outsider differ from the theory of corporations given here and would require suitable changes to reckon with the constraints on transfers of ownership.

Because the shares are fungible and the owner of a share may sell it to anyone without the consent of any other owner, there must be a single price per share of stock independent of the identity of the buyer or the seller. Let p denote the current market price of a share of stock in a corporation. Let h_j denote the number of shares held by investor j. If $ph_j > \overline{W}^j$ then investor j is inclined to sell his shares at the market price instead of retaining them. The buyer, a new owner of the corporation, pays p per share and expects a positive gain to result from his purchase. The proceeds from the sale of the shares to the new owner go to the seller of the shares and not to the corporation unless, of course, the latter is the seller. Why would a new investor be willing to pay more per share than $\overline{W}^j/h_j$? It must be because the buyer expects a bigger profit than the seller. Therefore, the new owner must place a valuation on the prospects of the corporation that is above the seller's.

Perhaps a corporation having realized the returns from its ventures decides to reinvest some of its profits. If so, the present owners must agree to raise their investments in the corporation by the amount of the profit retained. Each owner increases his stake in the corporation by the amount of profit per share that the corporation does not pay out in the form of dividends. This does not alter the proportion of the total capital owned by each of the current shareholders. Still another possibility is the sale of new shares by the corporation either to existing shareholders or to new ones. In this case the situation resembles the one discussed in the preceding about the creation of new joint ventures.

2. Willingness to Pay Function for an Individual Investor

There are t_j investors of type $j, j = 1, \ldots, n$, who are interested in a proposed joint venture. An investor type is defined with respect to two attributes: his belief in the prospects for success of the ventures he considers and his willingness to contribute to them in order to obtain a share of their profits. The first attribute refers to his beliefs or subjective probabilities about the ventures. The second refers to how much he is willing to invest in them. The latter depends on his total wealth, his estimates of the profits from these ventures, and other personal factors such as his age, family status, and health. The analysis begins with a description of the random process assumed to generate the returns to the ventures. Next is a discussion of how an individual determines the most he is willing to pay for participation in the coalition that would undertake the ventures. A von Neumann–Morgenstern utility function is one of the alternatives considered. This is followed by technical material on the relevant probability distributions. The section concludes with an extended example.

Let $F^i(z, x_i)$ denote the cumulative distribution function (cdf) of the random variable, z, from project i and let x_i denote the amount that the joint enterprise proposes to invest in this project. Assume there are m projects so that $i = 1, \ldots, m$. The term F^i is a nonnegative, nondecreasing function of z that approaches the upper bound one as z approaches infinity. The cdf is as follows:

$$F^i(z, x_i) = \int_0^z f(\zeta, x_i)d\zeta,$$

and the probability density function (pdf) is $f(.) > 0$. According to this formulation the random return has a lower bound of zero. More generally there would be a finite lower bound on the return, and we may take this to be zero (cf. chap. 3, sec. 2). The larger the investment outlay, x_i, the bigger is the probability that the random variable, ζ, will exceed a prescribed level, z. This translates into the following inequality:

$$\frac{\partial F^i(z, x_i)}{\partial x_i} < 0. \tag{1}$$

Figure 1 shows two cdfs for two different levels of x_i. Here OA_1A_1' is the cdf for the smaller and OA_2A_2' the cdf for the larger x_i. The probability of drawing a value of the random variable ζ that exceeds z is bigger for the cdf OA_2A_2' than it is for OA_1A_1'. If the cdf for the larger investment outlay promises a higher probability of a return above z for all levels of z there is said to be stochastic dominance. Figure 1 illustrates this. Strictly decreasing marginal returns with respect to the investment are shown by the inequality

$$\frac{\partial^2 F^i(.)}{\partial x_i^2} > 0.$$

To help rule out the possibility that no finite optimal x_i may exist, let $F^i(z, x_i)$ be bounded below by a cdf that does not depend on x_i. We see that the hypothesis that the amount invested in an enterprise enters as a parameter of the probability distribution is not without complications. These are worthwhile if a result is a useful theory of joint ventures.

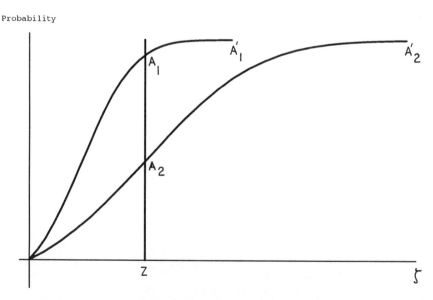

Fig. 1. Cumulative distribution function of returns for two types of investors with stochastic dominance

Disagreement about the prospects for success can take different forms. Figure 1 also shows how two investors regard the same joint venture. The type 1 investor is uniformly more pessimistic than is the type 2 investor. Figure 1 shows this because the cdf, labeled A_1', for the type 1 investor lies uniformly to the left of the cdf for the same project as viewed by the type 2 investor, labeled A_2'. Disagreement need not be uniform. Figure 2 illustrates nonuniform disagreement. The type 1 investor is more optimistic than the type 2 investor at low values of ζ but is less optimistic at high values. Uniform disagreement, since it can be represented by a single parameter, is easier to analyze than nonuniform disagreement. Figure 3 shows differences in the credibility of the investment projects in terms of the density functions. Even with uniform disagreement, the density functions must intersect. It is, accordingly, simpler to represent disagreement in terms of the distribution functions than in terms of the density functions.

Let a_{ij}, a number between 0 and 1, represent the credibility of venture i to a type j investor. The credibility factor shifts the cdf laterally. The more credible the venture, the farther to the right the investor believes it to lie. Credibility increases with a_{ij}. An investor who is fully confident in the venture sets $a_{ij} = 1$, and the most skeptical investor sets $a_{ij} = 0$. It may be worth noting that this way of looking at credibility does not affect an investor's estimate of the coefficient of variation (standard deviation divided by the mean) of the random variable giving the return to the joint venture. Moreover, investors of all types agree on the coefficient of variation for a given venture. For now assume that

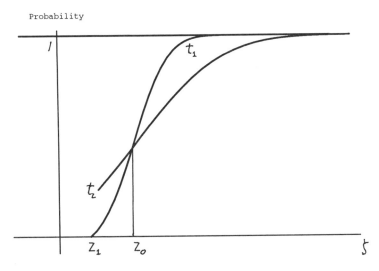

Fig. 2. Cumulative distribution function of returns for two types of investors without stochastic dominance

Probability

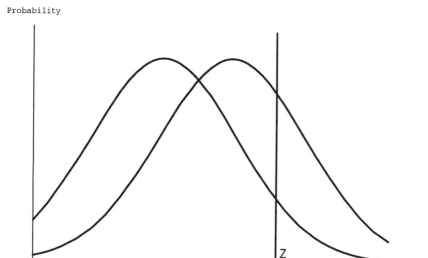

Fig. 3. Probability density functions for two types of investors

the credibility coefficients are given. Subsequently we shall study a more general model in which the costs of obtaining and disseminating information about the ventures can affect their credibility.

The random variable r_j is the perception by a type j investor of the return in money to the venture. It is not the return that the investor himself would receive. The return to an investor depends on how much he puts into the project. Because the coalitions compete for potential investors, it is this competition that determines how much an investor pays in order to become a member, that is, an owner, of shares in the joint venture. A detailed analysis of this competition among coalitions for investors is the topic of the next section. Here we study the relation between the return to the coalition and the size of its investment in the projects. Let ζ_i denote the random variable representing the return to venture i.

$$r_j = \sum_{i=1}^{m} \zeta_i a_{ij} \tag{2}$$

shows how investor j forms his perception of the total return of the m projects from the credibility coefficients and the returns of the individual ventures. Because the credibility coefficients are given nonrandom parameters, the expected value of r_j, call it $E(r_j)$, is

$$E(r_j) \equiv \sum_i E(\zeta_i)a_{ij} \equiv \sum_i \mu_i a_{ij}, \tag{3}$$

where $\mu_i \equiv E(\zeta_i)$ holds by definition. The expected return to a type j investor shown in equation (3) applies to a combination of m feasible projects for a coalition.

At this stage of the analysis one could introduce a von Neumann–Morgenstern utility indicator and assume the money return is an argument of this indicator. It is useful to see the consequences of doing so in order to understand why it would not serve our purposes. The expected return to a venture from an investment of x satisfies the following equation:

$$\int \zeta f(\zeta, x) d\zeta = \bar{\zeta}(x), \tag{4}$$

in which the subscript i for x is omitted. We shall study the problem of choosing the optimal level of x that maximizes the expected value of some random variable. If the objective is a continuous differentiable function of x then it must be locally concave at the optimal value of x. Suppose the objective is the maximal expected profit that is given by the expected return minus the cost of the investment. We seek useful sufficient conditions for the existence of an optimal x. If the cost of the investment is a linear function of x then the existence of an optimum depends on how the expected return varies as a function of x. Given that the expected return is continuously differentiable in x, we may conclude that it must also be concave with respect to x in a neighborhood of the optimal x. The von Neumann–Morgenstern approach introduces a utility indicator in place of the actual return. Instead of the expected return, it assumes the individuals choose x to maximize the expected utility defined as follows:

$$\int U(\zeta) f(\zeta, x) d\zeta = \bar{U}(x).$$

It is not difficult to verify the following result.

PROPOSITION. *If $\bar{\zeta}(x)$ defined in equation (4) is a concave function of x and U is an increasing concave function of ζ then $\bar{U}(x)$ is an increasing concave function of x.*

A sketch of the proof goes like this. The expected return given by equation (4) actually is a special case of a concave von Neumann–Morgenstern utility indicator because it is a linear function of ζ. It is also the least concave member of the class of concave von Neumann–Morgenstern indicators since it has zero curvature. If x increases by Δx then $\bar{\zeta}(x)$ becomes $\bar{\zeta}(x + \Delta x)$. Because U is more concave than ζ,

$$\bar{U}(x + \Delta x) - \bar{U}(x) < \bar{\zeta}(x + \Delta x) - \bar{\zeta}(x).$$

Thus, if $\bar{\zeta}(x)$ is concave in x then it increases with x at a decreasing rate. A fortiori, $\bar{U}(x)$ must also increase with x at a decreasing rate giving the desired conclusion that it is concave in x.

This result says that if the expected return is a concave function of the amount invested as is virtually required by the hypothesis that a finite maximum exists, then it would be superfluous to introduce a concave von Neumann–Morgenstern utility indicator as well to ensure the existence of a finite maximum.

There are two better reasons for not using a von Neumann–Morgenstern utility indicator in this analysis. First, we wish to study the optimal investments in alternative ventures by coalitions of individuals. Hence we want to describe the aggregate valuations of the projects by the different investors. It is meaningful to sum money valuations across individuals, but it is not meaningful to sum individual utility indicators across different individuals. The second reason is that we want to compute the expected net return. This requires subtracting the money cost of the investments from the valuations, which, therefore, must also be measured in money.

The approach we shall take postulates that each individual decides the most he is willing to pay for participation in a joint venture. It starts with a simple case. Let d denote a discount rate and $P = r/d$ is the present value of a perpetual, certain, and continuous income stream at d. Although an investor may believe that this income stream is worth P, he may be unwilling to pay this much for it either because of the constraint imposed by the size of his wealth, for other personal reasons, or because of the nature of his preferences for various kinds of assets. The most he is willing to pay may be a fraction of his total valuation of this income stream. Thus, the most an investor may be willing to pay for the fraction q of the income stream r with a present value of P is qP. Owing to the nature of the demand for this income stream by other potential investors, it may turn out that qP is the amount that this investor must pay for the income stream. In this case, he expects no gain from his participation in the venture that generates this certain income stream.

Assume that a potential investor can also decide the most he is willing to pay for an uncertain income stream. It may be less than or equal to a linear function of the expected value of the income stream. In the second case the investor is said to be risk neutral, and in the first case he is said to be risk averse. Let $W^j(r)$ denote the function showing the most that investor j is willing to pay for the income stream r. Writing r instead of r_j means that all the investors have the same subjective probability or beliefs about r. Let $f(r, x)$ denote this common pdf of r that depends on the size of the investment x. Consequently, the expected willingness to pay by an investor of type j is as follows:

$$E(W^j(x)) = \int W^j(r)f(r, x)dr. \tag{5}$$

The term $W^j(r)$ is a random variable via r which is a random draw from the pdf $f(r, x)$ that depends on the investment x in the project. The expected willingness to pay resembles the von Neumann–Morgenstern expected utility as is apparent from the equation (5) defining the expected willingness to pay. While $W^j(r)$ is measured in money, the utility indicator $U^j(r)$ is not and is indeterminate up to increasing linear transformations. Nevertheless one may say that the willingness to pay function is a special case of a von Neumann–Morgenstern utility indicator.

Since $W^j(r)$ is an increasing function of r, it poses the problem that the expected willingness to pay may not be finite. In order to ensure that the expected willingness to pay is finite for any admissible pdf as described in the preceding, one must assume that $W^j(r)$ is a bounded function of r. Savage's (1954, 93–98) discussion of various proposals to resolve the St. Petersburg paradox shows that only a bounded utility function can have a finite expected utility. His reasoning applies herein so we shall accept his conclusion.

The expected willingness to pay is assumed to be a suitably concave function of x that will ensure the existence of a finite optimal x. An investor acting alone could undertake the project by investing x in it. A coalition of investors can choose x. Risk aversion must be present at least asymptotically owing to the assumption that the willingness to pay function is bounded above. Since the willingness to pay function shows the most that an investor is willing to put into a venture, it is measured in money, it is commensurate with the investment outlays of the coalition, and it is meaningful to sum it across different individuals. The aggregate willingness to pay function for a coalition is the sum of its members' willingness to pay functions.

Before continuing our analysis of the properties of the willingness to pay functions, we must study some aspects of the relevant integrals. A typical integral is as follows:

$$J(\infty, y) = \int_0^\infty h(u)g(u, y)du.$$

In terms of the preceding integrals, h corresponds to the willingness to pay function, g to the pdf, and y to investment. The main theorem for our purposes is given as follows:

SECOND THEOREM OF THE MEAN (Graves 1946, 231). *Let h be a bounded nondecreasing function of u and let g be an integrable function of u for every z. There exists c_0 such that $0 \leq c_0 \leq c$, where c may be infinite, and*

$$J(c, y) = L \int_0^{c_0} g \, du + M \int_{c_0}^{c} g \, du$$

with $L \leq h(0)$ and $M \geq h(c)$. In addition, if h is nonnegative we can take $L = 0$ and

$$J(c, y) = h(c) \int_{c_0}^{c} g(u, z) \, du.$$

(The latter result is known as Bonnet's theorem [Apostol 1957, 217].) These results apply to the distribution of the sums of independent random variables. First, consider the sum of two independent random variables. Write

$$\Pr\{\zeta_1 + \zeta_2 \leq z\} = \Pr\{\zeta_2 \leq z - \zeta_1\}.$$

Therefore, the cdf of the sum, z, call it $G(z, x_1, x_2)$, is

$$G(z, x_1, x_2) = \int_0^\infty f^1(\zeta_1, x_1) F^2(z - \zeta_1, x_2) d\zeta_1.$$

The pdf f^1 is nonnegative and while the cdf F^2 is increasing in its first argument, $z - \zeta_1$, so that it is decreasing in ζ_1, the second theorem of the mean still applies to the integral $G(.)$ provided h is a bounded monotonic function of u. Hence

$$\begin{aligned} G(z, x_1, x_2) &= F^2(z - 0, x^2) \int_0^{c_1} f^1(\zeta_1, x_1) d\zeta_1 \\ &+ F^2(z - \infty, x_2) \int_{c_1}^\infty f^1(\zeta_1, x_1) d\zeta_1 \\ &= F^2(z, x_2) F^1(c_1, x_1) \end{aligned} \qquad (6)$$

because for given finite z, $F^2(z - \infty, x_2) = 0$. Moreover, equation (6) generalizes to m independent random variables so that

$$G(z, x) = F^m(z, x_m) F^{m-1}(c_{m-1}, x_{m-1}) \ldots F^1(c_1, x_1). \qquad (7)$$

If $F^i(.)$ is absolutely continuous uniformly in x_i then the operations, integration, and differentiation commute (Graves 1946, 215). Let each F^i have a partial derivative with respect to x_i everywhere, and, in short, let each F^i have such properties as will allow interchanging integration and differentiation.

For our present purposes two facts about the cdf of z are pertinent. First, G is a decreasing function of x_i just as each F^i is a decreasing function of x_i. Second, the cross-partial derivatives of G are all positive. To prove the first assertion, write

$$G_{x_1}(z) = \int_0^\infty f^1_{x_1}(\zeta_1, x_1) F^2(z - \zeta_1, x_2) d\zeta_1.$$

Now F^2 is a nonnegative monotonically decreasing function of ζ_1 so that the second theorem of the mean applies yielding

$$\begin{aligned} G_{x_1}(z) &= F^2(z - 0, x_2) \int_0^{c_1} f^1_{x_1}(\zeta_1, x_1) d\zeta_1 \\ &+ F^2(z - \infty, x_2) \int_{c_1}^\infty f^1_{x_1}(\zeta_1, x_1) d\zeta_1 \\ &= F^2(z, x_2) \int_0^{c_1} f^1_{x_1}(\zeta_1, x_1) d\zeta_1 < 0 \end{aligned}$$

because as noted previously $F^2(z - \infty, x_2) = 0$. To prove the second assertion about the cross partials, we have

$$G_{x_2 x_1}(z, x_1, x_2) = F^2_{x_2}(z, x_2) \int_0^{c_1} f^1_{x_1}(\zeta_1, x_1)d\zeta_1 > 0$$

owing to the hypothesis that both factors on the right are negative. Finally,

$$G_{x_1 x_1}(z, x_1, x_2) = F^2(z, x_2) \int_0^{c_1} f^1_{x_1 x_1}(\zeta_1, x_1)d\zeta_1 > 0$$

because F^i is a convex function of x_i by hypothesis.

LEMMA 1.   *If the returns from the m projects are independent random variables then*

$$G_x(z, x) = \int_0^z g_x(\eta, x)d\eta < 0 \quad \text{and} \quad \int_0^\infty g_x(\eta, x)d\eta = 0.$$

PROOF.   The first assertion relies on independence, that x_i is an argument of $f^i(., x_i)$ and is not an argument in any other f and that each $F^i_{x_i}(., x_i) < 0$.

To prove the second assertion, $F^i(\infty, x_i) \equiv 1$ implies $F^i_{x_i}(\infty, x_i) \equiv 0$. QED

Reconsider the expected willingness to pay function for a type j investor written as follows:

$$\overline{W}^j(x) = \int_0^\infty W^j(r)g(r, x)\, dr, \tag{8}$$

where g is the pdf of the profits r from m independent ventures. Let $s = \{s_1, \ldots, s_n\}$ denote a coalition composed of s_j members of investor type j. The coalition chooses the investments that maximize its expected gain. Let x_i stand for the amount of money invested in project i. The expected net gain to s is given by the characteristic function of the coalition, $V(S)$, defined as follows:

$$V(s) = \max_x \sum_{j=1}^n s_j \overline{W}^j(x) - \sum_{i=1}^m x_i. \tag{9}$$

The first-order necessary condition for optimal investments by the coalition s is given by the following inequality:

$$\sum_{j=1}^n s_j \overline{W}^j_{x_i}(x) - 1 \leq 0.$$

Therefore, the optimal investment will be undertaken at a positive level only if there are positive levels of investment at which the first-order partial derivatives of the expected willingness to pay are actually positive. Hence we are led to evaluate the following expression:

$$\overline{W}^j_{x_i}(x) = \int_0^\infty W^j(x) g_{x_i}(x, r)\, dr.$$

The Second Mean Value Theorem applies to this integral. If W^j is a bounded, positive, and increasing function of r and if g_x is an integrable function of r for every x then

$$\overline{W}^j_{x_i} = W^j\,(\infty) \int_c^\infty g_{x_i}\,(r, x)\,dr > 0 \tag{10}$$

by virtue of Lemma 1. Because the cross partials of $G(z)$ are positive and since $\int_0^\infty g_{x_h x_i}\,(.)\,d\eta \equiv 0$, we also know that

$$\overline{W}^j_{x_h x_i} = W^j\,(\infty) \int_c^\infty g_{x_h x_i}\,(x, \eta)d\eta < 0. \tag{11}$$

Therefore, a coalition that undertakes two projects h and i reduces its marginal expected return from each of them and would accordingly invest less in each than if it were to invest in only one of them. Also note that formula (11) holds for $h = i$ as well as for $h \neq i$.

A twice differentiable objective function can have an interior maximum only if the $m \times m$ matrix $s\overline{W}_{xx}$ is negative semidefinite at the optimal x's where

$$s\overline{W}_{xx} = \sum_j s_j \overline{W}^j_{xx} \quad \text{and} \quad \overline{W}^j_{xx} = \left[\overline{W}^j_{x_h x_i}\right]. \tag{12}$$

This fact furnishes a second-order necessary condition for an interior maximum. A differentiable objective function cannot have a maximum at an interior point satisfying the first-order necessary conditions unless it is locally concave at that point. Using equation (8), that defines the expected willingness to pay as a function of the amounts invested, and the expression for $\overline{W}^j_{xx}(x)$ given by equation (11), the second-order necessary condition in terms of the pdf $g(.)$ requires that the matrix

$$A(x, c) = \left[\left[\int_c^\infty g_{x_h x_i}\,(x, \eta)d\eta\right]\right] \tag{13}$$

be negative semidefinite. For the subsequent analysis a stronger condition is more useful, that this matrix is negative definite. The hypothesis asserts that each cdf for the random variable ζ_i giving the return to project, $F^i(\zeta_i, x_i)$, is a decreasing, convex function of x_i with a lower bound given by the cdf $H^i(\zeta_i)$ that does not depend on x_i so that for all $\zeta_i \geq 0$,

$$F^i(\zeta_i, x_i) \geq H^i(\zeta_i). \tag{14}$$

We wish to know whether these conditions imposed on the cdfs imply that the symmetric matrix $A(x, c)$ defined by equation (13) is negative definite in x for all c.

We begin with the case for two projects so that $m = 2$ and employ the expression for the cdf $G(z, x)$ given by equation (6). Define the function $B(z)$ as follows:

$$B(z, x) = 1 - G(z, x) = 1 - F^2(z, x_2)F^1(c_1, x_1). \tag{15}$$

In the form shown by equation (15), we can compute the elements of the matrix $A(z, x)$ from the second-order partials of $B(.)$ with respect to the x's. We obtain the following results:

$$A(z, x) = \begin{bmatrix} -F^2(z)F^1_{11}(c_1) & -F^2_2(z)F^1_1(c_1) \\ -F^1_1(c_1)F^2_2(z) & -F^2_{22}(z)F^1(c_1) \end{bmatrix}.$$

The subscripts denote the partials with respect to the x's. The matrix is negative definite if and only if the diagonal terms are negative, which is true by hypothesis, and the determinant of the matrix is positive. The determinant of $A(z, x)$ can be positive only if for either $i = 1$ or $i = 2$, the following inequality is satisfied:

$$F^i_{ii}F^i - (F^i_i)^2 > 0. \tag{16}$$

A sufficient condition for the determinant of A to be positive is that inequality (16) holds for $i = 1, 2$. Inequality (16) is equivalent to the following inequality:

$$\partial^2 \log F^i/\partial x^2_i > 0, \tag{17}$$

which means that $\log F^i$ is a convex function of x_i. Therefore, in case $m = 2$, a sufficient condition for the existence of a maximum is that $\log F^i$ is a convex function of x_i, $i = 1, 2$. Using these results we can solve the problem for the general case, $m > 2$. We begin with a lemma.

LEMMA 2. *Let $K(x) = \log [1 - B(x)]$. If $K(x)$ is a convex function of x then $B(x)$ is a concave function of x (and conversely).*

PROOF. Since $B(x) = 1 - \exp K(x)$, the desired conclusion follows directly from the expression:

$$B_{xx} = -\exp K(x)[K_x K^T_x + K_{xx}],$$

where K_x is an $m \times 1$ column vector, K^T is the transpose, and K_{xx} is a positive definite matrix. QED

Our goal is the next result.

THEOREM 1. *Let the willingness to pay function, W^j, be a positive, increasing, and bounded function of income. Let F^i be uniformly twice continuously differentiable in x_i. Also, let F^i be a decreasing convex function of x_i and let $\log F^i$ be a convex function of x_i. Then the expected willingness to pay function, $\overline{W}^j(x)$, is a concave, bounded, and increasing function of x.*

PROOF. Most of the work has been done. Let

$$K(x) = \sum_{i=1}^{m} \log F^i(x_i).$$

Since K is a sum of convex functions, it is convex. By Lemma 2, $B(x)$ is a concave function of x. Therefore, since W^j is a positive, increasing, bounded function of income, formula (11) applies, and we may conclude that $\overline{W}^j(x)$ is a bounded concave function of x. Lemma 1 and formula (10) show that it is an increasing function of x.   QED

The next corollary is an immediate implication of the theorem.

COROLLARY.   *Under the hypotheses of Theorem 1, $\sum_{j=1}^{n} s_j \overline{W^j}(x)$ is an increasing, bounded concave function of x.*

Observe that the concavity of the expected willingness to pay function depends on how the scale of the investments affects the cdf of profits. No assumptions about the shape of a valuation function other than that it is a positive, increasing, and bounded function of income are needed to conclude that the expected willingness to pay is a concave function of the investments.

We now study an example—a Pareto distribution. Let

$$F(y, x) = 1 - y^{-\alpha(x)}, \tag{18}$$

where $\alpha(x)$ has a positive lower bound and y, the random variable, is not less than 1. Let $z = y^{-\alpha(x)}$ so that $F(y, x) = 1 - z$. For large enough x, $\log F(y, x) \approx -z$ so that $\log F$ is a convex function of x if z is a concave function of x. Also, F itself is a convex function of x if and only if z is a concave function of x. Therefore, we shall focus on z as a function of x.

$$\log z = -\alpha(x)\log y$$

$$\frac{z_x}{z} = -\alpha_x \log y \Leftrightarrow z_x = -\alpha_x z \log y \tag{19}$$

$$z_{xx} = -\log y(\alpha_{xx}z + \alpha_x z_x) = -\log y \left(\frac{\partial}{\partial x} \right)(\alpha_x z).$$

Because $\log y$ is nonnegative, it follows from (19) that z is concave in x, which is equivalent to $z_{xx} < 0$ if and only if $\alpha_x z$ is an increasing function of x. Since the hypothesis asserts F is a decreasing function of x, it follows that α must be a decreasing function of x. Therefore, both α_x and z are increasing functions of x. Although the product of two *positive* increasing functions must be increasing, this result does not apply here because while z is positive, α_x is negative. Hence we cannot conclude that the product, $\alpha_x z$, is increasing in x although both factors are increasing in x. Given $\log y$, the following inequality will hold for all large enough x:

$$\frac{\alpha_{xx}}{\alpha_x^2} > \log y \tag{20}$$

provided the ratio α_{xx}/α_x^2 is an unbounded increasing function of x. For instance, let

$$\alpha(x) = \alpha_0 + \frac{\alpha_1}{(x + \alpha_2)^{\alpha_3}} \tag{21}$$

with $\alpha_i > 0$, $i = 1, 2, 3$. For each y, this function will satisfy inequality (20) provided x is large enough. In equation (21), $\alpha(x)$ is finite for $x = 0$. This means y

is a random variable even if the investment outlay is zero. However, if $\alpha_2 = 0$ then $\alpha(0) = \infty$ and the random variable y collapses to one for sure. This lengthy analysis of an example shows there are functions that can satisfy the hypotheses of Theorem 1.

3. Expected Gain of a Coalition and the Status of the Core

A joint venture is undertaken by a coalition of n types of investors that decides how much to invest in each project. Let s denote a coalition composed of s_j investors of type $j, j = 1, \ldots, n$, so that

$$s = \{s_1, \ldots, s_n\} \quad \text{and} \quad 0 \le s_j \le t_j \quad \text{with } t_j > 0.$$

A coalition s chooses the amounts of the investments in each of the m projects represented by the coordinates of the m-vector $x = \{x_1, \ldots, x_m\}, x_i \ge 0$, in order to maximize its aggregate expected gain, $V(s)$, defined as follows:

$$V(s) = \max_x \left[\sum_{j=1}^n s_j \overline{W}^j (x) - \sum_{i=1}^m x_i \right]. \tag{1}$$

The term $V(s)$ is a weighted sum of the expected willingness to pay of each of the investor types who are in the coalition with weights given by the number of investors of each type in the coalition minus the sum of the total cost of the investments. It seems open to the objection that it introduces subjective and therefore unobservable elements into the picture. This objection is answered by pointing out that the most an investor would be willing to put into a coalition is measurable in the same sense as the most that a consumer would be willing to pay for a commodity (see chap. 1). The market is the testing ground. From the $\overline{W}^j(x)$ functions one can derive the optimal investment outlays of a coalition as well as the amounts that the investors would place at the disposal of a coalition. These amounts are determined by competition among coalitions for members. Both the actual investment outlays of the coalitions and the investors' contributions to the coalitions are observable. These observables are the subject of the theory. Properties of the investors' willingness to pay functions supply deductions about the observables.

The optimal investment of a coalition s must satisfy the first-order condition as follows:

$$\frac{\partial}{\partial x_i} \left\{ \sum_j s_j \overline{W}^j (x) - \sum_i x_i \right\} \le 0. \tag{2}$$

These optimal investments depend on who is in the coalition s. To make this explicit write the optimal investments for s as $x(s)$, an m-vector whose coordinates depend on s.

Some pertinent facts about $V(s)$ are in the following theorem.

THEOREM 1.   *Under the hypotheses of Theorem 2.1, $V(s)$ is an increasing convex function of s.*

PROOF.   Write $V(s)$ in vector notation as the difference between two scalar products as follows:

$$V(s) = s \circ \overline{W}(x(s)) - \ell \circ x(s),$$

where $\ell = \{1, 1, \ldots, 1\}$, an m-vector all of whose coordinates are 1, $x(s)$ is the m-vector of the optimal investments by the coalition s, and $\overline{W}(x(s))$ is an n-vector whose jth component is $\overline{W}^j(x(s))$. The gradient of V with respect to s, V_s, is given by

$$V_s(x) = \overline{W}(x(s)) + s\overline{W}_x \circ \frac{dx}{ds} - \ell \circ \frac{dx}{ds} \tag{3}$$

$$= \overline{W}(x(s)) + (s\overline{W}_x - \ell) \circ \frac{dx}{ds} = \overline{W}(x(s))$$

because the term $(s\overline{W}_x - \ell) \circ dx/ds = 0$ by virtue of the fact that $x(s)$, being optimal for x, must satisfy the first-order necessary condition. Therefore $\overline{W} > 0$ implies $V(s)$ is an increasing function of s.

Next we prove that $V(s)$ is convex. To simplify the notation write $\overline{W}(t)$ in place of $\overline{W}(x(t))$ and so on. The hypothesis asserts that $\overline{W}^j(x)$ is a concave function of x. It follows that

$$\overline{W}^j(t) - \overline{W}^j(s) \le \overline{W}_x^j(s) \circ (x(t) - x(s)).$$

Rearranging terms, multiplying through by s_j, and summing over j, we obtain

$$\sum_j s_j \overline{W}^j(t) - \sum_j s_j \overline{W}_x^j(s) \circ x(t) \le \sum_j s_j \overline{W}^j(s) - \sum_j s_j \overline{W}_x^j(s) \circ x(s). \tag{4}$$

The first-order necessary condition and complementary slackness imply that

$$\sum_j s_j \overline{W}_x^j(s) \circ x(s) = \sum_i x_i(s).$$

Therefore, the right-hand side of inequality (4) becomes $V(s)$, and on the left-hand side there is

$$\sum_j s_j \overline{W}^j(t) - \sum_i x_i(t) + \sum_j t_j \overline{W}^j(t) - \sum_j t_j \overline{W}^j(t),$$

which becomes

$$V(t) - \sum_j (t_j - s_j) \overline{W}^j(t).$$

Therefore,

$$V(t) - V(s) \leq \sum_j (t_j - s_j) \, \overline{W^j}(t) = V_t(t) \circ (t - s).$$

This inequality shows that V is a convex function.   QED

As we shall see, the necessary and sufficient conditions for a nonempty core can be described in terms of an observable variable, namely, how much an investor places in the joint venture. For now it is better to describe the status of the core in terms of the profit expected by the investor. Let w_j denote the expected profit to a type j investor. A nonempty core requires the existence of a set of expected profits $\{w_j : j = 1, \ldots, n\}$ that no individual investor or coalition of investors could improve upon. This means the n-vector $w = \{w_j\}$ must satisfy the following conditions for all $s = \{s_1, \ldots, s_n\}$ with $0 \leq s \leq t$:

$$\sum_j s_j w_j \geq V(s) \quad \text{and} \quad \sum_j t_j w_j = V(t). \tag{5}$$

According to Appendix Theorem 3.B.2, a necessary condition for a nonempty core is that

$$V_t(t) \circ s \geq V(s) \quad \text{for all } s \text{ with } 0 \leq s \leq t, \tag{6}$$

given that $V(s)$ is a differentiable function of s so that V has partial derivatives. Inequality (6) is true if V is weakly superadditive by Appendix Theorem 3.B.2. Weak superadditivity is a necessary condition for a nonempty core according to Appendix Theorem 3.A.2. Under the hypothesis that $x(t) > 0$, Theorem 5 that follows shows that the expected returns based on the Lindahl prices defined in equation (12) do satisfy the core constraints. Hence inequality (6) would follow as an implication of Theorem 5.

Another necessary condition for a nonempty core is that

$$V_s(s) \circ s \geq V(s) \quad \text{for all } s \text{ with } 0 \leq s \leq t.$$

This inequality says that the expected profit to the coalition s must be a superhomogeneous function of s. That this is so is a consequence of the inequality

$$V_s(s) \circ s - V(s) = \sum_i x_i(s) \geq 0,$$

which proves

THEOREM 2.   *The expected profit to the coalition s is a superhomogenous function of s.*

Shapley (1971) gives an important sufficient condition for a nonempty core. It needs some preparation starting with the

DEFINITION. v is called a supermodular (set) function if for all sets S and T in its domain,

$$v(S) + v(T) \leq v(S \cup T) + v(S \cap T).$$

Every supermodular function for which $v(\varnothing) = 0$ is superadditive. To verify this from the definition take nonoverlapping S and T so that $S \cap T = \varnothing$. However, a superadditive function is not necessarily supermodular.

SHAPLEY'S THEOREM.   *Every n-person game with a supermodular characteristic function has a nonempty core that coincides with its von Neumann–Morgenstern stable set.*

Shapley also describes the extreme points of the core. Let P_i denote player i. An extreme point of the core is given by calculating the incremental contributions of the players to a sequence of coalitions such as the following:

$$a_1 = V(P_1), \qquad a_2 = V(P_2, P_1) - V(P_1),$$
$$a_3 = V(P_1, P_2, P_3) - V(P_1, P_2), \ldots,$$
$$a_n = V(P_1, P_2, \ldots, P_n) - V(P_1, P_2, \ldots, P_{n-1}).$$

Here a_i denotes the return to player i so that the n-vector $a = \{a_1, a_2, \ldots, a_n\}$ is an extreme point of the core. There are $n!$ extreme points, each determined by the order that players enter the grand coalition.

This theorem has an extension to continuous games that have strictly convex characteristic functions. Convexity of the characteristic function ensures that the conditions which apply to coalitions at the vertexes extend to all admissible coalitions including those in the interior. We begin with definitions of the union and intersection of vectors.

DEFINITION.   The union of the vectors r and s, denoted by $r \cup s$, is the smallest vector that contains r or s. The intersection of the vectors r and s, denoted by $r \cap s$, is the biggest vector contained in r and s.

The term *contains* and *contained* for vectors are defined as follows:

DEFINITION.   The n-vector s contains the n-vector r if $s_i \geq r_i$ for $i = 1, \ldots, n$. Likewise, the vector r is contained in the vector s if the coordinates satisfy the same inequalities.

On the basis of these definitions we have

DEFINITION.   Let $q_i = \max \{r_i, s_i\}$ and $p_i = \min \{r_i, s_i\}$ for $i = 1, \ldots, n$. Then $q = r \cup s$ and $p = r \cap s$.

Thus, q is the vector that is the least upper bound of r and s and p is the vector that is the greatest lower bound of r and s. For example, if $r = \{3, 7\}$ and $s =$

$\{4, 6\}$ then $r \cup s = \{4, 7\}$ and $r \cap s = \{3, 6\}$. Therefore, $r \leq r \cup s$, $s \leq r \cup s$, $r \geq r \cap s$, and $s \geq r \cap s$ as required. By Lemma 6.7.2,

$$r \cup s + r \cap s = r + s.$$

These definitions apply to the vectors that measure the sizes of the coalitions containing the individual members of the various types. It is always assumed that the union of two coalitions does not have overlapping membership (see chap. 2, append.). To apply these concepts to a function of vectors, we start with the

DEFINITION.   The function f is supermodular if

$$f(r \cup s) + f(r \cap s) \geq f(r) + f(s).$$

Rewrite this supermodular function as follows:

$$f(r \cup s) - f(r) \geq f(s) - f(r \cap s).$$

Make the following correspondences:

$$r + t \to r \cup s; \qquad t \to r; \qquad r + s \to s; \qquad s \to r \cap s.$$

On the left of each arrow are the vectors giving the sizes of the coalitions and on the right are the vector arguments for the supermodular function. As required there is

$$s \leq t \Rightarrow (r \cap s) \subset r.$$

These correspondences imply that a supermodular function of vectors satisfies the following inequality for all $0 \leq s \leq t$ and $r \geq 0$:

$$f(t + r) - f(t) \geq f(s + r) - f(s). \tag{7}$$

Inequality (7) says that if a supermodular function is differentiable then its gradient is nondecreasing. The result proved in Telser 1987, chap. 4, part 1, sec. 5, prop. 4, p. 98 implies the following:

LEMMA 1.   *Let $V(s)$ be a strictly convex, differentiable, characteristic function of the n-vector s on the domain $0 \leq s \leq t$. If the gradient of V is nondecreasing so that the elements of the matrix V_{ss} are nonnegative then V has a nonempty core for all $t \in \Omega_n$.*

Keep in mind that this lemma gives a sufficient but not a necessary condition for a nonempty core of a convex characteristic function defined on the entire nonnegative orthant, namely all $t \in \Omega_n$. A convex characteristic function may have a nonempty core for some but not for all $t \in \Omega_n$ when V_{ss} is not nonnegative. Theorem 5 that follows shows this by giving another and different set of sufficient conditions for a core of a convex characteristic function. The characteristic function in Theorem 5 is pertinent for the theory of corporations, and it applies for a given t. Nor is this all. All the elements of V_{ss} need not be non-negative. They would all be nonnegative if and only if the negative definite matrix $(s\overline{W}_{ss})^{-1}$ had only nonpositive elements. However, as formula (2.11) shows, the matrix $s\overline{W}_{xx}$ is negative definite and has negative elements. Therefore its inverse cannot have only nonpositive elements unless it is a diagonal matrix. The matrix can be diagonal given that the returns from the projects are independent random variables if the willingness to pay functions were linear. However, linear W could not assure a finite expected willingness to pay for all admissible pdf's as noted previously. Therefore, a strictly convex characteristic function can have an empty core. For a strictly convex characteristic function to have a core it must also be nondecreasing. These results have some important consequences.

To derive them we study how the status of the core depends on the number of investment projects and on the number of investment types. We shall obtain the following results. Coalitions restricted to a single type of investor but with an arbitrary number of projects can have a nonempty core. Coalitions restricted to a single project but with an arbitrary number of investor types who all have a positive marginal expected willingness to pay for the project can have a nonempty core. The status of the core is in doubt only if there are several investor types considering more than one project. In this general case there is an explicit imputation of the expected gains from the joint ventures that can satisfy all the core constraints provided the optimal investment in each of the projects is positive.

First, with only one investor type and an arbitrary finite number of investment projects, the vector representing a coalition reduces to a scalar so that $V(s)$ is a convex increasing function of a scalar. As the function of a scalar the situation is simple. The core is nonempty if and only if V is strictly superhomogeneous according to Theorem 3. Since in the present case this holds even if s were a vector, surely it is satisfied in the special case of a scalar. This proves

THEOREM 3.   *For convex V and coalitions consisting of a single investor type, if V is positive for large enough coalitions, so that V is strictly superhomogeneous, the coalition t is stable because there is an implication of a nonempty core for an arbitrary number of investment projects undertaken by t.*

A coalition with only one type of investor that has many projects would invest less in each the more projects it undertakes. This is so because of formula (2.11) which shows that the marginal expected willingness to pay for one project varies inversely with the amount spent on another.

The second assertion is given by

THEOREM 4.   *For a single investment project the coalition t is stable if it includes only those types of investors who agree on the desirability of the project in the sense that*

$$\overline{W}_x^i(t)\,\overline{W}_x^h(t) > 0. \tag{8}$$

PROOF.   To prove this requires an explicit expression for V_{ss}. Equation (3) says

$$V_s = \overline{W}\big(x(s)\big).$$

Therefore,

$$V_{ss} = \overline{W}_x\,\frac{dx}{ds}. \tag{9}$$

In equation (9), dx/ds is an $m \times n$ matrix, $\overline{W}_x$ is an $n \times m$ matrix, and V_{ss} is an $n \times n$ matrix. We can compute dx/ds from the first-order necessary conditions that $x(s)$ must satisfy given as follows:

$$s\overline{W}_x - \ell = 0.$$

Differentiate this equation with respect to s and obtain

$$\overline{W}_x + \big(s\overline{W}_{xx}\big)\frac{dx}{ds} = 0 \Rightarrow \frac{dx}{ds} = -\big(s\overline{W}_{xx}\big)^{-1}\overline{W}_x. \tag{10}$$

Substitute the expression for dx/ds from (10) into equation (9) to obtain

$$V_{ss} = -\overline{W}_x\big(s\overline{W}_{xx}\big)^{-1}\overline{W}_x. \tag{11}$$

In that special case in which the coalition has a single investment project, the middle term in equation (11) reduces to a negative scalar. Hence the $n \times n$ matrix V_{ss} is a product of the $n \times 1$ and $1 \times n$ vectors, $\overline{W}_x\,\overline{W}_x$, each of whose elements is nonnegative by virtue of the hypothesis inequality (8). Therefore, all the elements of V_{ss} are positive and by Lemma 1 there is an implication of a nonempty core.   QED

Under the hypothesis of Theorem 4, the bigger the number of types of investors who agree on the worth of the project in the sense of inequality (8), the larger is the optimal investment in that project. A useful interpretation of Theorems 4 and 5 is this. A joint venture that specializes on one project attracts a more heterogeneous group of investors than one that spreads its investments among many different projects.

Theorem 4 asserts that a coalition with a single investment project is stable for as many investor types as can agree on the marginal expected valuation of the project in the sense of inequality (8). A single-venture corporation can have a heterogeneous group of shareholders and be a stable coalition. It is consistent with this theory that there is an investor who owns stock in many different corporations. This means that stable coalitions can have overlapping membership. We do observe individuals who do own stocks in many different corporations. Hence this observation is consistent with the theory.

However, Theorem 4 also raises an issue that does not seem to square with the facts. A coalition with a single project and many types of investors is stable. Does this mean that *all* investor types must be present in *every* stable coalition? Put differently, let there be stable coalitions in the sense of Theorem 4. It may appear from this theorem that each investor type makes an investment in each stable coalition. If this were an implication of Theorem 4, the theory would be overturned by observing some investor types who invest in some but not in all single-venture coalitions.

Theorem 4 does not make this prediction. It does say that if one investor type has a high enough positive valuation for a project that would attract his funds then all investors of the same type would behave in the same way. But different investors have different views about the profitability of the possible ventures, and they are not all willing to invest in the same venture. Only those invest in a venture who value it highly enough. It is consistent with the theory to find some investors who place their funds in one project but not in another. Theorem 4 allows diversity with respect to the investment policies of different investors.

A stable coalition in the sense of Theorem 3 resembles a closed-end mutual fund with a diversified portfolio. On this interpretation, a closed-end mutual fund can attract a single investor type. Therefore investors in a given closed-end mutual fund should tend to be similar, and they would tend to invest the same amount in the fund. This suggests an empirical test of the theory. The concentration of ownership in a corporation or closed-end mutual fund describes the relation between the fraction of the shares held and the fraction of the investors who own these shares. Highly concentrated ownership means a small fraction of the shareholders accounts for a large fraction of all the shares. If the prediction about closed-end mutual funds is correct then ownership of a closed-end mutual fund should be less concentrated than ownership of a specialized corporation. It follows that the Lorenz curve for a closed-end mutual fund should be more nearly linear than for a specialized corporation. Whether this is so is unknown.

The general case is a joint venture with many projects and many investor types. It poses a matching problem. Such a coalition can be stable depending on the affinity between the projects and the investors. If such coalitions can be stable it would follow there are closed-end mutual funds with overlapping membership and diversified corporations with overlapping shareowners. We now prove an important result giving a sufficient condition for a stable coalition in these two senses.

THEOREM 5.   *Let each $\overline{W}^j(x)$ be a concave nondecreasing function of the investments that are restricted to be nonnegative. Let x(t), the m-vector of the* *optimal investments for the coalition t, be strictly positive so that the first-order necessary condition for the optimal investments is satisfied with equality. Then t is a stable coalition.*

PROOF.   The proof consists in showing that the following imputation is in the core.

$$w_j = \overline{W}^j(t) - \sum_i \overline{W}^j_{x_i}(t) x_i(t). \tag{12}$$

The second term on the right of the equal sign is the Lindahl price for the optimal investments of the coalition t. This imputation for a type j investor, his expected gain for participation in the coalition t, is his expected willingness to pay minus his Lindahl price. We begin by showing that $\sum_j t_j w_j = V(t)$.

$$\sum_j t_j w_j = \sum_j t_j \overline{W}^j(t) - \sum_j t_j \sum_i \overline{W}^j_{x_i}(t) x_i(t)$$

$$= \sum_j t_j \overline{W}^j(t) - \sum_i \sum_j t_j \overline{W}^j_{x_i}(t) x_i(t)$$

$$= V(t)$$

because $x(t) > 0$ by hypothesis so that the necessary condition is $\sum_j t_j \overline{W}^j_{x_i}(t) = 1$.

Next we show that $\sum_j s_j w_j \geq V(s)$ for all s such that $0 \leq s \leq t$. By concavity of $\overline{W}^j$,

$$\overline{W}^j_x(t) \circ \left(x(t) - x(s) \right) \leq \overline{W}^j(t) - \overline{W}^j(s).$$

Rearranging terms,

$$\overline{W}^j(s) - \overline{W}^j_x(t) \circ x(s) \leq \overline{W}^j(t) - \overline{W}^j_x(t) \circ x(t) = w_j.$$

Therefore,

$$\sum_j s_j w_j \geq \sum_j s_j \left[\overline{W}^j(s) - \overline{W}^j_x(t) \circ x(s) \right]$$

$$= \sum_j s_j \overline{W}^j(s) - \sum_i x_i(s) + \sum_i x_i(s) - \sum_j s_j \overline{W}^j_x(t) \circ x(s)$$

$$= V(s) + \sum_i x_i(s) - \sum_j s_j \overline{W}^j_x(t) \circ x(s)$$

$$+ \sum_j t_j \overline{W}^j_x(t) \circ x(s) - \sum_j t_j \overline{W}^j_x(t) \circ x(s)$$

$$= V(s) + \sum_j (t_j - s_j) \overline{W}^j_x(t) \circ x(s) \tag{13}$$

since the hypothesis that $x(t) > 0$ implies that the first-order necessary condition is an equation so that

$$\sum_i x_i(s) - \sum_j t_j \, \overline{W}_x^j(t) \circ x(s) = 0.$$

Now $t_j - s_j \geq 0$, $x(s) \geq 0$, and $\overline{W}_x^j(t) \geq 0$ so that all the terms on the last line of (13) are nonnegative. Therefore, as claimed $\sum_j s_j \, w_j \geq V(s)$. Hence w_j given by equation (12) does satisfy all the core constraints.   QED

For a more general result, see Telser 1987, chap. 4, part 3, sec. 2, prop. 1.

Figure 4 illustrates the equilibrium. The marginal expected willingness to pay for all the investors in a corporation except for the type 1 investors is shown by the curve $D_0 D_0'$. This curve approaches the horizontal axis asymptotically because the expected willingness to pay is an increasing, concave function of the amount invested. The line CC' shows the marginal cost of the investment. The optimal investment OX_0 is determined by the intersection of the two curves at A_0. The total cost of the investment is the area of the rectangle OCA_0X_0. The expected gain of these investors is shown by the area of the curvilinear triangle, CD_0A_0. This area corresponds to w_j given in equation (12). Let type 1 investors join the coalition. This raises the expected marginal willingness to pay from D_0D_0' to D_1D_1'. The new optimal investment is at the point X_1 as determined by

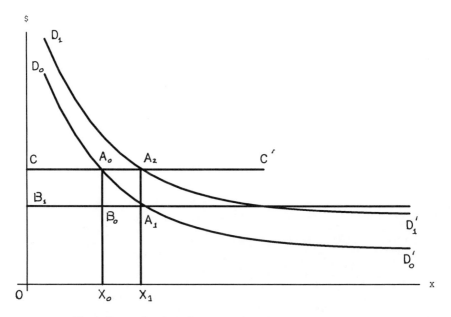

Fig. 4. Determination of optimal investment for a joint venture

the intersection of $D_1 D_1'$ with CC'. The original investors contribute $OB_1 A_1 X_1$ to defray the new total cost given by the area of the rectangle $OCA_2 X_1$, and the type 1 investors contribute $B_1 CA_2 A_1$. Because of the entry of the new investors into the coalition, the expected gain of the original investors rises from $CD_0 A_0$ to $B_1 D_0 A_1$. The increase of their expected gain is shown by the area of the rectangle $B_1 CA_0 B_0$ plus the area of the curvilinear triangle $B_0 A_0 A_1$. The first component is the cost they save that is now borne by the new members of the coalition, and the second component of their increased gain comes from the larger optimal investment due to the addition of the new members. Hence the existing members of the coalition expect a larger gain because of the addition of the type 1 investors to the coalition. The type 1 investors will join the coalition if they also anticipate a positive gain from so doing. Their gain will be positive if the area $D_0 D_1 A_2 A_1$ is bigger than the area $B_1 CA_2 A_1$. We see that this is true if and only if the area $D_0 D_1 A_2 A_0$ exceeds the area $B_1 CA_0 A_1$. Figure 4 shows how the total cost of the optimal investment OX_1 is shared between the two groups. The original members pay $OB_1 A_1 X_1$, and the new members pay $B_1 CA_2 A_1$.

The results of Theorem 5 are important for several reasons. First, they describe a unique point in the core that satisfies all the proper core constraints with strict inequality. This means that all members of the coalition expect to gain more than the minimal amount they would be willing to accept. Second, this particular point in the core shows how much each investor type contributes to the total cost of the investments of the coalition. A type j investor contributes

$$c_j = \sum_i \overline{W}_{x_i}^j(t) x_i(t),$$

which is his Lindahl price. Third, the stability of the coalition t follows from the hypothesis that the expected willingness to pay is both a concave and an increasing function of the amount invested. Consequently the marginal willingness to pay is positive for each investor type. The members of the coalition agree on the usefulness of their investment projects in this sense. Fourth, it is possible to compute how changes in the composition of the coalition affect w_j, the expected gains of the present members. This expected gain depends on the other members solely via their effect on the total optimal investments of the corporation. We now study this in more detail.

Differentiate w_j in equation (12) with respect to t_k and obtain

$$\frac{dw_j}{dt_k} = \overline{W}_x^j \frac{dx}{dt_k} - \overline{W}_x^j \frac{dx}{dt_k} - x(t) \overline{W}_{xx}^j(t) \frac{dx}{dt_k} = -x(t) \overline{W}_{xx}^j(t) \frac{dx}{dt_k}. \tag{14}$$

Assume that type t_k belongs to t and differentiate the first-order necessary condition with respect to t_k.

$$\overline{W}_x^k + \sum_j t_j \overline{W}_{xx}^j \frac{dx}{dt_k} = 0 \Rightarrow \frac{dx}{dt_k} = -\left(\sum_j t_j \overline{W}_{xx}^j \right)^{-1} \overline{W}_x^k. \tag{15}$$

Substitute this expression for dx/dt_k from equation (15) into equation (14) and obtain

$$\frac{dw_j}{dt_k} = x\,\overline{W}^j_{xx} \left(\sum_j t_j\,\overline{W}^j_{xx} \right)^{-1} \overline{W}^k_x. \qquad (16)$$

The following corollary is an immediate implication of equation (16).

COROLLARY. *Let a corporation specialize on a single project, so that x is a scalar. Under the hypotheses of Theorem 5, $dw_j/dt_k > 0$.*

This corollary says that the entry of more investor types into a specialized corporation who all have an increasing concave expected willingness to pay for its single project must raise the expected profit of the incumbent investors in that corporation (cf. fig. 5).

The effect on the expected profits of the present investors resulting from a replacement of an old type by a new type is more complicated. The departure of old type investors from the corporation is explained by a lowering of their expected willingness to pay because they have become less optimistic about the prospects for success of the corporation's ventures. The entry of new investors into the corporation shows their greater willingness to contribute to its ventures owing to their more optimistic view of its prospects than they held before. Formally, if type k replaces type h then

$$\Delta t_k + \Delta t_h = 0.$$

The effect of this replacement on the profits expected by an incumbent investor type j is as follows:

$$\frac{dw_j}{dt_k}\,\Delta t_k + \frac{dw_j}{dt_h}\,\Delta t_h = \left(\frac{dw_j}{dt_k} - \frac{dw_j}{dt_h} \right) \Delta t_k.$$

Reconsider equation (16). It implies that

$$\sum_j t_j\,\frac{dw_j}{dt_k} = x \circ \sum_j t_j\,\overline{W}^j_{xx}(t) \left(\sum_j t_j\,\overline{W}^j_{xx} \right)^{-1} \overline{W}^k_x = x \circ \overline{W}^k_x = c_k.$$

This result says that a linear combination of the rates of change of the expected gains to the present investors in the corporation with respect to a change in the number of type k investors equals the cost to a type k investor of joining the corporation.

The sufficient condition for a stable coalition in Theorem 5 reveals much about the nature of these coalitions. Consider a coalition t such that at least one of the following two conditions does *not* hold:

i. Each $\overline{W}^j(x)$ is strictly increasing and concave;
ii. $x(t) > 0$.

As a consequence *t* may not be stable. Theorem 5 asserts that stability of *t* would be assured if those investor types leave *t* so a new coalition can form for which conditions i and ii do hold. For single-project corporations or for single-type and closed-end mutual funds, these conditions do not apply. Theorems 3 and 4 give sufficient conditions for stability of such coalitions. Conditions i and ii create enough affinity among investors and projects to form a stable corporation.

We now derive some consequences of a nonempty core. Assume there is the affinity among investors and projects that implies a nonempty core so that the coalition *t* is stable. We seek some general properties of the returns to the investors. The value of participation in the coalition to investor *j* is given by his expected willingness to pay, $\overline{W}^j(x(t))$. This depends on the other members of the coalition solely through $x(t)$. Investor *j* expects a profit w_j as a member of *t*. As before, let c_j denote his cost of membership so this is how much he pays to *t*. Since

$$\overline{W}^j\left(x(t)\right) - c_j = w_j, \qquad c_j = \overline{W}^j\left(x(t)\right) - w_j.$$

Equation (12) gives an explicit expression for c_j. It follows readily from this equation and from Theorem 5 that shows an explicit w_j in the core that

$$\sum_j c_j t_j = \sum_i x_i(t). \tag{17}$$

The amount that the corporation collects from its members equals the total cost of its optimal investments. According to this theory, each different investor type may put a different amount into the corporation. The amount depends not only on the expected willingness to pay as a member of the corporation but also on competition for members among the various corporations. Those who belong to a corporation value its prospects more highly than those who do not belong to it. Therefore the shareholders of a corporation value their shares to be worth at least the current market price. To put it another way, the current market price of a share does not exceed the expected value of the stock to any of its current shareholders.

A budget constraint is often invoked to explain why someone does not buy a commodity. It is said that the commodity is too expensive or that the person cannot afford to buy it. This explanation is especially inappropriate here. An investor considers putting funds at the disposal of a venture hoping for a profit. Hope for profit is the spur, and fear of loss is the rein. A budget constraint in the ordinary sense has no place in this decision.

However, a condition akin to a budget constraint does have an important place in the model. It is equation (17) that equates the sum of the costs of the optimal investments by the corporation to the sum of the amounts invested by the members of the corporation. This equation is analogous to Walras's law that asserts the sum of the purchases equals the sum of the receipts. Equation (17) is an implication of the model not an assumption of it. It is a necessary condition for a core.

Nothing has been said yet about a salient aspect of corporations—the limited liability of their shareholders. Limited liability means that the loss to a shareholder cannot exceed his initial investment. It must not escape our attention that this theory does not assume limited liability—it predicts that it must be present to have a nonempty core. Thus, c_j, which is the investment of investor type j in the coalition t, is the maximal loss he can sustain. Limited liability is an implication of a nonempty core provided the funds supplied by the shareholders are the only source of capital to the corporation. The model assumes the corporation does not borrow (cf. chap. 3, append.). If the corporation did borrow then it would be necessary to describe what would happen in the event of bankruptcy. Real corporations who borrow and thereby obtain funds in addition to those furnished or owned by their shareholders have limited liability as an explicit part of their corporate charter. The owners of real corporations incur no residual liability to the creditors of the corporation. Hence no shareholder in a real corporation can lose more than his investment no matter how badly the corporation does. Moreover, limited liability is also necessary for the fungibility of shares traded in the market. Lacking limited liability, no shareholder would be allowed to sell his stake in the corporation without the consent of the other shareholders, nor would a new investor be allowed to become a shareholder in the corporation without the consent of the existing shareholders.

4. The Market for Shares of Ownership

The analysis so far applies to the circumstances that would lead to the formation of a stable coalition. A coalition t is stable when it can offer its members the prospect of a profit big enough to deter them from joining a subcoalition. This means no subcoalition of t can offer its members more than they could get by remaining in t. An investor type j who is a member of t expects a gain of w_j and pays c_j to the coalition. The sum of these payments equals the total cost of the optimal investments of the coalition. In the preceding section the analysis of stability focuses on the choice and size of the optimal investments by the coalition. Theorem 3.5 and the discussion of figure 4 center on the optimal sizes of the projects. We now examine the stability of a coalition in terms of the composition of its membership. This leads to a study of the market for shares.

Consider figure 5. The axes show the number of investors of each type. The point t is the coalition of all the investors. The subcoalitions of t are the points in the rectangle southwest of t. The coalition t is stable with respect to the subcoalitions in this rectangle if and only if none of these subcoalitions can promise more profit to their members than they could get as members of t. Next,

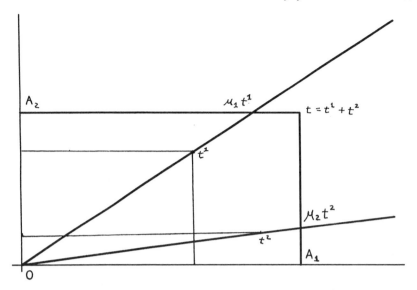

Fig. 5. Space of stable coalitions for two types of investors

consider two coalitions, t^1 and t^2, that sum to $t(t^1 + t^2 = t)$. Convexity of the willingness to pay functions implies that a stable coalition must include either all or none of the individuals of a given type. Because the hypothesis about the nature of the returns to a project implies that the willingness to pay function of each coalition is a convex, superhomogeneous function of its membership, neither t^1 nor t^2 is stable since neither includes all the members of any type that belongs to it. The only possible stable coalitions are those shown by the points on the frontier $A_2 t A_1$. Choose two points on this frontier, say, $\mu_1 t^1$ and $\mu_2 t^2$. Once again, neither of these is a stable coalition because each fails to include all investors of that type already in it. Thus, $\mu_1 t^1$ leaves out some type 1 investors, and $\mu_2 t^2$ leaves out some type 2 investors. Given there are two types of investors, the only possible stable coalitions are those represented by the vertexes, A_2, t, and A_1.

Suppose t were unstable. It means that some investors believe that they would get more profit by leaving t and forming their own coalition. They may even choose the same investment projects as t but of a different size. In this case, Theorem 3.4, not Theorem 3.5, is pertinent. Since projects are semiprivate goods, they have no external effects. In this theory even specialized corporations that choose the same venture but at different sizes do not directly affect each other's profits even though they may be rivals and consequently may be subject to some common forces of supply and demand.

Distinct corporations can include the same investor types. However, if a given type is a shareholder of a corporation then all investors of that type must also be shareholders. To illustrate, say there are three investor types and that a coalition including all three types would be unstable. Therefore, there can be at most three coalitions with two types of investors; these are as follows: a coalition with investor types 1 and 2, a coalition with types 1 and 3, or a coalition with types 2 and 3. If each of these were a stable coalition then no coalition with only one investor type could be stable. This is because each of the stable two-investor–type coalitions could promise their members more profit than any sub-coalition that has all the investors of a single type. It is also possible that some of the two-investor–type coalitions are unstable or even that none is stable. In the latter case the only stable coalitions would be composed of all investors of one type.

This theory does allow a wide variety of stable coalitions with respect to the size and composition by investor types. Nor is this all. Stable coalitions with investors of the same type can exist side by side. As far as we can determine from the available statistics, there are many more investors than organizations in the form of corporations or mutual investment funds. This does not contradict the theory. Even if each individual were a distinct investor type, individuals may gain by combining in joint ventures.

Next consider this situation. Start with stable coalitions. As time passes, things change. Some individual investors wish to sell their shares while others, not the original shareholders, wish to buy shares and become shareholders in the corporation. Because of limited liability, no investor risks more than his stake in the corporation. He is not liable for the debts of the other shareholders. Consequently, he can ignore the creditworthiness of the other shareholders in the corporation. This renders shares of ownership in a corporation fungible and easily traded. It must be emphasized that limited liability is necessary for the fungibility of the shares. Joint ventures without limited liability do not allow their members to sell their shares to anyone who is not approved by the current members. There are many examples of organizations that require the approval by all the present members of a prospective new member who wants to replace a current member. Among these are partnerships, real estate cooperatives, organized markets such as the New York Stock Exchange, the Chicago Board of Trade, the Chicago Mercantile Exchange, and Lloyd's of London. Shares in such ventures are not fungible.

A type j investor has a number of shares that shows his proportionate ownership in the company. When the company started, this investor expected a profit of w_j, he paid c_j to the company, and his proportionate share of the initial assets of the company is $q_j = c_j / \Sigma_k t_k c_k$, which implies that $\Sigma_j t_j q_j = 1$. Let z_j denote the number of shares he owns. In terms of shares of stock, he owns a fraction of the company given by the ratio $z_j / \Sigma_k t_k z_k$ and this ratio equals q_j. After the corporation begins, a shareholder can sell any number of his shares to anyone he pleases without the consent of the other shareholders. If the share-holder did not change his views about the prospects of the company then the least he would be willing to accept for his total interest in the company is the most he was willing to pay for his interest in it, namely, $\overline{W}^j$. Expressed in terms of the valuation per share, the minimal price a type j owner would be willing to accept for his share of the company is a price given by the ratio $\overline{W}^j/z_j$. Those who want to buy stock in the company presumably are willing to pay an amount depending on their views about the prospects for the company. This amount sets an upper bound on the maximum price they are willing to pay for a share of stock in the company. Analysis of the market for shares of stock can use the model of pure exchange in chapter 1. Owing to the fact that in the present application the characteristic function of a coalition is a convex function of the number of its owners, the theory makes definite assertions about this situation. First, if any individual investor values the prospects of the ventures undertaken by the coalition highly enough to join the coalition then this must be true of all investors of the same type. Second, if some investor of a given type does not value the coalition's prospects enough to be willing to invest in it then all in-vestors of that type have the same belief. Therefore, purchase of shares by one type of investor implies that all investors of that type would be willing to buy the stocks at the same price per share. Similarly, the desire by one investor type to sell his shares at some price entails the willingness of all investors of that type to do the same.

Figure 6a shows the supply curve of shares of stock of the existing own-ers ordered with respect to their expected valuation per share from the lowest to the highest. The coordinate of these valuations is shown on the horizontal axis. The cumulative proportion of the number of shares is shown on the verti-cal axis. Thus, the point $\overline{W}^1/z_1$ shows that the fraction $t_1q_1/\Sigma_j t_j q_j$ has a valua-tion given by $\overline{W}^1/z_1$. The next point, $\overline{W}^2/z_2$, shows the cumulative fraction of the shares $t_1q_1 + t_2q_2$ with a valuation up to $\overline{W}^2/z_2$, and so on. Say that the cur-rent market-clearing price per share in the corporation is p. A current type k owner in the corporation expects a nonnegative profit of $\overline{W}^k - pz_k$ or he would sell his stock. In figure 6a, investor types 1, 2, and 3 would sell their shares, and types 4 and 5 would retain their shares at the market price p. Another schedule shows the valuations of those who are not currently shareholders in the corpo-ration. This is the demand for shares shown by the step function $\overline{B}^5 \, \overline{B}^4 \, \overline{B}^3 \, \overline{B}^2 \, \overline{B}^1$ that decreases from left to right in figure 6a. The market-clearing price is at the intersection of the two schedules. The equilibrium fraction of the shares traded is $\Sigma_1^4 t_j q_j$, and the equilibrium share price must satisfy the inequali-ties $\overline{W}^4/z_4 \le p < \overline{B}^2$. There is no unique equilibrium price for the situation shown in figure 6a.

Both price and quantity would be uniquely determined if the supply and demand curves were both continuous and at least one curve had a nonzero slope

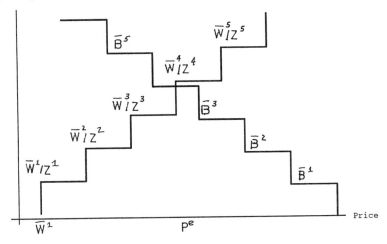

Fig. 6a. The supply and demand for shares of stock: Finite number of investor types

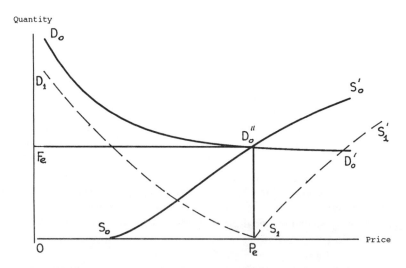

Fig. 6b. The supply and demand for shares of stock: Continuum of investor types

at the point of intersection. The curves would be continuous if there were a continuum of trader types. Figure 6b illustrates this case. Note that price is on the horizontal axis and that the fraction of shares held is on the vertical axis. The continuous curve $S_0 S_0'$ shows the cumulative distribution function for the expected willingness to pay, that is equivalent to the reservation prices of the current owners. This curve shows the fraction of the outstanding shares that would be offered at various prices. In algebraic terms, the cumulative distribution function of the current owners as follows,

$$A(p) = \int_0^p a(\xi)d\xi,$$

is the equation for the supply curve. The demand curve $D_0 D_0'$ shows the expected willingness to pay of those who are not among the current owners of the company. At OP_e there is a demand for the fraction OF_e of the outstanding shares. At this price the nonowners are willing to pay at most OP_e to acquire the fraction OF_e of the company. The equation of the demand curve,

$$B(p) = \int_p^\infty b(\eta)d\eta,$$

gives the fraction of the nonowners who are willing to pay up to p per share. Hence it is the fraction who believes the stock is worth at most p per share. This fraction decreases with p. The price that clears the market is OP_e. Trades between those current owners whose valuations of their shares are below p and the nonowners whose valuations are above p transform the function $A(.)$ from $S_0 S_0'$ to $S_1 S_1'$. As a result of these trades none of the current owners, including those who have just bought the stock, puts a value on their holdings that is below the market-clearing price. Also, these trades change the curve showing the valuations of the nonowners of the stock from the initial $D_0 D_0'$ before the trades to $D_1 P_e$ after the trades. Consequently, no nonowner has a value per share above the current market-clearing equilibrium price. All the old valuations between S_0 and P_e are replaced by the new valuations of the new owners on the section of the demand curve $D_0'' D_0'$. The new supply curve begins at the point P_e on the horizontal axis and goes up the line cutting the vertical axis at 1. The shape of the new supply curve may differ from that of the old supply curve because it includes the new owners of shares who bought their shares at the price OP_e.

It is instructive to derive the details for the simplest case where the distributions are linear functions. The pertinent graphs are in figures 7a and 7b. The valuations of the current owners are given by the upward sloping linear function $s_1 s_2$ while the maximum willingness to pay of prospective owners is shown by the downward sloping curve $d_1 d_2$. The market-clearing price is p^e, and the corresponding fraction of the outstanding shares exchanged is q^e. As a result of these trades, the new valuation function of the owners becomes the dashed

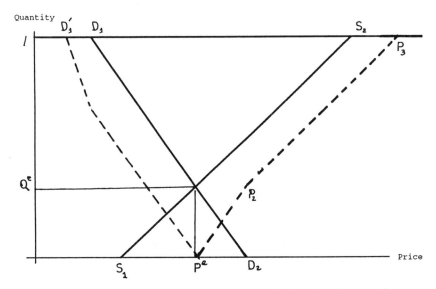

Fig. 7a. Effects of trades on the distribution of valuations for a continuum of traders

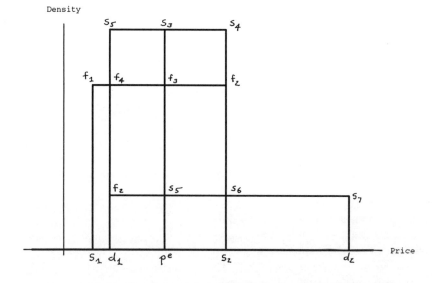

Fig. 7b. Effects of trades on the distribution of valuations for a finite number of traders

curve shown by $p^e p_2 p_3$ while the maximum willingness to pay of prospective owners becomes the curve shown by the dashed line $d_1 p^e$. In order to verify these results begin with the function showing the valuations of the current owners as follows:

$$A(p) = \int_{s_1}^{p} \frac{d\xi}{S_2 - S_1} = \frac{p - S_1}{S_2 - S_1}.$$

The willingness to pay of the prospective owners is given by the function

$$B(p) = \int_{p}^{d_2} \frac{d\eta}{D_2 - D_1} = \frac{D_2 - p}{D_2 - D_1}.$$

The market-clearing price is the solution of the pair of linear equations

$$A(p^e) = B(p^e) = q^e.$$

Figure 7b shows the density function of the valuations of the current owners. It is a uniform density in the interval from s_1 to s_2. The distance $f_1 s_1$ equals $1/(S_2 - S_1)$ so that the area of the rectangle $s_1 f_1 f_2 s_2$ is 1. The density function of the prospective owners is uniform over the interval from d_1 to d_2. The trades between the prospective owners and the current owners change the density function of the owners because the prospective owners who are willing to pay more than p^e replace the current owners whose valuations are below p^e. Hence the rectangle $p^e s_5 s_7 d_2$ of the prospective owners replaces $s_1 f_1 f_3 p^e$ of the current owners. Note that the area of $s_1 f_1 f_3 p^e$ equals the area of $p^e s_5 s_7 d_2$ and that $f_3 s_3 = p^e s_5$. As a result of these trades, the new density function of the owners is $p^e s_3 s_4 s_6 s_7 d_2$ and is no longer uniform. To the old density of the owners who retain their shares is added the density of the new owners. The area $p^e s_5 s_6 s_2$ equals the area $f_3 s_3 s_4 f_2$. Therefore, the length of the segment $f_3 s_3$ equals $p^e s_5$. Analytically, the new distribution function of the owners is as follows:

$$\int_{p^e}^{p} \left(\frac{1}{S_2 - S_1} + \frac{1}{d_2 - d_1} \right) d\xi = (p - p^e) \left(\frac{1}{S_2 - S_1} + \frac{1}{d_2 - d_1} \right)$$

if $p^e \leq p \leq s_2$ and

$$(s_2 - p^e) \left(\frac{1}{S_2 - S_1} + \frac{1}{d_2 - d_1} \right) + \int_{s_2}^{p} \frac{d\xi}{d_2 - s_2}$$

$$= (s_2 - p^e) \left(\frac{1}{S_2 - S_1} + \frac{1}{d_2 - d_1} \right) + \frac{p - s_2}{d_2 - s_2}$$

if $s_2 \leq p \leq d_2$. The new distribution function of the owners is shown by the dashed lines in figure 7a.

The new density of the nonowners includes the former owners who have sold their shares. Hence it is $s_1 f_1 f_4 s_5 s_3 f_3 p^e$. The new distribution function of the nonowners is as follows:

$$B(p) = 1 \quad \text{if } p < s_1,$$

$$B(p) = 1 - \frac{p - S_1}{S_2 - S_1} \quad \text{if } s_1 \leq p < d_1,$$

$$B(p) = 1 - \frac{D_1 - S_1}{S_2 - S_1} - (p - D_1)\left(\frac{1}{S_2 - S_1} + \frac{1}{D_2 - D_1}\right) \quad \text{if } d_1 < p < p^e,$$

$$B(p) = 0 \quad \text{if } p \geq p^e.$$

As a result of the trades the densities of the owners and nonowners separate at the market-clearing price p^e so that the density of the owners is now to the right of the market-clearing price and that of the nonowners to the left. The new cdf of the nonowners is shown by the line going to the left from p^e.

The general case where the distribution functions are nonlinear, while more complicated, is essentially the same as the linear case. Note that as a result of the trades, the distribution function changes from continuous to piecewise continuous so that it is not differentiable everywhere. This has implications for the statistical theory and affects tests of the distribution of the market-clearing prices.

This theory also applies to the market for share prices of n different stocks. Let $F(p)$ denote the cdf of the current owners of n stocks as a function of the n-vector p, where the ith coordinate of p is the minimally acceptable price to owners of the ith corporation. Let $A_i(p_i \mid \hat{p}_i)$ denote the conditional cdf of the owners of stock i where $\hat{p}_i$ is the $(n - 1)$-vector of prices leaving out the minimally acceptable price of share i. Let $F_i(p_i)$ denote the marginal distribution of the owners of stock i.

$$F(p) = A_i(p_i \mid \hat{p}_i) F_i(p_i).$$

Similarly, for the nonowners of these n stocks, there is

$$G(p) = B_i(p_i \mid \hat{p}_i) G_i(p_i),$$

in which the p's are the maximal acceptable prices and the cdfs go from these prices to infinity as described previously. It follows from these definitions that

$$\partial A_i(.)/\partial p_i > 0, \qquad \partial F_i(.)/\partial p_i > 0, \qquad \partial B_i(.)/\partial p_i < 0, \qquad \partial G_i(.)/\partial p_i < 0.$$

The n-vector of asymptotic market-clearing prices satisfies the n equations

$$A_i(p_i \mid \hat{p}_i) = B(p_i \mid \hat{p}_i) \Leftrightarrow G(p) / G_i(p_i) = F(p) / F_i(p_i) \qquad i = 1, \ldots, n.$$

The existence and uniqueness of these equations raise the standard questions, and we need not tarry over them.

One must recognize that these curves show the expected *total* valuations, not the expected *marginal* valuations, of the capital assets of the company. Consequently, the value of the company at the current market-clearing price is not the value of its current owners, who must believe their shares are worth more than the current price or they would not keep their stocks. Therefore, the market value given by multiplying the number of shares by the current price is the lower bound on the value of the company to the current owners (see chap. 3, sec. 2 for more on this point).

The investment outlays of a stable coalition depend on the number of each investor type belonging to that coalition. As a result of the trades, the membership changes, and this changes the total valuation function. If the marginal valuation function also changes (recall that the marginal valuation function is $\sum_{j}^{n} t_j \overline{W}_x^j$), then the theory predicts that the investment outlays of the company will also change. Investment outlays of a company would be correlated positively with changes in the composition of the ownership of that company, provided the coalition of the new owners with the incumbent owners results in a new marginal valuation function. However, this theory does not predict that the market value of a company evaluated at the market price of its shares and the investment outlays of the company must always move together. Such a positive link occurs if and only if the expected *total* valuation and the expected *marginal* valuation always move together. (See also chap. 3, sec. 2 on the neoclassical theory of investment.)

This argument can be stated in another way. According to this theory, the investment outlays of a corporation are an increasing function of the expected marginal valuations. If it were true that the higher the share price, the higher are the expected marginal valuations, then investment and the share price would be correlated positively. It does not follow that a higher total valuation due to the sale of shares by those who value them less to those who value them more always raises the expected valuations at the margin. It would not refute the theory to find that the market value of a company and its investment outlays are not positively correlated. Finding a positive correlation between these two variables is explained in this theory as due to a positive relation between the marginal and the total expected valuations. Grunfeld (1960) did find a positive association between market value and investment outlays for 8 corporations. More recently, Barro (1989) reports a significant positive association between investment in fixed assets by business firms and the lagged value weighted normal return at an annual rate for all New York Stock Exchange listed firms for the periods 1931–40, 1947–87. The *t*-ratio of the dependent variable, investment, on the explanatory variable, the return, is nearly 9.7. The R^2 is 0.74 for the regression equation that includes the lagged value of the dependent variable, business investment in fixed assets.

Still another implication of the theory refers to takeover bids. The theory predicts that the larger the fraction of the outstanding shares sought in a takeover, the higher is the bid price. This is because the bid price must be high enough to be acceptable to the present owners of that number of shares which the buyer wishes to acquire. The supply of shares of the current owners is an upward sloping curve as we have seen. This curve, $S_0 S_0'$ in figure 6b, ranks the current owners from those who value their shares the least to those who value them the most. The expected valuations of the current owners cannot be below the current market-clearing price. Therefore, the larger the fraction of the shares sought by the buyer, the higher is the price he must bid.

Bradley, Desai, and Kim (1988) have empirical results directly pertinent to this prediction. One of their regressions shows how much a takeover bid lifts the share price of the target firm. On the basis of the unweighted regression that they kindly furnished me, the elasticity of the share price of the target firm with respect to the fraction of the shares sought by the bidder evaluated at the sample means of the regression variables is 0.27. (For the weighted regression in the published article it is 0.34.) When there is more than one bidder, the price of the target firm rises by 13.6 percent relative to the price with one bidder, assuming the fraction of outstanding shares sought is independent of the number of bidders seeking to acquire the firm.

The price of the acquiring firm may also change. The price may decline if some current owners of the acquiring firm who oppose the acquisition sell their shares. The shares sold must be a small fraction of the total number of shares so that the depression of the price of the acquiring firm must be less than the rise in the price of the acquired firm. There may be other individuals who are not presently shareholders of the acquiring firm who raise their valuation of this firm and who buy shares because they favor the planned acquisition. It does not seem possible a priori to determine the total effect on the share price of the acquiring firm of these opposing forces.

There are other implications resulting from the realized earnings of the corporation. These depend on how the current owners revise their expected valuations of the company's prospects when they compare the actual to expected earnings. Earnings are funds that the corporation can retain for investment or can distribute to its shareholders. It will distribute the earnings if the shareholders have not changed their assessment of the company's prospects after having observed the profits. It will retain the earnings if the shareholders increase their marginal valuations of the company's prospects because of unexpectedly large profits. It follows that a company pays dividends because investing all of its profits is not optimal. The shareholders of a company that pays no dividend and that has positive profits believe that company has brighter prospects than one that does pay dividends. Of course, a company may not pay a dividend for quite another reason—it has a large loss and a slender chance of profits. Chapter 3, section 3 studies these problems.

5. Credibility

We now turn our attention to credibility—a topic that raises some hard problems. Money spent on credibility by a corporation does not literally change the probability of success of its investment projects although such expenditures may affect an individual's perception of the value of these projects as if it had this power. It would be as if your belief about the probability of a coin coming up heads affects the actual probability of this random event. Implicit in this statement is the opinion that there is a valid distinction between the subjective and the true probabilities of an event. Admittedly, to the subjectivist probability school, this distinction is meaningless, but for others it raises troublesome issues. We shall explore those that are relevant to this study of corporations.

Let a corporation spend $1 to enhance the credibility of its investment project. Say that this outlay has the effect of persuading an investor to put $0.50 into the project expecting a 10 percent rate of return. Hence the expenditure on credibility can raise the return of a corporation in this model via its effect on investors who finance the purchase of actual capital goods, machinery, buildings, and so on, hoping for a profit to result from these purchases. However, expenditures on credibility may also enable a corporation to deceive potential investors. This raises very troublesome problems about these outlays.

You could also interpret credibility in terms of a familiar problem of statistical inference. Suppose you had the results for a simple random sample of size n. The sample mean is $\bar{x}$, and the standard deviation of the sample mean is $s_{\bar{x}} = s/\sqrt{n}$. A 95 percent confidence interval for the mean is given by $\bar{x} \pm 1.96 s_{\bar{x}}$. The length of this interval measures the credibility of the estimate. There is more credibility, the bigger the sample size. By spending more, you could increase the sample size and increase credibility. If the value of credibility is an increasing function of credibility then you can figure out the optimal sample size and the consequent optimal outlay on credibility. This makes the outlay on credibility a way of finding out about something unknown, the true mean. It does not furnish a way of altering the true mean.

Let the credibility of project i to a type j investor depend on the amount, y_i, that the coalition spends in order to disseminate information about the project. If all the information about the project is favorable then it is plausible to assume that credibility, a_{ij}, is an increasing function of y_i. However, some investors will not interpret favorably the information they get about these ventures. An investor may learn enough about a venture to conclude that it is unsuitable for him. In either case, whether outlays to disseminate information about projects enhance or diminish their attraction to potential investors, the current members of the coalition can have an influence on the credibility of the projects by making such outlays. That credibility is an increasing function of these outlays is made explicit by writing $a_{ij}(y)$. Let $y = \{y_1, \ldots, y_m\}$ denote the m-vector of outlays on credibility for each of the m investment projects. The return to a type j investor becomes

$$r_j(y) = \sum_i \zeta_i a_{ij}(y).$$

The coalition chooses the optimal y. Hence in place of equation (3.1), there is

$$V(s) = \max_{x,y} \left\{ \sum_{j=1}^n s_j \overline{W}^j(x, y) - \sum_{i=1}^m (x_i + y_i) \right\},$$

and in addition to the first-order condition for the optimal x given by equation (3.2), there is the first-order condition for the optimal y as follows:

$$\frac{\partial}{\partial y_i} \left[\sum_j s_j \overline{W}^j(.) - \sum_i y_i \right] \leq 0.$$

Up to now how investment outlays affect the expected willingness to pay relies on the readily acceptable assumption that this willingness is a strictly increasing function of profit. However, as the next result demonstrates, the situation with respect to outlays on credibility is more delicate. To help ensure the existence of a finite expected willingness to pay with respect to the outlays on credibility, I shall make a more restrictive assumption about their effect. I shall assume that the willingness to pay is an increasing, bounded, and concave function of the expenditures on credibility. I shall also assume that the marginal credibility of each project, which is $\partial a/\partial y$, diminishes rapidly enough with respect to the credibility outlay y to overcome possible cross effects. Therefore, not only must $\partial^2 a/\partial y^2$ be negative but it must also be big enough to ensure the existence of a finite maximum. Before proving the main results given in Theorem 1, we need to establish some pertinent facts about how credibility enters the density function. As we shall see, credibility enters the density function similarly to the way that the sample size enters the pdf for the sample mean.

Write the basic probability distribution as follows:

$$F(z_0) = \int_0^{z_0} f(z)dz.$$

Let $z = a\zeta$ so that $\zeta = z/a$. Therefore,

$$\Pr\{z \leq z_0\} = \Pr\left\{\zeta \leq \frac{z_0}{a}\right\} = F\left(\frac{z_0}{a}\right).$$

We must show from this equation that $\partial F/\partial a \leq 0$. This follows from

$$F_a(.) = f\left(\frac{z_0}{a}\right)\left(\frac{-z_0}{a^2}\right) < 0.$$

Next compute the second derivative of F as follows:

$$F_{aa}(.) = \left(\frac{1}{a^2}\right)\left[\nabla f\left(\frac{z_0}{a}\right)\left(\frac{z_0}{a}\right)^2 + 2f\left(\frac{z_0}{a}\right)\left(\frac{z_0}{a}\right)\right]$$

$$= \left(\frac{1}{a^2}\right)\left(\frac{d}{d\xi}\right)[\xi^2 f(\xi)].$$

If $\lim \xi^2 f(\xi) = 0$ as $\xi \to \infty$ then because $\xi^2 f(\xi) > 0$, the term $\xi^2 f(\xi)$ must decrease for big enough ξ. Consequently, F_{aa} is asymptotically negative.

To insert the credibility factor into the pdf, begin with

$$F(a\zeta) = \int_0^{a\zeta} f(z)dz$$

and change variables from z to w so that $w = az$. The integral becomes

$$F(\zeta) = \int_0^\zeta f\left(\frac{w}{a}\right)\left(\frac{1}{a}\right)dw. \tag{1}$$

The integrand in equation (1) shows the pdf with the credibility factor appearing explicitly. As remarked previously, because a is in the denominator, it affects w just as the sample size affects the standard deviation of the sample mean.

In the following development there is no loss of generality and a gain of simplicity by confining attention to two investment projects. Let $m = 2$. Also, it simplifies the notation without causing ambiguity to drop the superscript j that denotes the investor type.

LEMMA 1.

$$\overline{W}(a_1, a_2) = \int\int W(a_1\zeta_1 + a_2\zeta_2)f^1(\zeta_1)f^2(\zeta_2)d\zeta_1\,d\zeta_2. \tag{2}$$

PROOF.   It follows from the analysis leading to equation (1) that

$$\overline{W} = \int\int W(z_1 + z_2)f^1\left(\frac{z_1}{a_1}\right)f^2\left(\frac{z_2}{a_2}\right)\left(\frac{1}{a_1 a_2}\right)dz_1\,dz_2.$$

Change variables as follows:

$$\zeta_1 = z_1/a_1 \quad \text{and} \quad \zeta_2 = z_2/a_2,$$

and the determinant of the Jacobean is $a_1 a_2$. With this transformation we obtain equation (2).   QED

THEOREM 1.   *In addition to the hypotheses of Lemma 1, let each W^j be a bounded, increasing concave function of profit. Let each a_i be concave so that its second derivative approaches minus infinity as the credibility outlay becomes unboundedly large. Then the expected willingness to pay $\overline{W}^j(x,y)$ is an increasing function of y.*

PROOF.   First, it follows from equation (2) that

$$\overline{W}_{a_i} = \int \int \nabla W(.)\zeta_i f^1(.) f^2(.) d\zeta_1 \, d\zeta_2 > 0 \tag{3}$$

because all the terms of the integrand are positive. Therefore, the willingness to pay is an increasing function of the outlay on credibility. Second, it follows from equation (3) that

$$\overline{W}_{a_i a_j} = \int \int \nabla^2 W(.)\zeta_i \, \zeta_j f^i f^j d\zeta_i \, d\zeta_j . \tag{4}$$

Next we need the mean value theorem for multiple integrals (Apostol 1957, 269).

Assume that g is in R and f is in R on a compact connected set S in R^n. Suppose that g is nonnegative and that f is continuous on S. There exists x_0 in S such that

$$\int_S f(x)g(x)dx = f(x_0) \int_S g(x)dx.$$

Approximate the integral in equation (4) over a bounded set from zero to large enough finite numbers as closely as desired so that the region of integration satisfies the hypotheses of this theorem. This allows the theorem to apply under the following correspondences:

$$g \leftrightarrow \zeta_i \zeta_j f^i f^j \quad \text{and} \quad f \leftrightarrow \nabla^2 W.$$

The term $\nabla^2 W(.)$ can go outside the integral because there is an r_0 such that

$$\overline{W}_{a_i a_j} = \nabla^2 W(r_0) \int \int \zeta_i \zeta_j f^i f^j d\zeta_i d\zeta_j = \nabla^2 W(r_0) E(\zeta_i) E(\zeta_j).$$

The hypothesis that W is concave now implies that $\overline{W}_{a_i a_j}$ is negative. Hence the matrix $[\,\overline{W}_{a_i a_j}\,]$ is symmetric with negative terms on the diagonal. This matrix can be expressed as follows:

$$\begin{bmatrix} E(\zeta_1) & 0 \\ 0 & E(\zeta_2) \end{bmatrix} \begin{bmatrix} W''(r_{11}^0) & W''(r_{12}^0) \\ W''(r_{12}^0) & W''(r_{22}^0) \end{bmatrix} \begin{bmatrix} E(\zeta_1) & 0 \\ 0 & E(\zeta_2) \end{bmatrix}.$$

By hypothesis, the credibility of project i depends only on the outlays for credibility directed to that project so that it depends only on y_i. Therefore,

$$\overline{W}_{y_i} = \overline{W}_{a_i} \frac{\partial a_i}{\partial y_i} \quad \text{and} \quad \overline{W}_{y_i y_j} = \overline{W}_{a_i a_j} \frac{\partial a_i}{\partial y_i} \frac{\partial a_j}{\partial y_j} + \delta_{ij} \overline{W}_{a_i} \frac{\partial^2 a_i}{\partial y_i^2} ,$$

where δ_{ij} denotes the Kronecker delta so that $\delta_{ij} = 1$ if $i = j$ and $\delta_{ij} = 0$ if $i \neq j$. The main conclusion is that

$$\overline{W}_{yy} = \begin{bmatrix} \overline{W}_{11} + \overline{W}_1 a_1'' & \overline{W}_{12} a_1' a_2' \\ \overline{W}_{12} a_1' a_2' & \overline{W}_{22} + \overline{W}_2 a_{21}'' \end{bmatrix}$$

so that if the terms $\overline{W}_i a_i''$ are big enough then $\overline{W}_{yy}$ will be a negative definite matrix giving the implication that $\overline{W}(y)$ will be a strongly concave function of the outlays on credibility.   QED

It can also be shown that similar hypotheses give the conclusion that the expected willingness to pay functions will be concave in both the investment and the credibility expenditures. That is, $\overline{W}^j(x,y)$ is a concave increasing bounded function of x and y for each type j investor. Therefore, the same conclusion holds for every coalition s because its aggregate willingness to pay is the scalar product of s with the vector whose components are the individual willingness to pay.

Figure 8 shows the locus of x and y holding constant the aggregate willingness to pay of the corporation s. The optimal combination of x and y is at that point on the locus AA' where the slope is one. As the figure shows, there is a sense in which outlays on credibility and investment are substitutes. However, the smaller the investment outlay, the less substitutable are the two kinds of expenditures. The two are complements along the line GG'. Figure 8 assumes it is increasingly difficult to raise the expected willingness to pay by raising the outlays on credibility as the total investment becomes larger. Figure 8 also shows that the optimal credibility outlay becomes unboundedly large as the investment outlay approaches X_0. This is the feature that prevents a corpo-

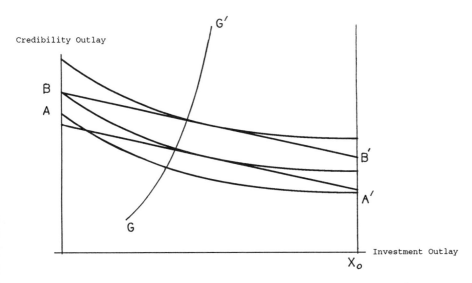

Fig. 8. Relation between outlays on credibility and outlays on tangible capital

ration from becoming unboundedly large by raising its credibility outlays without more investment in real bricks and mortar.

Finally, the reasoning about the budget constraint readily generalizes to encompass the two kinds of outlays. Now in place of equation (3.17) there is

$$\sum_j c_j t_j = \sum_i (x_i + y_i),$$

where, as before, c_j denotes the amount invested by each type j in the corporation.

It is undeniable that corporations have outlays on credibility. Therefore, such outlays are a proper subject of investigation. The complications they raise are instructive in themselves. There is also the interesting question of how the outlays on credibility vary with the size of the company. A sufficient condition for the stability of the corporation is markedly decreasing incremental returns with respect to its size. Is this consistent with the known facts?

Some implications of the model seem to have empirical support. First, investors are more likely to finance nearby corporations. Probably this is because it is less costly for investors to acquire information about closer than more distant corporations. Second, friends and relatives are likely to be among the first to finance a new company because its prospects are more credible to them than to strangers. Also, perhaps they are more trusting of its officers. Third, the more capital a corporation wishes to raise, the more it spends on promoting the new issue of capital.

6. Studies of Share Ownership

1. Introduction

An investor is the main actor in this theory that assumes there are many types of investors and many individual investors of the same type. Identical investors possess the same information and have the same willingness to pay functions. Consequently, all investors of the same type make the same decision about the projects available to them. Although we cannot see an individual's willingness to pay function, it would be possible in principle to observe his assets and liabilities. By looking at balance sheets for individuals, one could draw inferences about how similar they are. One might infer that those who make the same decisions are alike although this is not strictly true. Sorting individuals according to size and nature of their holdings would gather all those who do belong to the same investor class as well as some who do not. Even so, the main point is simple. People who do the same things are also more likely to be similar in other ways than those who do different things.

Although the idea is simple, exploiting it is not simple. This is because so little is known about the composition of individual assets and liabilities. The theory makes assertions about the holdings of common and preferred stock in corporations by investor types and about their holdings of mutual funds. However, there is a paucity of data about individual portfolios and a dearth about the shareholders of corporations. What follows is a survey of the available material and a discussion of its pertinence for the theory.

2. The Evidence Available

The most straightforward way to find out about shareholders is to ask them directly, but this is difficult, costly, and seldom done. The reasons can be seen in studies of wealth based on decedent estate tax returns. It appears from these studies, Lampman 1962 being among the best, that a very large fraction of all common stocks belongs to the wealthiest adults, an elusive group to study. For selected years between 1922 and 1953 Lampman reports that the richest 1 percent of adults accounts for more than 60 percent of the holdings of common stock. In 1953, the figure reached 76 percent. The top 1 percent of adults held more than 22 percent of total wealth in 1953; the peak was in 1929 when this group owned 37.7 percent of the total, and the trough was in 1949 when it was 22.2 percent of the total. Lampman describes other studies, and these all agree that holdings of common stock bulk very large among the total assets of the wealthiest individuals. Using similar data Smith and Franklin (1974) bring the figures up to 1969. In that year the richest 1 percent owned over 50 percent of common stock and about 25 percent of total net worth. Their figure for 1953 is over 86 percent, even higher than Lampman's. The particular number we accept for share holdings is unimportant since all agree that this number is very high.

Another way to find out about common stock holdings is to ask the wealthiest individuals. Projector and Weiss (1966) did this, and I shall use some of their results in the following. Crockett and Friend (1963) and Blume, Crockett, and Friend (1974) try another approach. It seeks to learn about individuals' share holdings from their income tax returns. Earlier, Atkinson (1956) did this in his study of Wisconsin income tax returns. However, this approach faces a major obstacle because it must rely on reported dividends. Some corporations pay no dividends on their common stock. This group includes both highly successful and very unsuccessful corporations. Nor is this all. Individual tax returns do not necessarily show the dividends received from corporations if the shares are held in a brokerage account or in some other way such as a trust. This avenue of research has furnished little useful material as a reader of these results soon discovers.

Atkinson (1956, 114–28) has two findings that are somewhat relevant for the theory. First, his study classifies traded stocks by industry. Suppose there is more disagreement among investors about the prospects of firms, the riskier is the industry. It would follow that corporations in riskier industries have a more heterogeneous group of owners than those in safer industries. Atkinson finds that the riskier the industry, the bigger is the percentage held by the higher income individuals. Therefore the sizes of the holdings of the owners of a corporation differ more, the riskier the industry. The second finding uses a more direct measure of risk. Atkinson classifies stocks according to a quality rating of the Fitch Publishing Company. A weighted index of stock quality is a decreasing function of individual income. This seems to imply that higher income people own riskier stocks. However, an equally weighted index of riskiness shows a convex relation between riskiness and income so that it is the middle income individuals who own the riskiest stocks. The unanswered question is the degree to which riskiness of the corporation attracts owners in the same income class. Also, neither of these relations takes account of the age of the individual nor the relation between the riskiness of the holding and the total wealth of the individual. Although the Atkinson evidence is consistent with the Projector–Weiss findings, it does not supply independent confirmation of their results owing to the lack of data on total wealth in his study. Such data are in the Projector–Weiss study.

Yet another route is via the records of brokerage firms (Cohn et al. 1975; Lease, Lewellen, and Schlarbaum 1974; Lewellen, Lease, and Schlarbaum 1977; and Schlarbaum, Lewellen, and Lease 1976 and 1978). Lacking guidance from any theory these studies provide little useful information about the behavior of investors. These articles ask and answer only the most rudimentary questions. Even these are hard to interpret due to the diverse ways stocks are held. To name a few, some stocks are held by individuals and are not in brokerage accounts, some are held by banks, and some individuals have more than one brokerage account.

The study by Projector and Weiss (1966) illuminates many of the factors underlying the willingness of investors to hold risky assets. The chief conclusion I derive from their study is that two factors are especially important—age and total wealth of the investor. Holdings of risky assets tend to decline with age and to rise with total wealth. Because wealth also tends to rise with age the interaction between these two factors explains the change in the composition of people's assets as they grow older. Middle aged people tend to hold the riskiest assets. Young people tend to hold riskier assets, the richer they are. As individuals grow older, they tend to shift their holdings to safer forms.

The Projector–Weiss study, sponsored by the Board of Governors of the Federal Reserve System, is a survey of households designed to elicit information about the components of household wealth. Starting with an initial sample of 3,551 individuals from households, they could obtain usable data only from 2,557 so that there were 994 nonrespondents. In order to have a big enough sample in the upper income and wealth groups, relatively large initial samples were drawn from these strata. Even so, the fraction of nonresponse as a function of

TABLE 1. Nonresponse Discrepancies in Projector–Weiss Study of Household Wealth

Income ($)	Actual Sample Size (1962 Income)[a]	pdf of Actual Sample (Percent)	pdf of Planned Sample (Percent)	Ratio of Col. 2 to Col. 3	Planned Number in Sample (1960 Income)[b]	Number Responding (1962 Income)[b]	Number Not Responding (1962 Income)[b]	Number Refusing Financial Data[b]	Financial Nonresponse Rate of Total Sample (Percent)	Refusal Rate (Percent)
Negative	8	0.31								
Under 3,000	403	15.76	9.21	1.4190	327	284	43	24	7.34	55.81
3,000–4,999	346	13.53	10.59	1.0328	376	335	41	24	6.38	58.54
5,000–7,499	405	15.84	11.29	1.1877	401	341	60	54	13.47	90.00
7,500–9,999	340	13.30	11.38	1.0149	404	335	69	58	14.36	84.06
10,000–14,999	349	13.65	11.86	1.0480	421	333	88	79	18.76	89.77
15,000–24,999	242	9.46	11.52	0.8121	409	298	111	92	22.49	82.88
25,000–49,999	196	7.67	12.98	0.6490	461	302	159	137	29.72	86.16
50,000–99,999	173	6.77	10.70	0.9058	380	191	189	162	42.63	85.71
Over 100,000	95	3.72	10.48	0.6884	372	138	234	190	51.08	81.20
Total	2,557	100.01	100.01	1.0000	3,551	2,557	994	820	23.09	82.49

Source: Projector and Weiss (1962).
[a]Projector–Weiss table A 35.
[b]Projector–Weiss table 15.

income rises with income as table 1 shows. It is also noteworthy that the sample overrepresents the lowest and third lowest income strata relative to the number that were planned to be drawn from these. For all these reasons I believe that the results are downward biased estimates of share holdings in the upper reaches of the wealth distribution.

The main value of the Projector–Weiss study is their estimates of the elasticities of the major components of household assets with respect to total financial wealth. Estimates of two different aspects of elasticities are presented; the elasticity of the *proportion* of households who own the given asset and the elasticity of the *amount* of the asset for those who do own it. The total elasticity is the product of these two components. The estimates are probably more reliable, the more accurate the estimates of the asset price. Hence I have more confidence in the estimated elasticities for most of the financial assets and less in components of consumer wealth such as housing, automobiles, and stocks in closely held companies that are seldom traded.

There are two main categories of financial assets in the study called liquid and investment assets. Liquid assets include checking accounts, savings in banks and in savings and loan associations, and U.S. savings bonds. Investment assets cover publicly traded stocks, mutual funds, mortgage assets, investment real estate, business assets not managed by the consumer unit, and company saving plans. Tables 25 and 26 in Projector and Weiss (p. 83) give estimated elasticities for these assets by age group for the best-fitting regressions. These have the following form:

$$p = a_{31} + k(1 - e^{-cw}) \quad \text{and} \quad y(H) = a_{32}w(H)^{b_{32}},$$

in which p is the proportion of the households with the given type of asset, $y(H)$ is the value of their holding of this asset, and w is their wealth (Projector and Weiss 1966, tables 22 and 23, p. 82). The elasticity of both liquid and financial assets rises with age. However, the investment asset elasticity rises more rapidly with age than does the liquid asset elasticity. The two types of elasticities differ in another way. The elasticity of the proportion of households holding liquid assets is quite low, between 0.03 and 0.08, so that most of the total elasticity is accounted for by the total amount held by households, an elasticity that is about 0.7 and that is nearly independent of age. In contrast, the elasticity of the proportion of households with investment assets is between 0.53 and 0.67, and the elasticity of the amount of these assets with respect to wealth is an increasing function of age, going from 0.9 in the youngest stratum, head under 35, to 1.2 in the oldest stratum, head over 65. The elasticities of both liquid and investment assets seem to decrease with wealth, the former going from 0.7 to a little below. The pattern for the investment elasticity is more complicated owing to an interaction with age. The investment elasticity is lower, the bigger the wealth. However, at first it rises with age and then drops for the over 65 group

(Projector and Weiss 1966, table 26, p. 84). The elasticity of investment assets is about twice as high as the elasticity of liquid assets. In some cells the investment asset elasticity is more than 1.8, and it is never less than 0.9. This description does not fully convey the regular fashion in which the elasticity of investment assets is a strongly concave function of age and wealth with a peak in the middle age and middle wealth stratum. Most of the variability of the total elasticity with respect to wealth seems to be explained by the sensitivity of the proportion of households owning the asset to wealth. Projector and Weiss's tables 31 and 32 (pp. 87–88) show the elasticities of the components of investment assets with respect to wealth as a function of age and wealth. Publicly traded stocks and investment real estate (as distinct from household-owned real estate) have the biggest total elasticities. Checking accounts have the lowest elasticities. The elasticities of checking accounts with respect to wealth are sometimes even negative in the wealthiest strata.[1] Marketable securities other than stock, that include mutual funds, have lower total elasticities than publicly traded stocks. Savings accounts and U.S. savings bonds have similar total wealth elasticities that are decreasing with wealth leveling off at somewhat higher levels than the elasticities of checking accounts.

One interpretation of these findings assumes that we can rank investment assets according to risk. Checking accounts are the least risky among these assets because they are payable on demand and are insured by an agency of the federal government. The principal of U.S. savings bonds and savings accounts is similar to checking accounts with respect to default risk, but the nominal return can vary over time. Hence they are more risky than checking accounts. Marketable securities other than stock, presumably including most mutual funds, are more risky than the preceding items. This tier also includes company savings plans. However, Projector and Weiss (p. 47) believe that estimates by households of their investments in these plans are especially prone to error. The most risky assets are publicly traded stocks, investment real estate, and mortgage assets. The category business investments not managed by the household unit includes equity in farms, partnerships, and closely held corporations in which no household member was active as a manager (p. 46). This component is also subject to especially large measurement error because it is difficult to obtain the prices of these assets.

The general pattern is this. The riskier the asset, the bigger is the wealth elasticity. Taking this at face value, it seems that risk aversion rises with age. Older and wealthier households are subject to conflicting effects—those with more wealth have a bigger proportion of their total wealth in the form of riskier assets, but those who are older have a smaller proportion of their total wealth

---

1. No data on currency holdings are available in this study.

in a riskier form. However, there is a different interpretation that reverses the role of wealth and asset type. Instead of saying that wealth determines asset type, it is at least as plausible to say that asset type is a determinant of wealth. Those who hold risky assets in ventures that were highly successful, like a winning lottery ticket, become wealthy. The group of wealthy households includes many winners among the owners of publicly traded stocks. These data are also consistent with the view that risk aversion or the willingness to bear risk is independent of age and wealth. The positive relation between the riskiness of asset holdings and wealth is due to the luck of the winners, who become wealthy as a result of their good fortune but who may be no more willing to bear risk than the luckless and less wealthy households.

The final study in this survey looks at share holdings in corporations. Demsetz and Lehn (1985) analyze data on the distribution of share holdings for the 511 largest corporations in 1980. These data are subject to the same criticisms as apply to an earlier TNEC-SEC study (Goldsmith and Parmelee 1940; Granby 1941) owing to the difficulty of stripping away the veil shielding individual share holdings from public view. "Holdings by diversified financial holding companies, investment banks, brokerage firms and investment company managers are listed in the 'street names' of the firms when the firms are not holding the shares in a management capacity" (p. 1163).

Three of their findings are pertinent for the theory. First, Demsetz and Lehn give the distribution of the holdings of the 5 largest shareholders in their sample (table 1, p. 1157). The figures show that this group holds a big fraction of the total shares in the firm. The mean share of the top 5 holders is 24.81 percent and the standard deviation is 15.77 percent. The minimum is 1.27 percent and the maximum is 87.14 percent. Given the big number of shareholders in these corporations, the large fraction of the total held by the top 5 shareholders is a remarkable fact ruling out descriptions of the data using a normal or log normal distribution. Since the values of the holdings are widely different, this finding is consistent with the theory that asserts the owners of corporations are a heterogeneous group of investors. Second, their study shows a significant inverse relation between the concentration of share ownership and riskiness of the enterprise as measured in various ways including the standard deviation of rates of profit. This result is the same as Atkinson's discussed previously. Third, they find that the bigger the firm, the less concentrated is the ownership.[2] Their first finding of high owner concentration is consistent with a Pareto distribution with the exponent α close to 1 giving a good fit to the individual holdings. Let us see why.

---

2. Collet and Yarrow also relate their estimates of α to company size. They find that α is bigger, the bigger the company (1976, 262). Their study estimates α for a Pareto distribution of the number of shares held but not for the value of the share holdings.

Let a simple random sample of size n be ordered from the smallest to the largest so that

$$x_{(i)} \leq x_{(i+1)} \qquad i = 1, \ldots, n - 1.$$

The ordered observations correspond to the quantiles of the distribution (Feller 1966, vol. 2, chap. 9, sec. 8). For a Pareto distribution

$$F(x) = 1 - \left(\frac{x}{x_0} \right)^{-\alpha} \qquad \alpha > 0, \qquad x \geq x_0 \tag{1}$$

the ith quantile from the bottom is given by

$$\frac{i}{n+1} = 1 - \left(\frac{x_{(i)}}{x_0} \right)^{-\alpha} \Leftrightarrow \left(\frac{x_{(i)}}{x_0} \right)^{-\alpha} = 1 - \frac{i}{n+1}. \tag{2}$$

It follows that

$$\left(\frac{x_{(i)}}{x_0} \right) = \left(\frac{n+1}{n+1-i} \right)^{1/\alpha}. \tag{3}$$

Let $T(5, n, \alpha)$ denote the sum of the holdings of the top 5 shareholders and let $T(n, \alpha)$ denote the total number of shares held by all n shareholders. Hence

$$T(5, n, \alpha)x_0^{-\alpha} = \sum_1^5 x_{(i)} \quad \text{and} \quad T(5, n) x_0^{-\alpha} = \sum_1^n x_{(i)}. \tag{4}$$

The share of the total held by the top 5 shareholders is the following ratio:

$$Sh(5, n) = \frac{T(5, n, \alpha)}{T(n, \alpha)}. \tag{5}$$

It is easily verified using equation (3) that this share can be written as follows:

$$Sh(5, n) = \frac{\displaystyle\sum_1^5 \frac{1}{i^\beta}}{\displaystyle\sum_1^n \frac{1}{i^\beta}} \qquad \beta = \frac{1}{\alpha}. \tag{6}$$

We can use expression (6) to see how close the Demsetz–Lehn data are to a Pareto distribution. The denominator of equation (6) is a well-known series that is convergent if and only if $\beta \geq 1$ and is divergent if $\beta \leq 1$. Therefore, for n large enough, the share of the top 5 owners approaches zero if $\beta \leq 1$ and has a positive limit if and only if the denominator is convergent so that $\beta > 1$. But $\beta = 1/\alpha > 1$ if and only if $\alpha < 1$. This yields the desired result. The fraction of total holdings of the top 5 shareholders can be as large as observed if α is below one. The small value of α means that the owners are a heterogeneous group with respect to the size of their holdings.

3. Conclusions

The theory says there are three kinds of stable organizations.

   a. corporations with specialized activities and heterogeneous types of in-
      vestors;
   b. mutual funds with diverse investments and a single type of investor;
   c. a combination of these two extremes where a corporation pursues dif-
      ferent activities and has a heterogeneous group of owners.

Case c imposes the most demanding conditions on the affinity among investor
types and the projects they are willing to finance. Condition a requires a measure of specialization. Lacking measures of this, if we suppose all corporations
are equally specialized then different types of investors may be identified by
differences among the sizes of their holdings. Hence corporations in category
a should have owners with more disparity in the sizes of their holdings than do
the organizations in the other two categories. Because the disparity in holdings
is bigger, the smaller is α, the estimates of α implied by the Demsetz–Lehn
study imply there is indeed much disparity among shareholders of these corporations.

APPENDIX: CONTINUOUS NONATOMIC GAMES

This appendix has material on continuous nonatomic games for the analysis in
the text.

1. Bond-Core and First-Core

In a continuous game a real number like a social security number stands for a
particular individual. Take a closed interval such as from 0 to 1. A point in this
interval is an individual. Since a point is infinitesimally small relative to the
interval, the same is true for each individual, and so the individuals are said to
be nonatomic. A set of points is a coalition of individuals. The size of a coalition measures how many points are in the set. Assume there are many individuals of the same type and that there is a finite number of different types, m,
a positive integer. The total number of type i individuals, $i = 1, \ldots, m$, in the
game is given by a positive real number, t_i. These numbers are the coordinates
of the m-vector $t = \{t_1, t_2, \ldots, t_m\}$ and show how many of each of the m types
are in the game. A subcoalition leaves out somebody. Let s_i denote how many
type i individuals are in the coalition s so that $0 \le s_i \le t_i$. Because s does not
include everybody, there must be strict inequality for at least one coordinate
of s so write $s \le t$. The coalition with nobody in it, $s = 0$, completes the pos-

sibilities. Let e^i denote the m-vector whose ith coordinate equals one and whose remaining $m - 1$ coordinates equal zero. A pure coalition has only one type. A pure type i coalition of size s_i is represented by multiplying the vector e^i by the scalar s_i. The coalition s is a linear combination of pure coalitions, $s = \Sigma_i s_i e^i$. Because individuals of the same type are identical, they are indistinguishable so that only the number of each type in a coalition affects the return to the coalition.

THEOREM 1.   *Let T denote the domain of admissible coalitions, a closed subset of* Ω_n, *the nonnegative orthant of* R_n. *Assume that*

   i. $0 \in T$;
   ii. $t \in T \Rightarrow s \in T$ *if* $s \leqq t$;
   iii. $r, s \in T \Rightarrow r + s \in T$.

Then T is a closed convex cone.

PROOF.   Assumptions i and iii imply that mr and ns are in T for all integers $m, n = 0, 1, \ldots,$. Therefore assumption iii also implies that $mr + ns$ is in T. Here T is a convex cone if

$$r, s \in T \Rightarrow (\alpha r + \beta s) \in T \quad \forall \alpha, \beta \geq 0.$$

Now $m \leq \alpha \leq m + 1$ and likewise for β. The desired conclusion follows from assumption iii.   QED

Since T is a convex cone, there is no upper bound on the size of an admissible coalition. Also, since any linear combination of pure coalitions is admissible, the set of admissible coalitions is the whole nonnegative orthant of R_n.

An alternative to the third assumption is given by

   iii.' $r, s \in T$ and $r + s \leqq t \Rightarrow r + s \in t$.

THEOREM 1'.   *Assumptions i, ii, and iii' imply T is a closed convex set.*

PROOF.   We must show that $r, s, r + s \in T \Rightarrow \theta r + (1 - \theta)s \in T \; \forall \; \theta : 0 \leq \theta \leq 1$. This is true if $\theta r + (1 - \theta)s \leq t$. Since $\theta r \leq r \leq t$ and $(1 - \theta)s \leq s \leq t$, it follows from iii' that

$$\theta r + (1 - \theta)s \leq r + s \leq t$$

so the desired conclusion is true. Finally, T is closed by hypothesis.   QED

In case T satisfies assumptions i, ii, and iii', let $T(t)$ denote the set of admissible coalitions.

Let $f(s)$ denote the function describing the return to the coalition s. Thus f

maps T into the reals. However, as we shall see, there are compelling reasons for assuming that $f(s)$ is nonnegative for all admissible coalitions. The various kinds of superadditivity are described by the following:

DEFINITION

1. The function f is said to be *superadditive* on T if for *all* r, s, and $r + s$ in T,
   a. $f(r + s) \geq f(r) + f(s)$.
2. f is *weakly superadditive* on T if for all s in T
   b. $f(t) \geq f(s) + f(t - s)$.
3. f is *individually superadditive* on T if for all s in T,
   c. $f(\Sigma s_i e^i) \geq \Sigma f(s_i e^i)$.
4. f is *weakly individually superadditive* on T if

   d. $\displaystyle\sum_{i=1}^{m} f(t_i e^i) \leq f\left(\sum_{i=1}^{m} t_i e^i\right)$.

Note the distinction between a superadditive and a weakly superadditive function. A function is superadditive on $T(t)$ when condition a holds for any triplet r, s, and $r + s$ in T while weak superadditivity applies only to s and its complement, $t - s$. Every superadditive function is weakly superadditive but not conversely. The relevance of the distinction between individual and weakly individual superadditivity will emerge when we consider the First-core and the Bond-core for continuous games (see also chap. 6, sec. 2).

The variants of superadditivity apply to the union of pure coalitions. In addition the size of a pure coalition can change, and one must be able to study the consequences.

DEFINITION.   The function f is superhomogenous if

$$f(\lambda t) \geq \lambda f(t)$$

for all $\lambda \geq 1$ and for all λt in the domain of f.

Assume that all players of the same type get the same return. This entails no loss of generality. Let x_i denote the return to a type i player. The coordinates of the m-vector $x = \{x_1, x_2, \dots, x_m\}$ show the returns to each of the m types. The characteristic function f describes the maximum payoff that any admissible coalition can assure itself under the most adverse conditions. Therefore a coalition s would not accept a return $\Sigma_{i=1}^{m} s_i x_i$ that is below $f(s)$. Write the sum more concisely as the scalar product $x \circ s$ so that $x \circ s = \Sigma_{i=1}^{m} s_i x_i$. Hence an acceptable return to s equals the min $\{x \circ s, f(s)\}$. The most that the coalition of everybody, the coalition t, has available for distribution is $f(t)$. Hence x is a feasible vector of returns only if $x \circ t \leq f(t)$.

DEFINITION. The Bondereva-core, call it the Bond-core, is the set of all m-vectors, x, such that

$$x \circ s \geq f(s) \quad \text{for all } s: 0 \leq s \leq t \quad \text{and} \quad x \circ t \leq f(t). \tag{1}$$

Just as for a game with a finite number of players we would like to have a definition of an imputation for a continuous game. However, this raises a technical difficulty for an infinitesimally small pure coalition that would correspond to a singleton in a finite game. It is better at this stage to avoid imposing special properties on the characteristic function such as continuity or differentiability in an attempt to contrive a correspondence between a singleton in a discrete game and a very small pure coalition in a continuous game. Therefore define an imputation for continuous games as follows:

DEFINITION. An imputation is a nonnegative vector x such that $x \circ t = f(t)$.

This definition makes sense only if $f(.) \geq 0$ for all $s \geq 0$ and $s \leq t$, so let us agree to assume this.

DEFINITION. The imputation x is dominated by the imputation y via the coalition s, written $y \succsim_s x$ if $y_i > x_i$ for the positive coordinates of s and y is feasible for s so that $y \circ s \leq f(s)$.

DEFINITION. The First-core is the set of undominated imputations.

Undominated imputations capture the essence of the core for economic applications. It appears in the first economic use of what became core theory in the study of pure exchange by Edgeworth (1881). It is therefore imperative to study the relation between the Bond-core and the First-core.

LEMMA 1. *The Bond-core is included in the First-core.*

PROOF. By contradiction. Assume x is in the Bond-core and suppose it is not in the First-core. Then there would be an imputation y and a coalition s such that $y \succsim_s x$. But then $f(s) \geq y \circ s > x \circ s$ giving a contradiction. QED

LEMMA 2. *Let f be nonnegative, weakly superadditive, and individually superadditive. It follows that the First-core is included in the Bond-core.*

PROOF. By contradiction. Assume x is in the First-core and suppose it is not in the Bond-core. Then there would be an $s \geq 0$ such that $x \circ s < f(s)$. It would follow that there would be an imputation y such that $y \succsim_s x$ where y satisfies

$$y_i = x_i + \frac{f(s) - x \circ s}{ns_i} \quad \text{for } s_i > 0$$

and

$$y_i = \frac{f[(t_i - s_i)e^i] + f(t) - f(s) - \sum_i f[(t_i - s_i)e^i]}{(t_i - s_i)} \quad \text{for } t_i - s_i > 0$$

provided y can meet the following three conditions:

a. $y_i > x_i$ and $s \circ y \le f(s)$ for $s_i > 0$;
b. $y_i \ge 0$ for $t_i - s_i > 0$;
c. $t \circ y = f(t)$.

Since $f(s) > x \circ s$, summing y_i over $s_i > 0$, it would follow that condition a is true.

b. By weak superadditivity, $f(t) - f(s) \ge f(t - s)$. By individual superadditivity, $f(t - s) \ge \Sigma f[(t_i - s_i)e^i]$. Therefore, $f(t) - f(s) - \Sigma f[(t_i - s_i)e^i] \ge 0$. Since f is nonnegative by hypothesis, condition b is true.

c. $t \circ y = s \circ y + (t - s) \circ y = f(s) + f(t) - f(s) = f(t)$ so condition c is true. Hence y is an imputation that dominates x via s contradicting the hypothesis that x is in the First-core so that x must be undominated.   QED

With the aid of these two lemmas the following result holds.

THEOREM 2.   *Let f be nonnegative, weakly superadditive, and individually superadditive. The First-core and the Bond-core are equivalent.*

Under the hypotheses of this theorem the distinction between the First-core and the Bond-core vanishes.

2. Varieties of Kindness

Four distinct situations arise depending on the relation between f and the status of the core on the domain of f. These require careful descriptions of the admissible coalitions for which it is sought to determine the status of the core.

DEFINITION.

1. If $f(.)$ admits a nonempty core for *some* $t \ge 0$ then f is called *weakly kind*.
2. If $f(.)$ admits a nonempty core for all t such that $0 \le t \le t_0$ then f is called *partly kind*.
3. If f admits a nonempty core for all $t \ge 0$ then f is called *totally kind*.
4. If f has an empty core for all $t \ge 0$ then f is called *unkind*.

There are several reasons for these distinctions owing to the nature of the economic applications. In the theory of corporations we seek the largest corporation in terms of the number of shareholders that would constitute a stable coalition in the sense of a nonempty core. Therefore, we seek the biggest t_0 for which f is partly kind. Second, there are important differences among the characteristic functions depending on the nature of their kindness. Every totally kind function is partly kind, and every partly kind function is weakly kind. Hence every property that is owned by a weakly kind function is inherited by a partly kind function and in turn is inherited by a totally kind function. Therefore, a necessary condition for weak kindness is also necessary for partial and for total kindness. The differences run deeper than this, especially for convex functions. Superadditivity is both necessary and sufficient for total kindness of a strictly convex function (Telser 1987, chap. 4, part 1, prop. 4). However, superadditivity is not necessary for partial kindness of a strictly convex function. Example 3 that follows shows this. Thus there are fundamental differences between total and partial kindness in the class of strictly convex functions. Because a weakly kind function is subject to the fewest restrictions, it is also the most difficult to handle. I mainly studied totally kind functions in Telser 1978. In Telser 1987 I did study all three types, but I did not distinguish between weak and partial kindness. Proposition 1 (1987, chap. 4, part 1) asserts that superadditivity is necessary for kindness. This is incorrect. Only *weak* superadditivity is necessary for *weak* kindness; however, superadditivity is necessary for *total* kindness. Some of the chief distinctions between weakly and partly kind functions are given in the next theorem and corollary.

THEOREM 3.   *Let f be weakly kind and let x(t) be in the core. Then*

A. *1. $f(\theta t) \leq \theta f(t)$ $\forall \theta : 0 \leq \theta \leq 1$;*
   2. f must be weakly superadditive.
B. *Let f be differentiable and let $f^*(s)$ denote its gradient at s so that the ith coordinate of $f^*(s)$ is the partial derivative of f with respect to s_i. Then*
   1. $x(t) \leqq f^*(t)$.
   2. $f^*(t) \circ s \geq f(s)$ for all s in $T(t)$.

PROOF.   To prove A.1, observe that by hypothesis, $x(t) \circ t = f(t)$. Since $\theta t \leq t \Rightarrow \theta t \in T(t)$,

$$\theta f(t) = \theta x(t) \circ t = x(t) \circ (\theta t) \geq f(\theta t).$$

A.2. By hypothesis, $x(t) \circ s \geq f(s)$ and $x(t) \circ (t - s) \geq f(t - s)$ so that $f(t) = x(t) \circ (s + t - s) \geq f(s) + f(t - s)$.

B. Define the function $h(s) = x(t) \circ s - f(s)$ that is nonnegative since the hypothesis asserts $x(t)$ belongs to the core. But $h(t) = 0$ so $s = t$ gives the minimum of $h(s)$ on $T(t)$. Because f is differentiable, so is h. Therefore, for arbitrary $\varepsilon > 0$

$$\left| h(s) - h(t) - h^*(t) \circ (s - t) \right| \leq \varepsilon \|s - t\| \text{if } \|s - t\| < \delta.$$

where δ may depend on both t and ε. Hence

$$0 \leq h(s) - h(t) \leq h^*(t) \circ (s - t) + \varepsilon \|s - t\|$$

for all $s \leq t$ because t gives the minimum of $h(.)$. Since $s - t \leq 0$, write

$$h^*(t) \circ (t - s) \leq \varepsilon \| t - s \|,$$

and the upper bound of $h^*(t)$ must be zero. Therefore, $h^*(t) = x(t) - f^*(t) \leq 0$. It follows that

$$f^*(t) \circ s \geq x(t) \circ s \geq f(s). \qquad \text{QED}$$

COROLLARY 1.   *Let f be partly kind on $T(t_0)$. Then f is superadditive and superhomogeneous on $T(t_0)$.*

PROOF.   Since f has a core for any t in $T(t_0)$, it is weakly kind on $T(t_0)$. The conclusions will follow from A of the theorem. To prove superhomogeneity, take $s = \theta t$ so that $t = \lambda s$ and $\lambda = 1/\theta \geq 1$. Hence A.1 implies that $\lambda f(s) \leq f(\lambda s)$ $\forall \lambda \geq 1$. To prove superadditivity take $r + s = t$ for t in $T(t_0)$ and the desired conclusion follows from A.2. \qquad QED

For $x(t)$ to be in the core, it must not exceed the gradient of f at t. The latter is the incremental contribution of t. Hence $f^*(t) - x(t)$ is the excess of the incremental contribution over the return to t, if any. Define the n-vector a as follows:

$$a = f^*(t) - x(t).$$

The coordinates of a are the excess of the incremental contributions over the returns to the m types of players. The next result follows from the preceding theorem and Corollary 1.

COROLLARY 2.   *Under the hypotheses of Theorem 3, f is weakly kind on $T(t)$ if and only if there is a nonnegative m-vector a such that*

> i. $a \circ s = f^*(t) \circ s - x \circ s \leq f^*(t) \circ s - f(s)$,
> ii. $a \circ t = f^*(t) \circ t - x \circ t \geq f^*(t) \circ t - f(t)$.

COROLLARY 3. $a = 0$ *can be in the core only if for all $s \leq t$, $f^*(t) \circ t - f(t) \leq f^*(t) \circ s - f(s)$.*

PROOF.   Take $a = 0$ in conditions i and ii of Corollary 2. \qquad QED

When $a = 0$ is in the core, the return to each type equals its incremental contribution to the grand coalition. It can be shown that a concave function that satisfies the inequality in this corollary must be weakly kind.

3. Superadditivity Again

Reconsider the concept of superadditivity. The characteristic function of a coalition as defined by von Neumann and Morgenstern (1947, 25.2–25.3) must be superadditive. Their reasons are as follows. Let r and s be any two coalitions with $f(r)$ and $f(s)$ their returns if separate and $f(r + s)$ their returns if joined together. Let v denote the von Neumann–Morgenstern characteristic function. Since the characteristic function shows the optimal choice for the coalition and since remaining separate or merging are both feasible, it satisfies

$$v(r + s) = \max \{f(r) + f(s), f(r + s)\}. \tag{1}$$

Therefore, the von Neumann–Morgenstern characteristic function $v(.)$ is superadditive.

Alternatively, one may wish to study the status of the core directly for f without imposing prior conditions in order to find under what conditions f does furnish incentives for forming larger groups. The next result sees how much superadditivity a weakly kind f must have.

LEMMA 3.   *Let f be weakly kind on $T(t)$. For any s in $T(t)$ such that the core constraint is an equality, it follows that*

$$f(s) \geq f(p) + f(s - p) \quad \text{for all } p \text{ and } s - p \text{ in } T(t). \tag{2}$$

PROOF.   The hypothesis asserts the existence of $x(t)$ such that $x(t) \circ t = f(t)$ and $x(t) \circ s \geq f(s)$ for all s in $T(t)$, $s \neq t$. If $x(t) \circ s = f(s)$ then $x(t) \circ p \geq f(p)$ and $x(t) \circ (s - p) \geq f(s - p)$ giving the implication that $x(t) \circ [p + s - p] \geq f(p) + f(s - p)$ so that $f(s) \geq f(p) + f(s - p)$.   QED

A weakly kind function must be weakly superadditive. Lemma 3 establishes superadditivity on a certain subset of $T(t)$ given by those coalitions for which the core constraints hold with equality. However, a weakly kind function may have no proper core constraint satisfied with equality. For example, if f is concave and weakly kind then all proper core constraints are strict inequalities. Owing to these considerations, it is desirable to see how much superadditivity is needed for a nonempty core.

Assume there is an s in $T(t)$ and a partition of s into p and q so that f is not superadditive for s. Therefore,

$$f(s) < f(p) + f(q), \qquad s = p + q. \tag{3}$$

Assuming f is weakly kind, there is an $x(t)$ such that $x(t) \circ p \geq f(p)$ and $x(t) \circ q \geq f(q)$. Consequently,

$$x(t) \circ s \geq f(p) + f(q) > f(s). \tag{4}$$

This completes the proof of

LEMMA 4.   *Let f be weakly kind on $T(t)$. For any s in $T(t)$ such that inequality (3) holds, the core constraint for s must hold as a strict inequality.*

This result shows that $f(s)$ is not the minimally acceptable return to s. By splitting s into the parts p and q, the members of s could enforce a larger demand from the grand coalition t. Also, s itself is not a stable coalition. The next definition names the subset of $T(t)$ on which f is subadditive.

DEFINITION.   SubAd$(t) = \{s: s, p$ and $s - p$ are in $T(t)$ and $f(s) < f(p) + f(s - p)\}$.

For a weakly kind f, because $x(t) \circ r = f(t)$, the grand coalition t itself cannot belong to SubAd(t). If f is partly or totally kind then SubAd(t) must be an empty set because the corollary of Theorem 2 asserts that f is superadditive on all of $T(t)$.

DEFINITION.   Let f be weakly kind on $T(t)$. Call the set of points such that a core constraint holds as a strict inequality, Plus(T). Let $x(t)$ be a point in the core of f.

Plus$(T) = \{s : s \quad$ in $T(t) \quad$ and $\quad x(t) \circ s > f(s)\}$.

According to lemma 3, if f is weakly kind then Plus(T) contains SubAd(t). The next result shows what happens if SubAd(T) is all of $T(t)$.

THEOREM 4.   *A subadditive function is unkind so it has no core.*

PROOF.   Let $t_i e^i, i = 1, \ldots, m$ denote the m extreme pure coalitions. Since f is subadditive by hypothesis,

$$f(t) < \sum_{i=1}^{m} f(t_i e^i) \quad \text{and} \quad t = \sum_{i=1}^{m} t_i e^i. \tag{5}$$

Choose some $x(t)$ such that $x(t) \circ t = f(t)$. Plainly $x(t)$ cannot satisfy any core constraint as an equality for which the coalition is a sum of two or more of the m extreme pure coalitions. Since any s can be written as a linear combination of the e^i's so that

$$f(s) = f\left(\sum_{i=1}^{m} s_i e^i\right) < \sum_{i=1}^{m} f(s_i e^i),$$

no core constraint for such an s can hold with equality. Therefore, only the extreme pure coalitions could satisfy the core constraints so that there would be

$$x \circ t_i e^i \geq f(t_i e^i). \tag{6}$$

It would follow that

$$f(t) = x \circ t = x \circ \Sigma t_i e^i \geq \Sigma f(t_i e^i) \quad \text{and} \quad \Sigma f(t_i e^i) < f(t)$$

giving a contradiction.   QED

4. Convex Characteristic Functions

The following results are pertinent for convex characteristic functions, which are important for the theory of joint ventures.

THEOREM 5.   A. *Let f be convex. Let $a = f^*(t) - x(t)$. Then $a = 0$ can be in the core only if f is linear.*

B. *Let f be strictly convex and weakly kind. Only $a > 0$ can be in the core.*

PROOF.   A. If f is convex then $f^*(t) \circ (t - s) \geq f(t) - f(s)$. Rearranging terms,

$$f^*(t) \circ t - f(t) \geq f^*(t) \circ s - f(s). \tag{1}$$

It follows from Corollary 3 that $a = 0$ can be in the core only if $f^*(t) \circ t - f(t) \leq f^*(t) \circ s - f(s)$. Hence

$$f^*(t) \circ t - f(t) = f^*(t) \circ s - f(s) \quad \text{for all } s \leq t \tag{2}$$

so $f(s)$ must be a linear function of s.

B. By contradiction. Suppose the first k coordinates of a were zero and choose r so that its first k coordinates are positive. Hence $r \circ (t - r) = 0$, $a \circ r = 0$, and $a \circ (t - r) = a \circ t = f(t) > 0$. Since f is weakly kind by hypothesis, $a \circ t \geq f^*(t) \circ t - f(t)$ and $a \circ (t - r) \leq f^*(t) \circ (t - r) - f(t - r)$. But then

$$f^*(t) \circ t - f(t) \leq f^*(t) \circ (t - r) - f(t - r) \tag{3}$$

giving a contradiction because f is strictly convex by hypothesis, so that

$$f^*(t) \circ t - f(t) > f^*(t) \circ (t - r) - f(t - r). \qquad \text{QED}$$

According to B, a game with a strictly convex characteristic function cannot have a point in the core such that any player gets a return equal to his incremental contribution to the grand coalition. Every point in the core has the property that the return to each player is strictly less than his incremental contribution to the grand coalition. Convex characteristic functions have some other important properties.

LEMMA 5.   *Let f be convex. It has a nonempty core on $T(t)$ if and only if it is possible to satisfy the core constraints at the vertexes of $T(t)$, which are the extreme pure coalitions.*

PROOF.   Necessity is obvious since it must be possible to satisfy the core constraints at the vertexes. Sufficiency. Assume all the core constraints at the vertexes were satisfied. Take s not a vertex so that it can be written as a convex combination of the m vertexes

$$s = \sum_{i=1}^{m} \theta_i t_i e^i, 0 \leq \theta_i \quad \text{and} \quad \sum_{i=1}^{m} \theta_i = 1.$$

By convexity, $f(s) \leq \sum_{i=1}^{m} \theta_i f(t_i e^i)$. The hypothesis asserts that the core constraints at all the vertexes are satisfied. Therefore,

$$x(t) \circ s = \sum_{i=1}^{m} x(t) \circ \theta_i t_i e^i \geq \sum_{i=1}^{m} \theta_i f(t_i e^i) \geq f(s). \qquad \text{QED}$$

THEOREM 6.   *If f is weakly kind and strictly convex then every core constraint at a nonvertex of T(t) is satisfied with strict inequality.*

PROOF.   By contradiction. Assume s is not a vertex of $T(t)$ and suppose $x(t) \circ s = f(s)$. By strict convexity,

$$f(s) < \sum_{i=1}^{m} \theta_i f(t_i e^i) \leq \sum_{i=1}^{m} \theta_i t_i e^i x(t) = x(t) \circ s, \tag{4}$$

thereby giving a contradiction.   QED

We now study three examples of convex functions that illustrate different aspects relevant to their kindness.

EXAMPLE 1.   Let the return to a coalition s be given by

$$f(s) = g(s) - k(s), \tag{5}$$

where $g(s)$ is convex and homogeneous of degree 1 and $k(s) \equiv \sum_{i \in s} \delta_i k_i$ so that $\delta_i = 1$ if $s_i > 0$ and $\delta_i = 0$ if $s_i = 0$. It follows that $k(s)$ is subadditive so that $k(r + s) \leq k(r) + k(s)$. Let $f(0) = 0$. Therefore, f is convex on $\Omega_m - \{0\}$. This example also has the complication that f is not continuous on all of $T(t)$. Whenever a coalition absorbs a new type, f jumps downward. Thus f is discontinuous as its argument goes from one vertex of $T(t)$ to another. Because g is convex and homogeneous of degree one, it is subadditive, and $g*(s) \circ s = g(s)$. For orthogonal r and s, $r \circ s = 0$ and $k(r + s) = k(r) + k(s)$. Hence for these r and s,

$$f(r + s) \leq g(r) + g(s) - k(r) - k(s) = f(r) + f(s),$$

and f is subadditive. Therefore, $\mathrm{SubAd}(T)$ is not empty.

We now verify that this f has no core. Let

$$x_i = g_i^*(t) - a_i \geq 0 \quad \text{and} \quad a_i \geq 0$$

as required for x to be in the core for f. It is also necessary that

$$\Sigma \, x_i t_i = f(t) = \Sigma \; g_i^*(t) t_i - \Sigma \, a_i t_i = g(t) - k(t)$$

so that

$$\Sigma \, a_i t_i = k(t) . \tag{6}$$

Consider a pure coalition including all of type i. For such a coalition we must have

$$g_i^*(t) t_i - a_i t_i \geq a_i t_i - k_i. \tag{7}$$

Because $g(s)$ is convex and homogeneous of degree one,

$$g^*(t) \circ (t - s) \geq g(t) - g(s) \Leftrightarrow g^*(t) \circ t - g(t) \geq g^*(t) \circ s - g(s),$$

and it follows from the equation $g^*(t) \circ t - g(t) = 0$ that

$$g^*(t) \circ s - g(s) \le 0. \tag{8}$$

Applying this to equation (7) yields (9)

$$a_i t_i - k_i \le 0 \tag{9}$$

so that in conjunction with equation (6) there is an implication of equality in (9). Hence in order to satisfy the core constraints it is necessary that

$$a_i = k_i/t_i. \tag{10}$$

Since f is convex, Theorem 6 is relevant and directs our attention to consider core constraints only at the vertexes of T. Let s be a vertex so that its coordinates are either 0 or t_i. For a weakly kind f, x must satisfy $x \circ s \ge f(s)$ so that

$$\sum_{i \in s} \left[g_i^*(t) - \frac{k_i}{t_i} \right] s_i \ge g(s) - k(s).$$

Consequently,

$$g^*(t) \circ s - g(s) \ge \sum_{i \in s} \left(\frac{s_i}{t_i} - 1 \right) k_i = 0. \tag{11}$$

By virtue of (8), it follows from (11) that

$$g^*(t) \circ s - g(s) = 0 \tag{12}$$

at every vertex s of T. But equation (12) can hold only if g is a linear function. Therefore, the f defined by equation (5) can be weakly kind if and only if g is linear. A nonlinear f must be unkind.

The common interest expressed by the nature of the fixed cost, k_i, is specific to each type and furnishes too small an incentive to have a core. The situation changes dramatically as shown by the following modification.

EXAMPLE 2.   Instead of (5) define the return to a coalition s as follows:

$$f(s) = g(s) - k \tag{13}$$

with k a positive constant the same for all types. Hence

$$f(r + s) = g(r + s) - k \le g(r) - k + g(s) - k = f(r) + f(s) + k,$$

an inequality consistent with superadditivity of f because it depends on the size of k. Also, unlike Example 1, f is now a continuous function on T and has first-order partials.

$$f^*(s) \circ s = g^*(s) \circ s = g(s) - k + k = f(s) + k$$

so that

$$f^*(s) \circ s - f(s) = k > 0$$

as required for weak kindness. Let

$$a_i = \theta_i \frac{k}{t_i} \quad \text{with } \theta_i \geq 0 \quad \text{and} \quad \sum_i \theta_i = 1. \tag{14}$$

The argument leading to equations (6) and (10) is valid here and it is possible to choose θ's to satisfy (6). A core constraint at a vertex s now requires that

$$0 \geq g^*(t) \circ s - g(s) \geq \sum_{i \in s} \left[\theta_i \frac{s_i}{t_i} - 1 \right] k = \sum_{i \in s} (\theta_i - 1)k. \tag{15}$$

However, if all the θ's are positive then provided $s \neq t$, $\sum_{i \in s}(\theta_i - 1) < 0$. There-fore, it is possible to satisfy (15) without imposing condition (12) because in this case the number on the right-hand side of the equality sign in (12) is neg-ative, not zero. The presence of a common fixed cost k that is the same for all coalitions enlarges the common interest by enough among the various types to bring about a nonempty core in the second example. In contrast in the first ex-ample, with a distinct fixed cost for each type, the common interest is too weak to have a core.

EXAMPLE 3.   A chief purpose of this example is to show that superaddi-tivity is not necessary for a nonempty core.[3] The function giving the return to a coalition is defined by

$$f(s) = s^T \circ A \circ s = (1/2)s^T \circ (A + A^T) \circ s \tag{16}$$

where A is an $m \times m$ matrix. Let $B = A + A^T$ so that B is symmetric. There is convexity if B is positive semidefinite.

PROPOSITION.   *The function f defined in equation (16) is weakly kind if and only if it is weakly superadditive.*

PROOF.   Necessity holds by Theorem 3. Sufficiency. Assume f is weakly superadditive. Hence

$$(1/2)s^T \circ B \circ s + (1/2)(t - s)^T \circ B \circ (t - s) \leq (1/2)t^T \circ B \circ t. \tag{17}$$

Inequality (17) is equivalent to

$$(t - s)^T \circ B \circ s \geq 0. \tag{18}$$

---

3. Weak supperadditivity is necessary for a weakly kind characteristic function however. See Theorem 3.

Let $b = (1/2)Bt$. We must show that b satisfies the core constraints. This is plainly true for $s = t$. For $s \leq t$ we must have $s^T \circ b = (1/2)s^T \circ B \circ t \geq f(s)$. This follows from inequality (18).   QED

Next we use this example to show that superadditivity is not necessary for partial kindness. The function $(t - s)^T \circ B \circ s$ is *concave* in s so it attains its minimum at a vertex of $T(t)$. This means that to check whether (18) holds for all s in T it suffices to look at the vertexes. Take the case $m = 3$. There are 8 vertexes as follows:

$$\{0, 0, 0\}, \quad \{t_1, 0, 0\}, \quad \{0, t_2, 0\} \quad \{0, 0, t_3\}, \quad \{t_1, t_2, 0\},$$
$$\{t_1, 0, t_3\}, \quad \{0, t_2, t_3\}, \quad \{t_1, t_2, t_3\}.$$

Because B is symmetric, there is an implication of weak superadditivity if the following inequalities can be satisfied:

$$t_2 b_{12} + t_3 b_{31} \geq 0$$
$$t_1 b_{12} \qquad + t_3 b_{32} \geq 0$$
$$t_1 b_{13} + t_2 b_{23} \qquad \geq 0. \qquad (19)$$

If $b_{12} < 0$, $b_{31} > 0$, and $b_{32} > 0$ then there is a t that can satisfy inequalities (19). It is not difficult to verify that f can be superadditive if and only if all the elements of B are nonnegative. Hence for these b's, f would not be superadditive although it is weakly superadditive. This means a convex weakly superadditive function can have a core although it is not superadditive. Moreover, (19) also implies that f is individually t-superadditive since $\Sigma f(t_i e^i) \leq f(\Sigma t_i e^i)$. More generally, it is not difficult to verify that for this class of functions weak and individual superadditivity are independent properties if $m > 3$.

Because it is possible to satisfy (19) while some off-diagonal elements are negative, this example shows that there can be a core although the hypothesis of the Proposition does not apply. It would apply if all the elements of A were nonnegative. When some elements of A are negative and (19) holds, f is weakly kind. It is partly kind for all t that can satisfy (19). Given negative off-diagonal elements of B while preserving its positive semidefinite character supplies examples of f that are not superadditive but are weakly superadditive and weakly kind. This shows superadditivity is not necessary for weak kindness.

CHAPTER 3

Valuation of Joint Ventures

1. Introduction

The most an individual is willing to invest in a company is a key element in the theory of corporations given in chapter 2. This chapter determines what underlies this valuation under two conditions; first, when there is certainty about the prospects of the company and second, when there is uncertainty. Certainty is taken to be equivalent to perfect and complete knowledge about everything that can affect the profit of a company. Despite the unrealism, it is a useful theoretical construct. Individuals can have no reason to disagree about the value of a company when its future is known for sure. Differences among intelligent and reasonable investors depend on there being uncertainty. The differences are greater, the more the uncertainty. It is easier to understand the effects of uncertainty by seeing what happens when there is none, the next topic.

2. The Neoclassical Theory of Investment for a Company in a Perfectly Competitive Industry under Perfect Certainty

The analysis herein serves three purposes: first, to describe the neoclassical theory of the optimal stock of capital and labor for a profit-maximizing firm in a perfectly competitive industry under perfect certainty; second, to see when that theory says there is a positive association between changes in the real stock of capital and changes in the market value of the firm, and third, to see how the price level affects the market value of the firm.

The stock market crash of October 1987 is the most recent and dramatic event that shows why it is desirable to study the relation between investment in capital goods by firms and the market value of the firms. In that case the sharp drop in share prices did not presage a sharp drop in investment, and no recession followed the crash, unlike the situation in October 1929 that preceded the Great Depression. We want to see what theoretical relation, if any, exists between the market value of a company as measured by the price of its shares and its real output, employment, and stock of capital goods. If only because of the contrast between the events following the two biggest stock market crashes, it is desirable to see what the standard theory has to say about these matters. The third topic concerns the relation between the general price level and the market value of the company. Assuming there is a constant equilibrium real rate of return on capital for the whole economy, we seek necessary and sufficient conditions on the firm's discount function that will supply a measure of the real market value of the firm.

A neoclassical theory that assumes there is complete information about the relevant factors affecting the prospects of the firm can ignore the role of investors in the firm and treat it as a single entity. There is no room for disagreement among potential investors about the value of a firm when there is perfect certainty. In contrast, the theory of corporations in chapter 2 emphasizes differences among the investors' willingness to pay functions owing to the uncertainty surrounding the prospects of the firm and to their differing personal situations such as their wealth, age, family, and state of health. The optimal investment in a corporation is a semiprivate good to the owners. Also, according to that theory, the market value of the company defined by the price per share multiplied by the number of shares outstanding is a lower bound on the true value of the company to its owners. None of this matters in a neoclassical theory that assumes perfect certainty.

Consider a firm that can produce an output $q(t)$ at time t with inputs of homogeneous labor services $l(t)$ and a stock of homogeneous capital goods $k(t)$. This makes a dichotomy of the factors of production so that in one category there is the flow of services the firm can hire instantaneously, here taken to be the services of labor, and in the other category, there are the stocks of capital goods. Capital goods yield a flow of productive services, but, unlike labor, a company can own capital goods. A firm can buy labor services, but it cannot buy or sell the workers who furnish these services. The situation is more complicated than this. First, the firm can finance that training of its workers that creates firm-specific human capital. Second, it is sometimes important to emphasize differences among the abilities of the workers and how well they can work harmoniously and productively together in teams. Third, there are costs of hiring and firing workers that can impede the continuous adjustment of actual labor services to the amount desired by the firm. Fourth, there are categories of capital goods, such as the stock of knowledge resulting from outlays on research, that are unlike the capital goods such as machines that the neoclassical theory has in mind. Knowledge that helps one firm can be useful to another not only because it allows a firm to learn what a rival firm can do but also because it allows a firm to be an imitator. Typically, imitation is cheaper than the cost of original discovery. The hypothesis there is perfect certainty is at odds with the fact that there is knowledge that a firm tries to keep for itself. All these complications are put aside in a theory that assumes the firm knows the production function, knows all the prices of the output, capital goods, and wages from the present to the remote future, and can buy and sell any amount without any effect on these prices and wages. The theory also assumes there are no costs of changing output, the stock of capital goods, or the flow of labor services.

The relation between the firm's output and the two types of inputs is stated by the following production function:

$$q(t) = f[l(t), k(t)]. \tag{1}$$

Let output be a continuous, increasing, differentiable, and concave function of the inputs. Assume that nothing can be produced without using a positive amount of at least one input. Hence $f(0, 0) = 0$. The stock of capital goods is measured in physical units like the number of machines. Let $x(t)$ denote the number of units of capital goods bought by the firm at time t. It corresponds to real gross investment. Let the stock of capital depreciate at a constant rate independent of its rate of use and let δ denote the rate of depreciation. Consequently, an accounting identity relates the rate of change of the stock of capital goods to the purchase of new capital goods and the depreciation rate shown as follows:

$$\frac{dk}{dt} = x(t) - \delta k(t). \tag{2}$$

At time t the wage rate is $w(t)$, the price of a capital good is $s(t)$, and the output price is $p(t)$. All these prices can change over time and do not depend on the firm's purchases or sales. Let $\pi(t)$ denote the firm's profit at time t. It is defined as follows:

$$\pi(t) = p(t)q(t) - w(t)l(t) - s(t)x(t). \tag{3}$$

This formula is somewhat unusual because it subtracts the *whole* cost of the machines bought at time t from the total revenue at time t. It does not attempt to estimate the cost of the services of capital goods. Since it subtracts total outlays whenever they occur from total current receipts, this definition of profits corresponds to a cash flow.[1]

Before proceeding, it is desirable to clarify the relation between the real and the nominal variables. Let $z(t)$ be a measure of the general price level at time t. The real profit, call it $\hat{\pi}(t)$, is given by

$$\hat{\pi}(t) = \pi(t)/z(t).$$

Let α denote the equilibrium real rate of return on capital goods in the economy so it is the real discount rate. The real present value at time 0 of the firm's profit is defined by the following integral:

$$P\hat{V}(0) = \int_0^\infty e^{-\alpha t}\, \hat{\pi}(t)dt.$$

---

1. This assumption and the following model are similar to Sargent 1979, chap. 6.

Let $g(t)$ denote the discount function for an income stream in nominal terms. It is defined by

$$g(t) = \alpha t + \log z(t).$$

The rate of change of this discount function is α, the real rate of return, plus the percentage rate of change of the price level.

$$\int_0^\infty e^{-g(t)} \pi(t)dt = \int_0^\infty e^{-\alpha t} \pi(t)/z(t)dt = \int_0^\infty e^{-\alpha t} \hat\pi(t)dt = P\hat V(0).$$

These equations say that application of the *nominal* discount function $g(t)$ to the *nominal* profit stream $\pi(t)$ gives the present value in *real* terms. The nominal present value must also satisfy the following equilibrium condition:

$$PV(0) = z(0) P\hat V(0)$$

because the real present value is independent of the price level. That is, at the initial time 0, the nominal present value equals the real present value multiplied by the price level. However, the real present value of a company's profit stream is not observable directly. Instead only the nominal present value is observable. Say this nominal present value is equal to the share price multiplied by the number of shares outstanding. The present value in real terms can be deduced from this nominal amount by dividing this nominal amount by a measure of the price level. This analysis furnishes another independent estimate of the present value in real terms given by discounting the nominal profit stream by the nominal discount factor.

The real present value at time τ is as follows:

$$P\hat V(\tau) = \int_\tau^\infty e^{-\alpha(t-\tau)} \hat\pi(t)dt.$$

This expression implies that

$$\partial P\hat V(\tau)/\partial\tau = -\pi(\tau) + \alpha P\hat V(\tau). \tag{4}$$

Therefore, a necessary condition for a finite real present value is that

$$\lim \partial P\hat V(\tau)/\partial\tau = 0 \quad \text{as } \tau \to \infty.$$

Hence there is a finite present value in the limit only if

$$P\hat V(\tau) \to \hat\pi(\tau)/\alpha.$$

The real present value would remain constant over time if and only if

$$P\hat V(\tau) = \hat\pi(\tau)/\alpha.$$

Equation (4) also suggests a useful empirical estimate of the value of α since that equation is equivalent to the following expression:

$$\partial \log PV(\tau)/\partial\tau = \alpha - \pi(\tau)/PV(\tau). \tag{4'}$$

Assume that the market value of a company equals the present value of its profit. Take a random sample of companies and approximate the percentage change of the real present value of their profit stream by the percentage change in their real market value. Regress these on the ratio of profit to market value. Equation (4) says that the constant term is an estimate of α and that the coefficient of the profit rate should be -1.

The next application applies the theory to preferred stock. A preferred stock is a security that pays a fixed nominal amount forever. Let $B(\tau)$ denote the nominal present value of a preferred stock that pays \$1 forever so that $\pi(\tau) = 1$ for all τ. Hence the real present value, $\hat{B}(\tau)$, satisfies

$$B(\tau) = z(\tau)\, \hat{B}(\tau).$$

Use the expression for $P\hat{V}(\tau)$ and replace $P\hat{V}(\tau)$ by $\hat{B}(\tau)$. After some routine calculations we obtain the following expression:

$$\partial B(\tau)/\partial\tau = B(\tau)[\partial \log z(\tau)/\partial\tau + \alpha] - 1 = B(\tau)[\partial g(\tau)/\partial\tau] - 1.$$

It is an implication of this equation that

$$\frac{\partial B(\tau)}{\partial\tau} \begin{bmatrix} > \\ = \\ < \end{bmatrix} 0 \quad \text{according as} \quad B(\tau) \begin{bmatrix} > \\ = \\ < \end{bmatrix} \frac{1}{\dfrac{\partial g(\tau)}{\partial\tau}}.$$

The nominal price of the preferred stock remains constant over time if and only if

$$B(\tau) = \frac{1}{\alpha + \dfrac{\partial \log z(\tau)}{\partial\tau}},$$

a familiar result. When this equation is satisfied, it is also true that

$$\frac{\partial \log \hat{B}(\tau)}{\partial\tau} = -\frac{\partial \log z(\tau)}{\partial\tau}$$

so that the percentage rate of change of the real value of the preferred stocks varies inversely with the percentage rate of change of the price level.

If the price level remains constant over time so that $z(t) = 1$ for all t then the distinction between the real and the nominal value vanishes. It is convenient to assume this for the rest of this section.

Let a firm choose $l(t)$ and $k(t)$ starting from the initial time $t = 0$ to $t = \infty$ in order to maximize $PV(0)$. Because the model assumes there is no cost of changing the stock of capital, the given initial stock of capital puts no constraint on the firm. It can costlessly move from $k(0)$ to another optimal level at

$t = 0$. (See Arrow 1962 and Telser and Graves 1972 for more on this point.) If there is a maximum then $k(t)$ and $l(t)$ must satisfy the following Euler equations:

$$\frac{\partial}{\partial k} e^{-\alpha t} \pi - \frac{d}{dt}\frac{\partial}{\partial k'} [e^{-\alpha t} \pi] = 0, \tag{5}$$

$$\frac{\partial}{\partial l} e^{-\alpha t} \pi - \frac{d}{dt}\frac{\partial}{\partial l'} [e^{-\alpha t} \pi] = 0. \tag{6}$$

It is convenient to use equation (2) to eliminate $x(t)$ from the expression for π and rewrite π so that

$$\pi = pq - wl - s(k' + \delta k). \tag{7}$$

Using this formula for π, the Euler equations (5) and (6) become

$$e^{-\alpha t}(pf_k - \delta s - \alpha s + s') = 0$$

$$e^{-\alpha t}(pf_l - w) = 0.$$

Since the factor $e^{-\alpha t}$ is positive, it can be divided out, and the Euler equations reduce to

$$f_k = (s/p)\,(\alpha + \delta - s'/s) \tag{8}$$

$$f_l = (w/p). \tag{9}$$

The variables on the right-hand side are the givens that determine the optimal values of the variables on the left-hand side. The firm can maximize the present value of its profits only if it chooses the stock of capital and the flow of labor services that satisfy equations (8) and (9) given the real rate of return on capital, which equals the discount rate, the rate of depreciation of the real stock of capital, and the relative prices of labor and capital goods.

We now study how the market value of the firm, MV, depends on the firm's choice of capital and labor in response to the givens, the prices, the discount rate, and the depreciation rate. Assume that the market value of the firm equals the present value of its profits. Hence $MV = PV$. This is plausible by virtue of the assumption of perfect certainty. Also assume that the firm chooses the optimal levels of labor and capital so that these always satisfy the Euler equations (8) and (9). We can compute the market value of the firm from these hypotheses. The expression for $\pi(t)$ has a term involving k'. Replace it by one involving s' using integration by parts. Omitting the details, which are routine, yields

$$PV = \int e^{-\alpha t} \{pf - wl - k[s(\alpha + \delta) - s']\}dt - e^{-\alpha t} s(t)k(t)\Big|_0^\infty .$$

By virtue of the hypothesis that the firm chooses k and l in order to maximize PV so that k and l satisfy the Euler equations (8) and (9), PV becomes

$$PV = \int e^{-\alpha t} p(t)[f - lf_l - kf_k]dt - e^{-\alpha t} s(t)k(t)\Big|_0^\infty. \qquad (10)$$

If f is homogeneous of degree one, the term [.] vanishes. In addition if the present value of the firm's stock of capital in the remote future is zero (a transversality condition) so that

$$\lim e^{-\alpha t} s(t)k(t) = 0 \quad \text{as } t \to \infty$$

then it follows that

$$PV(0) = s(0) \, k(0). \qquad (11)$$

This formula says that the market value of the firm at time $t = 0$ equals the stock of its capital goods multiplied by the price per unit of capital goods at time 0. If the firm maximizes the present value of its profits and chooses the best amounts of its inputs of labor and capital then this maximum present value looking forward in time equals the current value of its stock of capital goods provided there are constant returns to scale. This says that the book value of the firm's stock of capital goods in terms of the current prices of these goods equals the market value of the firm. Equation (11) is a consequence of optimality in conjunction with constant returns. Without constant returns a more complicated expression, equation (18), which follows, applies.

Still assuming that f is homogeneous of degree one, the present value as of time τ is

$$PV(\tau) = s(\tau)k(\tau). \qquad (12)$$

Therefore,

$$\frac{dPV(\tau)}{d\tau} = k(\tau)\frac{ds(\tau)}{d\tau} + s(\tau)\frac{dk(\tau)}{d\tau}. \qquad (13)$$

Both equations (12) and (13) follow from the necessary conditions for profit maximization when the production function is homogeneous of degree one. They are equilibrium, not structural, relations.

In the more general case the production function is still concave but is not homogeneous of degree one. Concavity of f implies that

$$kf_k + lf_l \le f(k, l) - f(0, 0) \Rightarrow f(k, l) - kf_k - lf_l \ge 0,$$

recalling that $f(0, 0) = 0$. Therefore,

$$PV(0) \ge s(0)k(0) \quad \text{and} \quad PV(\tau) \ge s(\tau)k(\tau). \qquad (14)$$

This means that a concave production function that is not homogeneous of degree one implies a maximum present value that exceeds the current book value of its capital goods. The excess does not mean disequilibrium. It expresses the departure from constant returns to scale by a concave production function.

To find the rate at which the market value of the firm changes over time, use the following expression for $PV(\tau)$:

$$PV(\tau) = \int_\tau^\infty e^{-\alpha t} p(t)[f - lf_l - kf_k]dt - e^{-\alpha t} s(t)k(t)\Big|_\tau^\infty . \qquad (15)$$

Equation (15) together with the transversality condition implies that

$$\frac{dPV(\tau)}{d\tau} = -p(\tau)(f - lf_l - kf_k) + \alpha[PV(\tau) - s(\tau)k(\tau)] + \frac{d}{d\tau}s(\tau)k(\tau). \qquad (16)$$

Equation (16) shows the equilibrium relation among time series of the market value of the firm, profits, and the firm's stock of capital goods. Like equation (13) it is an equilibrium, not a structural relation.

A strictly concave production function, one with decreasing returns to scale, can explain why the present value of a firm can exceed the current value of its stock of capital goods as shown by equation (14). Equation (16) shows that strict concavity allows no simple unambiguous relation between the rate of change of the present value of the firm and the optimal stock of its capital goods. The first term on the right-hand side of equation (16) is negative, the second term is positive, and the sign of the third term is indeterminate. The ambiguity remains even assuming equality between the present value and the market value of the firm.

There is an empirical observation that would contradict the model, a market value of the firm that is below the replacement cost of its current stock of capital goods. Such a finding would be inconsistent with inequality (14).

A more useful relation between the market value of the firm and its determinants takes a different approach. It studies how the market value of the firm responds to changes in two of the exogenous variables, the discount rate, α, and the product price, p. Begin with the definition of the function F as follows:

$$F(k, l) = f - kf_k - lf_l \geq 0. \qquad (17)$$

This allows the present value to be expressed by

$$PV(0) = \int_0^\infty e^{-\alpha t} pF dt + s(0)k(0) \qquad (18)$$

$$\partial PV/\partial \alpha = -\alpha \int_0^\infty e^{-\alpha t} pF dt + \int_0^\infty e^{-\alpha t} p[F_k \, dk/d\alpha + F_l dl/d\alpha]dt \qquad (19)$$

$$F_k = -(kf_{kk} + lf_{kl}) \quad \text{and} \quad F_l = -(kf_{lk} + lf_{ll}). \qquad (20)$$

We obtain from the Euler equations the following:

$$\begin{bmatrix} f_{kk} & f_{kl} \\ f_{lk} & f_{ll} \end{bmatrix} \begin{bmatrix} dk/d\alpha \\ dl/d\alpha \end{bmatrix} = \begin{bmatrix} s/p \\ 0 \end{bmatrix}. \tag{21}$$

It follows from equations (20)–(21) that

$$F_k(dk/d\alpha) + F_l(dl/d\alpha) = -ks.$$

Substituting the latter into equation (19) gives

$$\frac{\partial PV}{\partial \alpha} = -\int_0^\infty e^{-\alpha t}(\alpha pF + ks)dt < 0. \tag{22}$$

This says that the real present value varies inversely with the real discount rate. By a similar calculation it can be shown that the real present value varies inversely with the rate of depreciation.

Next consider how a permanent change in the product price affects the present value. To represent such a price change, write βp so that a change of the factor β shifts the whole price path.

$$\frac{\partial PV(0)}{\partial \beta} = \int_0^\infty e^{-\alpha t} pF dt + \int_0^\infty e^{-\alpha t} \beta p \left[F_k \frac{dk}{d\beta} + F_l \frac{dl}{d\beta} \right] dt. \tag{23}$$

The Euler equations imply that

$$\beta \begin{bmatrix} f_{kk} & f_{kl} \\ f_{lk} & f_{ll} \end{bmatrix} \begin{bmatrix} dk/d\beta \\ dl/d\beta \end{bmatrix} = - \begin{bmatrix} f_k \\ f_l \end{bmatrix}. \tag{24}$$

It is an implication of equation (24) that

$$\beta\{k\ l\}[.]\begin{bmatrix} dk/d\beta \\ dl/d\beta \end{bmatrix} = -\{kf_k + lf_l\}. \tag{25}$$

From equations (17), (20), and (25), the expression in (23) reduces to

$$\frac{\partial PV(0)}{\partial \beta} = \int_0^\infty e^{-\alpha t} pf dt > 0. \tag{26}$$

Hence the present value moves in the same direction as a permanent change in the product price. A similar calculation shows that the present value is a decreasing function of a permanent change of the input prices s and w.

More information about the response of the inputs to changes in the exogenous variables can be derived from equations (22) and (24). Solve (21) and obtain

$$dk/d\alpha = (s/p)f_{ll} / \det[.] \quad \text{and} \quad dl/d\alpha = -(s/p) f_{kl}/\det[.]. \tag{27}$$

By concavity, $f_{ll} < 0$ and $\det[.] > 0 \Rightarrow dk/d\alpha < 0$. The higher is the real discount rate, the lower the optimal stock of capital. The relation between the discount rate and the optimal amount of labor services depends on whether labor and capital are complements or substitutes. If they are complements so that f_{kl} is positive then the optimal labor input varies inversely with the real discount rate. If they are substitutes so that f_{kl} is negative then the labor input moves in the same direction as the real discount rate.

Equation (28) shows how a permanent change in the product price affects the optimal inputs of labor and capital.

$$dk/d\beta = -(1/\beta)(f_k f_{ll} - f_l f_{kl})/\det[.]$$

$$dl/d\beta = -(1/\beta)(f_l f_{kk} - f_k f_{kl})/\det[.]. \tag{28}$$

If labor and capital are complements then both $dk/d\beta$ and $dl/d\beta$ are positive. Hence both inputs rise and fall together in response to permanent rises and falls of the product price. It is still true but a weaker relation if labor and capital are substitutes.

This analysis shows how changes in the real present value of profits respond to changes in the amounts of the inputs caused by changes in the exogenous variables. There is no direct structural relation between investment in capital goods and the present value of real profits. For instance, consider the effect of a reduction in the real rate of return on capital. It raises the present value of profits and it raises the optimal stock of capital goods so these two endogenous variables move together. But one does not cause the other. The positive association is due to the common effect on both of a change in the real rate of return on capital. Not all changes in the various exogenous variables are like this. Thus a lower real wage rate raises the present value of profits but lowers the optimal stock of capital provided labor and capital are substitutes.

This model can illuminate the effect of a stock market crash on the amounts of the inputs. A crash does not necessarily lead to a decrease in all the inputs. The present value of profits and the level of inputs depend on common exogenous forces. These common forces affect the complementary inputs in the same way and the competing inputs in opposite ways.

3. A Theory of Capital for a Firm Facing Uncertainty

Let the sequence of profits of a corporation behave as if generated by random draws from a probability distribution. A potential investor observes past profits, estimates future profits, and reckons how much he would be willing to invest in that corporation. This section describes how an investor might do this.

The random shocks to which a corporation is subject make its profits a random variable over time. Unfavorable shocks can impose such large losses that the owners of the corporation decide to end its existence. The theory herein asserts that sooner or later this happens to every firm. Although stopping is certain, the date of stopping is uncertain. Following the theory in chapter 2, let the corporation obtain all its capital from its owners and borrow none. Even though the firm has no debt, has no creditors who can force it into bankruptcy, and has no risk of ruin, it stops eventually. This is because the owners of the firm, who are the claimants to its residual income, decide to close down the firm when they believe it does not have a future bright enough to warrant going on.

Although the theory assumes the firm has no debt, it is still useful to discuss briefly how debt would enter the picture in order to understand better what happens in its absence. Debt has distinct traits. The borrower promises to repay the loan on a schedule and on terms agreed to when the loan is made. The payments made by the borrower to the lender may be fixed in nominal terms or may depend on some factor outside the control of either party. For example, the interest payment may depend on some standard interest rate or on a price index. The loan agreement states what will happen if the borrower fails to satisfy its terms. Sometimes a tangible object is designated as collateral for the loan. In case the borrower defaults, the lender can seize the collateral and in so doing absolve the borrower of all remaining indebtedness. Such a loan is called a nonrecourse loan. However, the terms may give the lender the right to full repayment of the loan even in case of default so that any part of the loan not covered by the value of the collateral when the lender seizes it remains a liability of the borrower. The amount of the loan that is secured by the collateral is usually below the market value of the collateral at the time the loan is made. The more fungible, the more liquid, and the more stable in value the collateral, the bigger is the amount of the loan relative to the value of the collateral. Some loans are not secured by any collateral, and the lender must rely on the faith and credit of the borrower. The principal of a loan secured by tangible collateral is usually safer than the other kinds of loans. A lender needs to know less about the affairs of a borrower than do the owners of equity capital.

This analysis also applies to the Modigliani–Miller theorem (1958). This theorem asserts that the debt–equity ratio does not affect a firm's cost of capital because an investor in a firm can undo the effects of the firm's debt–equity ratio by his own borrowing or lending. Yet one must admit that debt secured by tangible collateral stands on a different footing than do other kinds of debt. An individual is seldom in a position like a corporation that has tangible assets which it can use as collateral for its loans. Often the bulk of the individual's wealth is human capital that is neither fungible, liquid, nor stable. In practice a firm may have an optimal debt–equity ratio depending on the nature of its business, its collateral, and the preferences of its current owners. The theory of corporations presented in chapter 2 and here does not accept the Modigliani–Miller theorem.[2]

The theory described here assumes the firm does not borrow. Neither a discount factor nor an interest rate affects its strategy. Yet as we shall see something akin to an interest rate is present in the form of the probability the firm will continue.

Because a series of independent random variables does not form a differentiable function of time though it can trace a continuous path, the model with uncertainty assumes time is a discrete variable. Hence differences replace derivatives. This is in contrast to the neoclassical theory with certainty as described in the preceding section.

Let z_t denote profit at time t, a random variable drawn from the pdf $\phi(.)$. Let the firm decide to cease operations the first time that its profit falls below a prescribed level, $-a$. The decision to stop on the first occasion of a big enough loss does not mean ruin. Stopping is a deliberate and voluntary decision of the firm. Let q denote the probability of stopping.

$$q = \Pr\{z \leq -a\} = \int_{-\infty}^{-a} \phi(z)dz. \tag{1}$$

To clarify the situation, introduce the truncated random variable π as follows:

if $z > -a$ then $\pi = z$;   if $z \leq -a$ then $\pi = -a$.

Consequently the firm can lose at most a when it stops. The expected value of π,

$$E(\pi) = \int_{-\infty}^{\infty} \pi\phi(\pi)d\pi = \pi^* - aq, \tag{2}$$

where

$$\pi^* = \int_{-a}^{\infty} z\phi(z)dz \equiv \int_{-a}^{\infty} \pi\phi(\pi)d\pi.$$

Let $p = 1 - q$ so p is the probability that the profit will be ample enough to induce the firm to continue its activities for one more period. Conditional on continuing, the expected profit of the firm for one period is $E(\pi \mid \pi \geq -a) = \pi^*/p$.

To say the firm continues for one more period if its net revenue is above $-a$ denies the adage that sunk costs are irrelevant. Moreover, since the firm has no debt, it has no creditors who can force it into bankruptcy. Only the owners

---

2. Stiglitz (1974) shows that the Modigliani–Miller theorem holds only if it is certain that bankruptcy cannot take place. Since the risk of bankruptcy or equivalently the probability of stopping lies at the heart of the following analysis, the results of Stiglitz, especially at p. 862, supply good reason for putting aside the Modigliani–Miller theorem.

themselves can freely decide whether or not to continue or to stop. Why should the *t*-period net return affect their decision?

One answer to this question explores the consequences of the hypothesis that the owners of the firm do not know the probability density function, $\phi(.)$, assumed to generate the net return. Their current knowledge about $\phi(.)$ depends on their experience. A simple analogy may explain why this is reasonable.

Say that a gambler who does not know the odds is betting on the outcome of a coin toss. The gambler only knows or believes that the same coin is used for each coin toss. This means he believes the true probability of heads is the same at each toss of the coin. If the coin comes up heads, he wins the amount one, and if it comes up tails, he gets nothing. He must pay $y < 1$ before each coin toss so that y is the cost of each toss. In short y is his bet. Let β denote the unknown probability of heads. The gambler decides on the basis of what he has seen up to and including trial n whether he should pay y to toss the coin or whether he should stop. Say that he wants to maximize his expected return and that he has won x times on the n preceding coin tosses. His realized net gain is $x - ny$. Therefore, $\bar{x} = x/n$, the sample mean, is the fraction of his wins in n trials. Whether he stops or continues, the realized net gain is the same. Evidently, however, it should affect his decision. If he plays one more time, his net gain will go up by $1 - y$ if he wins and it will go down by $-y$ if he loses. Hence his expected profit from continuing is the expected value of β minus y, the cost of continuing, $E(\beta) - y$. A sensible estimator of the expected value of β is the sample mean. The gambler believes continuing will be more profitable than stopping if $x > ny$. Therefore, the past frequency of success does affect his decision because it conveys information about the future. However, the sample mean is subject to random fluctuations. Even if the true mean is bigger than y, the cost of a bet, the sample mean may be below y. Therefore, stopping whenever the sample mean is less than y would lead the gambler sometimes to forego a profitable opportunity. To reduce the chance of this, the gambler may set a critical stopping level below y and thereby lower the chance of missing a profitable opportunity. For instance, if the gambler sets the stopping level two standard deviations below y, then he would falsely reject a favorable gamble a little more than 2 percent of the time. This rule says that the gambler should stop as soon as his past receipts, x, fall below his past costs, ny, by an amount that depends on the variability of the receipts. This procedure translates into the very rule in the model that determines whether the firm decides to continue or to stop. Even if the owners need not put more funds into their company and their liability is limited, they still have a cost of continuing like the size of the bet. This cost includes the salvage value of the firm.

The past is pertinent for the present when it furnishes the best forecast of the future prospects assuming the underlying circumstances remain the same.

We abandon a project not because the past losses are large but because they portend little hope of future profits. The same precept applies when underlying conditions change over time, but then there is more likelihood of a mistaken decision.

Let u_t denote the probability of continuing for t periods so that stopping occurs at time $t + 1$. The probability that the firm survives for at least n periods, call it v_n, is given by

$$v_n = \sum_{i=n+1}^{\infty} u_i. \tag{3}$$

Let $E(w)$ denote the expected value of the firm. It is the expected value of the sums of the profits of the firm conditional on survival for n periods multiplied by the probability of survival for n periods, n running from zero to infinity. Let the critical lower bounds on profits vary over time so that it is $-a_t$ at period t. Let π_{ij} denote the profit at period i *after* period j so that $i \geq j$. If the firm survives for i periods then it will have obtained a total profit equal to $\pi_{i,0} + \pi_{i,1} + \ldots + \pi_{i,i-1}$. The following tableau shows the alternatives:

Period	Profit	Probability
0	$-a_0$	u_0
1	$\pi_{10} - a_1$	u_1
2	$\pi_{20} + \pi_{21} - a_2$	u_2
	$\ldots$	
n	$\pi_{n0} + \pi_{n1} + \ldots + \pi_{n,n-1} - a_n$	u_n

and so on. The hypothesis of independent random shocks implies that

$$\pi_{10} = \pi_{20} = \pi_{30} = \ldots = \pi_{n0} = \pi_0,$$

$$\pi_{21} = \pi_{31} = \pi_{32} = \ldots = \pi_{n1} = \pi_1,$$

$$\pi_{n,n-1} = \pi_{n+1,n-1} = \pi_{n+2,n-1} = \ldots = \pi_{n-1},$$

because the time when the venture stops cannot affect the profits that were realized before the stopping time even if the stopping time does depend on the size of the preceding profits. Hence we may drop the first subscript from π, and the tableau simplifies to:

Period	Profit	Probability
0	$-a_0$	u_0
1	$\pi_0 - a_1$	u_1
2	$\pi_0 + \pi_1 - a_2$	u_2
	$\ldots$	
n	$\pi_0 + \pi_1 + \ldots + \pi_{n-1} - a_n$	u_n

Let

$$\bar{\pi}_t = \int_{-a_t}^{\infty} \xi\phi(\xi)d\xi \Big/ \int_{-a_t}^{\infty} \phi(\xi)d\xi$$

denote the expected profit in period t conditional on the profit not less than $-a_t$. Sum the preceding sequence of profits, multiply by the probabilities, take the conditional expectations, and obtain

$$E(W) = u_0(-a_0) + u_1(\bar{\pi}_0 - a_1) + u_2(\bar{\pi}_0 + \bar{\pi}_1 - a_2) + \dots$$
$$+ u_n(\bar{\pi}_0 + \bar{\pi}_1 + \dots + \bar{\pi}_{n-1} - a_n) + \dots$$
$$= (-a_0 u_0 - a_1 u_1 - \dots) + \bar{\pi}_0(u_1 + u_2 + \dots) + \dots$$
$$+ \bar{\pi}_{n-1}(u_n + u_{n+1} + \dots) + \dots.$$

Use the definition of v_n given in equation (3), collect terms and obtain

$$E(W) = \overline{W}_0 = -\sum_0^{\infty} a_t u_t + \sum_0^{\infty} v_t \bar{\pi}_t, \tag{4}$$

where $\overline{W}_0$ denotes the expected value calculated at the beginning of period 0 before observing the results of that period. As we shall see, the formula for the expected value given in equation (4) resembles a present value in which the t-period discount factor corresponds to the probability that the profits will continue after period t.

There is another illuminating way of deriving the expected valuation. Let W_0 denote the valuation of the prospect before having seen the outcome at the initial period. Let z be the random variable representing the revenue at the initial period. Let W denote the valuation of the prospect after observing the initial period results.

$$W_0 = z + W.$$
$$z \le -a_0 \Rightarrow \pi_0 = -a_0, \qquad W = 0, \quad \text{and} \quad \Pr\{z \le -a_0\} = q_0,$$
$$z > -a_0 \Rightarrow \pi_0 = z, \qquad W = W_1, \quad \text{and} \quad \Pr\{z > -a_0\} = p_0.$$

Taking expectations gives

$$\overline{W}_0 = -a_0 q_0 + p_0 \bar{\pi}_0 + p_0 \overline{W}_1.$$

Stationarity means the underlying conditions are the same in each period so that

$$a_t = a \quad \text{and} \quad \bar{\pi}_t = \bar{\pi} \quad \text{for all } t, \, v_t = p^{t+1}, \quad u_t = p^t q,$$

and

$$\overline{W}_0 = -aq \sum_0^\infty p^t + \bar{\pi}\ p/(1-p)$$

$$= -aq/(1-p) + \bar{\pi}\ p/(1-p)$$

$$= -a + \bar{\pi}\ p/q. \tag{5}$$

The expected life of the firm is $E(T) = p/q$. Formula (5) says that the expected value of the firm before observing the results of the initial period equals the stopping level, $-a$, plus the expected profit conditional on continuing multiplied by the expected life of the firm. Hence the relation between $\overline{W}_0$ and $\overline{W}_1$ is given by $\overline{W}_0 = p\overline{W}_1 + \mu_0$ where $\mu_0 = p\pi_0 - qa$ is the expected value of the truncated profit. With stationarity, $\overline{W}_0 = \overline{W}_1$ so that $\overline{W}_0 = \mu_0/q$. There is a close resemblance between this expression for the expected valuation and the present value of the certain income stream $\{\mu, \mu, \ldots\}$. Let ρ denote the discount rate and let payments be made at the end of each period. The present value of this income stream is given by

$$PV = \mu/(1+\rho) + \mu/(1+\rho)^2 + \mu/(1+\rho)^3 + \ldots = \mu/\rho.$$

Owing to this formula, q, the probability of stopping, plays the same role as the discount rate ρ.

It should not escape attention that the hypotheses of stationarity and independence imply that the age distribution of firms is a negative exponential and that the time when a firm stops does not depend on its age. In this case equation (5) gives the valuation of the firm.

Next consider what factors determine profits. Let y_t denote the t-period output of the firm. Let k_t denote the stock of capital at the beginning of period t. Let x_t denote the purchases of capital goods during period t. As in the model with certainty, let the depreciation of capital goods be proportional to the stock of these goods. The accounting identity relating these variables is

$$k_t = x_{t-1} + (1 - \delta)k_{t-1},$$

which says that the stock of capital goods available at the beginning of period t equals the purchases of these during the preceding period plus the stock of capital net of depreciation from the preceding period. The production function with the t-period output as a function of the t-period capital stock is

$$y_t = f(k_t). \tag{6}$$

This formulation ignores variable inputs that can adjust in response to current random shocks. It focuses instead on the firm's commitments before it can see the consequences of its commitments. Let r_t denote the t-period output price and s_t the t-period price per unit of the capital good. The unconditional profit during period t that corresponds to the random variable z is

$$z_t = r_t y_t - s_t x_t. \tag{7}$$

Like the theory with certainty described in the preceding section, profit is defined as a cash flow. Hence t-period total outlays are subtracted from t-period total receipts. Say the firm can control its output and its stock of capital so these are not subject to random shocks, but it cannot control prices. Hence these are the conduits of the random shocks into profit. Therefore, profit, z, in equation (7) is a random variable because the prices r and s are random variables.

Stationarity is the simplest case. It implies a constant stock of capital goods. The purchase of new capital goods serves only to replace the worn-out machines. From the definition of the unconditional profit given by equation (7), it follows that

$$z = ry - s\delta k = r f(k) - s\delta k. \tag{8}$$

Stationarity also implies that $u_t = p^t q$ and $v_t = p^{t+1}$. Hence the stopping time does not depend on the age of the firm.

It is worthwhile to see whether equation (5) is sensible by asking what it says about the price–earnings ratio (PE ratio) of a firm. The standard definition of a PE ratio is the current share price divided by the sum of the earnings per share during the preceding 12 months. In order to relate these numbers to the theoretical variables, assume that the current share price measures the expected value of the firm and that the past 12-month earnings measure the expected profit. It is an implication of equation (5) that

$$PE = -a/\bar{\pi} + E(T) < E(T). \tag{9}$$

Equation (9), that accepts the several assumptions—stationarity, independence, and those relating the empirical measures to the theoretical concepts—implies that the price–earnings ratio does not exceed the expected life of the firm, $E(T)$. Thus a price–earnings ratio of 15 would mean that the firm is expected to survive for at least 15 years. If one believes the firm can expect to survive for 30 years then a PE ratio of 15 means that $-a/\bar{\pi} = -15$. Hence the critical stopping level is a loss of \$15 per share when the conditional expected profit per share is \$1. This means a firm that expects a profit of \$1 per share and that sustains a loss of \$15 per share would go out of business. The following tableau shows some other alternatives.

PE Ratio	10		12		15	
$E(T) = p/q$	15	30	15	30	15	30
$-a/\pi$	−5	−20	−3	−18	0	−15

Despite the extreme assumptions underlying this tableau, including stationarity, independence of the random shocks over time, and expected profits equal to actual profits during the preceding 12 months, the numbers are plausible. Therefore, equation (9) is a reasonable guide for judging the price–earnings ratio with respect to several pertinent parameters.

Let the firm choose its capital input k in order to maximize the expected value $E(W)$ given by equation (5). This equation rewritten in a somewhat more useful shape is as follows:

$$E(W) = -a + \pi^*/q,$$

with π^* as defined in equation (2). Since a is constant, if the optimal k is positive, it must satisfy

$$\frac{\partial}{\partial k}\left(\frac{\pi^*}{q}\right) = 0 \Rightarrow q\,\frac{\partial \pi^*}{\partial k} - \pi^*\,\frac{\partial q}{\partial k} = 0. \tag{10}$$

Because both q and π^* are positive, equation (10) can have a solution only if the partials have the same sign. To see whether this is true, let us take a closer look at π^* and q. First, solve equation (8) for s and introduce the function $h(k, z)$ so that

$$s = h(k, z) = [r\,f(k) - z]/\delta k.$$

Let $g(r, s)$ denote the bivariate density function of the two random variables, r, the output price, and s, the price of the capital good. By hypothesis all the firms in the industry face the same prices that their individual actions cannot affect. This assumption poses a question. Given that all firms face the same pdf $g(.)$, why do they not all have the same stock of capital goods? One answer is that the firms have different lower bounds, the a's. Even though all the firms face the same prices, they do not choose the same quantities of inputs and outputs. Some firms are luckier or wiser than others. Therefore, their profit streams differ and have different standard deviations leading them to have different a's.

The cdf of profits, z, is as follows:

$$\Phi(z) = \Pr\{Z \le z\} = \int_0^\infty \int_{h(k,z)}^\infty g(r, s)\,ds\,dr.$$

To verify this equation, observe that $Z \le z$ corresponds to $h(k, z) \le s \le \infty$. Call the pdf of z, $\phi(z) = \partial\Phi(z)/\partial z$. Therefore,

$$\phi(z) = \int_0^\infty \frac{g[r, h(k, z)]}{k\delta}\,dr. \tag{11}$$

It follows from equation (11) that the pdf of profits depends on k as claimed.

The probability of stopping is

$$q = \Pr\{z \le -a\} = \int_{-\infty}^{-a} \int_{0}^{\infty} \frac{g[r,\, h(k,\, z)]}{kd} \; dr\, dz. \tag{12}$$

In terms of the density for prices, r and s, there is

$$\pi^*(k) = \int_{-a}^{\infty} \int_{0}^{\infty} \frac{z\, g[r,\, h(k,\, z)]}{k\delta} \; ds\, dr. \tag{13}$$

It is consistent with the main theme of this theory to explain differences among the firms as due to differences in their a's.

The first-order necessary condition for the optimal k yields a positive k only if $\partial q/\partial k$ and $\partial \pi^*/\partial k$ have the same sign.

$$\frac{\partial q}{\partial k} = \int_{-\infty}^{-a} \int_{0}^{\infty} \frac{1}{k^2 \delta} \left\{ -g(r,\, .) + \frac{g_s(r,\, .)}{k\delta} \left[z - r(f - kf_k) \right] \right\} dr\, dz \tag{14}$$

$$\frac{\partial \pi^*}{\partial k} = \int_{-a}^{\infty} \int_{0}^{\infty} \frac{z}{k^2 \delta} \left\{ -g(r,\, .) + \frac{g_s(r,\, .)}{k\delta} \left[z - r(f - kf_k) \right] \right\} dr\, dz. \tag{15}$$

If f is increasing and concave and $f(0) = 0$ then $f - kf_k > 0$. Because $z \le -a$, the term $\{.\}$ in equation (14) is negative. Therefore, $\partial q/\partial k$ would be negative if g_s were positive. But g_s can change sign so it is not possible to fix the sign of $\partial q/\partial k$ a priori. Also, in equation (15) z itself is positive over some of the region of integration in contrast to the situation in equation (14) where it is always negative. Therefore, $\partial q/\partial k$ and $\partial \pi^*/\partial k$ can have the same sign so that the optimal k can be positive.

Next consider how a enters the picture. To see how k depends on a start with the necessary condition for the optimal k, equation (10). At the outset note that

$$q = \int_{-\infty}^{-a} \phi(z)dz \Rightarrow \frac{\partial q}{\partial a} = -\phi(-a) < 0 \tag{16}$$

and

$$\pi^* = \int_{-a}^{\infty} z\phi(z)dz \Rightarrow \frac{\partial \pi^*}{\partial a} = -a\phi(-a) < 0. \tag{17}$$

Therefore, the bigger the loss the owners will tolerate, the less likely is stopping and the smaller is π^*. Differentiate the first-order condition for the optimal k with respect to a. After some straightforward algebra we obtain

$$(q\pi^*_{kk} - \pi^* q_{kk}) \frac{\partial k}{\partial a} = (q_k \pi^*_a - \pi^*_k q_a). \tag{18}$$

Because the optimal k must satisfy the first-order necessary condition, which is equation (10), that gives the values of q_k and π_k^*, equation (18) reduces to

$$\frac{\partial k}{\partial a} = \left(\frac{q_k}{q}\right) \frac{\pi_a^* - \dfrac{\pi^*}{q} q_a}{\pi_{kk}^* - \dfrac{\pi^*}{q} q_{kk}}. \tag{19}$$

If π^*/q is a twice differentiable and strongly concave function of k then it can be shown that at the optimal k,

$$\pi_{kk}^* - \frac{\pi^*}{q} q_{kk} < 0. \tag{20}$$

It is an implication of equations (16) and (17) that

$$\pi_a^* - \frac{\pi^*}{q} q_a = \phi(-a) \, \overline{W} > 0. \tag{21}$$

Consequently, $\partial k/\partial a$ and $\partial q/\partial k$ are of opposite sign. This completes the proof of the following

THEOREM 1.   *If π^*/q is a twice differentiable and strongly concave function of k which implies that a unique optimal k exists for each a then inequality (20) is true. Therefore,*

$$\frac{\partial k}{\partial a} = \frac{\left(\dfrac{q_k}{q}\right) \phi(-a) \, \overline{W}}{\pi_{kk}^* - \dfrac{\pi^*}{q} q_{kk}},$$

and there is the implication that $\partial k/\partial a$ and $\partial q/\partial k$ are of opposite sign.

This result says that if the probability of stopping varies inversely with the optimal capital, then firms with bigger a will have more capital. On the other hand, a bigger optimal capital may entail a bigger chance of stopping ($q_k > 0$). If so, then it is the firm with the smaller a that has the larger optimal capital. This theory does not determine the relation between the size of the optimal capital, k, and the size of the stopping probability, q. Nor is this all. Experience does not show that stopping and the size of capital are always inversely related. It does suggest that younger firms are more likely to stop than older firms. However, we do not know whether holding age or firm experience constant there is a regular empirical relation between the optimal size and the stopping probability. An apparent inverse relation between size and stopping may come from confounding age with size, or it may show that the firms doing badly are shrinking so that the smaller they become, the more likely they are to stop. This means that the available evidence does not refute the hypothesis of a constant stopping probability.

Even this highly abstract theory that takes the critical lower bound of stopping as a constant, that assumes no growth, that assumes the production function does not change so that the firm neither learns nor forgets, that has a constant rate of depreciation of capital, and that has a constant probability of stopping predicts relations consistent with many of the known facts. Before embracing more complicated models there should be good reasons for abandoning this simpler one.

4. Predicting Stock Prices

The models presented in the preceding two sections readily lend themselves to empirical tests. This section describes how well they can predict stock prices using monthly data for two periods. The first period starts in January 1919 and ends in December 1940. The second starts in January 1947 and ends in December 1991. Both periods include dramatic episodes such as the two stock market crashes, October 1929 and October 1987. The Great Depression is the major event of the first period. The second includes the Korean and Vietnam Wars as well as the high rates of inflation during the 1970s after the October 1973 Arab oil embargo.

We begin with a concise description of the model. Let d_t denote the discount rate at the beginning of month t, s_t the price per share at the beginning of month t, π_t the dividend per share paid at the *end* of month t, and y_t the revenue of the firm during month t. Let $E(s_{t+1})$ denote the share price expected to prevail at the beginning of month $t + 1$ and let $E(\pi_t)$ denote the dividend expected to be paid at the end of month t. The formula relating share prices, dividends, and the discount rate is

$$s_t = \frac{E(\pi_t) + E(s_{t+1})}{1 + d_t}. \tag{1}$$

Solving for $E(s_{t+1})$ yields

$$E(s_{t+1}) = (1 + d_t)s_t - E(\pi_t). \tag{2}$$

If all the profits were retained by the company so that $E(\pi_t) = 0$, then the expected price per share would increase by an amount depending on the size and use of these retained profits. Therefore, substituting expected profits for expected dividends in equation (2) would give a negative coefficient that is bigger, the more of the expected profit that is paid to the owners.

The empirical work replaces the share price per firm by the S&P Index of stock prices. Hence it applies to that group of firms whose share prices are in the S&P Index. The regressions use the 90-day Bankers' Acceptance Rate in New York as a proxy for the discount rate. The empirical proxy for the dividends of the firms in the S&P Index is an estimate of total nominal production for the whole U.S. economy.[3] One may justify this replacement if dividends are a linearly increasing function of profits and if profits in turn are a linearly increasing function of revenue so that

$$\pi_t - \bar{\pi} = \gamma[y_t - \bar{y}], \qquad \gamma > 0, \tag{3}$$

where $\bar{\pi}$ and $\bar{y}$ are the long-run expectations.[4] Hence the coefficient γ depends on two assumptions, linearity between dividends and profits together with linearity between profits and revenue. This poses the question of the shape of the relation between dividends and profits. Let $s_{t+1} = E(s_{t+1}) + u_{t+1}$ (see equation (5)) so that the observed and expected share prices in each period $t + 1$ coincide up to the addition of a random variable u_{t+1}. Therefore,

$$s_{t+1} - (1 + d_t)s_t = -E(\pi_t). \tag{4}$$

Using equation (4), one can see if $s_{t+1} - (1 + d_t)s_t$ is linearly related to proxies for $E(\pi_t)$.

No monthly data are available for nominal income or profits for the first sample period. Consequently, one must estimate these variables with the available data. Moreover, since it is desirable to compare the results for the two sample periods, the empirical work for the second period uses the same estimates of nominal income as the first period. The monetary or nominal value of total production, y_t, is estimated by multiplying together two monthly indexes, the Federal Reserve Board Index of Production and the Bureau of Labor Statistics Wholesale Price Index. Let $FRBProd_t$ denote the former and WPI_t denote the latter.[5] Hence

$$y_t = FRBProd_t \times WPI_t.$$

---

3. Starting in January 1926 monthly figures giving the dividend yield for the stocks in the S&P Index are available. "It [dividend yield] is obtained each week by dividing the aggregate cash dividend (based on the latest known annual rates for the stocks included in the index) by the total market value for a single day during the week. . . ." (Federal Reserve Board 1966, sec. 12, p. 16). Regressions based on these estimates are reported in the following.

4. It is also plausible to postulate that $\bar{\pi} = \theta \bar{y}$, $0 < \theta < 1$, but this relation will play no role in the subsequent analysis.

5. Owing to revisions of the Wholesale Price Indexes and the Federal Reserve Board Indexes of Production it is necessary to splice old indexes to the new ones in order to maintain the numbers on a comparable basis. In the pre–World War II sample this procedure is necessary for the Wholesale Price Index. The old index has the base 1913 so $P(1913) = 100$, and the new index has base 1926 so $P(1926) = 100$. The old index is available until October 1925 and the new index starts in January 1923, so they overlap for 34 months. Let newpri denote the new index and oldpri the old index. Fitting the new price index to the old one by least squares gives the following regression:

newpri =   −2.8058 +   0.6366 oldpri   adjusted $R^2 = 0.781$
             0.295   10.898   sample size = 34

The numbers below the regression coefficients are the t-ratios. Estimates of the new price index for the months when only the old price index is available come from this regression.

The Federal Reserve Board published an extensively revised Index of Production in August

To continue, one must replace the theoretical variables in equation (2) by observable counterparts. First, assume that the expected profit $E(\pi_t)$ coincides with actual profit, π_t. It follows from equation (2) that $E(s_{t+1}) = (1 + d_t)s_t - \pi_t$. Next, use expression (3) to replace π_t by $\bar{\pi} + \gamma[y_t - \bar{y}]$ and obtain

$$E(s_{t+1}) = (1 + d_t)s_t - \bar{\pi} - \gamma[y_t - \bar{y}]. \tag{5}$$

Lastly, assume that the observed stock price at the beginning of month $t + 1$ is related to the price that was expected at the beginning of the preceding month t by the equation $s_{t+1} = E(s_{t+1}) + u_{t+1}$, where u_{t+1} is a random variable with mean zero. The behavior of the sequence of random variables, $\{u_t\}$, provides another test of the model. These random variables should be mutually independent if $E(s_{t+1})$ is a good predictor of s_{t+1} and should have a common mean equal to zero.

The regression implied by the model and fitted to the monthly data for each of the two samples and the various subsamples is given by

$$s_{t+1} = a(1 + d_t)s_t + b\,y_t + c + u_t. \tag{6}$$

The model makes two testable predictions about this regression; first, that a should equal 1 and, second, that b should be negative. In addition, equation (4) furnishes another test of the model to see whether $s_{t+1} - (1 + d_t)s_t$ is a linear function of y_t.

Before describing the regression results, we should note some salient features of the data for the two sample periods. Some major differences between the two sample periods are apparent especially for the relation between dividends and nominal income.

1940. Estimates of the model using the new index give results very similar to the old index used in the text. In some cases the estimates are somewhat better with the old than the new index so there is all the more reason to stick with the old index. A more detailed examination of the new index does not create a compelling case for using it instead of the old index.

For the post–World War II period it is necessary to splice both the price index and the production index owing to revisions. Let $WPI(57)$ denote the Wholesale Price Index with base 1957 and $PPI(82)$ denote the Producer Price Index with base 1982. The two indexes overlap for 24 months, January 1963 to December 1964. The regression relating the two price indexes during these overlapping 24 months is

$$PPI(82) = -1.32636 + 0.33505\ WPI(57), \quad \text{adjusted } R^2 = 0.599$$
$$ 0.234 \qquad 5.942 \qquad\qquad\quad \text{sample size} = 24$$

The Federal Reserve Board Index of Production was revised from the base 1967 to the base 1987. Let $FRB(67)$ denote the former index and $FRB(87)$ the latter. The two indexes overlap for 24 months from January 1982 to December 1983. The following regression is used to convert the $FRB(67)$ index into figures comparable to the $FRB(87)$ index.

$$FRB(87) = 24.21244 + 0.41346\ FRB(67), \quad \text{adjusted } R^2 = 0.950$$
$$ 8.342 \qquad 20.0 \qquad\qquad\quad \text{sample size} = 24$$

Monthly figures are available starting in January 1926 giving the dividend yield for the stocks in the S&P Index (see footnote 3). These allow a comparison between the estimates of the dividends paid to the shareholders and the estimates of nominal income. Let r_t denote the estimated dividend yield for month t. The estimated dividend, call it π_t, is obtained by multiplying the estimated dividend yield by the stock price index as follows:

$$\pi_t = r_t \times s_t. \tag{7}$$

Certain difficulties are inherent in the dividend estimates. First, some companies do not pay dividends, unprofitable companies that are losing ground and new innovative companies that are gaining ground. Second, estimates of dividends are probably biased estimates of profits that depend on the state of the economy. Dividends underestimate expected profits for a growing and prosperous economy and overstate them in the reverse situation. Third, the estimated dividend yields are highly variable from month to month. Companies usually pay dividends 4 times per year. The denominator of the estimated yield is the price of the stock on one day per week during the month while the numerator is an estimate of the quarterly dividend from the payments of the preceding year. It is problematic whether the investors' estimates of profits coincide with these estimates. It should be decided on the basis of the evidence which is a better predictor of stock prices, nominal income from equation (3) or π_t from equation (7).

Now consider some of the evidence. From January 1926 to December 1940, the coefficient of variation of estimated dividends, π_t, and estimated nominal income, y_t, are very nearly the same, 0.302 for dividends and 0.282 for nominal income. However, the adjusted R^2 between the two series is only 0.36. For January 1947 to December 1991, the adjusted R^2 for these two series is 0.97. In both samples the residuals of nominal income regressed on estimated dividends are highly autocorrelated; the first-order autocorrelation is 0.96 for the 1926–40 sample and is 0.99 for the 1947–91 sample. Figures 9 and 10 show striking differences between the two periods with respect to the relation between estimated dividends and nominal income. As figures 11 and 12 show, there is little doubt that changes in the estimated dividends lag changes in nominal income. This conclusion is very strongly confirmed by the pattern of cross correlations between the two series shown in figures 13 and 14. Figure 13 shows that estimated dividends are highly correlated with past values of nominal income. The large drop in nominal income during the Great Depression emphasizes this. No equally dramatic event occurs in the second sample period, and figure 14 shows a flat cross correlogram between the two series. Last, we see that share prices were more volatile during the 1930s than in any other period in this study.

Consider the regression results for the prewar period in table 2. In the re-

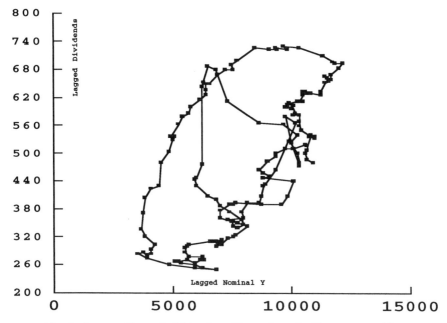

Fig. 9. Scatter of lagged dividends and lagged nominal income monthly, January 1926 to December 1940

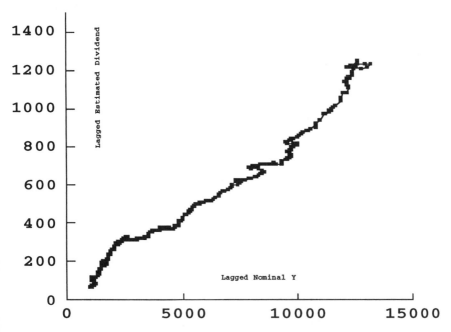

Fig. 10. Scatter of lagged dividends and lagged nominal income monthly, January 1947 to December 1991

Fig. 11. Time series of estimated dividends and nominal income
monthly, February 1926 to December 1940

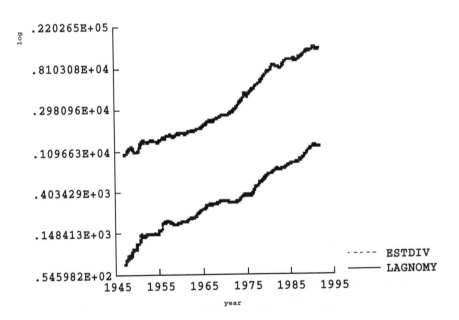

Fig. 12. Time series of estimated dividends and nominal income
monthly, January 1947 to December 1991

```
LAG    CORR    SE -1.0  -.8   -.6   -.4   -.2    .0    .2    .4    .6    .8   1.0
                     |----|----|----|----|----|----|----|----|----|----|
-24  -0.192  0.080                              (•••|     )
-23  -0.174  0.080                             •(••|    )
-22  -0.158  0.080                              (••|    )
-21  -0.146  0.079                              (••|    )
-20  -0.133  0.079                              (••|    )
-19  -0.118  0.079                              (••|    )
-18  -0.099  0.079                              (••|    )
-17  -0.076  0.078                              ( •|    )
-16  -0.049  0.078                              ( •|    )
-15  -0.018  0.078                              (  |    )
-14   0.016  0.078                              (  |    )
-13   0.050  0.077                              (  |• )
-12   0.085  0.077                              (  |••)
-11   0.123  0.077                              (  |••)
-10   0.163  0.077                              (  |••)•
 -9   0.205  0.076                              (  |••)••
 -8   0.247  0.076                              (  |••)•••
 -7   0.289  0.076                              (  |••)••••
 -6   0.331  0.076                              (  |••)•••••
 -5   0.374  0.076                              (  |••)••••••
 -4   0.419  0.075                              (  |••)•••••••
 -3   0.465  0.075                              (  |••)••••••••
 -2   0.509  0.075                              (  |••)•••••••••
 -1   0.553  0.075                              (  |••)••••••••••
  0   0.600  0.075                              (  |••)•••••••••••
  1   0.645  0.075                              (  |••)•••••••••••••
  2   0.690  0.075                              (  |••)••••••••••••••
  3   0.732  0.075                              (  |••)•••••••••••••••
  4   0.772  0.075                              (  |••)••••••••••••••••
  5   0.803  0.076                              (  |••)•••••••••••••••••
  6   0.826  0.076                              (  |••)••••••••••••••••••
  7   0.845  0.076                              (  |••)••••••••••••••••••
  8   0.862  0.076                              (  |••)•••••••••••••••••••
  9   0.874  0.076                              (  |••)•••••••••••••••••••
 10   0.881  0.077                              (  |••)••••••••••••••••••••
 11   0.886  0.077                              (  |••)••••••••••••••••••••
 12   0.886  0.077                              (  |••)••••••••••••••••••••
 13   0.881  0.077                              (  |••)••••••••••••••••••••
 14   0.872  0.078                              (  |••)••••••••••••••••••••
 15   0.859  0.078                              (  |••)•••••••••••••••••••
 16   0.846  0.078                              (  |••)••••••••••••••••••
 17   0.832  0.078                              (  |••)••••••••••••••••••
 18   0.817  0.079                              (  |••)•••••••••••••••••••
 19   0.801  0.079                              (  |••)•••••••••••••••••••
 20   0.784  0.079                              (  |••)••••••••••••••••••
 21   0.767  0.079                              (  |••)•••••••••••••••••
 22   0.749  0.080                              (  |••)••••••••••••••••
 23   0.729  0.080                              (  |••)•••••••••••••••
```

Fig. 13. Cross correlations of nominal income and estimated dividends for up to 48 lags, January 1926 to December 1940

```
LAG   CORR    SE  -1.0   -.8   -.6   -.4   -.2    .0    .2    .4    .6    .8   1.0
                  |----|----|----|----|----|----|----|----|----|----|----|
-24  0.793  0.044                                ( |•)••••••••••••••••••
-23  0.801  0.044                                ( |•)••••••••••••••••••
-22  0.809  0.044                                ( |•)••••••••••••••••••••
-21  0.817  0.044                                ( |•)••••••••••••••••••••
-20  0.826  0.044                                ( |•)••••••••••••••••••••
-19  0.834  0.044                                ( |•)••••••••••••••••••••
-18  0.842  0.044                                ( |•)••••••••••••••••••••
-17  0.850  0.044                                ( |•)••••••••••••••••••••
-16  0.859  0.044                                ( |•)••••••••••••••••••••
-15  0.867  0.044                                ( |•)••••••••••••••••••••
-14  0.875  0.044                                ( |•)••••••••••••••••••••
-13  0.884  0.044                                ( |•)••••••••••••••••••••
-12  0.892  0.044                                ( |•)••••••••••••••••••••
-11  0.901  0.044                                ( |•)••••••••••••••••••••
-10  0.909  0.043                                ( |•)••••••••••••••••••••
 -9  0.917  0.043                                ( |•)••••••••••••••••••••
 -8  0.925  0.043                                ( |•)••••••••••••••••••••
 -7  0.933  0.043                                ( |•)••••••••••••••••••••
 -6  0.941  0.043                                ( |•)••••••••••••••••••••
 -5  0.949  0.043                                ( |•)••••••••••••••••••••
 -4  0.957  0.043                                ( |•)••••••••••••••••••••
 -3  0.964  0.043                                ( |•)••••••••••••••••••••
 -2  0.972  0.043                                ( |•)••••••••••••••••••••
 -1  0.979  0.043                                ( |•)••••••••••••••••••••
  0  0.987  0.043                                ( |•)••••••••••••••••••••
  1  0.982  0.043                                ( |•)••••••••••••••••••••
  2  0.976  0.043                                ( |•)••••••••••••••••••••
  3  0.971  0.043                                ( |•)••••••••••••••••••••
  4  0.965  0.043                                ( |•)••••••••••••••••••••
  5  0.960  0.043                                ( |•)••••••••••••••••••••
  6  0.954  0.043                                ( |•)••••••••••••••••••••
  7  0.949  0.043                                ( |•)••••••••••••••••••••
  8  0.943  0.043                                ( |•)••••••••••••••••••••
  9  0.938  0.043                                ( |•)••••••••••••••••••••
 10  0.932  0.043                                ( |•)••••••••••••••••••••
 11  0.926  0.044                                ( |•)••••••••••••••••••••
 12  0.920  0.044                                ( |•)••••••••••••••••••••
 13  0.913  0.044                                ( |•)••••••••••••••••••••
 14  0.906  0.044                                ( |•)••••••••••••••••••••
 15  0.899  0.044                                ( |•)••••••••••••••••••••
 16  0.892  0.044                                ( |•)••••••••••••••••••••
 17  0.885  0.044                                ( |•)••••••••••••••••••••
 18  0.878  0.044                                ( |•)••••••••••••••••••••
 19  0.872  0.044                                ( |•)••••••••••••••••••••
 20  0.865  0.044                                ( |•)••••••••••••••••••••
 21  0.859  0.044                                ( |•)••••••••••••••••••••
 22  0.852  0.044                                ( |•)••••••••••••••••••••
 23  0.845  0.044                                ( |•)••••••••••••••••••••
```

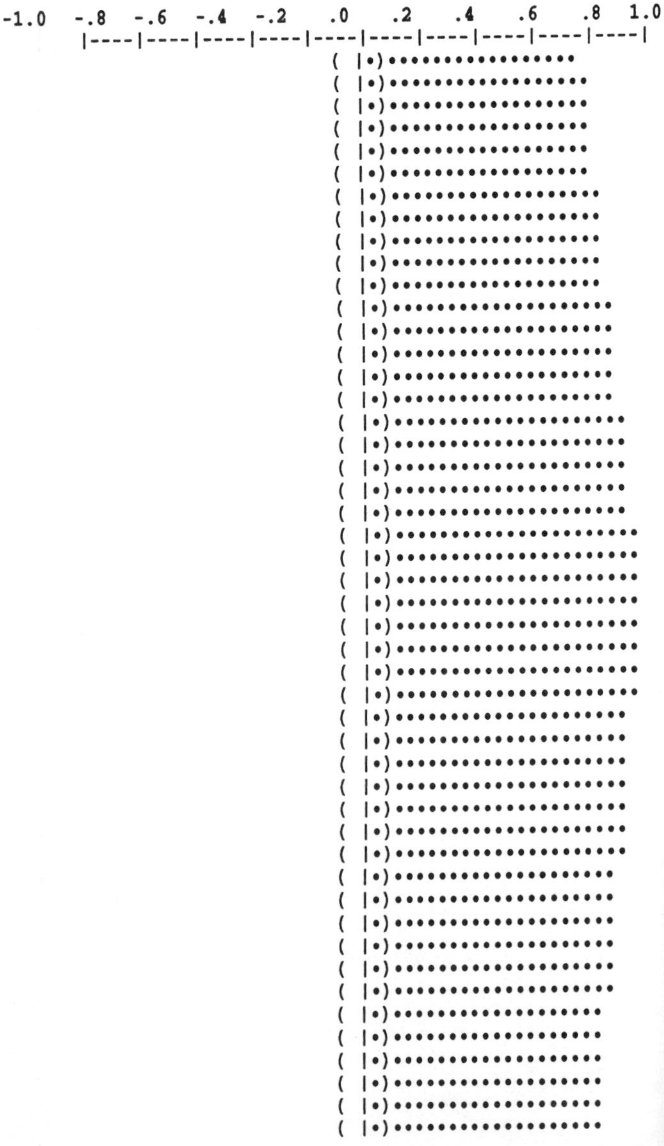

Fig. 14. Cross correlations of nominal income and estimated dividends
for up to 48 lags, January 1947 to December 1991

TABLE 2.   Pre–World War II: Regression Estimates of the Model Using 263 Consecutive Months, January 1919 to December 1940, to Predict s_{t+1}

	Estimate	t-Ratio	Estimate	t-Ratio	Estimate	t-Ratio	Tolerance[a]
Coefficient of $(1 + d_t)s_t$			0.94334	94.0	0.94534	80.2	0.788
Coefficient of y_t	0.00694	8.010			−.00017	−0.899	0.788
Constant	37.818	4.872	3.102	2.938	4.54	2.86	
Adjusted R^2	0.194		0.970		0.969		
Standard error of estimate	33.790		6.515		6.679		
F-ratio	64.2		8,900.0		4,032.0		

[a]Tolerance measures the correlation among the explanatory variables of the regression. The tolerance of a variable is $1 - R^2$ where R^2 is the multiple correlation of that variable regressed on the remaining explanatory variables of the regression equation. Hence the closer the tolerance to 1, the lower is the collinearity among the explanatory variables.

gression without the variable $(1 + d_t)s_t$, the coefficient of y_t is positive with a t-ratio over 8. However, as the model predicts, the estimate of b is negative in the regression that includes both y_t and $(1 + d_t)s_t$ although its t-ratio is only 0.9. The coefficient of $(1 + d_t)s_t$ is 0.943 in the regression without y_t, and it increases slightly to 0.945 in the regression with y_t. The first-order autoregression coefficient of the residuals is 0.407 with an asymptotic estimate of the t-ratio equal to 6.58. The 2d and 3d order autoregression coefficients of the residuals are negative, and the sum of the three coefficients is 0.19. This indicates some autocorrelation of the residuals.

Figure 15 shows the residuals. The October 1929 crash is clearly visible. Moreover, as figure 15 plainly shows, the residuals are much more stable before than after October 1929. Although the model does not predict the crash, an ex post analysis of how well the model fits the data for the two subperiods before and after the crash is well advised.

Table 3a has the results. There are two important findings. First, the estimates for the subperiod preceding the October 1929 crash are much closer to the predictions of the model than for the subperiod following the crash. The Great Depression dominates the latter subperiod. For October 1929 to December 1940, the coefficient of y_t is positive while the model says it should be negative. The coefficient of $(1 + d_t)s_t$ that estimates b is 0.83, decidedly different from 1, the prediction of the model. Also the model for the period after the October 1929 crash does not fit the data as well as before the stock market crash. The standard error of the estimate is almost twice as big postcrash as precrash.

Table 3a also has estimates for another regression for April 1933 to De-

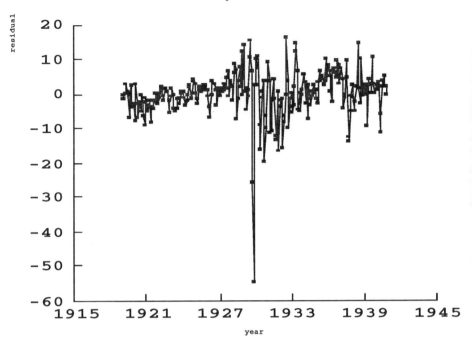

Fig. 15. Time series of residuals for stock prices monthly, February 1919 to December 1940

cember 1940 that omits October 1929 to March 1933, the Great Depression itself. While the regression for the whole subperiod October 1929 to December 1940 does not conform to the predictions of the model, the one for the period April 1933 to December 1940 conforms closely to the model. For the second regression, the coefficient of lagged nominal income is negative as the model predicts albeit with a t-ratio of only -1.61 (but see table 3b). The coefficient of $(1 + d_t)s_t$ is 0.98; that differs from the prediction of 1 by only ½ of one standard deviation. Therefore, even for the turbulent 1930s, the regression estimates are close to the predictions of the model.

The results in table 3b test the validity of linearity assumed by equation (4). The dependent variable in these regressions is $p_{t+1} - (1 + d_t)p_t$, so that the hypothesis is $a = 1$ in equation (6). There are three ways to look at this. First, the coefficient of nominal income should be significantly negative. Not only is this true, but also the t-ratios in table 3b exceed the corresponding t-ratios in table 3a. Second, the standard errors of estimates in table 3b are smaller than the corresponding ones in table 3a. Third, the scatter diagrams between the residuals and lagged nominal income, not shown, are consistent with linearity.

TABLE 3a. Pre–World War II: Regression Estimates of the Model for Three Subsamples, January 1919 to September 1929, October 1929 to December 1940, April 1933 to December 1940, to Predict $s_t + 1$

	Jan. 1919 to Sept. 1929 (128 obs.)			Oct. 1929 to Dec. 1940 (135 obs.)			Apr. 1933 to Dec. 1940 (93 obs.)		
	Estimate	t-Ratio	Tolerance	Estimate	t-Ratio	Tolerance	Estimate	t-Ratio	Tolerance
Coefficient of $(1 + d_t)s_t$	0.99951	130.0	0.856	0.83029	30.0	0.475	0.98149	22.0	0.410
Coefficient of y_t	−0.00039	−2.317	0.856	0.00112	2.196	0.475	−0.00084	−1.606	0.410
Constant	1.32348	0.815		6.40857	2.416		8.24679	2.918	
Adjusted R^2	0.993			0.941			0.922		
Standard error of estimate	3.48971			7.94070			5.24193		
F-ratio	9,245.0			1,077.0			528.46		

TABLE 3b.   Regression Estimates of $p_{t+1} - (1 + d_t)p_t$ on y_t to Test Equation (4)

	Jan. 1919 to Sept. 1929		April 1933 to Dec. 1940	
	Estimate	t-Ratio	Estimate	t-Ratio
Constant	1.31408	0.816	7.80635	2.994
Coefficient of y_t	−0.00040	−2.539	−0.00101	−3.021
Adjusted R^2	0.041		0.081	
Standard error of estimate	3.47588		5.21804	
F-ratio	6.449		9.124	

Figures 16, 17, and 18 plot the residuals and stock prices to see if there is homoscedasticity. There is no evidence against this hypothesis.

Next consider the results from the postwar period shown in tables 4, 5a, and 5b. The coefficient of y_t in the regression where it is the sole independent variable is 0.022 with a t-ratio of 53 and an adjusted R^2 of 0.837. However, the estimate of b in the regression with both independent variables is negative as

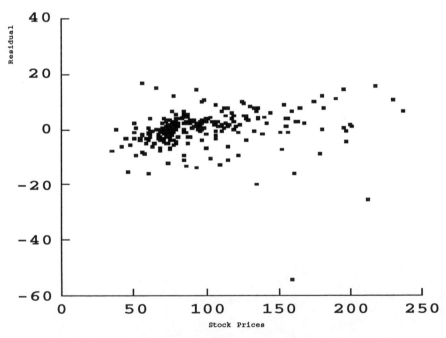

Fig. 16. Scatter relating residuals of stock prices to stock prices monthly, February 1919 to December 1940

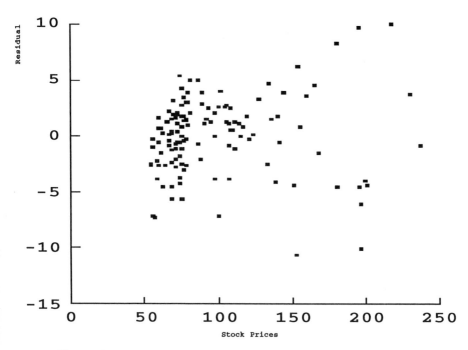

Fig. 17. Scatter relating residuals of stock prices to stock prices monthly,
February 1919 to September 1929

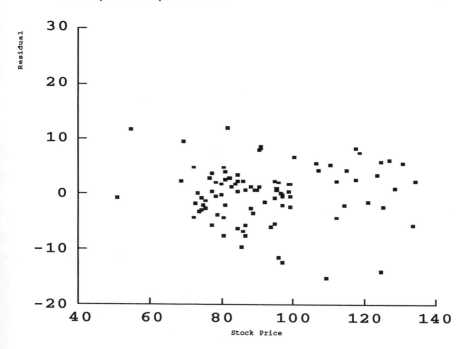

Fig. 18. Scatter relating residuals of stock prices to stock prices monthly,
April 1933 to December 1940

TABLE 4. Post–World War II: Regression Estimates of the Model Using 539 Consecutive Months, January 1947 to December 1991, to Predict s_{t+1}

	Estimate	t-Ratio	Estimate	t-Ratio	Estimate	t-Ratio	Tolerance
Coefficient of							
$(1 + d_t)s_t$			0.93104	390	0.97114	140.0	0.146
Coefficient of y_t	0.02187	53.0			−.00112	−6.435	0.146
Constant	10.541	4.378	1.087	3.275	1.510	3.866	
Adjusted R^2	0.837		0.996		0.996		
Standard error							
of estimate	35.609		5.557		5.703		
F-ratio	2,770.0		154,025.		64,184.		

TABLE 5a. Post–World War II: Regression Estimates of the Model for Two Nonoverlapping Subsamples, January 1947 to September 1973 and October 1973 to December 1991, to Predict s_{t+1}

	Jan. 1947 to Sept. 1973 (320 obs.)			Oct. 1973 to Dec. 1991 (219 obs.)		
	Estimate	t-Ratio	Tolerance	Estimate	t-Ratio	Tolerance
Coefficient of						
$(1 + d_t)s_t$	0.97597	90.0	0.123	0.97361	69.0	0.167
Coefficient of y_t	−0.00257	−4.061	0.123	−0.00105	−2.088	0.167
Constant	3.89865	6.647		0.37350	0.176	
Adjusted R^2	0.995			0.992		
Standard error						
of estimate	2.27469			8.49910		
F-ratio	29,830.0			13,491.3		

TABLE 5b. Regression Estimates of $p_{t+1} - (1 + d_t)p_t$ on y_t to Test Equation (4)

	Jan. 1947 to Dec. 1991		Jan. 1947 to Sept. 1973		Oct. 1973 to Dec. 1991	
	Estimate	t-Ratio	Estimate	t-Ratio	Estimate	t-Ratio
Constant	1.24212	3.171	4.79646	11.0	2.44241	1.340
Coefficient of y_t	−0.00180	−27.0	−0.00387	−17.0	−0.00191	−9.232
Adjusted R^2	0.569		0.485		0.279	
Standard error						
of estimate	5.79285		2.28844		8.54796	
F-ratio	712.3		300.9		85.2	

predicted by the model and with a *t*-ratio −6.44. The coefficient of $(1 + d_t)s_t$ is 0.931 in the regression without y_t, and the estimate of a is 0.971, much closer to 1, the prediction of the model. Like the prewar residuals, the postwar residuals have some autocorrelation. The first-order autoregression coefficient of the residuals is 0.479 with an asymptotic *t*-ratio of 11.1. While both the 2d and 3d order autoregression coefficients are negative, they are much closer to zero than are the prewar sample estimates. The graph of the postwar residuals shown in figure 19 is very revealing. The residuals are more volatile in the 1970s with the onset of high rates of inflation than during the preceding years with more stable prices. The October 1987 stock market crash is plainly visible, and residuals are more volatile after this event than before. Owing to the change in the pattern of residuals after October 1973, it is useful to estimate the model separately for two subperiods, the first ending in September 1973 and the second starting in October 1973.

Table 5a has estimates of the model for the two postwar subperiods. Although the first subperiod includes the Korean War and most of the Vietnam War, the model fits the data better for this subperiod than for the second sub-

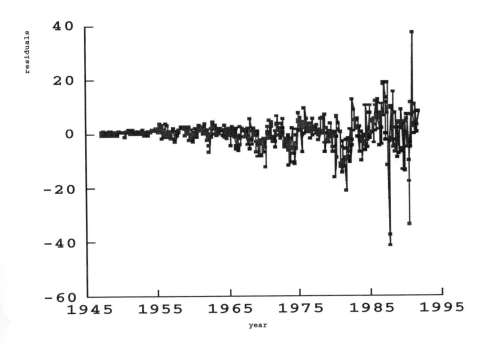

Fig. 19. Residuals of stock prices by months, February 1947 to December 1991

period. The estimate of b is negative for both subsamples, but the t-ratio is much bigger for the first than for the second. Both estimates of a are close to 1. The hypothesis that a is 1 could not be rejected at the 98 percent level.[6] The standard error of the estimate is 3.7 times bigger for the post–Arab oil embargo period than for the preembargo period. Hence, like the pre–World War II estimates of the model, the agreement between the predictions and the estimates is better for more normal periods.

The estimates in table 5b test the validity of equation (4) in the same way as the results in table 3b. In every case the coefficient of y_t is bigger with a much bigger t-ratio than in the corresponding regression in table 5a. However, the standard errors of estimates are slightly bigger for the regressions in table 5b than in tables 4 and 5a. Figures 20 and 21 show the scatters relating the residuals to stock prices. It appears that the standard error of the residuals increases with the level of stock prices. While it would be possible to raise the efficiency of the estimates by using weighted regressions, lacking a sound economically valid reason for so doing I chose to test the model using ordinary least squares. Recall that for the pre–World War II regressions there is no evidence of a similar positive relation between the size of the residuals and stock prices despite a very large range of stock prices. It is hard to justify a weighted regression in one period and not in the other merely on grounds of expediency.

Table 6 has estimates of a so-called naive regression. It is so described because it omits the discount factor. The naive regression is as follows:

$$s_{t+1} = As_t + By_t + C + v_t. \tag{8}$$

Thus s_t is not multiplied by the discount factor $(1 + d_t)$ in this equation as it is in equation (6). We wish to see whether the introduction of the discount factor as implied by the model improves the results.

First note that in contrast to equation (6), the estimates of B, the coefficient of y_t, are positive for both the prewar and postwar samples. The regression corresponding to the model, equation (6), has a negative coefficient for y_t as the model predicts. However, the coefficients of the lagged stock price index, A, are very close to 1 in the naive model for both samples, indeed closer to 1 than is the case for the estimates of a for equation (6). Finally, the naive regressions do fit the data somewhat better than the estimates of equation (6) and have somewhat lower autocorrelation of the residuals. The main difference between the estimates of equation (6), the model based on the theory, and equation (8), and naive regression, is the coefficient of y_t. It is negative in both samples for estimates of equation (6) and significantly so for the postwar period. While it

---

6. Two standard deviations above the estimate for a for the first subperiod is 0.99777 and for the second subperiod it is 1.00181. A 1-sided confidence interval for 2 standard deviations is at the 97.8 percent level.

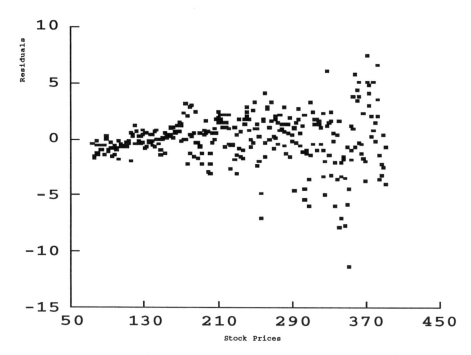

Fig. 20. Scatter of residuals of stock prices and stock prices monthly, February 1947 to September 1973

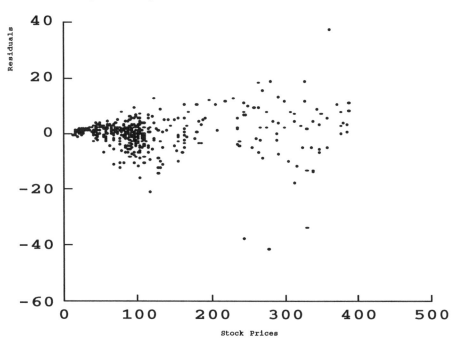

Fig. 21. Scatter of residuals of stock prices and stock prices monthly, February 1947 to December 1991

is positive for both periods for equation (8), the t-ratio is lower (1.98) in the postwar sample than the t-ratio of the negative coefficient of y_t for this period (-6.43). This is the best evidence for the model and against the naive regressions (see table 6).

Tables 7 and 8 show estimates of the naive regressions for the two subperiods corresponding to each of the two main sample periods before and after World War II. Start with table 7.

While the coefficient of y_t is negative in this regression like the coefficient for the corresponding regression in table 3, the t-ratio is -1.98, but in table 3 it is -2.3. The coefficient of the lagged stock price in table 7 is 1.046, but in table 3 the estimate of b is 1 as the model predicts. Hence for the first subsample the model comes through with flying colors by comparison with the naive regression. The naive regression for the second subsample that includes the Great Depression does not differ much from the estimates of the model. However, the latter, as we have seen, does agree with the model's predictions for the period April 1933 to December 1940.

Table 8 has estimates of the naive regression for the two subsamples of the post–World War II period. Here also like the prewar comparison, the decisive test is with respect to the estimate of b. The estimate of b for the model has a t-ratio of -4.1 while in the naive regression the coefficient of lagged nominal output has a t-ratio of $-.25$. The coefficient of lagged stock prices has a coefficient of 1 in the naive regression, and the coefficient of $(1 + d_t)s_t$ is 0.976 for the model. However, the model deserves more credit than the naive regression because it makes more specific assertions about the coefficients. For the second subsample of the postwar period there is little doubt that the model does better than the naive regression. Not only are the predictions of the model borne out

TABLE 6.   Naive Regressions to Predict s_{t+1} Pre– and Post–World War II, January 1919 to December 1940 and January 1947 to December 1991

	Pre–World War II (Jan. 1919 to Dec. 1940)			Post–World War II (Jan. 1947 to Dec. 1991)		
	Estimate	t-Ratio	Tolerance	Estimate	t-Ratio	Tolerance
Coefficient of s_t	0.97853	82.0	0.805	0.99588	160.0	0.163
Coefficient of y_t	0.00018	0.982	0.805	0.00028	1.981	0.163
Constant	0.57787	0.367		-0.13544	-0.395	
Adjusted R^2	0.970			0.997		
Standard error of estimate	6.556			4.976		
F-ratio	4,188.5			84,389.0		
No Obs	263			539		

TABLE 7.   Naive Regressions to Predict s_{t+1} Pre–World War II for Two Nonoverlapping Subsamples, January 1919 to September 1929 and October 1929 to December 1940

	Jan. 1919 to Sept. 1929 (128 obs.)			Oct. 1929 to Dec. 1940 (135 obs.)		
	Estimate	*t*-Ratio	Tolerance	Estimate	*t*-Ratio	Tolerance
Coefficient of s_t	1.04593	130.0	0.858	0.88271	32.0	0.460
Coefficient of y_t	−0.00032	−1.985	0.858	0.00072	1.426	0.460
Constant	0.07997	0.0518		5.10886	1.992	
Adjusted R^2	0.994			0.945		
Standard error of estimate	3.31364			7.67583		
F-ratio	10,260.4			1,157.3		

by the estimates of its parameters, but also the naive regression has a positive coefficient for y_t with a *t*-ratio of 1.8 while the estimate of *b* is negative as the model predicts and its *t*-ratio is −2.1. Hence the model fits very well in the second subsample of the post–World War II period despite a standard error of estimate 3.7 times bigger in the second than in the first subsample.

Before concluding this section we shall consider some alternative approaches closely related to those given in the preceding. These use the figures on dividends in various ways. Equivalent to equation (2) there is the following

$$\frac{s_{t+1}}{s_t} = 1 + d_t - r_t. \tag{9}$$

However, estimates of this equation give very poor results largely because the estimates of r_t fluctuate widely from month to month and do not adequately measure the effects of expected profits on stock prices. A more direct alterna-

TABLE 8.   Naive Regressions to Predict s_{t+1} Post–World War II for Two Nonoverlapping Subsamples, January 1947 to September 1973 and October 1973 to December 1991

	Jan. 1947 to Sept. 1973 (320 obs.)			(Oct. 1973 to Dec. 1991 (219 obs.)		
	Estimate	*t*-Ratio	Tolerance	Estimate	*t*-Ratio	Tolerance
Coefficient of s_t	1.00075	100.0	0.135	0.98635	79.0	0.186
Coefficient of y_t	−0.00013	−0.250	0.135	0.00076	1.817	0.460
Constant	0.47565	0.98232		−2.60562	−1.420	
Adjusted R^2	0.996			0.994		
Standard error of estimate	1.96874			7.43265		
F-ratio	39,874.8			17,673.7		

TABLE 9. Estimates of the Regression Coefficients and Selected Statistics Using Monthly Data and Estimates of Total Dividends for Three Samples

| | Coefficients and t-Ratios | | | | | |
Sample	$a(1 + d_t)$	b	c	Adj. R^2	F-Ratio	Obs. (N)
Oct. 1929 to	0.90110	−0.00959	11.8383	0.940	1,053.5	135
Dec. 1940	33.0	−1.414	5.181			
Apr. 1933 to	0.95183	−0.00933	8.23353	0.921	527.95	93
Dec. 1940	290.0	−1.580	2.910			
Jan. 1947 to	0.98087	−0.01603	2.02439	0.996	62,690.7	539
Dec. 1991	100.0	−5.295	4.770			

tive to equation (6) is the following equation that replaces nominal income y_t with π_t, an estimate of dividends.

$$s_{t+1} = a(1 + d_t)s_t + b\,\pi_t + c + u_t. \tag{10}$$

While the point estimates of the coefficients of this regression are close to those for equation (6) in each of the samples and subsamples, owing to the nature of the estimates of π_t as shown in equation (7), s_t and π_t are closely correlated. Hence the t-ratios for the estimates of b are somewhat lower for equation (10) than for equation (6). The estimated regression coefficients differ less across subsamples using estimates of nominal income than using the estimates for total dividends (see table 9). This is probably due to the higher multicollinearity among the explanatory variables for the regressions containing estimated dividends. It suffices to present three results comparable to corresponding ones in tables 3 and 4. Note that estimates are closer to predicted values for the sample period April 1933 to December 1940 than for the sample including the worst years of the Great Depression.

Recognizing that estimates of the model given in tables 2–5 depend both on the validity of the model and on how well the empirical variables approximate their theoretical counterparts, the results are good enough to accept the model even with respect to so simple and strong an alternative as the "naive regression." Many of the authors in White (1990) reach similar conclusions about the two stock market crashes.

APPENDIX. THE PROBLEM OF BORROWING

The theory of corporations presented in section 2 and in chapter 2 assumes that those who own the corporation are the only sources of its capital. The corporation has no debt, has no creditors, and consequently has no fixed obligations it is impelled to satisfy as a condition for staying in business. The decision to continue operations is the autonomous choice of its owners. It may seem strange to assume that corporations have no debt since many do borrow.[7] However, as the following analysis will demonstrate, the true problem is not to explain the absence of debt, but it is rather to explain why corporations borrow.

The simplest model containing the main elements of the problem assumes there is only one time period so that no intervening time is available to meet a temporary setback. Borrowing occurs at the beginning of the period, and repayment is at the end. Let K denote the total capital of the corporation and let θK denote how much capital it has borrowed, $0 \leq \theta < 1$. Note that θ cannot equal one. This is required because someone, not the bondholders whose return is subject to a fixed upper bound, must obtain the residual income, which is a random variable. Consequently, $\theta = 1$ is not possible.[8] The equity of the owners in the corporation is $(1 - \theta)K$. Let r denote the rate of interest demanded by the lenders. Therefore, the fixed obligation of the corporation to its creditors at the end of the period is the amount $\theta K(1 + r)$. This is the most the bondholders can expect to receive. Assume no collateral backs the loan. This simplifies the analysis without omitting any essential aspect of the problem. Let ξ be a random variable representing the contribution to overhead. The latter is the amount that the corporation has available to cover its fixed obligations so it is what remains from total receipts after paying out-of-pocket costs. As shown in section 2, the corporation will not continue in business unless this residual income exceeds some lower bound. For present purposes, there is no loss of generality in assuming the lower bound is zero so that $\xi \geq 0$. Last, let δ denote the default-free rate of return. If government debt were default free then δ would be the rate of return on government debt.

We start by calculating the bondholder's net return, denoted by β.

$\xi \geq \theta K(1 + r) \Rightarrow$ bondholder receives $\theta K(1 + r)$.

$\xi < \theta K(1 + r) \Rightarrow$ bondholder receives ξ and consequently loses

$\theta K(1 + \delta) - \xi$.

The term $\theta K(1 + \delta)$ is the total return on a default-free loan of θK. Let $X \equiv \theta K(1 + r)$. The expected net return to the bondholder, $E(\beta)$, is

$$E(\beta) = \int_X^\infty X f(\xi)d\xi + \int_0^X \xi f(\xi)d\xi - \theta K(1 + \delta). \tag{1}$$

---

7. Interest is a deductible expense while dividends are not under current U.S. tax laws. Hence the after-tax return on capital in the form of interest on debt is bigger than on dividends. That this cannot be the sole explanation is shown by the existence of corporate debt before there was either the corporate or the personal income tax.

8. The residual income claimants seem to be the workers in the case of Japanese corporations according to some scholars (Peck 1988; Matsumoto 1995).

If there is an optimal interior θ for the bondholder, then θ must satisfy $\partial E(\beta)/\partial\theta = 0$.

$$\frac{\partial E(\beta)}{\partial\theta} = -Xf(X)\frac{\partial X}{\partial\theta} + \int_X^\infty f(\xi)\frac{\partial X}{\partial\theta}\,d\xi + Xf(X)\frac{\partial X}{\partial\theta} - K(1+\delta)$$

$$= (1+r)K\int_X^\infty f(\xi)d\xi - K(1+\delta). \tag{2}$$

Consequently,

$$\frac{\partial E(\beta)}{\partial\theta}\bigg|_{\theta=0} = (r-\delta)K > 0 \quad \text{because} \int_0^\infty f(\xi)\,d\xi = 1$$
$$\text{and} \quad r-\delta > 0 \tag{3}$$

(see equation (5)),

$$\frac{\partial E(\beta)}{\partial\theta}\bigg|_{\theta=1} = (1+r)\,K\int_{K(1+r)}^\infty f(\xi)d\xi - (1+\delta)K \tag{4}$$

and

$$\frac{\partial E(\beta)}{\partial\theta} = 0 \Rightarrow \int_X^\infty f(\xi)d\xi = \frac{1+\delta}{1+r} \tag{5}$$

and

$$\frac{1+\delta}{1+r} < 1 \quad \text{because} \int_K^\infty f(\xi)d\xi < 1.$$

It follows that a loan is possible only if $r > \delta$. Note that nothing has been assumed about the relation between the interest rate demanded by the bondholders and the interest rate on default-free debt. It is an implication, not an assumption, of this theory that a necessary condition for a loan to the corporation is that the interest rate on the loan must exceed the default-free interest rate. Given that $r > \delta$, we may conclude that $\partial E(\beta)/\partial\theta|_{\theta=1} < 0$ for big enough K. In this case, equation (5) would be satisfied at θ between zero and 1. For small enough K it would be possible to satisfy equation (5) at $\theta = 1^-$ so that the share of the total capital in the hands of the owners would be arbitrarily small.

The next result shows that $E(\beta)$ is a strictly concave function of θ because

$$\frac{\partial^2 E(\beta)}{\partial\theta^2} = (1+r)Kf(X)\left(-\frac{\partial X}{\partial\theta}\right) < 0.$$

Now consider the prospects for the owners. Let π denote their profit. The equity of the owners is $(1-\theta)K$, and their default-free rate of return is the same as for the bondholders, namely δ. The owners' capital at risk is $(1-\theta)K(1+\delta)$.

$$\pi = \frac{\xi - X - (1 - \theta)(1 + \delta)K \quad \text{if } \xi \geq X}{0 - (1 - \theta)(1 + \delta)K \quad \text{if } \xi < X}.$$

Therefore,

$$E(\pi) = \int_X^\infty (\xi - X)f(\xi)d\xi - (1 - \theta)(1 + \delta)K$$

and

$$\frac{\partial E(\pi)}{\partial \theta} = -\int_X^\infty f(\xi)d\xi \, \frac{\partial X}{\partial \theta} + (1 + \delta)K$$

$$= -(1 + r)K \int_X^\infty f(\xi)d\xi + (1 + \delta)K.$$

Of critical importance is that $E(\pi)$ is a convex function of θ. Since the owners choose θ to maximize their expected profit, the optimal θ for them is at an extreme, either $\theta = 0$ or $\theta = 1^-$. The convexity of $E(\pi)$ is shown by

$$\frac{\partial^2 E(\pi)}{\partial \theta^2} = (1 + r)Kf(X) \, \frac{\partial X}{\partial \theta} > 0.$$

To find the optimal θ for the owners, note that

$$\left. \frac{\partial E(\pi)}{\partial \theta} \right|_{\theta=0} = -(1 + r)K + (1 + \delta)K = (\delta - r)K < 0$$

since $r > \delta$. Hence $E(\pi)$ is decreasing at $\theta = 0$. Necessarily,

$$E(\pi)_{\theta=0} = \int_0^\infty \xi f(\xi)d\xi - (1 + \delta)K > 0.$$

since otherwise the optimal K would be zero.

The nature of the problem is apparent. The expected net return to the bondholders is a concave function of θ while the expected profit to the owners is a convex function of θ. There are only two possible optimal solutions for the bondholders. The first is θ between zero and one, and the second is θ arbitrarily close to but less than one. There are also only two possible optimal solutions for the owners. The first is θ equal to zero, and the second is θ as close to one as possible. It would seem that only when the optimal θ is arbitrarily close to one can there be a meeting of minds between the creditors and the shareholders. However, θ arbitrarily close to one is not a possible equilibrium.

Figure 22 shows why. First, define the net return on the total capital K, η, as follows:

$$\eta \equiv \pi + \beta = \xi - (1 + \delta)K. \tag{6}$$

The total net return is independent of how it is financed. Hence in figure 22 the

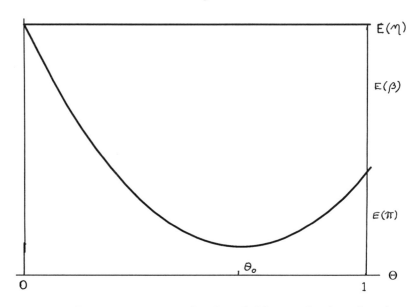

Fig. 22. Expected return as a function of debt as a fraction of total capital

expected total net return, $E(\eta)$, is a horizontal line, the same for all values of θ. While the *rate* of return to the owners is arbitrarily large as $\theta \to 1^-$, their *total* return is always a maximum at $\theta = 0$. This is owing to the fact that bondholders get a positive net return on average as their share of the capital approaches one. This means the expected profit of the owners is lower at $\theta = 1^-$ than at $\theta = 0$. The figure also shows why concavity of $E(\beta)$ with respect to θ necessarily entails convexity of $E(\pi)$ with respect to θ, a result implied by equation (6). While it is best for the bondholders to have an interior value of θ or to have $\theta = 1^-$, the best θ for the shareholders is always $\theta = 0$.

This analysis demonstrates that debt would not be optimal for a corporation. Since some corporations do have debt, it must be for reasons outside this model. Perhaps owners lack enough capital of their own to attain the minimal amount they need for the success of their venture. Perhaps owners must accept a suboptimal θ in order to induce lenders to furnish them with capital. Perhaps it is because interest payments but not dividends are deductible from profits and not subject to the U.S. federal corporation tax. If the last explanation were correct then corporations would raise more capital by borrowing than by issuing stock, the higher the U.S. Federal corporate tax rate.

CHAPTER 4

When an Alliance Can Survive

1. Introduction

The prevailing view among those who apply game theory to economics draws a sharp distinction between cooperative and noncooperative games. It is thought that noncooperative games are better for studying competition while cooperative games apply to noncompetitive situations. Because the players in a cooperative game can make binding agreements among themselves, may form coalitions, and may coordinate their actions, it is claimed that competition must be absent. Because the players in a noncooperative game act independently, cannot make binding agreements among themselves, and cannot form coalitions, by the same token it is claimed that competition must be present. Only self-enforcing agreements are possible in noncooperative games. While it is true that real games have definite rules about these things, it is more complicated in the real economy. Moreover, the dichotomy between cooperation and competition is illusory in economic applications of game theory. A well-known application shows why.

Consider the model of pure exchange as analyzed by Edgeworth (1881). Individuals begin with endowments of commodities, go to a market, and trade what they have for what they want. Any group of two or more individuals may agree among themselves on potential trades. Edgeworth calls these tentative agreements *contracts*. The individuals may seek other trading partners with whom they can make tentative agreements. Edgeworth calls this whole procedure *recontracting*. The result of this process is a set of final allocations of the commodities among the traders with several distinctive properties. First, the set of final allocations is not susceptible to improvement by any individual or group of individuals. Second, comparison between the individuals' initial and final allocations implies a set of constant-unit prices for every commodity. The monetary value of the initial bundle of commodities at these prices defines a budget constraint for each individual such that the final allocation is the best outcome attainable to each individual compatible with this budget constraint. This is the great classical example of a competitive equilibrium. Edgeworth's analysis constitutes the first use of what we now call the theory of the core. Yet because this theory speaks of coalitions, it is called a cooperative game with a

159

connotation of collusion though it is the very exemplar of unrestricted competition.

There is a great deal of misunderstanding about the nature of competition. Use of the terms *cooperative* and *uncooperative* serves only to enhance this misunderstanding. The real economy is a mixture of cooperation and rivalry. A useful model of what happens in a real economy should encompass both rivalry and cooperation and show how they serve each other. Edgeworth's analysis may contain another source of misunderstanding. The competitive equilibrium in his model implies a set of constant-unit prices that furnishes information to individuals which they can use in making the best choices for themselves. This is shown by the fact that the trades which occur at these prices allow the individuals to move from their initial positions to their preferred final positions and remain within the confines of their individual resources. However, these prices are ancillary to competition. The core of a market describes the set of undominated allocations that emerges from the competitive process. The existence of these prices is not an essential part of competition.

That individuals can advance their interest by forming groups is plain. However, history teaches us the power of self-interest. An individual does not stay in a group and serve the other members out of altruism. A group can survive only if it can solve the problem of how to enlist selfish humans to do things that will be of benefit to the group. Many different kinds of groups form in order to pursue their common economic interests. A business firm is a coalition of individuals with diverse tasks and interests. Each member of this coalition may also simultaneously belong to many other coalitions bound together by their common interests. Coalitions compete for members. They seek those who can make valuable contributions to the coalition, and they offer potential members returns commensurate with their contributions insofar as competition among coalitions for members compels this. Among coalitions there is competition and within them cooperation. While members of a coalition may promise to do certain things, an individual may gain more by treacherously failing to do so. A coalition or an alliance cannot survive unless it can prevent treachery by its members. This may not be possible without the intervention of third parties, people who are outside the given coalition. If treachery can be prevented without third-party intervention the alliance is self-enforcing. Otherwise, survival of the alliance depends on third-party enforcement. A chief goal of this analysis is to see when survival of the alliance requires enforcement by outsiders because self-enforcement is ineffectual.

The next section presents a model of an alliance among n individuals. It shows under what conditions the alliance is self-enforcing so that it can prevent treachery and secession. To prevent secession it must offer its members more than they could obtain from rival alliances. Self-enforcement can prevent treachery only if the allies themselves can impose suitable penalties.

Sections 3 and 4 describe situations in which a self-enforcing alliance is not possible. The model in section 3 has a principal and an agent. The principal, assumed to be honest beyond doubt, cannot ensure faithful performance by the agent without watching him, a costly alternative. In an optimal regime an agent cannot gain on average by cheating. It would seem to follow that the principal could save the cost of inspection if the agent promised to be honest. However, knowing that the principal who trusts the agent would not watch him, the agent would not keep his promise because he can gain by cheating. In this setting the theory of noncooperation is more useful than the theory of cooperation.

Section 4 is a model of conflict between two individuals. Both would obtain a higher return in a compromise than in a fight. However, compromise is not self-enforcing in this model because the situation will not recur. Therefore, even if the two parties were to agree on a compromise in advance, a violation of this agreement cannot be punished afterward. In addition the one who concedes is worse off than he would be in a compromise. Here, too, cooperation poses a dilemma. Without the possibility of the situation arising repeatedly, a self-enforcing agreement is not possible. In reality sometimes we do observe compromise, sometimes a concession by one party to another, and sometimes conflict. Hence a useful theory should be capable of predicting the frequency of these different results. Here is another case where the theory of noncooperation is better than cooperation.

2. Maxims for an Alliance

There are n identical individuals who are considering an alliance that can advance their mutual interests. By becoming allies each would agree to do certain things simultaneously that would be good for the alliance. The current return to each individual depends only on his own current actions and the actions of the other $n - 1$ individuals. We shall explore the consequences of the assumption that each one has but a single goal—to make his own profit as big as possible. The alliance cannot attain this goal for each person, but it can approach it closely by choosing actions that will maximize the total profit of the group.

Owing to the difficulties of this problem, it is advisable to have examples in mind. The traditional one is a group of competing firms who make commodities that their customers regard as close substitutes. The action is the price at which a firm offers to sell its product.[1] A second example refers to outlays for a common purpose. Let the action be advertising that is visible to everybody. Think of an individual seller of something who is advertising it to potential buyers. However, one should not assume that this is a special case applica-

---

1. This version overlooks the possibility that firms competing in the output market may sell inputs to each other and thereby have a means of enforcing adherence to a cooperative agreement.

ble only to advertising. It is more general than that. Any situation in which one individual is affected by the actions of the other individuals needs some method of approaching, attaining, and maintaining an efficient outcome, one without deadweight loss.

A third example is a group of firms that offer the same things under a franchise. McDonald's is a well-known instance. Gasoline service stations, new car dealers, specialized auto repair facilities, and motels are some other familiar examples. Because every franchisee is supposed to offer the same commodities and the same level of service, an individual franchisee faces the temptation of raising his profit by relying on the general reputation of the chain while failing to incur the costs that would maintain his goods and services at the level expected of all the franchisees. The larger is the transient trade, the bigger the gain to that individual and the greater the loss to the other members of the group.

Faithful adherence to the alliance means that each member lives up to the terms and fulfills his promises. Each individual can calculate what his return would be if everyone adheres to the terms of the alliance. Yet it is generally true that an individual can get more by breaking his promise provided everybody else keeps his promise. Someone who breaks his promise betrays the alliance. Such treachery lowers the returns of the loyal allies. An alliance needs some way to punish treachery after it happens in order to deter treachery at the outset. Punishment is possible only if there is time to act after the present action. Hence the alliance must continue for at least two successive periods. Since there is always one more period after the present, it is the same as lasting forever. At the beginning of every period the group makes a plan for the current period and for the next period. Treachery now can evoke punishment on the next occasion. This is a tit-for-tat strategy (Axelrod 1984). There is no relentless or grim retaliation for a current transgression. A violator of the terms of the alliance faces punishment only during the period immediately following the violation. The alliance has no definite time when it will conclude, and it can continue as long as its members desire. By virtue of this assumption one can study how and whether an alliance can prevent treachery by means of suitable punishment.

Punishment of treachery is always costly. Each person considering whether or not to join an alliance calculates how much his return would be reduced below the level he would get as a loyal ally and how much it would cost him to punish treachery in the next period. (It simplifies the analysis to ignore time discounting or, equivalently, to include it implicitly.) If an individual loses more as a victim of treachery than it would cost him to punish it then he has a credible incentive to punish treachery. He also calculates what his return would be were each person to act independently and pursue his self-interest as best as he can. Even if the punishment is credible, treachery may happen if a traitor gains more from treachery than he loses from the punishment he suffers for his treachery. Therefore, treachery will not occur if both of the following two conditions are satisfied:

1. the losses to the victims of treachery exceed their costs of punishing it;
2. a punished traitor incurs a net loss.

An alliance will not form in the first place unless it can offer prospective members more than they could get under other arrangements. Because any coalition with two or more members is vulnerable to treachery, a salient alternative arrangement is for everyone to shun alliances and always to act independently on his own. This alternative is called individualistic or atomistic noncooperation. Therefore, an alliance cannot form unless

3. each ally receives more in the alliance than under individualistic noncooperation and this return exceeds the net cost of punishing treachery.

These conditions apply to each individual calculating his own monetary gains and losses. No psychic factors intrude. An individual asks himself whether he would be willing to incur the cost of punishing treachery, whether he would lose more from treachery than it would cost him to punish it, whether he would gain more as a traitor than as a loyal ally, whether his return would be bigger as a faithful ally than it would be under individualistic noncooperation, and whether, after reckoning all of these gains and losses, his profit as a member of the alliance would be positive. The costs, the gains, and the losses depend on the actions of all the prospective members of the alliance. It is only by the choice of their actions that the individuals can determine their returns. This point is important. The individuals exchange no bonds among themselves and deliver no sureties to third parties who would judge whether anyone has violated the terms of the agreement and who could impose fines or other penalties on the offenders. Survival of the alliance depends only on what the members themselves do and not on what third parties can or may do. Detection of treachery is certain after it has taken place, and there is no doubt about the identity of the treacherous member of the alliance. Therefore, neither who is to be punished nor how is in doubt to anyone.

Summarizing, *n* individuals can form an alliance now and agree on appropriate actions. What is done next time depends on what happens now. If there was no treachery in the previous period, the alliance can repeat what it has done before. If there was treachery before, the alliance knows this and knows who was responsible so that now it can punish the treachery. The betrayer of the alliance on the previous occasion, anticipating punishment, because in the absence of any punishment treachery would surely be profitable and would therefore continue, loyalty would suffer, and the alliance would disintegrate, responds appropriately to the punishment in the current period. The alliance can continue indefinitely under suitable conditions.

Not only does an alliance have the problem of an internal traitor but it also has the problem of secession. One or more members of an alliance can quit and form their own smaller alliance if their return as members of this suballiance is higher than as members of the whole alliance. An alliance cannot survive unless it can furnish each member a return at least as large as he could get from any suballiance he can join. Therefore, the returns to the members of the alliance must be in the core or the alliance would disintegrate. Survival of the alliance is possible if and only if it can deter both treachery and secession.

Detailed study of an example is the best way to grasp the pertinent issues. Let r_i denote the return to individual i. It depends on the action of that individual as well as on the actions of the $n - 1$ other individuals. Let the coordinates of the n-vector $X = \{x_1, \ldots, x_n\}$ denote these actions and assume that the coordinates can be any nonnegative number. The relation between the return to individual i and the actions is given by the particular quadratic function as follows:

$$r_i = -\frac{a}{2}\left(x_i - \frac{c}{a}\right)^2 + \frac{b}{2}\sum_{j \neq i}\left(x_j - \frac{d}{b}\right)^2 + \frac{1}{2}\left[\frac{c^2}{a} - (n-1)\frac{d^2}{b}\right], \quad (1)$$

where a, b, c, and $d > 0$. To show that the individuals are alike, these parameters are the same for all of them. Among the advantages of this assumption is that it permits calculation of the effect of the number of individuals on the results. Since r_i is a concave function of x_i and a convex function of x_j, $j \neq i$, the function has a unique deterministic minimax (saddlevalue). The return to an alliance of n persons is the sum $\sum_{i=1}^{n} r_i$. This sum is a strongly concave function of X so that it has a unique maximum if and only if

$$-a + (n-1)b < 0. \quad (2)$$

The maximum is at

$$x_i^0 = x^0 = \frac{c - (n-1)d}{a - (n-1)b}, \quad (3)$$

and the optimal action is strictly positive if and only if

$$c - (n-1)d > 0. \quad (4)$$

From now on, let both inequalities (2) and (4) be true so that the alliance has a maximum joint return at x_0 given by equation (3).

The actions under the various alternatives are given as follows:

x^0 is the action of a loyal ally shown in equation (3);
x^t is the action of a traitor, and $x^t = c/a$;
x^d is the defensive action taken by a traitor while he is being punished, and $x^d = c/a$;

x^p is the action taken by a loyal ally in order to punish a traitor, and $x^p = d/b$;

x^e is the action of an individual in an individualistic noncooperative equilibrium, and $x^e = c/a$.

Owing to the special form of the quadratic function, an individual takes the same action in an individualistic noncooperative equilibrium as a traitor defending himself while being punished. For more general quadratic functions, this would not be true. One may also write the return to individual i in the somewhat more informative shape as follows:

$$r_i = -\frac{a}{2} (x_i - x^t)^2 + \frac{b}{2} \sum_{j \neq i} (x_j - x^p)^2 + \frac{1}{2} [cx^t - (n - 1)dx^p].$$

It is useful to compare the various actions directly. To begin, note that

$$\frac{\partial r_i}{\partial x_i} = -a \left(x_i - \frac{c}{a} \right) \quad \text{and} \quad \frac{\partial r_i}{\partial x_j} = b \left(x_j - \frac{d}{b} \right) \quad j \neq i.$$

Thus, r_i is increasing where $x_i < c/a = x^t$ and $x_j > d/b = x^p$. Owing to the symmetry, this means that if individual i cheats by choosing $x_i = x^t$, this can raise the return to individual j if c/a is bigger than d/b. Cheating by individual i has, of course, the opposite effect on the return of individual j if c/a is smaller than d/b. However, these interesting relations reveal little about the internal stability of the alliance. Also, as we shall see, what is decisive is the relative sizes of a and b.

The following formulas apply when the alliance has a single traitor.

$$x^t - x^0 = -b(n - 1) \frac{x^t - x^p}{a - b(n - 1)}$$

$$x^0 - x^p = a \frac{x^t - x^p}{a - b(n - 1)}.$$

Consequently, $x^t > x^p$ implies that x^0 is greater than both x^t and x^p. Thus when the x's represent outlays on advertising, it means that if a traitor's outlays are above the amount he would spend while being punished then the amount he had promised to spend as a loyal ally must exceed either x^t or x^p. Possibly, $x^t < x^p$ and in this case x^0 would be below both x^t and x^p. Thus cheating may entail spending an amount that is above or below what a loyal ally had promised to spend depending on the relation between x^t and x^p.

This example has two other important features. First, the minimax does not depend on the actions of anyone who is outside the alliance. Outsiders may act collectively or in some other way without changing the minimax of an individual member of the alliance. This is because the punishing action, x^p, does not depend on the number of the punishing individuals. Although this simplifies analysis of the example, it also limits the scope of the conclusions. Second, because punishment takes the form of an action as distinct from a fine, the feasibility of punishment is never in doubt. As long as the punishing action is feasible so is the punishment. Monetary penalties levied on the miscreant are not feasible without enforcement by a third party because a traitor would not voluntarily pay the penalty that the loyal members of the alliance would try to impose on him as a deterrent to his treachery.[2]

The returns of an individual under the various circumstances follow.

r^0 is the return to a loyal ally in alliance with loyal comrades;

r^t is the return to a traitor who betrays the loyal comrades;

r^v is the current return of the $n - 1$ loyal comrades as victims of the traitor;

r^p is the return of the $n - 1$ loyal allies while they punish the traitor;

r^d is the return to the traitor being punished after his treachery;

r^e is the return to an individual in an individualistic noncooperative equilibrium.

The action $x^t = c/a$ maximizes the return to an individual given the actions of all the other individuals. As equation (1) shows, choosing the action x^t removes the negative term $-(a/2)(x - c/a)^2$ from r_i so this action raises the traitor's return. The faithful allies subsequently respond by choosing the action $x^p = d/b$ that removes the positive term from the return of the traitor so that the traitor's return is reduced. It becomes the minimax K as follows:

$$K = (1/2)[cx^t - (n - 1)dx^p]. \tag{5}$$

Making the appropriate substitutions yields the equations as follows:

$$r^0 = -\frac{a}{2}(x^0 - x^t)^2 + \frac{b(n-1)}{2}(x^0 - x^p)^2 + K;$$

$$r^t = \frac{b(n-1)}{2}(x^0 - x^p)^2 + K;$$

$$r^p = \frac{b-a}{2}(x^t - x^p)^2 + K;$$

$$r^v = -\frac{a}{2}(x^0 - x^t)^2 + \frac{b(n-2)}{2}(x^0 - x^p)^2 + \frac{b}{2}(x^t - x^p)^2 + K;$$

---

2. Punishment in the form of a monetary penalty imposed on the miscreant may also fail if there is uncertainty in detecting treachery. Such uncertainty requires a penalty bigger than the amount that the traitor gains from his treacherous action. If the probability of detection is too low, a penalty big enough to deter treachery may be too big to be collectible.

$r^d = K;$

$r^e = \dfrac{b(n-1)}{2}(x^e - x^p)^2 + K.$

First an individual computes whether he would get more from the alliance than in an individualistic noncooperative equilibrium. The answer is yes because

$$r^0 - r^e = \frac{(bc - ad)^2(n-1)^2}{2a^2[a - b(n-1)]} > 0 \tag{6}$$

owing to inequality (2).

Next an individual calculates the return from treachery compared to the return as an honest ally.

$$r^t - r^0 = \frac{a}{2}\left(x^0 - \frac{c}{a}\right)^2 > 0 \tag{7}$$

shows that a traitor's immediate return exceeds his return as a loyal ally. However, a traitor is punished in the period following his treachery, and the punishment lowers the net gain. Each victim of the traitor chooses the punishing action x^p. While in this example the punishing action does not depend on the number of victims, the return to the punished traitor does depend on this. The best response of the traitor is the defensive action x^d that is in fact the same as the treacherous action of the traitor in the previous period. Punishment lowers the return of the traitor below what it would have been in an individualistic non-cooperative equilibrium because

$$r^e - r^d = \frac{b(n-1)}{2}\left(x^t - \frac{d}{b}\right)^2 > 0. \tag{8}$$

Because the minimax equals r^d, the return to a loyal ally is above the return to a punished traitor,

$$r^0 - r^d > 0. \tag{9}$$

A punished traitor suffers a net loss compared to loyalty if the punishment takes away more than the gain so that

$$r^0 - r^d > r^t - r^0 \Leftrightarrow r^0 > \frac{r^t + r^d}{2}. \tag{10}$$

In detail,

$$r^0 - \frac{r^t + r^d}{2} = (ad - bc)^2(n-1)\,\frac{a - 2b(n-1)}{2ab[a - b(n-1)]^2}. \tag{11}$$

This expression is positive, making condition (10) true if and only if

$$a - (n-1)b > (n-1)b. \tag{12}$$

It follows from inequality (2) that the left side of inequality (12) is positive, but none of the hypotheses so far implies that it is bigger than the right side. Therefore, even punishment of the traitor might allow him to have a positive gain if a is too small relative to $(n - 1)b$ because treachery has a large effect on the returns of the loyal allies.

Equation (11) measures the net gain of the traitor compared to his return as a faithful ally. More important is his net gain per period as a punished traitor compared to his net return in the individualistic noncooperative equilibrium. To this end there is the

LEMMA. $(r^t + r^d)/2 < r^e \Leftrightarrow a - b(n - 1)(\sqrt{2} + 2) > 0$.

PROOF.   First,

$$r^t + r^d - 2r^e = -(n - 1)(ad - bc)^2 \frac{[a - b(n - 1)(2 + \sqrt{2})][a - b(n - 1)(2 - \sqrt{2})]}{A}, \quad (13)$$

where $A = 2a^2b[a - b(n - 1)]^2 > 0$. Next

$$a - b(n - 1)(2 - \sqrt{2}) > a - b(n - 1) > a - b(n - 1)(2 + \sqrt{2}). \quad (14)$$

The middle term in (14) is positive because of concavity, and so the first term must be positive. Therefore, the sign of $r^n - (r^t + r^d)/2$ must be the same as the sign of $a - b(n - 1)(\sqrt{2} + 2)$.   QED

For big enough a relative to $b(n - 1)$ the return from treachery is lower than the return in an individualistic noncooperative equilibrium. But for small enough a, the opposite would be true owing to the great loss a traitor could inflict on all the loyal allies.

These results emphasize the importance of the shape of the profit function. Define the function $S(z)$ as follows:

$$S(z) = a - (n - 1)\, bz.$$

The total return of the alliance is a strongly concave function of their actions if $S(1) > 0$. The profit function is more curved, the bigger is S as a function of z. The effect of an individual's actions on the others is greater, the flatter is the profit function with respect to z. An individual has more autonomy and less effect on the others, the greater the curvature of the profit function. It follows that when the effect of an individual's action on the others is weak as shown by a highly curved profit function, treachery is less profitable than when there is a strong effect as shown by a flat profit function.

Now consider the credibility of the punishment. Punishment is surely credible if an avenging ally has a bigger return punishing the traitor in the period after treachery than his return as a victim of the traitor. The condition $r^p > r^v$ is sufficient but not necessary for the credibility of punishment.

$$r^P - r^v = -(ad - bc)^2 \frac{a - bn}{2b^2[a - b(n-1)]^2}.$$ (15)

Therefore,

$$r^P - r^v > 0 \Leftrightarrow a - bn < 0.$$ (16)

However, strong concavity of total return requires that $a - b(n-1) > 0$ so that

$$a - bn > -b.$$ (17)

While it is possible to satisfy both inequalities (16) and (17) simultaneously, it is more plausible that since $a - b(n-1) > 0$ then also $a - bn > 0$. Therefore, the return as a victim, r^v, exceeds the return as a punishing ally, r^P. Hence it is costly for the loyalists to punish the traitor. The borderline case occurs when $a - b(n-1) > 0$ and $a - bn < 0$ because then, while the total return is curved enough to be strongly concave and have a unique maximum, it is on the verge of losing this property if another person were to join the alliance. The borderline case is when the alliance is just big enough to have a unique maximal total return.

The preceding analysis settles another problem not yet discussed. It is assumed that punishment in the current period is punished in the following period, tit for tat. It would seem that punishment would be more effective if it went on for more than one period. Admittedly, by punishing longer the loyal allies can lower the return to the traitor, but it would be at the cost of reducing their own returns. When punishment is costly because r^v is bigger than r^P, then the longer lasting the punishment, the bigger is the cost. Therefore, this analysis, by supposing that punishment occurs only once in the period following treachery, seeks the cheapest punishment that may deter treachery.

Next

$$r^d - r^P = (a - b)\frac{(ad - bc)^2}{2(ab)^2} > 0$$

because $a > b$. This means the return to a traitor defending himself during his punishment exceeds the return to a loyal ally who is imposing the punishment on the traitor.

Summarizing, the results so far are as follows:

$$r^t > r^0 > r^e > r^d > r^P.$$

Notably absent from this sequence of inequalities is r^v. One may only say that $r^0 > r^v$. The indeterminacy of the location of r^v in this sequence has important consequences. First, an individual compares the return from treachery and the subsequent punishment that is $r^t + r^d$ to the sum of his returns as a victim of the traitor and an avenging loyal ally, $r^v + r^P$.

$$r^t > r^0 > r^v \quad \text{and} \quad r^d > r^P \Rightarrow r^t + r^d > r^v + r^P.$$

Therefore, the return to a punished traitor exceeds the return to the victim who punishes him. Apparently, it is more profitable to betray than to be betrayed even taking into account the loss from punishment that betrayal evokes. Yet everybody is better off in the alliance with faithful allies than in an individualistic noncooperative equilibrium.

Second, the relation between r^v and r^e is particularly important.

$$r^v - r^e = (ad - bc)^2(n - 1)\frac{a(n - 3) - b(n - 1)(n - 2)}{2a^2[a - b(n - 1)]^2}. \tag{18}$$

Because $a - b(n - 1) > 0$, it follows from equation (18) that for big enough n, $r^v > r^e$. However, if n is too small, then it is possible that $r^e > r^v$. This means that when n is small not only may a loyal ally receive a return below the individualistic noncooperative equilibrium while he is punishing the traitor, but also this can be true when he is the victim of the traitor. Hence we are led to calculate $r^e - (r^v + r^p)/2$. This is the difference between a person's return in the individualistic noncooperative equilibrium and his average return as a betrayed loyal ally who then punishes the traitor.

$$r^e - \frac{r^v + r^p}{2} = \frac{a^2(a - bn) - 2ab^2(n - 3)(n - 1) + 2b^3(n - 2)(n - 1)^2}{2(ab)^2[a - b(n - 1)]^2}.$$

$$\tag{19}$$

It follows that $r^e - (r^v + r^p)/2$ has the same sign as

$$a^2(a - bn) - 2b^2(n - 1)[a(n - 3) - b(n - 1)(n - 2)].$$

This expression can be positive for big enough a relative to b so that an individual might get a higher return in the individualistic noncooperative equilibrium than as a loyal, betrayed, and punishing member of an alliance. However, for big enough n, the sign of the expression in equation (19) can be negative so that $(r^v + r^p)/2$ exceeds r^e. Yet there is the tantalizing possibility of getting $r^0 > r^e$ if only treachery could be prevented.

The preceding calculations are shortsighted insofar as they fail to take into account an individual's gain from the alliance with respect to some pertinent alternatives. The long-term gain per period of a faithful ally compared to his return in an individualistic noncooperative equilibrium is $r^0 - r^e$, which is positive. His return as a victim of the traitor plus his return as an avenging ally is $r^v + r^p$ so that per period this return is $(r^v + r^p)/2$. Compared to the alternative of no cooperation, a farsighted person still gains from joining the alliance because he has a positive gain per period if

$$r^0 > (1/2) [r^e + (r^v + r^p)/2]. \tag{20}$$

Inequality (20) is true because $r^0 > r^v$ and $r^0 > r^p$ so that $r^0 > (r^v + r^p)/2$ and because $r^0 > r^e$. Nevertheless the alliance cannot survive unless it can prevent treachery.

The main proposition pertinent to the internal stability of the alliance is contained in the

THEOREM.   *Let punished treachery be unprofitable relative to independence. It follows that*

1. $r^v > r^e \Leftrightarrow n \geq 4$;
2. $r^v > r^p \Leftrightarrow n \geq 2$.

PROOF.   The hypothesis is equivalent to

$$a - b(n - 1)(\sqrt{2} + 2) > 0 \tag{21}$$

by virtue of the preceding lemma. To prove assertion 1 note that

$$r^v > r^e \Leftrightarrow a\,(n - 3) > b\,(n - 1)(n - 2)$$

according to (18). The claim is that

$$a(n - 3) - b(n - 1)(n - 2) > a - b(n - 1)(\sqrt{2} + 2) \tag{22}$$

if (21) is true. Inequality (22) is implied by

$$a - b(n - 1)\,\frac{n - 2}{n - 3} > a - b(n - 1)(\sqrt{2} + 2), \tag{23}$$

and the latter is equivalent to

$$\frac{n - 2}{n - 3} < \sqrt{2} + 2.$$

Hence if

$$n - 3 > \frac{1}{\sqrt{2} + 1} = \sqrt{2} - 1 \tag{24}$$

the desired conclusion will follow. Since $n > \sqrt{2} + 2$, inequality (24) holds for $n \geq 4$. This proves the first assertion.

To prove the second assertion, recall that $r^v > r^p$ is equivalent to $a - bn > 0$. Hence assertion 2 is true if

$$a - bn > a - b(n - 1)(\sqrt{2} + 2) > 0.$$

The first inequality is equivalent to

$$n < (n - 1)(\sqrt{2} + 2) \Leftrightarrow n > \sqrt{2},$$

and the latter is certainly true if $n > 2$.   QED

Plainly, if punished treachery is less profitable than independence, then it is surely less profitable than loyalty to the alliance.

The theorem shows the importance of the curvature of the profit function as the principal factor for the survival of the alliance. If the profit function is not too flat so that one traitor cannot harm loyal allies too much then his traitorous profit will be below his return as an independent. Therefore he would be better off as a loyal ally. However, under these conditions it is also true that it costs more to punish a traitor than to be his victim. Yet punishment is worthwhile because the long-run return to loyalty exceeds all the alternatives including the average return as a victim of treachery as well as the return from independence.

The alliance cannot survive unless it can deter secession. Secession occurs when one or more members of the alliance form their own suballiance. Without loss of generality consider the incentive to secede by individuals 1 to k and call this the k-coalition. Their total return is

$$\sum_{i=1}^{k} r_i = \frac{-a + b(k-1)}{2} \sum_{1}^{k} x_i^2 + [c - d(k-1)] \sum_{1}^{k} x_i$$
$$+ k \left[\frac{b}{2} \sum_{k+1}^{n} x_i^2 - d \sum_{k+1}^{n} x_i \right]. \tag{25}$$

This total return is a maximum at $x^0(k)$, the optimal action of the cooperating k individuals, and

$$x^0(k) = \frac{c - d(k-1)}{a - b(k-1)}, \qquad j = 1, \ldots, k.$$

Inequality (2) implies that $a - b(k-1) > 0$ and inequality (3) that $c - d(k-1) > 0$ so that $x^0(k) > 0$. Let $r_1(k)$ denote the return to individual 1 as a member of the k-coalition.

$$r_1(k) = -\frac{a}{2}\left[x^0(k) - \frac{c}{a} \right]^2 + \frac{b}{2}(k-1)\left[x^0(k) - \frac{d}{b} \right]^2$$
$$+ \frac{1}{2}\left[\frac{c^2}{a} - (n-1)\frac{d^2}{b} \right]. \tag{26}$$

Secession will not occur if and only if an individual obtains the biggest return as a member of the alliance of all n individuals. This holds if and only if $r_1(k)$ is a maximum at $k = n$. Hence we are led to study $\partial r_1 / \partial k$ as a function of k.

Treat k as a continuous variable instead of as an integer. This allows replacement of a first difference by a derivative and simplifies without distortion the job of finding the maximizing k.

$$\frac{\delta r_1(k)}{\delta k} = \frac{\partial r_1(k)}{\partial x} \frac{\partial x}{\partial k} + \frac{\partial r_1}{\partial k}$$
$$= \frac{\partial r_1}{\partial k} = \frac{b}{2}\left[x(k) - \frac{d}{b} \right]^2 > 0. \tag{27}$$

This uses the fact that x is optimal for k so that $\partial r_1/\partial x = 0$. Therefore, equation (27) shows that $r_1(k)$ is a strictly increasing unbounded function of k so it has a maximum at $k = n$. Therefore, no member of the alliance of n would wish to secede.

Since secession does not threaten the alliance, it can survive under the hypothesis of the theorem. This hypothesis says that if a potential traitor cannot inflict too much damage on the loyal allies because a is big enough relative to b in the sense that

$$a > b(n - 1)(\sqrt{2} + 2)$$

then an alliance among farsighted members can survive. Applied to an ordinary cartel, this result says that if the members make commodities that are too much alike then the cartel would be so vulnerable to treachery that it could not survive and presumably would not form.

Study of the problem of the internal stability of an alliance uncovers new conditions that determine when it can survive. Consequently, the class of stable alliances is more easily identified and distinguished from fragile alliances. More important, these results show how the nature of the effects of individuals' actions on each other determines the status of the core. When individuals trade commodities in a spot market for cash, a coalition refers to a group of buyers and sellers. Treachery can take the form of paying with counterfeit currency so that the seller is cheated or selling stolen goods so that the buyer is cheated should he subsequently lose title to his purchases. Core theory applied to market exchange usually ignores these possibilities so that internal treachery does not affect the status of the core in a spot market for cash. When the traders can buy on credit or all the conditions of the transaction are not consummated at once as is true of forward contracts, treachery can take the form of failure to carry out the terms of an agreement by defaulting on the payment or reneging on delivery. In standard core theory those who make agreements among themselves are assumed to abide by them. When this assumption is dropped so that an alliance survives only if it can rely on self-enforcing agreements then a core may fail to exist because the members of the alliance, being too vulnerable to the effects of treachery, internal stability is lacking. Only third-party enforcement of the rules can ensure internal stability of the alliance.

3. The Honest Principal and the Tempted Agent

New problems arise when treachery can be concealed and is costly to uncover. A surprisingly simple case contains most of them. Because the context of the situation in which the agent is supposed to advance the interests of the principal is important, let us consider some examples. The principal may own several retail stores that his agents manage for him. An agent may cheat the owner by concealing some of the proceeds from the retail sales. Another leading example is a landlord who rents a farm to a tenant. Suppose the rent depends on the profit of the farm. Profit is revenue minus cost. Owing to the difficulties of measuring profit, especially cost, and the opportunities for fraud in doing so, it is more common for rent to depend on gross proceeds that are easier to measure, an arrangement called sharecropping. Although both parties would be better off by gearing rent to profit, the lack of an impeccable measure of profit inclines the parties toward an arrangement recognizing this. In the third example, a principal manufactures something that his agents, the retailers, sell. The manufacturer wants the retailers to do certain things that will guard the quality of the product and promote its sale. However, an agent can raise his profit by not doing these things, by concealing his failure to do so from the principal, and by pocketing the savings in costs resulting from this broken promise. A fourth example is payment of taxes. Everyone knows the gains from evading taxes, the risk of an audit, and the penalties if the evasion is detected and punished.

The situation that contains most of the pertinent issues is given in the following matrix.

Principal

Agent	Doesn't Inspect	Inspects
Doesn't Cheat	$0, 0$	$0, -\delta_1$
Cheats	$\delta_2, -\delta_2 - \delta_3$	$-\delta_2 - \delta_3 - \delta_4, \delta_2 + \delta_3 + \delta_4 - \delta_1$

The first entry in each cell shows the return to the agent and the second the return to the principal. The cost of inspection is δ_1. Inspection by the principal is necessary in order to discover whether the agent has cheated him. Cheating in the past undetected by the principal remains forever hidden from him. If the agent cheats the principal who does not inspect so that the cheating is undetected and unpunished then the agent obtains and the principal loses δ_2. The principal may also lose the additional amount δ_3 because customers are less confident in the reliability of his product owing to effect of the cheating on the product quality. If this loss does not occur because the cheating of the agent takes the form of pocketing some of the receipts due the principal then δ_3 would be zero. By continuously inspecting the agent, the principal can ascertain whether or not the agent is honest. If cheating is discovered there is punishment in the form of a penalty equal to $\delta_2 + \delta_3 + \delta_4$. This penalty equals the loss to the principal from the agent's dishonesty, $\delta_2 + \delta_3$, plus the additional amount δ_4 that lawyers call punitive damages. The principal's return is this sum less the cost of inspection.

This example is asymmetric insofar as it assumes that although the principal is always honest the agent may be dishonest. Hence it ignores a possible complication—false accusations of cheating by the principal who wishes to extract the penalty from the agent. The parties can handle this in several ways. First, they may agree in advance to use a third party in order to adjudicate disputes. However, this remedy is not self-enforcing. Second, an agent not trusting the principal may demand valuable assets from the principal. These assets become the property of the agent when their relation ends. Third, the principal may be better known with a reputation to protect. False accusations raise the cost to the principal of enlisting new agents.

Before presenting the formal analysis, it is desirable to describe the dilemma facing the two parties. The agent has two alternatives. He can assure himself of a return equal to zero by never cheating the principal. Suppose he is occasionally honest so that his optimal strategy gives a positive probability to not cheating. It follows that his expected return from the optimal strategy must also equal zero since it must reckon with the chance of being found out and punished by the principal. Therefore, even under the optimal strategy an agent gains nothing from occasional cheating. Therefore, aware of this, the principal may seek a bargain with the agent whereby the agent does not cheat and the principal does not inspect. The principal would save the cost of inspection, and the agent is no worse off since his return is zero, the same as his expected return from the optimal strategy. However, the agent knows that the principal will not inspect so the agent has the tempting possibility of a positive gain from cheating without the loss from punishment. Because the principal also knows this, he cannot rely on the agent's promise not to cheat. The principal must inspect randomly with the probability of inspection optimally chosen. In this way the principal can raise his return above $-\delta_1$. Because inspection is necessary to detect cheating the two parties cannot have a self-enforcing agreement capable of eliminating cheating and the cost of inspection (Telser 1990).

Let α denote the probability that the agent will not cheat and let β denote the probability that the principal will not inspect. Let $E(\pi_p)$ denote the expected profit of the principal and $E(\pi_a)$ the expected profit of the agent.

$$E(\pi_p) = \beta[\alpha 0 - (1 - \alpha)(\delta_2 + \delta_3)] + (1 - \beta)[-\alpha\delta_1$$
$$+ (1 - \alpha)(\delta_2 + \delta_3 + \delta_4 - \delta_1)]. \tag{1}$$

$$E(\pi_a) = \alpha[\beta 0 + (1 - \beta)0] + (1 - \alpha)[\beta\delta_2 - (1 - \beta)(\delta_2 + \delta_3 + \delta_4)]$$
$$= (1 - \alpha)[\beta\delta_2 - (1 - \beta)(\delta_2 + \delta_3 + \delta_4)]. \tag{2}$$

Let the agent choose α to maximize his expected return given the optimal choice of β by the principal. Therefore the maximal expected return of the agent,

$$E(\pi_a^0) = \beta\delta_2 - (1 - \beta)(\delta_2 + \delta_3 + \delta_4) = 0. \tag{3}$$

Likewise, let the principal choose β to maximize his expected return given the

Π(P)

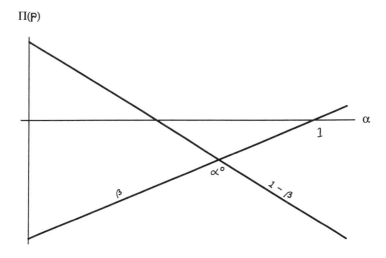

Fig. 23. Best strategy for the principal is nondeterministic

optimal choice of α by the agent. It follows that the maximal expected return of the principal,

$$E(\pi_p^0) = -(1 - \alpha)(\delta_2 + \delta_3) = -\delta_1 + (1 - \alpha)(\delta_2 + \delta_3 + \delta_4). \qquad (4)$$

Equation (3) shows that the maximal expected return of the agent is zero, the same as if he were never to cheat. Equation (4) shows that the maximal expected return to the principal exceeds $-\delta_1$, that is, his cost of inspection. Therefore, the principal gets a higher return by inspecting randomly with the optimal β chosen to satisfy equation (3) than by inspecting continuously. The maximal expected return to the principal is the optimal probability of cheating by the agent multiplied by the loss to the principal resulting from being cheated. The principal's expected loss is smaller than his cost of inspection.

Another way to derive these results uses a diagram. This has the advantage of showing easily how the equilibrium changes in response to changes in the values of the parameters. In figure 23, the vertical axis shows the return of the principal and the horizontal axis shows α, the probability that the agent is honest. The line segment labeled $1 - \beta$ means "inspect" and corresponds to the choice of the second column of the matrix that shows how the return to the principal varies with α. The minimum is at $-\delta_1$, where $\alpha = 1$ so that the agent is certainly honest. The line segment labeled β means "don't inspect" and shows the other strategy of the principal corresponding to the choice of the first column of the matrix. The α maximizing the expected return of the agent is at the intersection of the two line segments. The intersection must occur at an α be-

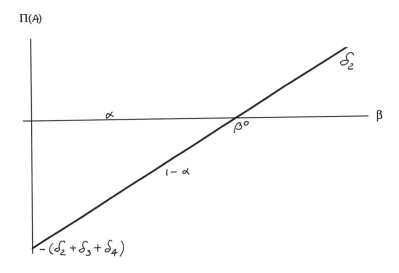

Fig. 24. Best strategy for the agent is also nondeterministic

tween zero and one so the equilibrium is nondeterministic. Since α is the probability of cheating, the best strategy for the agent entails randomly determined cheating with a frequency given by the optimal α^0. This diagram shows that the bigger is the principal's loss from cheating ($= \delta + \delta_3$), the lower is the agent's optimal probability of cheating. It also shows that the higher is the cost of inspection ($= \delta_1$), the bigger the agent's optimal probability of cheating.

Figure 24 shows the return to the agent on the vertical axis and the principal's probability of not inspecting, β, on the horizontal axis. The line segment labeled $1 - \alpha$ means "cheat," corresponding to the choice of the second row by the agent, shows the agent's return as a function of β. If the agent does not cheat so that he chooses the first row of the matrix then his return is shown by the locus of the points on the β-axis between zero and one labeled α, "don't cheat." The optimal β for the principal is at the β^0 where the line segment $1 - \alpha$ crosses the β-axis. This always occurs between zero and one so there is a nondeterministic equilibrium. Figure 24 shows that the maximum expected return to the agent is zero at the principal's optimal β. Figure 24 also shows that the bigger the return to the agent from cheating, the bigger is the optimal probability of inspection by the principal. Call δ_3 the indirect damage suffered by the principal from cheating of the agent. Call δ_4 the punitive penalty imposed by the principal on the agent caught cheating. The principal can collect from the agent who is caught cheating the sum of the direct loss, the indirect loss, and the punitive penalty. Given the agent's direct return from cheating, δ_2, the bigger the indirect damage and the bigger the punitive penalty, the lower is the optimal probability of inspection by the principal. It is noteworthy that when both the indirect damage and the punitive penalty are zero, then the optimal probability of inspection by the principal is 1/2. In this case, the optimal probability of cheating by the agent is $(1/2)(\delta_1/\delta_2)$.

Because the average return to the agent is zero while the average return to the principal is negative, one may ask why the principal uses an agent. It must be that employing an agent who is occasionally dishonest still yields the principal a bigger return than if he were to do the agent's job himself.

4. Conflict and Compromise

Each of the two parties wants something requiring the consent of the other. A compromise is possible. Without one, there would be conflict costly to both. If one party accedes to the demands of the other then they can avoid conflict. In this case the one making concessions may or may not be worse off than in a conflict. The main challenge to a theory of this situation is to show when conflict occurs although almost always a compromise would make both better off.

Examples where compromise dominates conflict come readily to mind, such as labor–management negotiations that can result in a strike or lockout, international disputes that can result in war, or marital discord that can result in separation or divorce. Every one of these examples poses the same problem, that conflict sometimes happens although both parties would be better off in a suitable compromise.

A standard model for many of these situations is bargaining between a buyer and seller. Assume the buyer has a maximally acceptable price he would be willing to pay for the item and that the seller has a minimally acceptable price that he would take for it. Neither knows the limit price of the other. Room for a bargain may be present if the buyer's maximum is above the seller's minimum. Owing to their ignorance of each other's limit price, the harm that each would suffer by revealing the limit price to the other, and the actual sequence of bids and offers from their effort to find a mutually acceptable price, it may be that trade does not occur and that both are worse off as a result. A price even chosen randomly between their two limits would be better for both.

Sometimes there is a third party at whose expense one trader can make a concession to the other. This was true at Munich in 1938. The third party, Czechoslovakia, was absent from the negotiations between the two trading partners, Hitler for Germany and Chamberlain for Great Britain. In this case the gain to one party is not the loss of the other because it is at the expense of a third party. This may sometimes occur in labor negotiations where the one who hires labor makes a product sold in a market not perfectly competitive and the one who offers labor services can prevent the entry of competing laborers. Consequently, the parties in the negotiation can prosper at the expense of the third parties who are the buyers of the product and the workers who are prevented from offering their services. A key problem in the theory of labor negotiations is to explain why strikes sometimes happen. However, it is surprising for one party to gain at the expense of the trading partner even when there are third parties ripe for plunder.

A model of these situations that lends itself to formal analysis assumes there are two parties, who each selfishly seeks the best possible outcome for itself. Let the parties believe that there are two possible matrices that describe the situation they face. In the first matrix conflict yields a payoff to each person that is lower than if one had been willing to make a concession to the other. In the second matrix the party willing to make a concession would be worse off than in a conflict. Matrix 1 resembles the situation studied in section 2 in which the victims of a traitor lose less than by punishing treachery. In matrix 2, punishment is credible even to shortsighted participants. The present model differs from the one studied in section 2 in two respects: first, the two parties are assumed to be in a nonrecurrent situation so that there is no repetition over time and no possibility of punishing a current violation of an agreement by suitable actions later; and second, the two parties do not know beforehand which of the two matrices describes their situation. They do know the outcome when they agree on a compromise but in the three remaining cases what happens is shrouded by Nature's choice of the matrix. Because compromise dominates conflict, it would seem that the two parties would compromise. However, even if they were to agree in advance on compromise, the one who reneges would do better. A compromise is not self-enforcing because the situation will occur only once. As is well known, recurrent situations are self-enforcing for a low enough discount factor (Telser 1980). Let the analysis begin with the first matrix as follows:

Column Player

		Concession	Tough
Row Player	Concession	$0, 0$	$-\delta_1 - \delta_2, \delta_1$
	Tough	$\delta_1, -\delta_1 - \delta_2$	$-\delta_1 - \delta_2 - \delta_3, -\delta_1 - \delta_2 - \delta_3$

MATRIX 1

The returns are normalized so that each player gets zero if both compromise. If one player compromises while the other does not then the return of the player who compromises is below zero while the return to the other is above zero. If both players are tough and stand fast then each has the same loss. Nor is this all. In matrix 1, conflict reduces the return to a level below what a conciliatory player would obtain. Thus a tough player can win against a player willing to compromise. A player loses less by conceding than if there is a fight.

Conservative people would choose strategies that would give them the largest possible returns under the most adverse conditions. This means they would choose to compromise because the minimax is in the upper left-hand corner of matrix 1. However, unless the same situation involves the two players repeatedly with a high enough probability, bilateral compromise is not self-enforcing.

Alternatively assume the players choose their strategies independently so as to maximize their expected returns. On this hypothesis matrix 1 has two pure noncooperative equilibria, one in the upper right-hand corner where one player concedes and the other is tough and the other in the lower left-hand corner where roles are reversed. There is a mixed, noncooperative equilibrium that we now derive. Let π_c denote the return to the column player and π_r the return to the row player. Let α denote the probability that the row player makes a concession so it is the probability the row player chooses row 1. Let β denote the probability of a concession by the column player so it is the probability that the column player chooses column 1. The expected return to the row player is as follows:

$$E(\pi_r) = \alpha[0\beta - (\delta_1 + \delta_2)(1 - \beta)]$$
$$+ (1 - \alpha)[\delta_1\beta - (\delta_1 + \delta_2 + \delta_3)(1 - \beta)]. \tag{1}$$

Owing to the symmetry of the situation the expected return to the column player is the same as to the row player with α and β interchanged. Let α^0 and β^0 denote the optimal values of these probabilities for the row and column players respectively. Therefore,

$$E(\pi_r^0) = -(\delta_1 + \delta_2)(1 - \beta^0) = \delta_1\beta^0 - (1 - \beta^0)(\delta_1 + \delta_2 + \delta_3), \tag{2}$$

giving the implication that

$$\delta_1\beta^0 = (1 - \beta^0)\delta_3,$$

which reduces to

$$\beta^0 = \frac{\delta_3}{\delta_1 + \delta_3}, \tag{3}$$

a number between zero and one. By symmetry, $\alpha^0 = \beta^0$. While δ_2, the loss of making a concession, does not affect the probability of so doing it does affect the expected return. Equation (3) implies that the probability of conflict, $1 - \beta^0$, is higher, the bigger the return from toughness that is δ_1.

Before going on to matrix 2, let us see what this theory says about the three equilibria, two of which are pure and the third mixed. The theory does not predict which will occur. However, it would be surprising to observe one party consistently gaining more than the other given the symmetry of their positions. The mixed equilibrium has the best credentials because it predicts the frequency with which each of the two pure equilibria will occur and it shows how the frequency depends on the components of the returns. Therefore it is the best candidate to guide empirical studies.

Matrix 2 depicts a different situation, one in which it is less costly to fight than to concede. The return to the row player is lower if he makes a concession than if he fights.

Column Player

Row Player		Concession	Tough
	Concession	$0, 0$	$-\delta_1 - \delta_2 - \delta_3, \delta_1$
	Tough	$\delta_1, -\delta_1 - \delta_2 - \delta_3$	$-\delta_1 - \delta_2, -\delta_1 - \delta_2$

MATRIX 2

Unlike the situation shown by matrix 1, for matrix 2 the optimal strategy for both players is always to fight.

Suppose the two players do not know which is the true matrix. This means they do not know which matrix correctly describes the world. There are two ways to interpret this. First, one may say that one matrix is true and the players begin with prior beliefs based on their experience. Eventually their beliefs solidify, and they find the true matrix. The second interpretation says that both matrices are true; sometimes it is one and sometimes the other. Nature chooses matrix 1 with probability θ and matrix 2 with probability $1 - \theta$. All any player can learn is the true probability governing the choice by Nature but not the actual choice itself. With enough experience the players can learn the true probability without ever knowing in advance which matrix applies to the current situation. I shall follow the second interpretation. Assume also that the players have learned the true probability, θ.

Simultaneously and in ignorance of which matrix is the choice of Nature, the players choose their strategies. In this case there is the ex ante matrix 3 as follows:

$$\text{Matrix } 3 = \theta \text{ matrix } 1 + (1 - \theta) \text{ matrix } 2. \tag{4}$$

The optimal strategies of the players refer to this matrix. Instead of the expression for the expected return to the row player given by equation (3) now there is

$$E(\pi_r) = \alpha\{0\beta - [\delta_1 + \delta_2 + (1 - \theta)\delta_3] (1 - \beta)\}$$
$$+ (1 - \alpha) [\delta_1\beta - (1 - \beta)(\delta_1 + \delta_2 + \theta\delta_3)]. \tag{5}$$

This expression differs from equation (1) in two places. First, the term showing the α-strategy has $\delta_1 + \delta_2 + (1 - \theta)\delta_3$ instead of $\delta_1 + \delta_2$. Second, in the term for the $(1 - \alpha)$-strategy, $\theta\delta_3$ replaces δ_3.

$\Pi(\Re)$

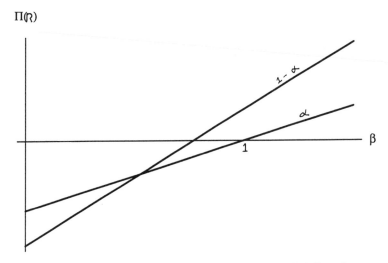

Fig. 25. Expected return to the row player and the probability of compromise by the column player

The equilibrium for matrix 3 differs markedly from either matrix 1 or matrix 2. The results for matrix 3 depend on the size of θ relative to 1/2. If $\theta \leq 1/2$ so that matrix 2 is not less probable than matrix 1 then toughness is optimal for each player and fighting is inevitable. However, if $\theta > 1/2$ then it is as if matrix 1 were true so there are two pure equilibria and one mixed equilibrium. Summarizing,

if $0 \leq \theta \leq 1/2$ then

$$E(\pi_r^0) = -(\delta_1 + \delta_2 + \theta\delta_3) \quad \text{and} \quad \beta^0 = 0; \tag{6}$$

if $1/2 < \theta$ then

$$E(\pi_r^0) = -(1 - \beta^0)[\delta_1 + \delta_2 + (1 - \theta)\delta_3] \tag{7}$$

and

$$\beta^0 = \delta_3 \frac{\theta - (1 - \theta)}{\delta_1 + \delta_3[\theta - (1 - \theta)]}. \tag{8}$$

Figure 25 shows the alternatives. The vertical axis is the return to the row player and the horizontal axis, the probability of compromise by the column player. The line segment labeled $1 - \alpha$ is the locus of return to the row player who chooses "tough" of matrix 3. The line segment labeled α is the locus of return if he chooses the first row of matrix 3, "concession." If $\theta = 1/2$ then the two lines intersect at the vertical axis and the equilibrium β, the probability of compromise, is zero as shown in equation (6). Therefore, there is always conflict for this case. If θ is below 1/2 then a fortiori conflict always dominates compromise. When $\theta > 1/2$ so that it is more probable that the world is represented by matrix 1 than by matrix 2 then the probability of compromise is positive as shown by where the two lines in the figure intersect. The probability of compromise is bigger, the more likely is matrix 1, that is, the bigger the θ. It is an implication of this theory that the probability of conflict is $(1 - \alpha^0)(1 - \beta^0)$ when $\theta > 1/2$. There is always conflict when $\theta \leq 1/2$.

This elaboration of the theory taking into account the players' beliefs about the state of the world gives predictions qualitatively similar to those for matrix 1. There are two pure equilibria and one mixed equilibrium. The latter is the more useful prediction of the theory because it not only shows the frequency of conflict but it also shows what this frequency depends on.

CHAPTER 5

The Agent's Incentive to Serve the Principal

1. Preamble

It is useful to classify organizations into two types, a hierarchy and an alliance. A hierarchy has the shape of a triangle in which those at the lower levels take orders from those at the higher levels and give orders to their subordinates. An alliance has the shape of a rectangle because its members are peers. The bulk of the preceding chapter analyzes the stability of an alliance in which the members make no direct payments to each other. The allies are supposed to do certain things for their common interest. If one ally is disloyal and does not do what he had promised then he can gain at the expense of the others. The loyalists cannot punish the disloyalists by imposing a direct financial penalty on them. Instead they must punish disloyalty by means of actions that impose a loss on a dishonest ally at the cost of losses to themselves. This chapter treats a different problem. Here a superior, the principal, wishes to furnish the subordinate, the agent, with incentives to do those things that advance the interests of the principal. Now the principal pays the agent directly so the problem of how to encourage good behavior and discourage bad behavior is in their agreement. The basic idea is simple. The agent gets paid more, the more he advances the interest of the principal. Surprisingly, making the payment a continuously increasing function of the agent's output does not have the desired effect, as we shall see. A two-part payment scheme can induce the appropriate behavior by the agent.

Reconsider the general setting. Several individuals combine to pursue a common goal. Their joint venture takes the form of a corporation, and each owns a part in proportion to his original investment. The owners delegate their authority to a smaller group—the board of directors—who will represent them and act accordingly. The board hires people who will do the things intended to attain the goal of the joint venture. These people, the managers, hire others to help them and to obey their orders. Step by step an elaborate structure is built up with layers of employees and with all the problems of overseeing, controlling, and directing the work of many individuals toward attaining the goal set by the owners and their direct representatives.

To assume there is such a structure seems to beg a question. A joint venture has other ways of attaining its goal without making an elaborate hierarchy. The market is the first that leaps to mind. Instead of layers in a single organization there are separate organizations, firms, that buy inputs from upstream entities and sell outputs to downstream entities. If the markets at every level have cores then an efficient equilibrium can emerge from competition among independent traders in these markets. A single vertically integrated organization would be superfluous. However, when a market at some level lacks a core then union into one coalition of the entities at that level and at surrounding levels can attain an efficient equilibrium. Given normal demand relations, the status of the core depends on the shapes of the cost curves of the entities at each level. For example, if there is a unique optimal scale for the units at some level then the market at that level would have no core. Chapter 7 studies these problems in detail. A combination of the units at the various levels into one firm can yield an efficient equilibrium when the markets at these levels would have no core. Therefore, a firm is an efficient alternative to entities that would like to be linked by competitive markets but cannot owing to empty cores. The firm is at the boundary of those activities it can control better than a market.

Compare the situation in which many individuals belong to a hierarchy to one in which one person aims at attaining his own goals. Knowing what he wants and how his actions will affect the chances of gratifying these wants, the individual will behave appropriately. He will try to avoid conflict between the effects of his actions and the attainment of his goals. The principal and the agent being one person, there can be no conflict between them. Robinson Crusoe alone on an island is the best-known example of this in English literature. When Friday arrived on the island, the principal–agent problem came with him. Two people on the island would be better off than each by himself because they could divide their work in ways that could obtain the benefits of specialization. Robinson Crusoe gave some tasks to Friday and had to ensure that these would be done properly without his constant supervision. Because Friday and Robinson Crusoe are different people, they need not have the same or consistent goals. Neither may know or even can know what the other wants or seeks. What is best for one is not necessarily best for the other. In the novel Robinson Crusoe must somehow induce Friday to cooperate with him so that Friday goes some way toward attaining his own goals by obeying Robinson Crusoe.

It is worthwhile pausing briefly now to consider the many situations where these problems arise and how they are solved. The principal may be the state and the agent an infantry platoon on the battlefield. The agents may be assigned tasks placing them in mortal danger. What induces the members of the platoon to obey orders? Is it patriotism, desire for fame, fear of punishment, avoidance of shame, bravado rooted in ignorance, training, hatred of the enemy, desperation, a mixture of some or all of these, or something entirely different? An extreme example is the kamikaze attacks at the end of World War II. Can "government" so motivate its employees that they will serve the "public"? Would the postal system provide the same services at lower cost if it were owned or operated by a private company? During World War II, the U.S. government did succeed in producing atomic bombs starting almost from scratch, an endeavor described as comparable to creating the entire then existing U.S. auto industry in about three years (Rhodes 1986, 605). What made Groves and Oppenheimer work so well as agents of the government in managing this huge enterprise?

Economics offers solutions to these problems on the hypothesis that individuals seek personal gain. In order to induce someone to help you, you must motivate him or reward him sufficiently. Either by persuading him to accept your goals or by giving him a suitable compensation when your goals differ, you can induce your agent to advance your interest. In the first case the agent and the principal are both better off because of what the agent does, and in the second case the principal must compensate the agent to obtain good work from him. The agent and the principal may have different skills and knowledge so that each does his own work better than the other. This may make it harder for the principal to obtain good work from the agent. For example, think of the agent who is a physician and the principal who is a patient ignorant of medicine.

Principal–agent relations also present many opportunities for fraud. Agents may shirk, steal, or malinger. Principals may cheat, lie, or renege. Each party must carefully watch the other and try to see whether promises are kept. When a violation is discovered, there must be suitable punishment. In this chapter a punishment is a reduction of the amount the principal pays the agent. The main problem is to figure out the relation between performance and payment.

This chapter studies various aspects of the principal–agent problem in an economic setting that is most relevant to joint ventures on the hypothesis that principals and agents are honest. There will be honesty if it costs the principal nothing to inspect the results of the actions of the agent. It means the agent cannot hide the results of his actions from the principal so that one kind of cheating cannot occur. Chapter 4, section 3 analyzes the problems that arise when it is costly for the principal to inspect the agent. In that case the best strategy for the principal is inspection at randomly chosen times, and likewise the agent's best strategy is cheating at randomly chosen times. The probabilities of these actions come from a noncooperative equilibrium if the principal and the agent independently choose the strategies that will maximize his expected profit.

We begin with an abstract version of the situation facing Robinson Crusoe as principal and Friday as agent. Next we consider the case with one principal and many agents. This case presents a new facet of the problem. Not only is there the problem of resolving conflict between the principal and the agent but there is also the problem of inducing many agents to cooperate in order to advance the interest of the principal.

The principal–agent problem raises an issue also present in the Coase theorem. That theorem poses two logically distinct questions that need separate answers. First, it poses an economic problem that must be studied to see if it is solvable. Second, there is the question of how to carry out the solution when there is one. A satisfactory analysis should state the conditions under which an economic problem has a solution with a description of how to implement it. It is tempting but wrong to say that if a solution does exist then it is always possible to find a way to carry it out. An example is helpful. Take the game of chess. It is a game of perfect information. A theorem of von Neumann asserts an optimal pure strategy exists for every game with perfect information, and so this is true for chess. However, knowing there is an optimal pure strategy does not reveal its nature or show us how to play a perfect game of chess. Closer to our interest, integer programming problems often occur in economic situations. These closely resemble a game of chess by virtue of the enormous number of alternative choices they have. Although almost always these integer programming problems have solutions, nobody knows what they are or how to find them. These problems raise complexity problems that are an active area of current research in computer science. The principal–agent problem also poses the same two questions. First, one must show whether an optimal solution exists. Second, one must show how to find it.

We shall consider two types of compensation schemes, profit sharing and a bonus paid if prescribed goals are met. The latter has several interpretations. One says when an employee will get a raise. The bonus resembles the present value of the raise. Another interprets a bonus as an option. The employee obtains an option such that his return is at one level if he meets a goal and is at a lower level if he does not. However, the return for successfully attaining the goal is a given reward not geared to the size of the goal. An important conclusion follows. There does exist an optimal bonus method of compensation, but there does not exist an optimal profit-sharing method of compensation. When there are several agents, bonuses exist such that the principal can induce the agents independently to choose strategies that will maximize their own profits. In this way a principal can induce an efficient noncooperative equilibrium from the agents. The principal can discover the optimal bonus by experimentation. Hence the analysis not only shows the existence of a method of payment that is optimal for the principal but it also shows how to find it.

Because optimal bonuses exist but optimal profit sharing does not exist, this raises the question of how to explain those instances in the economy, if there are any, in which it seems that profit sharing is present. One must be clear about the nature of the evidence that would contradict the theory herein. It does not refute the theory to see several individuals who share the total investment and the total profit. It would refute the theory that principals choose optimal compensation schemes to find an agent who invests nothing and still shares the profit with the principal.

2. Robinson Crusoe and Friday[1]

Let the gross return, r, depend on the input of the agent called x. The principal cannot observe directly the agent's input and does not know the nature of the relation between the gross return and the input, $r = R(x)$. This means the principal can see r but does not know how it depends on x. Hence the relation $R(x)$ is known to the agent but not to the principal. Assume the principal can observe the gross return ex post. Let the relation between the gross return and the agent's input be deterministic, not random, so the agent controls the outcome by choosing his input x. Assuming all this, we shall study the following problem. Can the principal devise a way of paying the agent that will induce him out of self-interest to choose that x which maximizes the net return to the principal? One answer this model allows is $x = 0$ so that the agent may quit. Thus the model also answers the question of whether the agent is willing to accept the terms of the principal.

Let the function R be strictly increasing and concave in x. Let $R(0) = 0$. Hence the principal knows when the agent quits or does not work. Let R be twice continuously differentiable. Therefore R_x is positive and decreasing because $R_{xx} < 0$. Let $P(x)$ denote the net return to the principal and $A(x)$ the net return to the agent.

Start with profit sharing as a way of paying the agent. The principal chooses the values of two parameters, k and θ. If the gross return is below k, the principal pays the agent the fixed amount a. If the gross return is at least k, then he pays the agent a plus an amount linearly proportional to the excess of the gross return over k. Therefore the principal and the agent share the excess of the return above k. Formally, the net return of the principal is as follows:

$$P(x) = R(x) - a \quad \text{if } R(x) < k$$
$$P(x) = k + (1 - \theta)[R(x) - k] - a \quad \text{if } R(x) \geq k. \qquad (1)$$

The agent has a cost, call it $W(x)$, known only to himself. It is an increasing, nonnegative, convex, and twice continuously differentiable function of the agent's input x. Hence $W_x(x) > 0$, $W_{xx}(x) > 0$, and $W(0) = 0$. The principal only knows that the cost to the agent goes up with his input. The net return to the agent is as follows:

$$A(x) = a - W(x) \quad \text{if } R(x) < k$$
$$A(x) = \max \{0, a + \theta[R(x) - k] - W(x)\} \quad \text{if } R(x) \geq k. \qquad (2)$$

Given this remuneration scheme, let the agent choose that x which maximizes his own return. This raises the possibility that the principal may be able to in-

---

1. Certain features of the payment scheme are related to those studied by Mirrlees (1976, sec. 3) and Holmstrom (1979 and 1982). Lazear and Rosen treat similar payment arrangements (1981, 855–56).

fer the true relation between r, which by hypothesis he can observe, and the parameters under his control, k and θ. Because the principal may be able to detect shirking or the like that the agent may wish to conceal, perhaps the agent would advance his self-interest more by maximizing an objective other than his true return. However, as we shall see, this would not serve the purpose of the agent. Therefore, we may study the implications of the agent's decision to maximize his true return and explain subsequently why this makes sense. Having introduced the constant a, it is apparent that setting $a = 0$ entails no loss of generality, so let us agree to this. I claim that profit sharing is not optimal for the principal.

At the outset several conclusions are plain. Because R is concave in x, R_x is decreasing. Let x_0 denote the root of the equation $R(x) - k = 0$. This gives the minimum input of x that can attain the goal set by the principal. Let x^* denote the optimal input of the agent so that x^* maximizes $A(x)$. The optimal input is either zero or positive. It is positive only if

$$\theta R_x(x_0) - W_x(x_0) > 0. \tag{3}$$

That is, from the definition of the agent's return given in (2), if

$$\theta R_x(x_0) - W_x(x_0) \leq 0$$

then $x^* = 0$, meaning that the agent would quit. The agent would work only if inequality (3) is true, so assume this. Given (3), the optimal x must satisfy

$$\theta R_x(x^*) - W_x(x^*) = 0. \tag{4}$$

Equation (4) shows the principal how his choice of θ and k affects his own return $P(\theta, k; x)$ without knowing x or the private cost of the agent. This raises two questions: first, is it optimal for the agent to choose that x which maximizes the true $A(x)$, and, second, what k and θ are optimal for the principal?

Start with the first question. Although the principal can see how r responds to his choice of k and θ, he cannot measure the true relation because he does not know and cannot discover the agent's private cost. Therefore, the agent cannot lose and surely gains by selecting that x which maximizes his true private return.

The second question refers to the optimal choice of θ and k by the principal. If the optimal x is positive so that the agent is working and $r \geq k$ then

$$P(\theta, k; x) = \theta k + (1 - \theta) R(x). \tag{5}$$

Take the partials of P with respect to θ and k as follows:

$$P_\theta = k - R(x^*) + (1 - \theta) R_x(x^*) \frac{\partial x^*}{\partial \theta}, \tag{6}$$

$$P_k = \theta + (1 - \theta) R_x(x^*) \frac{\partial x^*}{\partial k}. \tag{7}$$

Because x^* does not depend on k, it follows that $P_k = \theta$. If the optimal θ were positive then the optimal choice of k by the principal would be to make it as large as possible and the optimal response of the agent would be to quit. If the principal's optimal θ were zero, then again it would be optimal for the agent to quit. This proves that the profit-sharing formula given by (1) and (2) is not optimal for the principal.

Next consider a different scheme that rewards the agent if he attains the goal k set by the principal. Now the agent's net return is as follows:

$$A(x) = 0 - W(x) \quad \text{if } R(x) < k$$

$$A(x) = \max \{0, b - W(x)\} \quad \text{if } R(x) \geq k. \tag{8}$$

If the agent attains the goal set by the principal he gets a bonus b. The net return of the principal is

$$P(x) = R(x) \quad \text{if } R(x) < k$$

$$P(x) = R(x) - b \quad \text{if } R(x) \geq k. \tag{9}$$

The private cost to the agent of meeting the goal set by the principal is a minimum at $W(x_0)$. Even if the principal pays a bonus above $b_0 = W(x_0)$, the self-interest of the agent dictates the choice $x^* = x_0$. This means the best strategy of the agent is to select the smallest input that can attain the goal of the principal. The conclusion is this: the principal can be sure of obtaining $R = k$ and a nonnegative return only if $k - b \geq 0$.

The offer of a bonus raises the problem that the principal may cheat the agent by claiming falsely that the goal was not met. (See chap. 4, sec. 3 for more on this.) The agent has several defenses against this tactic. First, the agreement can be self-enforcing if it is recurrent. The agent can quit if he is cheated. The principal could cheat an agent once at most. Also a principal who cheats agents would incur the additional cost of replacing his victims. Depending on the cost of this and on how long it takes the principal to hire new agents, honesty may be best. Second, the bonus scheme may include third-party enforcement. In this case both sides agree in advance to accept the decision of a third party as arbitrator of their disputes. However, this would shift the problem of honesty to the shoulders of the arbitrator, whose livelihood may depend on having a steady stream of clients. Therefore, the competence and reliability of the arbitrator determine whether he can prosper or even survive in his work. Although the formal analysis does not explicitly assume a repeated situation, with a long enough horizon and the good reputation that can be built up, a principal may learn that honesty is best. Let us assume this from now on.

The claim is that there exists a principal-optimal bonus for a given k. Start with $b > b_0 = W(x_0)$, $k = R(x_0)$, and given k. Any bonus above the minimum needed to attain k is not optimal for the principal. This is because by lowering b, the principal could attain the goal k and lift his net return. In a sequence of iterations in which the principal makes offers to the agent who can accept or reject them, the principal can observe his profit from each and find the best bonus for each given goal. Hence the optimal bonus must just equal the minimal amount necessary to attain the prescribed goal and induce the agent to continue working. Therefore, the principal's optimal bonus must satisfy

$$b = W(x). \tag{10}$$

If so, $R(x) \geq k$ and $P(x) = R(x) - b$. The partial of P with respect to b is

$$P_b = R_x \frac{\partial x}{\partial b} - 1. \tag{11}$$

It follows from equation (10),

$$W_x \frac{\partial x}{\partial b} = 1 \Leftrightarrow \frac{\partial x}{\partial b} = \frac{1}{W_x}.$$

Therefore,

$$P_b \left\{ \begin{matrix} > \\ = \\ < \end{matrix} \right\} 0 \quad \text{according as } R_x \left\{ \begin{matrix} > \\ = \\ < \end{matrix} \right\} W_x. \tag{12}$$

Consequently, the best bonus for the principal and k satisfy.

$$R_x = W_x \quad \text{and} \quad R(x) = k. \tag{13}$$

This shows there is an optimal bonus given the goal k. This is a remarkable result. It says that although the principal cannot observe the private cost of the agent, he can still set the bonus at a level such that the marginal return, R_x, equals the private marginal cost of the agent given by equation (13).

Figure 26 does the analysis in another way. The vertical distance between R and W, the principal's profit, is a maximum where the slopes of the two curves are equal. This determines both the goal, k, and the bonus, b, that are optimal for the principal. A sequence of iterations for finding the maximum is straightforward.

Under the principal-optimal bonus scheme, even if the private cost of the agent is strictly convex, the agent would not get a surplus. The strict convexity of the private cost implies that $W_x x > W(x)$ while the surplus with the principal-optimal bonus is $b - W(x) = 0$. This raises a new point. It would serve the interest of the agent to allow the principal to see his input if the principal would agree to set a constant payment per unit of input. Thus, if the principal and the agent could agree on a return w per unit of input then at $w = W_x$ the agent would choose the input that would maximize the net return of the principal. At $w =$

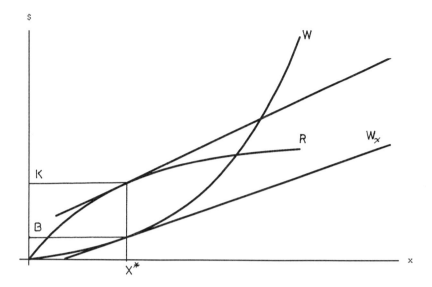

Fig. 26. Equilibrium bonus and the agent's goal

W_x, the agent would pick that input which maximizes the principal's profit and the agent would get a positive gain because $w \circ x = W_x \circ x > W$. However, the return to the principal would be smaller under this scheme because the agent would get more than if the principal were to pay a fixed bonus for attaining the goal k. We have now reached a well-known result describing the principal's best arrangement. The principal-optimal bonus corresponds to the profit-maximizing strategy of a monopsonist who presents his supplier with an all-or-none choice.

Formula (9) can be put in more familiar terms. It says that the principal pays the agent a bonus equal to b if the agent meets the goal k. Under a profit-sharing scheme the agent sets his own goal because he determines the gross profit by the choice of his own input. Under formula (9), the principal takes this power away from the agent. This induces the agent to choose that action which best advances the principal's interest. Since formula (9) can do this while formula (2) cannot, if principals do select optimal payment schemes, this is why bonuses are more common than profit sharing.

It is better to interpret the bonus scheme in another way. It shows when a principal will raise the salary of the agent. The raise can be considered as the return on the bonus, or, equivalently, the bonus can be considered as the present value of the raise.

3. One Principal and Many Agents

This theory also applies when the principal has several agents. The new problem it presents is this. How can the principal induce cooperation among the agents using a remuneration scheme that sets optimal bonuses for each of the agents? As we shall see, there is a unique noncooperative equilibrium that does this. This analysis also answers some objections to bonus schemes of Arrow (1985).

Two agents suffice to begin with. The net return to agent i, known only to himself, depends on his input x_i shown by the function $A_i(x_i)$. The gross return of the principal, r, depends on the inputs of both agents so that $r = R(x_1, x_2)$. The principal can observe the result, the gross return, r, but not the inputs of the agents nor the relation between r and these inputs. Hence the principal does not know the function $R(.)$. Assume as before that $R(.)$ is strictly increasing, concave, $R(0,0) = 0$, and that a positive return is possible even if only one agent works. Thus, $R(x_1, x_2) > 0$ if x_1 or $x_2 > 0$. It follows that the principal cannot infer from the gross return whether one agent is shirking. Of course, he knows when an agent quits. The gross return depends on the two individual inputs, not on their sum as would be true if the agent's inputs were perfectly substitutable. Each agent knows only his own private cost, and the principal knows neither. Let $W^i(x_i)$ denote the private cost of agent i. As in the preceding, let W^i be strictly increasing, twice continuously differentiable, convex and $W^i(0) = 0$. The counterpart to formula (2.8) is as follows:

$$A_i(x_i) = 0 - W^i(x_i) \quad \text{if } R(.) < k$$
$$A_i(x_i) = \max \{0, b_i - W^i(x_i)\} \quad \text{if } R(.) \geq k. \tag{1}$$

The net return of the principal is

$$P(x) = R(x) \quad \text{if } R(.) < k$$
$$P(x) = R(x) - \Sigma_i b_i \quad \text{if } R(.) \geq k. \tag{2}$$

Let $X_0(k)$ denote the set of inputs that can satisfy the principal's goal. It must be emphasized that the goal applies to the pair of agents and not to each individually.

$$X_0(k) = \{(x_1, x_2) \mid R(x_1, x_2) \geq k\}. \tag{3}$$

By virtue of the concavity of the function R, $X_0(k)$ is closed and convex. If the inputs of the agents were perfectly substitutable so that $r = R(x_1 + x_2)$ then $X_0(k)$ would be linear.

The claim is that there exists a pair of bonuses, given the goal for the team of agents, that can maximize the net profit of the principal and that can induce a unique noncooperative equilibrium for the agents. The principal chooses the

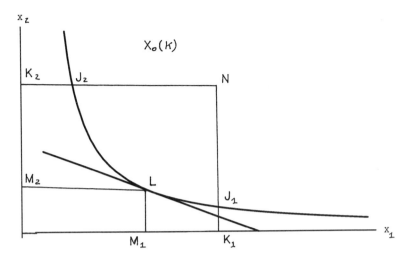

Fig. 27. Best bonuses for two agents

goal, k, for the pair of agents and the bonuses he pays each of them, b_i. The new feature in this situation is that the agents must cooperate in order to attain the goal set by the principal. However, depending on the circumstances, one agent can shirk and try to force the other to work enough to meet the goal set by the principal. The pertinent issues are best understood with the help of figure 27. In this figure, $X_0(k)$ is the convex set northeast of and including the curve $J_2 L J_1$. The minimal inputs that can attain the principal's goal are on the curve $J_2 L J_1$. The inputs of the agents are in the rectangle bounded by $K_2 N K_1$. These bounds are determined by the bonuses, b_i. Thus, given b_1, the maximum input of agent 1 is $W^1(b_1)^{-1}$, the inverse function of W. The locus of points $K_1 N$ corresponds to this upper bound. Similarly, for agent 2 the upper bound is $W^2(b_2)^{-1}$. Therefore, given the goal k and the bonuses b_i, the inputs must lie in the convex set $J_2 L J_1 N$. The agents' optimal choices are at the lower bound of this set. For agent 2 the best point is J_1 because it gives him the bonus b_2 at his least cost. If agent 2 could move first then he would choose the x_2 coordinate of J_1. As a result agent 1 could do no better than pick the x_1 coordinate of J_1. Moreover, given this choice by agent 1, agent 2's best response is the x_2 coordinate of J_1. Therefore, J_1 is a noncooperative equilibrium. On the other hand, J_2 is the best choice for agent 1. If agent 1 could move first he would pick the x_1 coordinate of J_2. The optimal choice of agent 2 would be the x_2 coordinate of J_2. Given this choice by agent 2, the best choice by agent 1 would be the x_1-coordinate of J_2. Hence J_2 is also a noncooperative equilibrium.

The two agents are in a noncooperative game. All the points on the curve J_2J_1 are noncooperative equilibria. To show this, take any input of one agent and calculate the net revenue-maximizing input of the other. Given the latter, find the net revenue-maximizing input of the former. The resulting pair of inputs is on the curve J_2LJ_1. Because there is a continuum of these non-cooperative equilibria, the outcome seems indeterminate. However, before accepting this conclusion, consider how the principal can affect the agents' choices.

There is a unique equilibrium if the principal chooses the bonuses and the goals optimally so that he maximizes his own net return. With such choices the principal can force the agents into a particular noncooperative equilibrium. Given k, the principal's optimal pair of bonuses must be on the curve $R(x_1, x_2) = k$. For the reasons given in section 2, we may confine our attention to that portion of the curve given by J_2LJ_1 because it includes the optimal point for the principal. The principal-optimal bonus pair is the solution of the following maximum problem:

$$\max R(x_1, x_2) - b_1 - b_2$$

with respect to b_1, b_2 subject to

$$b_1 = W^1(x_1) \quad \text{and} \quad b_2 = W^2(x_2). \tag{4}$$

The Lagrangian is

$$R(.) - b_1 - b_2 + \lambda_1[b_1 - W^1(x_1)] + \lambda_2 [b_2 - W^2(x_2)]. \tag{5}$$

Taking first-order partials with respect to the b's and x's,

$$-1 + \lambda_i = 0 \quad \text{and} \quad R_{x_i} - \lambda_i W^i_{x_i} = 0 \qquad i = 1, 2. \tag{6}$$

Therefore, the best choice of the b's for the principal satisfies

$$R_{x_i} = W^i_{x_i} \tag{7}$$

In figure 27, this optimum is the point L. By selecting b's optimally, the principal eliminates the indeterminacy and offers the unique noncooperative equilibrium point L to the two agents. The slope at L satisfies

$$\frac{R_{x_1}}{R_{x_2}} = \frac{W^1_{x_1}}{W^2_{x_2}}. \tag{8}$$

This result shows there is a pair of bonuses capable of supporting a unique non-cooperative equilibrium optimal for the principal given his goal, k. Moreover, even if the private costs of the agents are strictly convex functions of their inputs, they obtain no surplus under the principal-optimal bonus.[2]

It is also useful to consider some new features present when the return to the principal depends on the sum of the agents' inputs. This is when the agents' inputs are perfectly substitutable for each other. Because the term on the right-hand side of equation (8) represents the ratio $R_X/R_X = 1$, this equation becomes

$$\frac{W^1_{x_1}}{W^2_{x_2}} = 1, \tag{9}$$

$X = x_1 + x_2$, and $R_{x_i} = R_X$. In this case since $J_2 L J_1$ would be a straight line, the principal-optimal bonus is determined by the condition that the ratio of the private marginal costs is 1. However, in general the principal-optimal bonuses for the agents would be unequal. The situation resembles the analysis for a perfectly discriminating monopsonist (see sec. 2). Despite the linearity, by a suitable choice of the bonuses, the principal can still force the two agents into a unique noncooperative equilibrium. If the agents agree to reveal their inputs to the principal in exchange for payment linearly proportional to their inputs then the principal could pay the agents the same amount per unit input, w, in order to satisfy the necessary condition for maximizing his profit. Under this method of payment the agents would choose their inputs that maximize the profit of the principal, but the maximum would be lower than if the principal could offer each agent a particular take-it-or-leave-it bonus.

With two or more agents another feature enters the analysis—the possibility of cooperation among the agents so as to advance their joint interest against the principal. The best approach to this problem uses core theory. Let k denote the principal's goal set; let $r = R(x)$, $x = \{x_1, \ldots, x_n\}$; and let the return to the principal be an increasing, concave, twice continuously differentiable function of the inputs, x_i, of agent i. Let $b = \{b_1, \ldots, b_n\}$ denote the n-vector of the bonuses the agents obtain from the principal if they satisfy the goal, k, set by the principal. Agents may form coalitions and pay each other

---

2. "A Nash equilibrium of this game is for each individual to choose the appropriate action, a_i^* [$= x_i^*$ in the text], that is for each individual i, choosing a_i^* is optimal given the payoffs, providing each other individual, j, chooses a_j^*. But the proposed game is hardly satisfactory. It involves in effect collective punishment. More analytically, there are many Nash equilibria, of which $(a_1^*, \ldots, a_n^*)$ is only one. If some individuals shirk a little, it pays the others to work somewhat harder to achieve the same output. Hence the scheme does not enforce the optimal outcome, though it permits it" (Arrow 1985, 47).

As the text shows there is a principal-optimal bonus scheme that does enforce a unique Nash equilibrium. Hence it does meet one of Arrow's objections since it is unique. However, it also involves what he calls collective punishment, and he does not explain why he finds this objectionable.

amounts that can differ from the bonuses they receive from the principal. Let a = $\{a_1, \ldots, a_n\}$ denote the n-vector of returns to the agents resulting from competition among the coalitions for members who are agents of the principal. Let S be a subset of the n agents. For each coalition S, the members choose their inputs to solve the following maximum problem:

$$V(S) = \max \sum_{i \in S} [b_i - W^i(x_i)]$$

with respect to $x_i \in S$ subject to $R(x) \geq k$. The expression $V(S)$, the value of this objective, shows the security value of the coalition S assuming that everybody outside of S does it the most harm if they all shirk. The Lagrangian for this maximum problem is

$$\sum_{i \in S} [b_i - W^i(x_i)] + \lambda[R(x) - k].$$

If there is a maximum, the members of S must choose their inputs to satisfy

$$-W^i_{x_i} + \lambda R^i_{x_i} = 0$$

assuming the optimal inputs for all members of S are positive. This means nobody in S is a shirker. Call $x(S)$ the solution of this maximum problem.

There is a nonempty core if the n-vector a can satisfy the following inequalities:

$$\sum_{i \in S} a_i \geq V(S) \quad \forall S \subset N \quad \text{and} \quad \sum_{i \in S} a_i \leq V(N).$$

Here N denotes the set of all n agents. A sufficient condition for a nonempty core is plain. If every agent would have a smaller input as a member of the whole coalition N than as a member of any subcoalition of N then

$$a_i = b_i - W^i[x_i(N)]$$

is in the core. Moreover, the concavity of R together with the convexity of W^i implies that this sufficient condition for a nonempty core does hold. Therefore, there is the important conclusion that the coerced noncooperative equilibrium that is optimal for the principal is in the core for the group of n agents. Consequently, even if the agents form coalitions in order to raise their individual returns, they cannot do better than accept the terms offered by the principal.

4. Conclusions

I claim that bonus schemes are used more often than profit-sharing schemes owing to their advantages to the principal. Some may object that empirical evidence contradicts this assertion. Thus, high level executives own shares of stock in the company that employs them or have options to buy its stock. As stated previously, this does not mean their remuneration is a form of profit sharing. That executives have property rights in the firms that employ them does not refute my theory. It is true that the harmony of interest between executives and the owners of the firm is greater, the more shares the executives own in the firm. However, a more important reason explains ownership of shares or options by the company's executives. An executive may obtain shares or options to buy shares as a reward for achieving a goal. This is a much better way to align his interest with his employer. The bonus is usually much bigger than the capital gain the executive could receive from any action within his power to affect the company's profit. For instance, suppose an IBM executive owns 10,000 shares of stock in IBM that has a current market value of about $1,000,000. It is true that for each $1 rise in the price of an IBM share, the wealth of the executive would rise by $10,000. But 10,000 shares is a minor portion of the total number of IBM shares that may well accurately reflect how much this executive can influence the price per share of IBM stock as a result of his actions as an employee. Suppose, however, that his superiors set him a goal and promise him 10,000 shares of stock if he attains it. Is it not plain that he has an incentive worth $1,000,000 to make the attempt? The prospect of getting this bonus is a generous lure while ownership of the same amount of stock is not. Implicit in this argument is the view that shareholders know less about the incremental contributions of each company employee to its net revenue than do the supervisors of these employees.

CHAPTER 6

The Determination of Wages

1. Introduction

A firm can be regarded as a team of workers.[1] Let firms compete for workers with different productivities. A worker may leave one firm and work for another whenever it would advance his interest. The wages that result from this competition for workers are in the core of the market if no worker or group of workers can obtain higher wages for themselves. This concise description of a competitive labor market is in Frank Knight's *Risk, Uncertainty and Profit* (1921, 106–8) save that he did not say "in the core of the market." That Knight uses this approach is not surprising since he acknowledges his debt to Edgeworth (Knight 1921, n. 2, p. 82), who laid the foundations for core theory. Even Knight's later qualms (1934) about this approach do not diminish its attraction as a useful tool for studying the labor market.

Core theory illuminates a number of important yet neglected aspects of the labor market. First, a wage that results from competition need not be directly related to the productivity of the worker. A worker may receive a competitively determined wage that is below his incremental contribution to the firm that hires him. The distribution of competitively determined wages may be very different than the distribution of workers' productivities. Many different wage schemes may be in the core of the labor market, and all these are consistent with competition. This approach is especially useful for studying how specialization can raise productivity. According to Adam Smith in the *Wealth of Nations* ([1776] 1981, chap. 1 and Stigler [1951] (1968)), more division of labor enables greater production at a given total cost. Babbage's ([1835] 1971, chaps. 19–21) more elaborate analysis points out that there may be different optimal combinations of workers when their productivities differ. These combinations depend on how much of the commodity is wanted. Highly specialized workers are most valuable in firms big enough to utilize fully their special skills. This is an important source of increasing returns to scale. While large enough firms by virtue of their nonempty cores are stable, smaller ones may lack cores and be unable to survive.

The next section presents basic material on core theory and pertinent new

---

1. Matsumoto (1995) argues this is typical of Japanese firms.

results for labor markets. Of special interest is the distinction between the core as the set of undominated outcomes and the core as analyzed by Bondareva (1963). Her work leads to practical linear programming algorithms for calculating the points in the core. The section gives general necessary and sufficient conditions under which the two kinds of cores are equivalent.

Section 3 explains the meaning of an empty core in the labor market. Section 4 describes a production function for which the relative productivity of a worker does not depend on which firm he joins. For these production functions it is shown that there is a minimal firm size below which firms have no core and so could not survive. Section 5 derives many properties of these production functions.

Section 6 gives sufficient conditions for a nonempty core under two different wage schemes for the production function in Sections 4 and 5. In the first, the wage of a worker is proportional to his productivity. In the second it is proportional to his incremental contribution to the firm that hires him. When the firm is large enough both wage schemes are in the core. However, the minimal size of a firm that is stable in the sense of a nonempty core is smaller under the first wage scheme, wages proportional to productivity, than under the second scheme, wages proportional to the worker's incremental contribution. Wages proportional to productivity faithfully reflect it, but wages proportional to workers' incremental contributions to the firm do not. The density of wages is more skewed to the right than the density of productivity when wages are proportional to the worker's incremental contribution to the firm. Nor is this all. If wages are proportional to the workers' incremental contributions, the less productive workers get higher wages relative to their productivity than the more productive workers.

Section 7 studies more general production functions that allow the productivity of a worker to depend on the other workers. There is positive complementarity among the workers that diminishes with firm size. It is shown that a necessary condition for a stable firm in this case is stability of a firm with neutral complementarity. Neutral complementarity means the production function defined in the three preceding sections. Section 7 also describes the relation between the status of the core, the specialization of the workers, and the commodities that they make. Workers have many different skills in this model. By hiring suitable workers the firm forms a team with complementary skills able to make the commodities that require specific skills at the least total cost.

2. Core Constraints

The model has three elements:

    i. a set of n workers, $N = \{P_1, \ldots, P_n\}$, sometimes called the grand coalition;

ii. a characteristic function $V(.)$ defined for each subset of N giving the output of that subset;

iii. an n-vector $x = \{x_1, \ldots, x_n\}$ whose coordinates are the wages of each of the n workers.

The characteristic function $V(S)$ maps the subsets S of N into the nonnegative real numbers.[2] Workers may join a coalition or team S to make an output $V(S)$ that is the maximum which S can make using only its own resources. Coalitions compete for workers to join them. The n-vector of wages is the result of this competition. Let $\Phi(S)$ denote an n-vector called the *indicator function* that describes who belongs to the coalition S. If worker i belongs to S then the ith coordinate of $\Phi(S)$ is 1, and if worker i does not belong to S then the ith coordinate is 0. Thus all coordinates of $\Phi(N)$ are 1. For the coalition consisting of one worker, P_i, the indicator function is $\Phi(P_i)$, that has only one nonzero coordinate, the ith, which equals 1. The sum of the wages received by all the workers in the grand coalition N is the scalar product $\Phi(N)x$. Because $V(N)$ is the maximum total output, it imposes an upper bound on the total wage bill as follows:

$$\Phi(N)x \leq V(N). \tag{1}$$

Inequality (1) would make no sense as a constraint unless $V(N)$ were the maximum total output of the grand coalition. Workers can form teams and thereby can ensure themselves of a return given by the team's output. A team S would reject the wages it would receive under the vector x unless it were true that

$$\Phi(S)x \geq V(S). \tag{2}$$

---

2. For the applications herein it is reasonable to assume a nonnegative charactistic function which is not very restrictive.

DEFINITION. U and V are equivalent characteristic functions if they are related by a linear transformation such that

$$U(S) = \Phi(S)a + \beta V(S)$$

where $\beta > 0$ and a is an arbitrary n-vector.

THEOREM A.   *The status of the core is the same for equivalent superadditive characteristic functions.*

PROOF.   Let x be in the V-core so that $\Phi(S)x \geq V(S) \forall S \subset N$ and $\Phi(N)x \leq V(N)$. Let $y = \beta x + a$. Therefore, $\Phi(S)y \geq U(S)$ and $\Phi(N)y \leq U(N)$. Hence y is in the U-core. Conversely, by a similar argument if y is in the U-core then x is in the V-core.   QED

Given that U and V are equivalent, if V is individually superadditive then U can be assumed to be nonnegative. For singletons P_i, $U(P_i) = a_i + \beta V(P_i) = 0$ if $a_i = -\beta V(P_i)$. Hence $U(S) = \beta[V(S) - \Sigma_i V(P_i)] \geq 0$ if V is individually superadditive.

DEFINITION.   A vector x is in the Bondereva-core (abbreviated to the Bond-core) if it is feasible so that it satisfies inequality (1) and if it is acceptable to all proper subsets S of N, so that it satisfies inequality (2) for all $S \subset N$.

Depending on the nature of the characteristic function, perhaps no vector x is capable of satisfying inequalities (1) and (2). In this event the Bond-core is said to be empty.

Another way, indeed historically the first way, of describing the competitive process is in terms of domination. First, define the set A as follows:

$$A = \{x: \Phi(N)x = V(N) \quad \text{and} \quad \Phi(P_i)x \geq V(P_i)\}.$$

An x in A is called an *imputation*. It is group rational because the sum of the x's equals the upper bound, and it is individually rational because x_i is not less than the amount that individual P_i can assure himself, $V(P_i)$.

DEFINITION.   An imputation x is dominated by an imputation y if there is a coalition S such that $y_i > x_i$ for all P_i in S and y is feasible for S so that $\Phi(S)y \leq V(S)$.

An imputation x is in the First-core if it is undominated. This means there is no imputation y and no coalition S that can dominate an imputation x in the First-core.

DEFINITION.   The First-core is the set of all undominated imputations.

As one would expect, it turns out that these two different ways of defining the core are not only closely related but are also equivalent provided the characteristic function satisfies certain conditions. Before describing them, we have the next result valid for all characteristic functions.

LEMMA 1.   *The Bond-core is included in the First-core.*

PROOF.   By contradiction. Assume that x is in the Bond-core but suppose it is not in the First-core. There would be an imputation y and a coalition S such that y dominates x for all members of S and y is feasible for S. Formally,

$$y_i > x_i \quad \text{for all } i \in S \quad \text{and} \quad \Phi(S)y \leq V(S).$$

But then $\Phi(S)x < \Phi(S)y \leq V(S) \leq \Phi(S)x$, a contradiction.   QED

It follows from Lemma 1 that a *sufficient* but not a *necessary* condition for a nonempty First-core is a nonempty Bond-core. Because it is much easier to determine the status of the Bond-core than of the First-core by means of linear programming, this result is very useful.

The conditions on the characteristic function that imply equivalence between the two cores involve different types of superadditivity.

DEFINITION.

   i. $V(.)$ is superadditive if $V(R) + V(S) \leq V(R \cup S)$ for *all* disjoint subsets R and S of N;

ii. V is called weakly superadditive if $V(S) + V(N - S) \leq V(N)$ for all subsets S of N;

iii. V is called individually superadditive if for all subsets S of N, $V(S) \geq \Sigma_{i \in S} V(P_i)$;

iv. V is called individually N-superadditive if $V(N) \geq \Sigma_{i \in N} V(P_i)$.

Every superadditive function is both weakly and individually superadditive. If V is individually superadditive then the individuals who join to form a coalition S are collectively not worse off than they would be as separate individual coalitions, that is, as singletons. Individual superadditivity does not imply either superadditivity or weak superadditivity. Weak superadditivity does not imply superadditivity. Finally, individual N-superadditivity does not imply individual superadditivity. Examples of all these assertions appear subsequently.

LEMMA 2. *If the Bond-core is not empty then the characteristic function must be weakly superadditive.*

PROOF. By hypothesis there is an x such that for all S in N,

$$V(N) \geq \Phi(N)x = \Phi(S)x + \Phi(N - S)x \geq V(S) + V(N - S). \qquad \text{QED}$$

This means that weak superadditivity is necessary for a nonempty Bond-core. Simple examples show that it is not a sufficient condition.

DEFINITION. A partition of N is a set of nonoverlapping subsets of N, $\{S_j \mid j = 1, \ldots, k\}$, such that each P_i belongs to at least one S_j and none belongs to more than one. Hence

$$\Phi(N) = \sum_{j=1}^{k} \Phi(S_j).$$

COROLLARY. *If the Bond-core is not empty then $V(N) \geq \Sigma_j V(S_j)$ for every partition $\{S_j\}$ of N. In particular, V must be individually N-superadditive.*

PROOF. By hypothesis there is an x in the Bond-core. Therefore, for any partition $\{S_j\}$ of N,

$$V(N) \geq \Phi(N)x = \sum_{j} \Phi(S_j)x \geq \sum_{j} V(S_j).$$

Take the partition of N into singletons and it follows that V must be individually N-superadditive. Equivalently, individual N-superadditivity is necessary for a nonempty Bond-core. QED

Neither superadditivity nor individual superadditivity is necessary for a nonempty Bond-core.

LEMMA 3. *Let V be individually and weakly superadditive. Every imputation in the First-core is in the Bond-core.*[3]

PROOF.   By contradiction. Assume x is in the First-core and suppose it is not in the Bond-core. Then there would be a coalition S such that $\Phi(S)x < V(S)$. Let m_S denote the number of members of S. Choose y_i according to the following scheme:

i. $P_i \in S \Rightarrow y_i = x_i + \dfrac{V(S) - \Phi(S)x}{m_s}$;

ii. $P_i \in N - S \Rightarrow y_i = V(P_i) + \dfrac{\left[V(N) - V(S) - \displaystyle\sum_{j \in N-S} V(P_j) \right]}{n - m_s}$.

We must show that y would be an imputation that dominates the imputation x via the coalition S. This requires y to satisfy the following three conditions:

a. $P_i \in S \Rightarrow y_i > x_i$ and $\Phi(S)y = V(S)$;
b. $P_i \in N - S \Rightarrow y_i \geq V(P_i)$;
c. $\Phi(N)y = V(N)$.

Since $\Phi(S)x < V(S)$, the definition of y_i when $P_i \in S \Rightarrow y_i > x_i$. Because x is an imputation it also follows that $y_i > V(P_i)$. Here $\Phi(S)y = \Phi(S)x + V(S) - \Phi(S)x$. Hence condition a is satisfied. To verify condition b it suffices to show that

$$V(N) - V(S) - \sum_{j \in N-S} V(P_j) \geq 0. \tag{3}$$

By hypothesis, $V(.)$ is weakly superadditive so that

$$V(N) - V(S) \geq V(N - S) + V(S) - V(S) = V(N - S).$$

By individual superadditivity, $V(N - S) \geq \Sigma_{i \in N-S} V(P_i)$. Consequently, inequality (3) is true so condition b is true. Next,

$$\Phi(N)y = \Phi(S)y + \Phi(N - S)y = V(S) + \Phi(N - S)y \quad \text{and}$$

$$\Phi(N - S)y = V(N) - V(S)$$

gives the implication that $\Phi(N)y = V(N)$. Therefore, y is an imputation that dominates x contradicting the hypothesis that x is in the First-core.   QED

---

3. These results are slightly more general than Aumann's Lemma 6.3 (1989) because they impose somewhat weaker conditions on the characteristic function than his hypothesis of superadditivity.

The hypothesis of weak superadditivity is indispensable for this result. Aumann (1989, 112) gives an example of a characteristic function that is not weakly superadditive and that has an imputation in the First-core which is not in the Bond-core.

The main result is

THEOREM 1.   *Let the characteristic function be individually and weakly superadditive. Then the Bond-core and the First-core coincide.*

PROOF.   By Lemma 1, the Bond-core is included in the First-core. The hypotheses imply that Lemma 3 applies, which asserts the First-core is included in the Bond-core.   QED

There will be no ambiguity from now on if we simply refer to the core and drop the distinction between the Bond-core and the First-core when the properties of the characteristic function allow this.

One can determine the status of the core by studying solutions of a certain linear programming problem. Let x satisfy inequality (1). For each coalition S define the difference d_S as follows:

$$d_S = V(S) - \Phi(S)x.$$

If $d_S \leq 0$ then the members of the coalition S would be no worse off accepting $\Phi(S)x$ than by making the output $V(S)$ by themselves. However, if d_S is positive then the coalition S would be worse off by accepting $\Phi(S)x$ than by producing $V(S)$. An empty core means that for any globally feasible x, namely, any x that satisfies inequality (1), there is some S such that $d_S > 0$. We exploit this fact by solving a linear programming problem that finds points in the core when the core is not empty and comes as close as possible to satisfying the core constraints when the core is empty. This linear programming problem, call it the A-problem, finds the x that minimizes the maximal d_S. The primal for the A-problem is min α with respect to x and $\alpha \geq 0$ subject to

$$V(S) - \Phi(S)x = d_S \leq \alpha$$

$$\Phi(N)x \leq V(N). \tag{4}$$

The Lagrangian for this minimum problem is

$$\alpha + \sum_S \delta_S[V(S) - \Phi(S)x - \alpha] + \delta_N[\Phi(N)x - V(N)],$$

where δ_S and $\delta_N \geq 0$ are the Lagrangian multipliers. A solution of this linear programming problem must satisfy

$$1 - \sum_S \delta_S \geq 0$$

$$\delta_N \Phi(N) - \sum_S \delta_S \Phi(S) = 0. \tag{5}$$

The first necessary condition in (5) is an inequality because α must be nonnegative while the second condition in (5) is an equation because there is no sign restriction on x. Note that according to the first constraint in (4) for the singleton P_i there is

$$\Phi(P_i)x + \alpha \geq V(P_i).$$

This means that individual rationality is not imposed as a constraint in the A-problem. Therefore it seems that some individual P_i could obtain a return below the amount he could produce by himself, $V(P_i)$, if the solution of the A-problem gives a positive α. We shall reconsider these issues subsequently.

The dual of the A-problem is as follows:

$$\max \sum_S \delta_S V(S) - \delta_N V(N)$$

with respect to δ_S and $\delta_N \geq 0$ subject to (5). Under the hypothesis that $V(S)$ is nonnegative, the constraints of the primal and dual problems are feasible. Therefore the duality theorem of linear programming applies and yields the following conclusion:

$$\max \sum_S \delta_S V(S) - \delta_N V(N) = \min \alpha.$$

The next result is immediate.

THEOREM 2.   *The Bond-core is not empty if and only if min $\alpha = 0$.*

The next lemma describes some properties of solutions of the A-problem.

LEMMA 4.

   i. If min $\alpha = 0$ then every solution of the A-problem is individually rational.
   ii. Let $V(S) > 0$ for all S. If min $\alpha > 0$ then $\Phi(N)x = V(N)$.

PROOF.   The first assertion is obvious from the singleton constraint $x_i + \alpha \geq V(P_i)$ taking $\alpha = 0$.
ii. Because min $\alpha > 0$ and $V(S) > 0$ by hypothesis, it follows that at least one $\delta_S > 0$ so that $\delta_N > 0$. Therefore the second constraint in (4) must be an equality.   QED

Lemma 4, Part ii, says that if the Bond-core is empty then total wages must equal the upper bound so there is group rationality but not necessarily individual rationality. Lemma 4, Part i, says that if the Bond-core is empty then there must be individual rationality but not necessarily group rationality. The question of when $\alpha = 0$ implies group rationality is settled by Theorem 4, which follows.

Because individual rationality is not imposed by the constraints of the A-problem it is worthwhile to consider what would happen if it were a constraint. Change the A-problem to include individual rationality as a constraint so that x must satisfy

$$\Phi(P_i)x \geq V(P_i)$$

in addition to the constraints (4). If the A-problem has a solution then

$$V(N) \geq \Phi(N)x = \sum_{i=1}^{n} \Phi(P_i)x \geq \sum_{i=1}^{n} V(P_i).$$

This inequality would be true if and only if the characteristic function is individually N-superadditive. Consequently if individual rationality were imposed as a constraint on the A-problem then a solution could not exist unless the characteristic function were individually N-superadditive so that the total output of the whole group is not less than the sum of the outputs of the individual members of the group. This establishes the

COROLLARY. *If in addition to the constraints (4) the solution of the A-problem must be individually rational then a necessary condition for the existence of a solution is that the characteristic function be individually N-superadditive.*

Individual rationality is a very appealing postulate. It is hard to see why any individual would willingly accept a return below what he could assure himself acting alone if joining a group is a voluntary action.

Next we investigate under what conditions a solution of the A-problem gives a nonempty core and there is group rationality so that the sum of the x's is as large as possible. Since there is individual rationality when the core is not empty, if in addition there is group rationality, it would follow that the solution of the A-problem would be an imputation. In order to study this problem let us introduce a second linear programming problem, the B-problem. The primal for the B-problem is defined as follows:

$$\min \Phi(N)y \tag{6}$$

with respect to y subject to

$$\Phi(S)y \geq V(S) \quad \forall S \subset N.$$

The Lagrangian for this primal problem is

$$\Phi(N)y + \sum_{S} \eta_S[V(S) - \Phi(S)y],$$

where $\eta_S \geq 0$ are the Lagrangian multipliers. A solution of the B-problem must satisfy

$$\Phi(N) - \sum_S \eta_S \Phi(S) = 0. \tag{7}$$

The dual of the B-problem is

$$\max \sum_S \eta_S V(S)$$

with respect to $\eta_S \geq 0$ subject to equation (7). Because both the primal and dual constraints of the B-problem are feasible, the duality theorem of linear programming aplies and gives the conclusion that

$$\min \Phi(N)y = \max \sum_S \eta_S V(S). \tag{8}$$

Therefore, the Bond-core is not empty if and only if

$$\min \Phi(N)y = \max \sum_S \eta_S V(S) \leq V(N). \tag{9}$$

THEOREM 3.   *Let $V(S) > 0$ for all S. Assume the Bond-core is not empty. The dual of the A-problem has a nontrivial solution with $\delta_N > 0$ if and only if $\min \Phi(N)y = V(N)$.*

PROOF.   Given $V(S) > 0$ for all S and a nonempty Bond-core so that $\alpha = 0$, the dual A-problem has a nontrivial solution if and only if $\delta_N > 0$. Therefore the second constraint of (5) can be written

$$\sum_S \frac{\delta_S}{\delta_N} \Phi(S) = \Phi(N).$$

Hence $\eta_S = \delta_S/\delta_N$ satisfies equation (7) for the B-problem and

$$0 = \alpha = \sum_S \delta_S V(S) - \delta_N V(N) \Rightarrow \sum_S \eta_S V(S) = V(N).$$

Conversely, if $\min \Phi(N)y = V(N)$ then by means of the substitutions,

$$\delta_S = \frac{\eta_S}{\sum_R \eta_R} \quad \text{and} \quad \delta_N = \frac{1}{\sum_R \eta_R} \tag{10}$$

in equation (7), there is an implication of a nontrivial solution of the dual A-problem.   QED

When $\min \Phi(N)y < V(N)$, the dual A-problem has only trivial solutions so that $\delta_S = \delta_N = 0 \ \forall S$. Even so one may still make the substitutions given by equation (10) using the values of η from the solution of the dual B-problem. Thus

$$\delta_S^* = \frac{\eta_S}{\displaystyle\sum_R \eta_R} \quad \text{and} \quad \delta_N^* = \frac{1}{\displaystyle\sum_R \eta_R}$$

would satisfy the dual constraints (5) for the A-problem but would violate the nonnegativity of α. Hence the solution given by the dual variables of the B-problem would not be a solution for the dual A-problem.

Although Theorem 3 shows that a solution of the primal A-problem may fail to satisfy group rationality when there is a core, provided the characteristic function is individually superadditive, a solution of the A-problem will be an imputation. The next theorem shows this.

THEOREM 4.   *Let $V(S) > 0$ for all S, let V be individually superadditive, and let min $\alpha = 0$. Then the A-problem has a solution x such that $\Phi(N)x = V(N)$ so that x is group rational.*

PROOF.   The hypothesis implies a nonempty Bond-core because min $\alpha = 0$. Hence by Lemma 2 the characteristic function must be weakly super-additive. It is individually superadditive by hypothesis. Hence by Theorem 1 the Bond-core and the First-core coincide. Therefore every x in the First-core is an imputation that belongs to the Bond-core. For each x, $\alpha = 0$, so it is a so-lution of the A-problem.   QED

The next result describes some properties of an empty core.

THEOREM 5.   *Assume the core is empty and let the coalitions $C = \{S_j : j = 1, \ldots, m\}$ satisfy the constraints of the solution of the primal A-problem with equality so that*

$$\Phi(S_j)x + \alpha = V(S_j), \qquad j = 1, \ldots, m \quad \text{and} \quad \Phi(N)x = V(N). \tag{11}$$

Either V is not superadditive or C is not a partition.

PROOF.   The dual constraints (5) are $\sum_j \delta_j = 1$ and $\sum_j \delta_j \Phi(S_j) = \delta_N \Phi(N)$. Suppose C were a partition so that $\Phi(N) = \sum_j \Phi(S_j)$. Since the core is empty, $\delta_N > 0$, and it would follow that $\delta_j = \delta_N$. Hence

$$0 < \alpha = \sum_j \delta_j V(S_j) - \delta_N V(N) = \delta_N \left[\sum_j V(S_j) - V(N) \right]$$

giving the implication that V is not superadditive. Therefore, if V is superaddi-tive then C cannot be a partition, given that the core is empty.   QED

Say there is no core and the characteristic function is superadditive. Con-sequently, a solution of the A-problem implies some individual belongs to more than one of the coalitions in C, but this is not a hallmark of an empty core. Even with a nonempty core the coalitions in C need not form a partition.

The incremental contribution of P_i to the grand coalition N is $\Delta V(P_i) = V(N) - V(N - P_i)$. We seek the relation between x_i, the return to P_i, and $\Delta V(P_i)$. Assume the core is empty so that $\alpha > 0$ implying that $\Phi(N)x = V(N)$. For $N - P_i$, $\Phi(N - P_i)x \geq V(N - P_i) - \alpha$ so that

$$\Phi(N)x - \Phi(P_i)x \geq V(N - P_i) - \alpha \Rightarrow V(N) - V(N - P_i) + \alpha \geq x_i.$$

This means x_i cannot exceed the incremental contribution $\Delta V(P_i)$ plus α. Since the latter is positive when there is an empty core, P_i could get more than his incremental contribution. This cannot happen when there is a nonempty core. In this case

$$\Phi(N)x \leq V(N) \quad \text{and}$$

$$\Phi(N - P_i)x \geq V(N - P_i) \Rightarrow x_i \leq V(N) - V(N - P_i).$$

The status of the core shows whether the grand coalition can offer wages to the individuals capable of meeting competitive offers from constituent coalitions. Individuals will remain members of the grand coalition only if their returns are at least as good as their best alternative. According to the interpretation that $V(S)$ is the total production of a team of workers, S, the grand coalition N can survive only if it can pay S at least as much as it can produce. The n individuals would not remain in the grand coalition unless N can produce at least as much as any division of itself into two coalitions, S and its complement, $N - S$. Therefore, the n individuals would have no incentive to form N unless the production function is weakly superadditive. Moreover, they would have no incentive to form any S whatever unless S can produce more than the sum of the outputs of its individual members. Therefore, individual superadditivity is necessary for the formation of any team S. The grand coalition cannot survive unless the production function is both weakly and individually superadditive. These are necessary, not sufficient, conditions for the survival of N. When they apply in a strict sense, all the n individuals do have an incentive to work together in the team N. Suppose the production function meets these necessary conditions and the core is empty. The solution of the A-problem determines a minimum tax, α, that can maintain the grand coalition as a stable entity and preserves as much competition as is possible for an empty core. It does this by placing a tax on each coalition. If a coalition S forms then it cannot demand $V(S)$ but instead it can demand only the smaller amount $V(S) - \alpha$. This means a coalition S can secede from the grand coalition N only by paying a tax equal to α. The solution of the A-problem determines the smallest possible tax that is compatible with an empty core. The solution also determines the vector of wages that emerges from competition among all possible coalitions S who can threaten to leave the grand coalition N unless their total receipts are at least as large as

$V(S) - \alpha$. The wages given by this solution are feasible because they do not exceed the total production of the grand coalition. An individual P_i receives w_i, which is the ith coordinate of the w given by a solution of the A-problem. However, no coalition does pay the tax α because each is better off by staying in the grand coalition than by leaving it. In this fashion the solution of the A-problem gives a vector of competitive wages w that is an imputation and a minimum tax α that enables the group N to survive. However, if the production function were not weakly or individually superadditive, the individuals would not agree on the rules that underlie the competition given by the A-problem. Nor is this all. Given that the production function is individually superadditive, individual rationality may be imposed as a constraint on the primal A-problem while preserving the existence of solutions to the A-problem.

3. Significance of an Empty Core

When the core is empty the grand coalition is unstable because there is always at least one subcoalition that can do better on its own than by staying in the grand coalition. This is true no matter what distribution of the total output the grand coalition proposes. Although $V(N)$ is the maximum amount the grand coalition can produce, it may seem that the individuals can obtain a bigger return by forming the coalitions $\{S_j\}$ determined by the constraints that must be satisfied with equality by the solution of the B-problem. This seems possible because the solution of the dual B-problem satisfies the inequality $\sum_j \eta_{S_j} V(S_j) > V(N)$ when the core is empty. This section shows that the return $\sum_j \eta_{S_j} V(S_j)$ is *not* feasible for $\sum_j \eta_{S_j} \Phi(S_j) = \Phi(N)$.

Rewrite the dual constraints for the B-problem as follows:

$$\sum_S \eta_S \Phi(S) = \Phi(N). \tag{1}$$

Say that the nonnegative dual variable η_S describes the fraction of his time that an individual member of the coalition S spends working for it. Equation (1) means that the sum of these fractions is one for each individual in N. An individual is a whole person and cannot be present in more than one coalition at the same time. Therefore, it is physically impossible to produce the total output given by $\sum_j \eta_{S_j} V(S_j)$, the solution of the dual B-problem. The following example shows why.

Consider the 3-person situation for which the characteristic function is as follows.

$$V(P_i) = 0, \qquad V(P_i, P_j) = 1 \quad \forall P_i, P_j, \qquad i \neq j, \qquad \text{and}$$

$$V(P_1, P_2, P_3) = 1.$$

This characteristic function is superadditive so the necessary condition for forming the grand coalition is satisfied. It is not hard to verify that the solution of the dual B-problem is $\eta_S = 1/2$ for all 2-person coalitions S. The value of the objective given by the solution of the dual B-problem is $3/2 > V(P_1, P_2, P_3) = 1$. Hence there is an empty core. According to the solution of the dual B-problem, it seems that each person should spend half his time with each of a certain pair of 2-person coalitions. Thus, P_1 should spend half his time with the two coalitions (P_1, P_2) and (P_1, P_3), P_2 should spend half his time with the two coalitions (P_1, P_2) and (P_2, P_3), and, finally, P_3 should spend half his time with the two coalitions (P_1, P_3) and (P_2, P_3). The two members of a coalition to which they have been assigned must both be present at the same time so that they can work together simultaneously. Thus the available times for the three individuals are as follows:

P_1 1st half day   2d half day
P_2 1st half day   2d half day.
P_3 1st half day   2d half day

If P_1 and P_2 work together in the morning while P_1 and P_3 work together in the afternoon, then there is no common time available for P_2 and P_3. Consequently, the arrangement suggested by the solution of the dual B-problem is physically impossible. This means the total output 3/2 is not attainable. But then one may ask why there is an implication of an empty core. The answer is that each 2-person coalition *can* produce one unit of output and will refuse to join the grand coalition of the 3 persons unless it gets a return of 1 unit. This demand is feasible for each 2-person coalition but cannot be gratified by the 3-person coalition. Hence there is an implication of an empty core.

4. The Production Function

This section describes a particular production function based on some reasonable assumptions about complementarities among the workers in a team that makes a single commodity. Let p_i, a positive number, denote the productivity of worker P_i. When working alone, it is the output of the worker. When working in a team, p_i measures the relative effect on the output of the team of that worker. Assume that the relative effect is independent of the composition of the team. Let $F(S)$ denote the production function of the team S. The assumption that the relative effect on the total output of a team from the addition of P_i does not depend on who is in the team implies that

$$\frac{F(S, P_i)}{F(S)} = p_i. \tag{1}$$

Therefore, the production function is

$$F(S) = \prod_{i \in S} p_i. \tag{2}$$

Since $p_i > 0$, there is positive complementarity among the workers in the team.

We now derive necessary and sufficient conditions for the various kinds of superadditivity for this production function.

LEMMA 1.   *The production function $F(S)$ defined in equation (2) is*

a. weakly superadditive only if $p_i \geq 1$;
b. superadditive if and only if $(p_i - 1)(p_j - 1) \geq 1$ for all i and j;
c. superadditivity and individual superadditivity are equivalent for $F(S)$.

PROOF.   Let $\Pi_S \equiv \Pi_{i \in S} \, p_i$. With this notation, weak superadditivity entails

$$\prod_N \geq \prod_S + \prod_{N-S} \quad \forall S \subset N. \tag{3}$$

The next identity is readily verified.

$$\left(\prod_S - 1 \right)\left(\prod_{N-S} - 1 \right) \equiv \prod_N - \prod_S - \prod_{N-S} + 1.$$

From this identity it follows that weak superadditivity is equivalent to

$$\left(\prod_S - 1 \right)\left(\prod_{N-S} - 1 \right) \geq 1 \quad \forall S \subset N. \tag{4}$$

Assertion a says that inequality (4) is true only if $p_i \geq 1$. Suppose not, so that $p_i < 1$. By hypothesis $F(.)$ is weakly superadditive so inequality (4) holds. Take $S = P_i$ and it would follow that $p_i - 1 < 0$ and $\Pi_{N-S} < 1$, giving a contradiction of inequality (4). Hence assertion a is true.

b. Take any pair P_i and P_j. Superadditivity requires that

$$(p_i - 1)(p_j - 1) \geq 1 \tag{5}$$

so inequality (5) is necessary for superadditivity. To prove this condition is also sufficient, assume inequality (5) holds for all pairs. Hence at most one member of the pair can have $p < 2$ and, of course, $p \geq 1$ given that inequality (5) is true. However, at most one p out of all the n p's can be less than 2 since otherwise inequality (5) would be false. Therefore, for any pair of coalitions, R and S, each excluding the one P whose $p < 2$, it follows that

$$\left(\prod_R - 1 \right)\left(\prod_S - 1 \right) \geq 1$$

because all the p's in these coalitions are bounded below by 2. But then this inequality is also true if one of the two coalitions does include the P with p between 1 and 2. Therefore there is superadditivity as claimed.

c. There is individual superadditivity only if inequality (5) holds for all pairs. By condition b, inequality (5) implies superadditivity. Hence individual superadditivity implies superadditivity. The converse is obvious since superadditivity is equivalent to inequality (5) that implies individual superadditivity.

QED

According to Theorem 2.1, the Bond-core and the First-core are equivalent if there is both weak and individual superadditivity. In the present application, individual superadditivity is equivalent to superadditivity, but the production function is not necessarily weakly superadditive. Nor is this all. It is not necessarily individually superadditive even if it is weakly superadditive. Therefore the production function $F(S)$ defined by equation (2) need not yield equivalence between the Bond-core and the First-core. Even so, Lemma 2.1 says that because the Bond-core is included in the First-core, a nonempty Bond-core is *sufficient* for a nonempty First-core. It is also true that points in the Bond-core are undominated so they possess all the desirable properties of the core. These facts justify our interest in the status of the Bond-core.

The results in Lemma 1 verify the claim that superadditivity of the production function depends on the sizes of the p's. Figure 28 shows this. The curve DE is the hyperbola marking the lower boundary of the locus of points p and q for which the production function would be additive so that condition (6) would hold with equality. The hyperbola must pass through the point (2, 2). Its asymptotes are the lines AB and AC that intersect at (1, 1).

$$(p - 1)(q - 1) \geq 1. \tag{6}$$

Any pair in the shaded region satisfies condition (6) with strict inequality and so implies strict superadditivity.

It is tempting to believe that specialization is the source of superadditivity. The total output of a group of workers is bigger if each one specializes in some of the whole job than if everyone does all of it. Adam Smith argues this forcefully in the very first chapter of his *Wealth of Nations*. He gives three reasons for gains from specialization even if all workers are equally able. First, workers spend less time changing from one task to another so that more time is available for productive activities. Second, labor confined to simple tasks can become more proficient. Third, machines are more readily improved and new ones more likely to be invented, the simpler the tasks they perform.

The production function defined in equation (2) implies the output is biggest given the mean value of the p's when all the p's are equal. This does not contradict the proposition that more specialization can raise total production. Increased specialization means a bigger *average p,* not a bigger *dispersion* of the p's.

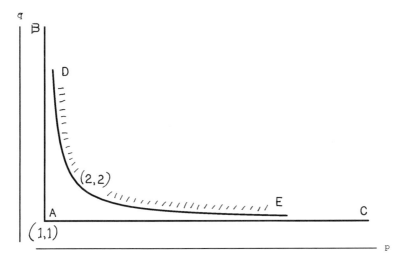

Fig. 28. Relation between superadditivity of the worker's production functions and their abilities

Let two equally able workers join forces so they make the total output p^2. By remaining separate their total output would be $2p$. They gain by working together if p^2 is bigger than $2p$, which is true if and only if $p > 2$. However, two disparate workers can gain by working together even if one of the p's is below 2. Inequality (6) can hold if $1 < q < 2$ when p is big enough. However, inequality (6) cannot hold when both p and q are between 1 and 2. The production function $F(S)$ shows that teams of workers can become more productive even when the individual members are not very productive owing to the presence of a few highly productive members. When abilities differ, a worker always prefers to join workers more productive than himself. With a nonempty core the more able worker must receive a high enough return that reflects his contribution to any coalition that he joins. In its present version this model explains the larger production of a team as due to the augmentation of the output of the less able by the more able members of the team.

It would be wrong to conclude that increasing specialization has unlimited power to explain why mean output per person rises as the size of the group increases. True as specialization increases it does allow the productive employment of those with less ability on more narrowly circumscribed activities. However, there are offsetting factors. Coordination becomes more costly as specialization increases. It also becomes more costly to detect and reduce malfeasance and shirking in groups big enough to take advantage of more specialization.

Another element also enters and lowers the return from specialization if the desired output is prone to unpredictable change. Highly specialized workers may lack the skill and flexibility to adapt easily to random shocks. The cost of using specialized workers outside the narrow range of their particular competence is often much higher than it is within the range best suited to their skills. Less specialized workers may be more costly in a narrower range but less so in a wider range. Therefore, depending on the sizes of the random disturbances the optimal arrangement may employ less specialized and more adaptable workers (Stigler 1939).

Adam Smith believed that the market could coordinate the activities of specialized producers. He even proposed that specialization is limited by the extent of the market. However, within the firm, indeed, within Adam Smith's pin factory, the market is no guide to the activities of the specialized workers. It is the supervisors and foremen who arrange the tasks and oversee the work. The better is the market as a coordinating tool, the less the need for the firm. The extent of the firm is limited by the failure of the market.

5. Some Specific Results

This section derives some specific results for the production function $F(S)$ defined in equation (4.2) and repeated as follows:

$$F(S) = \prod_{i \in s} p_i. \tag{1}$$

Finding sufficient conditions for a nonempty Bond-core is the focus of this analysis because a nonempty Bond-core implies a nonempty First-core. To this end we start with the B-problem.

The primal objective of the B-problem given in section 2 seeks the minimum of $\Phi(N)y$ with respect to nonnegative y subject to

$$\Phi(S)y \geq F(S) \quad \forall S \subset N. \tag{2}$$

This suggests finding the greatest lower bound for $\Phi(N)y$ from the inequalities (2). Sum these inequalities over all coalitions with k members. On the left-hand side this gives some integer multiple of $\Phi(N)y$. To find this multiple we reason as follows. Every y_i is present in N together with each of the other $n - 1$ individuals as often as the number of combinations of $n - 1$ things taken $k - 1$ at a time. Let $\binom{n}{k}$ denote the number of combinations of n things taken k at a time so that

$$\binom{n}{k} = \frac{n!}{k!(n-k)!}.$$

There are $\binom{n}{k}$ coalitions of size k. Summing the inequalities (2) over all coalitions of size k yields

$$\binom{n-1}{k-1} \Phi(N)y \geq \sum_{S} F(S). \tag{3}$$

The sought-for multiple is $\binom{n-1}{k-1}$. The terms on the right-hand side of inequality (3) can be simplified because they are the sums of the products of the p's taken k at a time. Let $A(z)$ denote the nth degree polynomial in z defined as follows:

$$A(z) = \prod_{i=1}^{n} (z + p_i) = z^n + a_1 z^{n-1} + \ldots + a_{n-1} z + a_n.$$

The coefficient of z^{n-k} is a_k, which is the sum of the products of the p's taken k at a time. The number of summands in a_k is the number of combinations of n things taken k at a time. Hence the mean value of a summand, call it b_k, is

$$b_k = \frac{a_k}{\binom{n}{k}}. \tag{4}$$

Therefore, dividing through inequality (3) by $\binom{n}{k}$ gives

$$\Phi(N)y \geq \frac{nb_k}{k} \tag{5}$$

because $\binom{n}{k}/\binom{n-1}{k-1} = n/k$. The next result establishes some useful properties of the b's.

LEMMA 1. *If $p_i \geq 1$ for all i then $\{b_k | k = 1, \ldots, n-1\}$ is nondecreasing and convex.*

PROOF. Because the lower bound of the p's is 1 and b_k is the arithmetic mean of the products of the p's taken k at a time, b_k is a nondecreasing function of k. In fact, if all the p's are bigger than 1 then the b's are strictly increasing with k. The sequence $\{b_k\}$ is convex if and only if the second differences satisfy the inequalities as follows:

$$(b_{k+1} - b_k) - (b_k - b_{k-1}) \geq 0.$$

These second differences can be represented better as follows:

$$(b_{k+1} - b_k) - (b_k - b_{k-1}) = \sum \prod p_{i_j}(p_{i_1} - 1)(p_{i_2} - 1). \tag{6}$$

Each term in the sum is the product of $k + 1$ distinct factors of which $k - 1$ are p's and the remaining two factors are different p's minus 1. The number of summands is the number of combinations of n things taken $k + 1$ at a time. Therefore, as asserted, the second differences are nonnegative, which shows that the sequence $\{b_k\}$ is convex. It is strictly convex if the second differences are positive. This is true if and only if all the p's are bigger than one.   QED

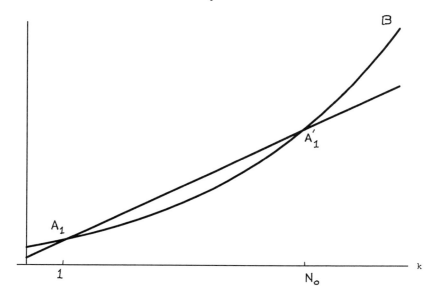

Fig. 29. Output of a coalition as a function of its size and the status of the core

It follows from this lemma and inequality (5) that the greatest lower bound for $\Phi(N)y$ is at an extreme, $k = 1$ or $k = n - 1$. Figure 29 shows this for the curve $A_1A_1'B$ that is the locus of the points b_k with smooth interpolations between adjacent k's. As the lemma requires, this curve is convex and nondecreasing.

Consider the maximum of b_k/k. It must be at one of the extremes, either at $k = 1$ or $k = n - 1$. In case the maximum is at $k = 1$ so that

$$b_1 > b_n/n \tag{7}$$

there is a violation of individual N-superadditivity. Individual N-superadditivity is necessary for a nonempty Bond-core by the corollary of Lemma 2.2 so that inequality (7) implies an empty Bond-core. Lemma 2.2 also states that weak superadditivity is necessary for a nonempty Bond-core. Lemma 4.1 gives a necessary and sufficient condition for weak superadditivity of $F(S)$ as follows:

$$\left(\prod_{S} - 1\right)\left(\prod_{N-S} - 1\right) \geq 1 \tag{8}$$

that must hold for all $S \subset N$. Index the p's so that $p_i \leq p_{i+1}$. Therefore,

$$(p_1 - 1)\left(\prod_{N-P_1} - 1\right) \leq \left(\prod_{S} - 1\right)\left(\prod_{N-S} - 1\right).$$

Consequently, inequality (8) is true if

$$\prod_{N-P_1} - 1 \geq \frac{1}{p_1 - 1} \Leftrightarrow \prod_{N-P_1} \geq 1 + \frac{1}{p_1 - 1}. \tag{9}$$

This completes the proof of the following

LEMMA 2.   *The production function F(S) has a nonempty Bond-core only if there is individual N-superadditivity so that $nb_1 \leq b_n$ and only if the p's satisfy inequality (9).*

The two necessary conditions given by Lemma 2 for $F(S)$ to have a nonempty Bond-core are independent as the next two examples demonstrate.

EXAMPLE 1. $p_1 = 1.414, p_2 = 1.8, p_3 = 1.9$

$$\sum_i p_i = 5.114 > \prod_i p_i = 4.836$$

so there is not individual N-superadditivity, but there is weak superadditivity because

$$(p_1 - 1)(p_2 p_3 - 1) > 1.$$

EXAMPLE 2. $p_1 = 6/5, p_2 = 5/4, p_3 = 9/5, p_4 = 21/8.$
There is individual superadditivity because

$$\sum_i p_i = 6.875 < \prod_i p_i = 7.0875,$$

but there is not weak supperadditivity because

$$(p_1 - 1)(p_2 p_3 p_4 - 1) = 0.98125 < 1.$$

Neither of these examples has a Bond-core.

   It is also useful to compute the division of N into that partition of two coalitions S and $N - S$ which gives the maximum total output. Given that $1 < p_i \leq 2k$, the expression $(\Pi_S - 1)(\Pi_{N-S} - 1)$ is a maximum when the members of S and $N - S$ are chosen to put Π_S and Π_{N-S} as close to 2 as possible.

   The next and sharper result shows explicitly how size of N enters.

THEOREM 1.   *There is an implication of individual N-superadditivity so that $nb_1 \leq b_n$ only if*

$$\prod_N > n^{\frac{n}{n-1}}. \tag{9'}$$

PROOF.   It follows from a formula of Newton (Hardy, Littlewood, and Polya, 1959, thm. 52) that

$$b_1 > b_2^{1/2} > b_3^{1/3} > \ldots > b_{n-1}^{1/n-1} > b_n^{1/n}.$$

Hence there is an implication of individual N-supperadditivity only if

$$b_n^{1/n} < b_1 < \frac{b^n}{n}. \tag{10}$$

Inequality (10) is valid if

$$b_n \left(\frac{b_n^{n-1}}{n^n} - 1 \right) > 0,$$

giving the desired result since $\Pi_N = b_n$. $\qquad$ QED

As n increases $n^{\frac{n}{n-1}}$ approaches 1 from above. By Lemma 4.1 weak su-peradditivity requires the smallest p to exceed one. Hence inequality (9') that is a necessary condition for a nonempty Bond-core holds for big enough n. This result is important. It means that a minimal size of the firm N is necessary for stability. This minimal size is larger, the less productive the workers.

Inequality (9') relates the geometric mean of the p's to the minimum size of the team that is necessary for its cohesion. Call GM_n the geometric mean of the p's so that $GM_n = b_n^{\frac{1}{n}}$. There is individual N-supperadditivity only if

$$GM_n \geq n^{\frac{1}{n-1}} \tag{11}$$

Because the arithmetic mean is not less than the geometric mean, inequality (11) gives the best possible result for the relation between the mean of the work-ers' abilities and the team size necessary for its stability. This lower bound shows an inverse relation between mean ability and team size.

These results supply a sufficient condition for weak superadditivity in terms of the least productive member of the team.

COROLLARY.   *If $p_1 > 1 + \dfrac{1}{n-1}$ and if GM_n satisfies inequality (11) then there is weak supperadditivity.*

PROOF.   According to Lemma 2 there is weak superadditivity if and only if

$$(p_1 - 1) \left(\prod_{N-P_1} - 1 \right) \geq 1. \tag{12}$$

By hypothesis inequality (11) holds so that

$$\prod_{N-P_1} \geq GM_n^{n-1} \geq \left(n^{\frac{1}{n-1}} \right)^{n-1} = n.$$

Therefore,

$$(p_1 - 1)\left(\prod_{N-P_1} - 1 \right) \ge (p_1 - 1)(n - 1).$$

Hence $(p_1 - 1)(n - 1) \ge 1$ implies inequality (12) so that

$$p_1 > 1 + \frac{1}{n - 1}, \tag{13}$$

which implies weak superadditivity.   QED

    There is another illuminating way of looking at the role of n. Let the p's be random draws from a symmetric density on the closed interval $[1, 2]$ so that the expected value of p is $3/2$. Lemma 1 says that there is the biggest difference between the production of the whole firm N and a partition of N when the latter is all the singletons. Therefore, the total output of N relative to all the singletons is a maximum when

$$\frac{3}{2} \, n < n^{\frac{3}{2}} \Leftrightarrow \frac{3}{2}\left[\left(\frac{3}{2} \right)^{n-1} - n \right] > 0.$$

The latter inequality is equivalent to

$$n^{\frac{1}{n-1}} < \frac{3}{2}. \tag{14}$$

Some numerical values are as follows.

n	2	3	4	5	6
$n^{\frac{1}{n-1}}$	2	1.732	1.587	1.495	1.431

	7	8	9	10	∞
	1.383	1.346	1.316	1.292	1.

The smallest n capable of satisfying inequality (14) is $n = 5$. These figures also shows the inverse relation between n and the lower bound on the geometric mean of the p's required for the stability of N.

    The next result is a necessary condition for a nonempty Bond-core.

LEMMA 3.   *Let the wage vector w belong to the Bond-core. The wage w_i of worker P_i cannot exceed his incremental contribution to the grand coalition N.*

PROOF.   The hypothesis says that w is in the Bond-core so it must satisfy

$$\Phi(N)w = \prod_{N} \quad \text{and} \quad \Phi(N - P_i)w \ge \prod_{N-P_i} = \prod_{N} \Big/ p_i,$$

which implies that

$$w_i \le \prod_N - \frac{\prod_N}{p_i} = \prod_N \left(1 - \frac{1}{p_i}\right). \tag{15}$$

The right-hand side of inequality (15) is the incremental contribution of P_i to N.   QED

By Lemma 2 there is a Bond-core only if there is individual N-superadditivity. However, this does not mean that the production function satisfies the more stringent condition of individual superadditivity that applies to arbitrary coalitions. Therefore, there is not always equivalence between the First-core and the Bond-core for this production function. Even so, a nonempty Bond-core is sufficient for a nonempty First-core though it is not necessary.

6. Two Wage Schemes

The preceding section shows that when n is large or the p's are large, many wage vectors can satisfy the Bond-core constraints. This section examines two plausible wage schemes and derives sufficient conditions for them to be in the Bond-core. In the first scheme the wage of a worker is proportional to his relative productivity. In the second scheme it is proportional to his incremental contribution to the total output. Index the p's in ascending order so that $p_i \le p_{i+1}$.

Let the wage of worker i be linearly proportional to his relative productivity. The wage w_i satisfies the following equation:

$$w_i = p_i \frac{\prod_N}{\sum_N}. \tag{1}$$

The term $\prod_N / \sum_N$ ensures that the sum of the w's equals the total output. We seek conditions on the relative productivity so that w given by formula (1) can satisfy all the Bond-core constraints.

LEMMA 1.   *The wages given by equation (1) are in the Bond-core for big enough n.*

PROOF.   According to Lemma 5.3, only wages that do not exceed the workers' incremental contributions to the grand coalition can be in the Bond-core. Hence it is necessary that w_i in equation (1) satisfy

$$p_i \frac{\prod_N}{\sum_N} \le \left(1 - \frac{1}{p_i}\right) \prod_N \Leftrightarrow \frac{p_i}{\sum_N} \le 1 - \frac{1}{p_i}.$$

The latter inequality is equivalent to

$$\frac{1}{1 - \dfrac{1}{p_i}} \le \sum_{N-P_i}.$$

The left-hand side of this inequality is a maximum at $i = 1$, and the right-hand side is bounded below by $(n - 1)p_i$. Therefore, the desired conclusion will follow if

$$\frac{1}{1 - \dfrac{1}{p_1}} \le (n - 1)p_1 \iff p_1 > 1 + \frac{1}{n - 1} \quad \text{if } p_1 > 1.$$

For n big enough this inequality is true.   QED

The core constraint for the first k individuals is

$$\prod_N \frac{\sum_1^k P_i}{\sum_N} \ge \prod_1^k p_i, \tag{2}$$

which reduces to

$$(p_1 + p_2 + \ldots + p_k)(p_{k+1}p_{k+2}\cdots p_n - 1) \ge p_{k+1} + \ldots + p_n. \tag{3}$$

Individual N-superadditivity implies inequality (2) is true for $k = 1$. Take $k > 1$. To get a sufficient condition for inequality (3), replace the terms on the left-hand side by the smallest representative and those on the right-hand side by the largest. Therefore if it is true that

$$k p_1 (p_{k+1}^{n-k} - 1) \ge (n - k)p_n \tag{4}$$

then a fortiori inequality (3) will be true. Indeed

$$k p_1 (p_1^{n-k} - 1) \ge (n - k)p_n \tag{5}$$

implies inequality (4), which implies inequality (3). Next we can prove

LEMMA 2.   *Let $p_i > 1$ for all i and let the production function be individually N-superadditive. If p_1 and p_n satisfy inequality (5) for $k = 2$ then inequality (2) is true for $k = 1, \ldots, n$.*

PROOF.   Define the polynomial $g(k) = k p_1(p_1^{n-k} - 1) - (n - k)p_n$.

$$g(k) \equiv k p_1^{n-k+1} + k(p_n - p_1) - np_n. \tag{6}$$

If $g(k) \ge 0$ for $k = 2, \ldots, n$ then inequality (5) will be true for these k. Inequality (4) will follow, and (4) implies inequality (3), which implies inequality (2) for these k. Let us verify this chain of implications. Take k as a continuous variable so that

$$\frac{dg}{dk} = p_1^{n-k+1} (1 - k \log p_1) + (p_n - p_1) \quad \text{and}$$

$$\frac{d^2g}{dk^2} = -p_1^{n-k+1} \log p_1 (2 - k \log p_1). \tag{7}$$

Since $p_1 > 1$ by hypothesis, it follows from (7) that g is concave for small values of k and becomes convex for large values. It is also true that g is an increasing function of k when k is small enough. Moreover, g is unimodal and is a maximum at an interior k. The smallest values of g in the range from $k = 2$ to $k = n - 1$ are at the extremes, 2 and $n - 1$. Now $g(n) = 0$ and $g(0) = -n\,p_n$. Hence $g(n - 1) > 0$. If $g(2) > 0$ then $g(k) > 0$ for $k = 2, \ldots, n - 1$ so inequality (3) is true for these k. This implies that inequality (2) holds for the same k's. Lastly, by hypothesis there is individual N-superadditivity so that inequality (2) holds for $k = 1$.   QED

From these results we can prove

THEOREM 1.   *Let $p_i > 1$ for all i and let the production function be individually N-superadditive. If $g(2) \geq 0$ then w_i given by equation (1) is in the Bond-core.*

PROOF.   Let $p = \{p_1, \ldots, p_n\}$ denote the n-vector of the workers' productivities. We must establish that the inequality

$$\frac{\Phi(S)p}{\Phi(N)p} \geq \frac{\prod_S}{\prod_N}$$

holds for all subsets S of N. Rearrange this inequality into the same form as inequality (3) and there is

$$\Phi(S)p \left[\prod_{N-S} - 1 \right] \geq \Phi(N - S)p. \tag{8}$$

If there is individual N-superadditivity then inequality (8) holds for all $S = P_i$, namely, the singletons. Using the same argument as in Lemma 2, if $g(2) \geq 0$ then inequality (8) is true for all coalitions with 2 or more members.   QED

The second wage scheme assumes the wage of the worker is proportional to his incremental contribution to the grand coalition. Let y_i denote the wage of worker P_i under this scheme and

$$y_i = \frac{\prod_N - \prod_{N-P_i}}{c},\qquad(9)$$

where the constant c is chosen to make the wages sum to the total production so that

$$c = \sum_j \left(1 - \frac{1}{p_j}\right).\qquad(10)$$

It follows from these two equations that

$$y_i = \prod_N \frac{1 - \dfrac{1}{p_i}}{\sum_j \left(1 - \dfrac{1}{p_j}\right)}.\qquad(11)$$

For this wage scheme the necessary condition for a nonempty Bond-core given by Lemma 5.3 requires $c \geq 1$. However, $p_i > 1$ does not yield a lower bound on n that can ensure $c \geq 1$. Consider

$$n\left(1 - \frac{1}{p_1}\right) \leq c \leq n\left(1 - \frac{1}{p_n}\right)$$

that bounds c because

$$1 - \frac{1}{p_1} \leq 1 - \frac{1}{p_2} \leq \ldots \leq 1 - \frac{1}{p_n}.$$

Let $p_1 = 1 + \varepsilon$. It follows that

$$\lim\left(1 - \frac{1}{1 + \varepsilon}\right) = 0 \quad \text{as } \varepsilon \to 0.$$

Therefore, the greatest lower bound of c is zero not 1. This means that the necessary condition imposed on c by Lemma 5.3 cannot be satisfied if p_1 can be arbitrarily close to 1. There is a fundamental difference between wages based on a worker's incremental contribution and wages proportional to ability as shown by Theorem 3, which follows.

We can use the same line of reasoning for y, the incremental wage scheme, as for w to obtain sufficient conditions placing y in the Bond-core. Begin with the core constraint for the k least able workers as follows:

$$\frac{1}{c} p_1 p_2 \cdots p_n \left[\left(1 - \frac{1}{p_1}\right) + \left(1 - \frac{1}{p_2}\right) + \ldots + \left(1 - \frac{1}{p_k}\right)\right] \geq p_1 p_2 \cdots p_k,$$

which simplifies to

$$p_{k+1}\cdots p_n\left[\left(1-\frac{1}{p_1}\right)+\ldots+\left(1-\frac{1}{p_k}\right)\right]$$

$$\geq\left[\left(1-\frac{1}{p_1}\right)+\ldots+\left(1-\frac{1}{p_n}\right)\right].$$

Rearrange terms so that

$$[p_{k+1}\cdots p_n-1]\left[\left(1-\frac{1}{p_1}\right)+\left(1-\frac{1}{p_2}\right)+\ldots+\left(1-\frac{1}{p_k}\right)\right]$$

$$\geq\left[\left(1-\frac{1}{p_{k+1}}\right)+\ldots+\left(1-\frac{1}{p_n}\right)\right].$$

Replace the terms on the left-hand side by the smallest elements and those on the right-hand side by the largest. This gives

$$k(p_{k+1}^{n-k}-1)\left(1-\frac{1}{p_1}\right)\geq(n-k)\left(1-\frac{1}{p_n}\right). \tag{12}$$

A fortiori inequality (12) will be true if

$$k(p_1^{n-k}-1)\left(1-\frac{1}{p_1}\right)\geq(n-k)\left(1-\frac{1}{p_n}\right). \tag{13}$$

Next define the function $f(k)$ as follows:

$$f(k)\equiv k(p_1^{n-k}-1)\left(1-\frac{1}{p_1}\right)-(n-k)\left(1-\frac{1}{p_n}\right). \tag{14}$$

Note that $f(k)$ resembles $g(k)$ defined previously. If $f(k)\geq 0$ for $k=1,\ldots,n$ then inequality (13) will be true. If inequality (13) is true then inequality (12) will be true. Thus $f(k)\geq 0$ for all k gives a sufficient condition for y to be in the Bond-core. Now $f(k)$ is positive given p_1 and p_n for large enough n. This completes the proof of

THEOREM 2.   *The wage scheme y_i based on the worker's incremental contribution shown in equation (11) is in the Bond-core, given p_1 and p_n, for big enough n.*

The two different wage schemes raise an interesting question. How do the distributions of wages under these two schemes compare to the underlying distribution of worker productivity? Under the first scheme where the wage of a worker is proportional to his productivity, equation (1) says

$$w_i=p_i\frac{\prod_N}{\sum_N}.$$

For wages proportional to incremental contribution, equation (11),

$$y_i = \prod_N \frac{1 - \dfrac{1}{p_i}}{\displaystyle\sum_j \left(1 - \dfrac{1}{p_j}\right)}.$$

Given n and the p's, y is proportional to $1 - 1/p$ while w is proportional to p. Thus under both schemes wages are higher for more productive workers. When wages are proportional to productivity, the distribution of wages is the same as the distribution of productivity. However, when wages are proportional to the worker's incremental contribution, the density of wages is asymmetric even with a symmetric density of productivity. Let us see why this is so.

Let $h(p)$ denote the probability density function (pdf) of productivity so that the cumulative distribution function (cdf) is $H(p)$ as follows:

$$H(p) = \int_0^p h(\xi)d\xi.$$

$$y = 1 - \frac{1}{p} \Rightarrow p = \frac{1}{1 - y}.$$

Therefore, the pdf of y is given by

$$\frac{1}{(1 - y)^2} h\left(\frac{1}{1 - y}\right).$$

Suppose h were symmetric. (See fig. 30a.) Therefore $h(p) = h(q)$ if $p - 3/2 = 3/2 - q$. The pdf of p is symmetric around the point 3/2, and the variables p and q are between 1 and 2. Hence for $p + q = 3$, $h(p) = h(q)$. The density of wages would be symmetric if and only if $p + q = 3$. The latter implies that $h(p)p^2 = h(q)q^2$. But $h(p)(p^2 - q^2) = 3h(p)(p - q)$ so that the difference has the same sign as $p - q$. Consequently the density of wages is not symmetric even if the density of productivity is symmetric when the wages of the workers are proportional to their incremental contributions to the total production. The height of the wage density at a wage to the left of that corresponding to a productivity level 3/2 is below the height of the density at an equal distance to the right of 3/2. Figure 30b shows this. Even so, the ratio of the wage of the most productive worker relative to that of the least productive given by

$$\frac{1 - \dfrac{1}{p_n}}{1 - \dfrac{1}{p_1}}$$

is much bigger than it would be for wages proportional to productivity. Although wages are an increasing concave function of productivity, it is still pos-

Frequency

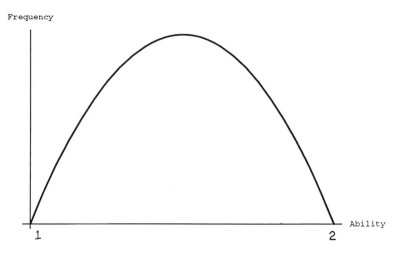

Ability

1

2

Fig. 30a. Probability density function of ability

sible that wages are higher relative to productivity at the higher than at the lower levels of productivity. Wages proportional to the incremental contribution allow this depending on how the firm selects workers. For example, suppose a selection of workers such that w_{n+1-k} is proportional to $1/2k$, which implies that p_{n+1-k} is proportional to $1 + 1/(2k - 1)$, $k = 1, \ldots, n$. In this case the ratio w_{n+1-k}/p_{n+1-k} is an increasing convex function of k so that the more productive the worker, the higher is his wage relative to his productivity.

It is also useful to compare the two wage schemes to see how the stability of a team of workers depends on the size of the team. This is the result. Wages proportional to productivity allow a smaller team to be stable than wages proportional to the worker's incremental contribution to the production of the team.

Under proportional sharing, the grand coalition N is stable if

$$k(p_1^{n-k} - 1)p_1 \geq (n - k)p_n. \tag{15}$$

It is stable for wages proportional to the worker's incremental contribution if

$$k(p_1^{n-k} - 1)\left(1 - \frac{1}{p_1}\right) \geq (n - k)\left(1 - \frac{1}{p_n}\right). \tag{16}$$

Therefore, to see how n affects the stability of N under the two wage schemes, compare

$$\frac{p_n}{p_1} \quad \text{to} \quad \frac{1 - \dfrac{1}{p_n}}{1 - \dfrac{1}{p_1}}.$$

Frequency

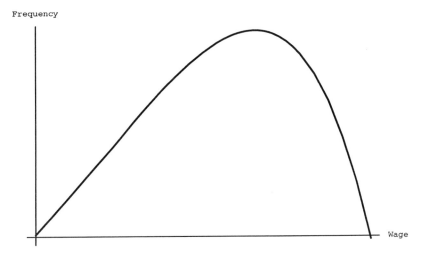

Wage

Fig. 30b. Probability density function of wages

A smaller n suffices for stability of the grand coalition when wages are proportional to productivity than when they are proportional to the incremental contribution if

$$\frac{1}{p_1}\frac{1}{1-\frac{1}{p_1}} < \frac{1}{p_n}\frac{1}{1-\frac{1}{p_n}}, \tag{17}$$

where $1 < p_1 < p_n < 2$ so $1 > 1/p_1 > 1/p_n$. The expression $z(1-z)$ is a maximum at $z = 1/2$ on the interval from $1/2$ to 1 and it decreases to zero as z goes from $1/2$ to 1. Consequently, inequality (17) is true. This proves

THEOREM 3.   *The firm N is stable for a smaller n when wages are proportional to productivity, equation (1), than when wages are proportional to the worker's incremental contribution to the total output, equation (11).*

It is also true that N, the grand coalition, is stable for smaller n, the closer together the p's. This holds for both wage schemes. Equations (15) and (16) explain why this is so. A smaller n can satisfy these equations, the closer together are p_1 and p_n.

The main results are as follows. The minimal size of a stable firm in the sense of a nonempty core is bigger when wages are proportional to the worker's incremental contribution than when wages are proportional to the worker's ability. The effect of the different wage schemes on the minimal firm size is least, the more homogeneous the abilities of the workers in the firm.

7. Some Generalizations

In the preceding analysis the output of a team does not cover the possibility that those individuals who learn each other's strengths and weaknesses may work better together than those who do not. Consequently the productivity of team members may depend on who they are. Let $F(S)$ denote the production function taking this into account. Let $\Pi(S)$ denote the production function used in the preceding analysis that ignores this consideration. Thus for the Π-function the relative productivity of a worker does not depend on the identity of the other members of the team. To put it another way, for the Π-function, p_i, the productivity of worker i is the same for any coalition that he joins. The Π-function is a benchmark for the general case in the following sense:

$$\frac{F(S)}{\Pi(S)} \begin{Bmatrix} > \\ = \\ < \end{Bmatrix} 1 \Rightarrow \begin{Bmatrix} \text{positive} \\ \text{neutral} \\ \text{negative} \end{Bmatrix} \text{complementarity.}$$

A coalition can create a culture among its present members, who can transmit it to new members. Traditions, expectations, norms, practices, and similar arrangements may form bonds that are reflected in the production function $F(S)$ but which are absent from the production function $\Pi(S)$. Although this does not specify an explicit F, still one can derive some useful results by comparing the status of the Bond-core for these two production functions.

DEFINITION.   There is uniformly positive complementarity for F if for all S, $F(S) > \Pi(S)$.

Suppose there were a positive scalar β and an n-vector a such that

$$F(S) \geq \beta \prod_S + \Phi(S)a \quad \forall S \subset N$$

$$F(N) = \beta \prod_N + \Phi(N)a. \tag{1}$$

If x is in the Bond-core for F so that

$$\Phi(N)x = F(N) \quad \text{and} \quad \Phi(S)x \geq F(S) \quad \forall S \subset N, \tag{2}$$

then y such that

$$x = \beta y + a \tag{3}$$

is in the Bond-core for the Π-function, as we may easily verify. It would follow that a nonempty Bond-core for the neutral production function Π is necessary for a nonempty Bond-core for a production function with positive complementarity. The question is whether there exist positive β and an n-vector a that can satisfy conditions (1). The difficulty lies in this: taking β and big enough a

to satisfy equality in the second condition of (1) may foil satisfying the first condition of (1). However, this is possible in one important case.

The ratio $F(S)/\Pi(S)$ always exceeds one if F has uniformly positive complementarity. Assume that the coalition for which this ratio is a minimum is N itself, the grand coalition. This means that the biggest team has the least positive complementarity, a plausible assumption. Choose $\beta = F(N)/\Pi_N$ and $a = 0$. It is easy to see that if x is in the Bond-core for F then $y = x/\beta$ is in the Bond-core for Π. The following theorem summarizes these results.

THEOREM 1. *If F has uniformly positive complementarity and if the ratio $F(S)/\Pi(S)$ is a minimum at $S = N$ then a nonempty Bond-core for the Π-function is a necessary condition for a nonempty Bond-core for F.*

However, when the minimum of the ratio $F(S)/\Pi(S)$ is not at N and even if there is uniform positive complementarity, then it is not generally possible to find $\beta > 0$ and a that can satisfy condition (1). For this reason, Theorem 1 gives the best possible result for a production function with uniform positive complementarity.

A second important generalization uses the obvious fact that ability is multidimensional. Say there are n different kinds of ability and measure the abilities of worker P_i by the coordinates of the vector $A_i = \{a_1, a_2, \ldots, a_n\}$. A host of interesting questions arises about the possible relations among different abilities. Some individuals may have high levels of all abilities. Some kinds of ability vary inversely with other kinds while complementarity may be the rule for some abilities. No doubt studying the implications of such special relations would be useful; however, it is better to begin with general results.

Assume there are m individuals. Let the ith row of the $m \times n$ matrix M represent the vector of abilities for individual i.

$$M = [a_{ij}]. \tag{4}$$

At the outset say there is only one commodity. Let the maximum quantity of this commodity that worker i can produce be as follows:

$$\min \{a_{i1}, a_{i2}, \ldots, a_{in}\}.$$

A coalition of workers, R, corresponds to a selection of rows of the matrix M. The output of R is defined by the following production function $f(R)$:

$$f(R) \equiv \min_{j} \ \max_{i \in R} \{a_{i1}, a_{i2}, \ldots, a_{in}\}. \tag{5}$$

According to definition (5), a coalition of individuals is equivalent to a person formed by taking the biggest element from each of the n columns of the submatrix given by the subset of the rows of M. The total output of the coalition R is the smallest coordinate of the resulting n-vector.

More generally, assume a commodity is defined by the inputs of certain required types of ability. Hence a commodity is a subset C of the *columns* of M. Let $g(C)$, the function giving the output of commodity C, be defined as follows:

$$g(C) \equiv \max_{j \in C} \min \{a_{1j}, a_{2j}, \ldots, a_{mj}\}. \tag{6}$$

Thus, $g(C)$ is the maximum quantity of commodity C that can be produced by the m individuals. Since a commodity is defined by the abilities represented by a subset of the columns of M, this approach can encompass $2^n - 1$ different commodities. This is the total number of nonempty subsets of all possible combinations of abilities.

Some simple and important observations are immediate. The minimum of a subset of columns is not less than the minimum of all the columns. The maximum of a subset of rows does not exceed the maximum of all the rows. Consider those commodities that each require a single unique ability and compare the outputs of these for those commodities that each require two of these abilities. Plainly, the outputs of commodities that require two abilities cannot exceed the output of a commodity that requires only one of them. More generally, therefore, a group of workers can produce more, the fewer the different abilities needed to make the commodity. This result may seem to contradict the view that specialization can raise productivity. However, specialization can change the coefficients of the matrix M as well as change the number of columns of M. This means a matrix showing the effects of more specialization has more columns and different elements than one representing a less specialized group of workers.

A commodity in this technology is a selection of columns from the matrix M. The principles are the same and the analysis is simpler for a commodity that requires all n abilities. Hence let us focus on the simpler case.

We begin by obtaining some properties of the production function. Define the n-vector $a(R)$ as a function of the subset of rows, R, as follows:

$$a(R) = \max_i \{a_{ij}\} \quad \text{subject to } i \in R. \tag{7}$$

The vector $a(R) \cup a(S)$ is defined to be the smallest vector that is not less than $a(R)$ or $a(S)$ so it is the least upper bound of these two vectors. That is, the ith coordinate of $a(R) \cup a(S)$ is the larger of the ith coordinate of the two vectors $a(R)$ and $a(S)$ for $j = 1, \ldots, n$. The n-vector $a(R \cup S)$ is obtained from the submatrix given by the union of the rows R and S by taking the largest element from the columns of each row of the submatrix. The next result is almost obvious.

LEMMA 1.

$$a(R) \cup a(S) = a(R \cup S). \tag{8}$$

PROOF.   Without loss of generality consider the first column of the vector $a(R) \cup a(S)$ given by the larger of the first pair of coordinates of $a(R)$ and $a(S)$. Each of these in turn is the largest of the first coordinates for their respective sets R and S. Consequently, there is an implication of equality for the first coordinates. The same argument applies for each coordinate.   QED

The vector $a(R) \cap a(S)$ is defined to be the biggest vector that does not exceed $a(R)$ or $a(S)$ so it is the greatest lower bound of these two vectors. Put differently, the ith coordinate of $a(R) \cap a(S)$ is the smaller of the ith coordinate of the two vectors $a(R)$ and $a(S)$.

LEMMA 2.

$$[a(R) \cup a(S)] + [a(R) \cap a(S)] = a(R) + a(S). \tag{9}$$

PROOF.   Equation (9) makes an assertion of equality for each of the n coordinates of the 4 vectors. The validity of this equation readily follows by considering only the first coordinate. Say the bigger coordinate is $a(R)$ so the smaller is $a(S)$. Then $a(R) \cup a(S)$ is the first coordinate of $a(R)$ and $a(R) \cap a(S)$ is the first coordinate of $a(S)$. Therefore equation (9) is true for the first coordinate, and so it is true for all coordinates.   QED

There is no counterpart to equation (8) for $a(R) \cap a(S)$ and $a(R \cap S)$. Moreover, in general, $a(R) \cap a(S) \neq a(R \cap S)$. This can be seen by taking the case where R and S have no rows in common so their intersection is null but $a(R \cap S)$ is not null.

By the definition of f (cf. equation (5)) and by equation (7),

$$f(R) = \min_j a(R). \tag{10}$$

The next result gives a sufficient condition for superadditivity of the production function.

LEMMA 3. $a(R) \cap a(S) = \varnothing \Rightarrow f(R \cup S) \geq f(R) + f(S)$.

PROOF.   It follows from Lemma 1, $\min [a(R) \cup a(S)] = \min [a(R \cup S)]$ $= f(R \cup S)$.

By Lemma 2 and by hypothesis

$$\min ([a(R) \cup a(S)] + [a(R) \cap a(S)]) = \min [a(R) + a(S)] = f(R \cup S)$$

$$\geq \min a(R) + \min a(S) = f(R) + f(S). \qquad \text{QED}$$

The vector $a(R) \cap a(S) = \varnothing$ if the scalar product of the two vectors $a(R)$ and $a(S)$ is zero. Because these are nonnegative vectors, the scalar product is zero if and only if one coordinate of each pair is zero. This result is interesting because it is an extreme form of complementarity and specialization. It means that each worker has a specific ability lacking in the other members of the group, that the members of the group perfectly complement each other, that a positive output requires the presence of each member of the group, and that the absence of even only one member prevents a positive output. Therefore each member of the group is indispensable. Under these conditions we prove

THEOREM 2.   *Under the hypotheses of Lemma 3, the Bond-core is non-empty.*

PROOF.   The hypotheses imply that $f(R) = 0$ for all subsets R of the matrix M. Only the group of all the workers is capable of producing a positive output. Therefore, the core constraints are as follows:

$$\Phi(R)w \geq 0 \quad \text{and} \quad \Phi(N)w = F(M).$$

Obviously these have a solution. Moreover the Bond-core is very big.   QED

For less extreme complementarity not only is superadditivity in doubt but also the core may be empty. Thus let each row of M have one coordinate equal to zero so that for every R and P_i, $a(P_i) \cap a(R) = \emptyset$ for $i = 1, \ldots, m$ and

$$f(P_i \cup R) \geq f(P_i) + f(R) = f(R) \quad \forall P_i \ \& \ R.$$

Therefore, a worker who joins any coalition cannot reduce the output of that coalition. Still for this case it is easy to give an example where the production function is not superadditive, indeed, not even weakly superadditive, so that it has no Bond-core.

The next example has the seed of a general result clearly showing the role of specialization in this model. There are three workers each with four different skills. Let $0 \leq x \leq y \leq z$. The following tableau gives the entries for the matrix M.

	Skills				Min	
	1	2	3	4	A	B
P_1	x	x	x	10	x	x
P_2	y	y	10	y	y	y
P_3	z	10	z	z	z	z
$P_1 \cup P_2$	$x \cup y$	$x \cup y$	10	10	y	y
$P_1 \cup P_3$	$x \cup z$	10	$x \cup z$	10	z	z
$P_2 \cup P_3$	$y \cup z$	10	10	$y \cup z$	z	z
$P_1 \cup P_2 \cup P_3$	$x \cup y \cup z$	10	10	10	z	10

There is superadditivity for the production of commodity A that requires all 4 skills if and only if

$$z \geq \max \{x + y, \ y + z, \ x + z, \ x + y + z\} = x + y + z.$$

Consequently, superadditivity requires $x = y = 0$. Assume this necessary condition. There is a nonempty Bond-core if wages can satisfy the following inequalities:

$$w_1 \geq 0 \qquad w_2 \geq 0 \qquad w_3 \geq 0 \qquad w_1 + w_2 \geq 0 \qquad w_1 + w_3 \geq 0$$

$$w_2 + w_3 \geq 0 \qquad w_1 + w_2 + w_3 \leq z.$$

The solution is $w_1 = w_2 = 0$, $w_3 = z$, equivalent to autarky, because the three workers have no incentive to cooperate in producing commodity A. The reason is clear. It is because the production of commodity A requires 4 skills and there are only three workers. There is a dramatic change if the workers decide to make commodity B that requires three skills since the first skill is not needed for B. The last column of the tableau shows the amounts of commodity B that the various teams can produce. Note that the outputs are the same for each team with less than three workers and there is a difference only for the team of the three workers. For this team the output of commodity B is 10 while the output of commodity A would be z. This difference is crucial. There is superadditivity in the production of commodity B if and only if

$$10 > \max \{y + z, \ x + z, \ x + y + z\}.$$

The core constraints are as follows:

$$w_1 \geq x \qquad w_2 \geq y \qquad w_3 \geq z \qquad w_1 + w_2 \geq y \qquad w_1 + w_3 \geq z$$

$$w_2 + w_3 \geq z \qquad w_1 + w_2 + w_3 \leq 10.$$

These inequalities have a solution, and so there is a nonempty core.

For the $m \times n$ matrix M let each worker be highly skilled in one specialty, let workers have different specialities, and let them make commodities that do not require more different skills than the number of workers. Under these assumptions there is a core. The critical constraints that set the limits on wages in the core are the singletons and the overall feasibility constraint.

This analysis illuminates a link between division of labor and the nature of the commodity. If production of a commodity needs many different skills then, depending on the number of available workers, it may be necessary for several to acquire more than one skill. This reduces the return from specialization because it is costly to acquire a skill and because the proficiency of each worker is lower, the more skills in which he must acquire competence. This theory can show the least number of skills each worker must have so that each will have enough incentive to join a team that makes a commodity which requires many different skills. The combinatorial problem that this involves is more easily grasped using a somewhat more complicated analysis than the preceding.

Let 4 workers make a commodity requiring 5 different skills. The entries in the matrix are chosen so that the team of all 4 workers can produce more than any team with fewer workers, so that there is strict individual superadditivity, and so that there is a core. The problem is to find the least number of skills per worker that can meet all these conditions. Choose the subscripts for the a's so that $a_i \leq a_{i+1}$ and let the a's be nonnegative. For the sake of simplicity this example omits the condition that a worker is less proficient in a skill, the more skills he has.

Skills

Teams	1	2	3	4	5	Min
P_1	10	a_1	a_1	a_1	10	a_1
P_2	a_2	10	a_2	a_2	a_2	a_2
P_3	a_3	a_3	10	a_3	a_3	a_3
P_4	a_4	a_4	a_4	10	a_4	a_4
$N - P_1$	a_4	10	10	10	10	a_4
$N - P_2$	10	a_4	10	10	10	a_4
$N - P_3$	10	10	a_4	10	10	a_4
$N - P_4$	10	10	10	a_3	10	a_3
N	10	10	10	10	10	10

The production function is strictly individually superadditive if and only if $\Sigma a_i < 10$. This matrix has the property that each worker has the minimal number of skills that is consistent with allowing the 4 workers to make the product and such that no smaller group of workers can make it. Consequently, each worker has an incentive to join the whole group instead of joining any subgroup or working alone. The following wages are in the core if there is strict individual superadditivity:

$$w_1 \geq a_1, \qquad w_2 \geq a_2, \qquad w_3 \geq a_3, \qquad w_4 \geq a_4, \qquad \text{and} \quad \Sigma w_i = 10.$$

The incremental contributions of workers P_1, P_2, and P_3 are the same, $10 - a_4$, and the incremental contribution of P_4 is $10 - a_3$. Therefore, the core does not contain wages equal to the individual's incremental contribution to the whole group. This example also shows that only one worker must be proficient in two different skills to enable the 4 workers to make the commodity requiring 5 skills. The general condition for m workers and n skills, $n > m$, is evident. The required $n - m$ additional skills should be distributed as sparsely as possible among the m workers so that each worker needs to acquire as small a number of skills as needed to make the commodity that requires n skills.

CHAPTER 7

Multiproduct Viner Industries with an Application to the Motion Picture Industry

1. Introduction

In a Viner industry with identical single-product firms, each firm has the same U-shaped unit cost curve intersected by a rising marginal cost curve at the unique scale of operation where the unit cost is a minimum. Such Viner industries have an empty core for nearly all rates of demand if it is optimal for more than one firm to be in the industry (Telser 1978, chap. 3). When firms make more than one commodity, this raises the problem of how to measure total output since unit cost cannot be measured in the same way for a multiproduct as for a single-product firm. It is not difficult to define a function that indicates whether a multiproduct firm operates where total cost is above, equal to, or below the revenue that would be generated by selling the commodities at prices equal to their marginal costs. The locus of outputs at which receipts equal total costs for a multiproduct firm corresponds to the output rate where unit cost would be a minimum for a single-product firm. This chapter presents the new features of a multiproduct Viner industry.

Section 2 describes the nature of the cost conditions for these industries. Analysis of these conditions is more general not only because the firms make more than one commodity that households want but also because there are intermediate commodities and services that households do not value directly but which are useful owing to their capability of lowering the costs of making those things that households do value directly. Some of these inputs are specific to some firms, and others affect the costs of all firms.

This elaboration of the cost conditions is related to an important contribution to core theory by Scarf (1986) that introduces a distributive cost function and shows there is a nonempty core if and only if the cost function is distributive. A simple way to understand distributive cost functions is as follows. Let y_j denote the quantity of input j and x_i the quantity of output i. The total cost of producing m outputs is given by

$$c = \sum_{j=1}^{m} w_j y_j \tag{1}$$

if each input j can be bought at constant unit prices, w_j. Consider the following minimum problem that seeks the least total cost of producing a bundle of commodities in quantities not less than given levels:

min c with respect to $y_j \geq 0$ subject to $x_i \geq x_i^0$,

where x_i^0 is the minimum required output of the ith commodity and the x's and y's are in the set of production possibilities. The solution of this minimum problem makes the inputs implicit functions of the required outputs so we may write

$$y_j = Y_j(x^0, w). \tag{2}$$

$$c = \sum_j w_j Y_j(x^0, w) \equiv C(x^0, w) \tag{3}$$

shows total cost as a function of those given outputs that households want. Inputs disappear as explicit variables from the cost function and become implicit functions of x. This brief analysis shows that suppression of inputs from the cost function does not seem to entail a loss of generality. However, it is still useful to see what modifications occur if the intermediate commodities do appear explicitly. Section 2 does this.

Scarf goes on to define a distributive cost function as follows:

DEFINITION.   A cost function induces a distributive set if there is a nonnegative price vector p such that $C(x) = p \circ x$ and $C(y) \geq p \circ y$ for all y such that $C(y) \leq C(x)$.

A distributive cost function is closely related to a supportable cost function (Sharkey and Telser 1978). It is not hard to verify that a distributive cost function must be subadditive and subhomogeneous. A useful counterpart to Scarf's distributive cost function is a distributive surplus function defined as follows:

DEFINITION. v is a distributive surplus function if there is a vector a such that $a \circ t = v(t)$ and for all s such that $v(s) \leq v(t)$, $a \circ s \geq v(s)$.

With these preparations we can prove the following

PROPOSITION.   *Let v be a nondecreasing distributive surplus function. Also let v be the minimum amount that a coalition can assure itself under the most adverse conditions. Then v has a nonempty core.*

PROOF.   We must show that for all $s \leq t$, there is an a such that $a \circ t = v(t)$ and $a \circ s \geq v(s)$ if $s \leq t$. By hypothesis, $v(s) \leq v(t)$ if $s \leq t$.   QED

Scarf's result seems to say that in a general equilibrium setting, a nonempty core requires either constant returns to scale or a single "firm" capable of making anything more cheaply than would be possible under any alternative arrangement. The first alternative says that the size of a firm is irrelevant. The second seems to suggest that it is only when one big firm can do everything better than many smaller firms that the whole economy can have a nonempty core. Neither alternative is attractive nor advances our understanding of what happens in the economy. Consequently, it is desirable to study situations in which a definite size distribution of firms is optimal. This is one purpose of the following material.

Section 3 introduces the concept of an optimal coalition. Because the core is usually empty in Viner industries in both single-product and multiproduct versions, for any efficient allocation of the total output there would be at least one proper coalition that could do better on its own than as part of the grand coalition. This raises the problem of explaining what would happen when this is true since it means an empty core. The grand coalition is unstable for an empty core so that it cannot resist the forces of secession. Only those coalitions capable of survival can be expected to form. An optimal coalition can survive because it can furnish each of its members a bigger gain than each could get as a participant in the grand coalition. This leads to a study of the nature and attributes of an optimal coalition.

Optimal coalitions form when the core is empty. Although there is equality between prices and marginal costs in an optimal coalition, global efficiency is absent. This is because the prices in the optimal coalition differ from those in the residual coalition, whose members are outside the optimal coalition. This inefficiency disappears only when the grand coalition is itself an optimal coalition.

Section 4 studies the relations between the cost condition and the optimal coalition. It describes how an optimal coalition can cover all of its costs including its overhead costs by means of marginal cost pricing.

The last section uses these concepts to study the motion picture industry in the period from 1920 to 1940. The arrangements between the producers of films and their affiliated exhibitors seem to constitute an optimal coalition. The analysis also explains many of the practices of the industry as devices designed to attain an efficient equilibrium when there is uncertainty. Among these is block booking.

2. Cost Conditions

Two facts underlie the specification of the cost conditions herein. First, there is more than one firm in most industries. Second, as demand increases, the number of firms in the industry also increases. A third less well-founded fact is also pertinent. It is that market shares of the incumbent firms tend to vary inversely with industry size. However, the evidence for the latter is impaired by the failure of many of the pertinent studies to adjust adequately for the multiproduct character of most firms. Nevertheless even just the first two facts suggest that a firm's cost function has a form that implies the existence of a finite upper bound on its size correctly measured.

First, assume that each producing entity encounters increasingly higher cost, the more it produces. Therefore, for a large enough total demand for the commodities, it is cheaper to spread production among several firms than to make everything in one firm. Second, assume that the firms make several different commodities because this is cheaper than specializing in the production of a single commodity. Let the coordinates of the n-vector x denote the quantities of the n commodities made by a producing entity. Let each firm have the same cost function, $f(x)$, such that $f(x)$ is increasing, twice continuously differentiable, and convex on the nonnegative orthant Ω_n. The firm is active if it produces a positive quantity of at least one of the n commodities so that $x \geq 0$. Let $f(x) > 0$ for any active firm. These assumptions imply that a given total of each of n commodities can be produced most cheaply if every active firm makes the same amount of each of the commodities that is produced. Even these assumptions about the nature of the firm cost function are not sufficient to ensure that costs rise rapidly enough with output to set an upper bound on firm size. Such a conclusion needs more conditions on the cost function.

Let f_x denote the gradient of f so that the ith coordinate of f_x is $\partial f(x)/\partial x_i = f_{x_i}$. Hence f_{x_i} denotes the marginal cost of making commodity i. Define the level set of f as follows:

$$L(\tau) = \{x : f(x) - f_x(x) \circ x = \tau\}. \tag{1}$$

The parameter τ is the total cost of producing x minus the receipts that would be obtained if the unit price of each commodity were equal to its marginal cost. Unit costs are above or below marginal costs according as τ is positive or negative. The loci of output rates for the n commodities where unit costs are said to be at their minima are the points in $L(\tau)$ where $\tau = 0$. Moreover and of equal significance, the outputs in $L(0)$ have the property that if they were sold at prices equal to their marginal costs then the total receipts would equal the total cost of producing them. If the total cost function were homogeneous of degree one, $L(\tau)$ would be an empty set for all $\tau \neq 0$, $L(0)$ would be the only nonempty level set, and it would include all output rates. Also in this case $f(0) = 0$ and there would be no fixed cost. Define the function

$$\psi(x) = f(x) - f_x(x) \circ x. \tag{2}$$

By hypothesis, $\psi(0) > 0$. If $\psi(x)$ is an unboundedly decreasing function of x then for large enough x, $\psi(x)$ must become negative so $L(0)$ is not empty. Also since $\psi(0) > 0$ there are $x > 0$ in $L(0)$. This completes the proof of

LEMMA 1.   *If $f(0) > 0$ and if $\psi(x)$ is an unboundedly decreasing function of x then there are positive x such that $x \in L(0)$.*

This is a useful result. It means there is a locus of positive output rates that can be sold at prices equal to marginal cost and that would yield enough revenue to cover their total cost. Under the hypotheses of Lemma 1 it follows that the gradient of $\psi(x)$ is

$$\psi_x = -x \circ f_{xx} \leqq -c, \tag{3}$$

where c is a strictly positive n-vector. Observe that convexity of f does not imply inequality (6). Next we prove

LEMMA 2.   *Let f be twice differentiable and have an unboundedly increasing gradient so that for all $\Delta x \geq 0$*

$$f_x(x + \Delta x) - f_x(x) > 0.$$

Then all the elements of the symmetric matrix $f_{xx}(x)$ are nonnegative, and at least one element in each row must be positive.

PROOF.   By hypothesis for $\varepsilon > 0$ there is a $\delta > 0$ such that for all $\|\Delta x\| < \delta$

$$\left| f_{x_i}(x + \Delta x) - f_{x_i}(x) - f_{x_i x}(x) \circ \Delta x \right| \leq \varepsilon \|\Delta x\|.$$

Therefore, for all $\Delta x \neq 0$ and $\|\Delta x\| < \delta$,

$$0 < f_{x_i}(x + \Delta x) - f_{x_i}(x) \leq f_{x_i x}(x) \circ \Delta x + \varepsilon \|\Delta x\|$$

giving the implication that

$$-\varepsilon \|\Delta x\| < f_{x_i x}(x) \circ \Delta x \Rightarrow 0 \leq f_{x_i x}(x) \circ \Delta x.$$

Since this holds for all $\Delta x \geqq 0$, we may conclude that $f_{x_i x}(x) \geqq 0$ and therefore that $f_{xx}(x) \geqq 0$. Because the gradient is increasing, there is no x for which all the coordinates of $f_{x_i x}(x)$ vanish.   QED

The hypotheses of Lemma 2 imply that for all $x \geq 0$ there is a positive vector c such that $x \circ f_{xx}(x) \geq c > 0$. These are sufficient conditions for Lemma 1. It can be shown using Taylor's series with remainder that if $f_{xx}(x)$ is a positive matrix for all x in an open convex set then f_x is strictly increasing on that set.

The hypotheses of Lemma 2 do not assert that f is a convex function. Moreover, a symmetric matrix with nonnegative elements and with at least one positive element in every row need not be positive semidefinite. The hypotheses of Lemma 2 do imply that f cannot be a strictly concave function of x because the diagonal elements of f_{xx} cannot be negative. Lemma 2 says that the marginal cost of each commodity is an unboundedly increasing function of the outputs of all n commodities.

To illustrate these results, consider the example of a quadratic function as follows:

$$f(x) = a + x \circ b + (1/2)x^T C \circ x. \tag{4}$$

where a is a positive scalar, b is a positive n-vector, and C is a symmetric positive definite $n \times n$ matrix. In this case,

$$L(0) = \{x | a - (1/2)x^T C \circ x = 0\} \quad \text{and} \quad f_x = b + C \circ x. \tag{5}$$

Hence f_x is an unboundedly increasing function of x if and only if all the elements of C are positive. This example can show how the scale of the firm varies in the level set $L(0)$.

Let us recall some well-known facts about positive matrices (Debreu and Herstein 1953). First, the eigen vector associated with the largest eigen value of a positive matrix is itself positive. Let x_0 denote this extreme eigen vector and let ρ denote the maximal eigen value. Hence $C \circ x_0 = \rho x_0$. The scale of x_0 is the number $\xi x_0 \in L(0)$. This scale ξ must satisfy the equation

$$a - (1/2)\xi^2 x_0^T C x_0 = 0.$$

Call ξ_0 the solution and obtain

$$\xi_0^2 = \frac{2a}{x_0^T C x_0} = \frac{2a}{\rho x_0^T x_0}. \tag{6}$$

The number ξ_0 is the scale of the output vector x_0 with the lowest unit cost. For an arbitrary set of outputs given by the coordinates of x, the unit cost would be a minimum at ξ that satisfies

$$\xi^2 = \frac{2a}{x^T C x}. \tag{7}$$

Second, the maximal eigen vector is such that

$$\max_x \frac{x^T C x}{x^T x} = \rho.$$

Therefore,

$$\frac{x^T C x}{x^T x} < \rho \quad \forall x \neq x_0. \tag{8}$$

Some simple calculations based on (6) to (8) imply

$$\xi_0^2 < \xi^2 \frac{x^T x}{x_0^T x_0}. \tag{9}$$

Without loss of generality let x and x_0 have the same length so that $x^T x = x_0^T x_0$. Inequality (9) says that on the locus of output rates where unit cost is a minimum, the smallest scale of a firm is at the output vector given by the maximal eigen vector of the matrix C. Figure 31 shows $L(0)$ for $f(x)$ defined in equation (4).

It is important to observe that the optimal scale ξ depends on x. Thus the

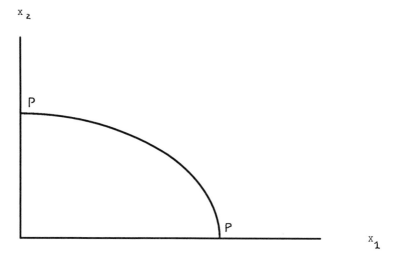

Fig. 31. Level set of outputs for a quadratic cost function

size of a multiproduct firm changes along the locus $L(0)$ although unit cost is a minimum everywhere on this locus. Many empirical studies of optimal firm size seem to overlook this fact. Even if output prices were equal to marginal cost and firms operate where their revenue equals their total cost so that their output is in $L(0)$, it does not follow that prices would be constant or that total revenue and total cost would be the same at different output vectors in $L(0)$.

The analysis so far studies the cost of making various quantities of different commodities and services that the final consumers want. There are many other commodities and services that do not go directly to households, that are inputs in production, that are costly to make, and that are produced because they can lower the cost of the final commodities and services that consumers want. Such things are in two classes. The first includes the things that are inputs for the factories that buy and use them on their own premises. These inputs have no effects outside the walls of their own users. Machinery in a factory is an example. Let y denote the total quantity of these inputs that includes labor. Although labor is the complement of leisure and households do value their leisure, in this model leisure is not among the commodities that enter household valuation functions (see sec. 3 for a discussion of the household valuation function). The reason is this. Leisure is purely personal. It is impossible to transfer the leisure of one person directly to another person although it can be done indirectly. A person who works more or produces more for someone else may permit the other to have as much goods as before, work less, and thereby have more leisure. The model allows this. The value of leisure appears indirectly in this model in the function showing that the cost to the firm of labor rises with the amount of labor it hires. This function is $\ell(y)$. The second class includes those commodities that can lower the production costs of all the factories. Let Z denote the total quantities of these commodities and services that may also include labor. Highways, railroads, and sewage systems are such inputs because, while they are inputs to individual firms, they are also available simultaneously to many firms. Research and development that expand knowledge and improve the technology of all firms are leading examples of these inputs. The function $k(Z)$ shows the cost of these general inputs.

Let X denote the total output of the goods that consumers want. Let μ denote the number of factories and σ the number of facilities that make the general inputs Z. Define the industry total cost function as follows:

$$C(x, y, z, \mu, \sigma) = \sigma g(z) + \mu[h(Z)f(x, y) + \ell(y)k(Z)] \tag{10}$$

and

$$Z = \sigma z, \qquad Y = \mu y, \qquad X = \mu x. \tag{11}$$

The cost function of a firm making the output vector x using the input vector y is given by $f(x, y)$. Thus x and y are the quantities per firm while X and Y are the total quantities. Assuming that f is a convex function of its arguments makes it optimal for x and y to be the same for all active firms. The y-input lowers the total cost of making x so that $f_y < 0$, and the y-input is costly so that $\ell_y > 0$. The cost function of a facility making the general inputs z is given by $g(z)$, and the cost function of the firm-specific inputs is $\ell(y)$. Let $g(z)$ and $\ell(y)$ be convex implying that it is best for each active facility to produce the same amounts of their respective outputs, y for the ℓ-facilities and z for the g-facilities.

The following development studies the solution of the problem of finding the minimal total cost of an industry that makes a prescribed total output X.

Min $C(x, y, z, \mu, \sigma)$

with respect to x, y, z, μ, and σ subject to $\mu x \geq X$. Although μ and σ are integers, for now let us agree to treat them as continuous variables. Let us also agree to ignore the nonnegativity constraints on the decision variables x, y, and z. The Lagrangian for the minimum problem is

$$C(x, y, z, \mu, \sigma) + p \circ (X - \mu x), \tag{12}$$

where p is the nonnegative vector of Lagrangian multipliers for the inequality constraint. The optimal values of the decision variables must satisfy the following first-order conditions.

$$C_x - \mu p = 0, \tag{13}$$

$$C_y = 0, \tag{14}$$

$$C_\sigma = 0, \tag{15}$$

$$C_z = 0, \tag{16}$$

$$C_\mu - p \circ x = 0. \tag{17}$$

The first-order partials of the cost function C are as follows:

$$C_x = \mu h(Z) f_x \qquad C_y = \mu[h(Z) f_y + k(Z) \ell_y]$$

$$C_z = \sigma g_z + \mu\left[f(x, y) h_z \circ \frac{\partial Z}{\partial z} + \ell(y) k_z \circ \frac{\partial Z}{\partial z}\right]$$

$$= \sigma\{g_z(z) + \mu[f(x, y)h_z + \ell(y)k_z]\}$$

$$C_\sigma = g(z) + \mu\left[f(x, y) h_z \circ \frac{\partial Z}{\partial \sigma} + \ell(y) k_z \circ \frac{\partial Z}{\partial \sigma}\right]$$

$$= g(z) + \mu[f(x, y)z \circ h_z + \ell(y)z \circ k_z]$$

$$C_\mu = h(Z)f(x, y) + K(Z) \ell(y).$$

In checking these results keep in mind that Z is related to the policy variable z by the definition given in equation (11) while X is a prescribed vector with given coordinates. Given that $\ell_y > 0$, equation (14) says there is an optimal y only at $f_y < 0$. This means the y-inputs must lower the cost of making x. Likewise, given $g_z > 0$, equation (16) says it is optimal to have positive quantities of the general inputs Z only if these inputs can lower the cost function either because $h_z < 0$, or lower the cost of y because $k_z < 0$, or both. Equation (16) implies that the optimal z satisfies $z \circ C_z = 0$. Together with equation (12) it follows that

$$g(z) - z \circ g_z = 0. \tag{18}$$

Therefore, at the minimal industry total cost of making the prescribed final output X, the optimal scale of a facility producing the general input z is on the locus where its unit cost is a minimum.

Next consider the conditions determined by the solution of the minimum problem for the entities that make x and that use the y inputs. From the necessary condition for the optimal number of firms, equation (17), and from equation (13) giving the first-order necessary condition for the optimal firm output rates, it follows that

$$h(Z)[f(x, y) - x \circ f_x] + \ell(y)k(Z) = 0. \tag{19}$$

Since $h(.)$, $\ell(.)$, and $k(.)$ are all positive, equation (19) says that in order to minimize the industry total cost of producing the given total output X, firms should produce x on the locus where its marginal cost is above its unit cost. This is where unit cost is rising. Section 4 uses this result.

Next reconsider the example of a quadratic cost function defined in equation (4). Once again it serves the purpose of illustrating the detailed results in the more complicated case where production cost depends on both the final output x and the input y. The presence of both x and y in the cost function turns out to have a major effect on the shapes of the level sets. In the preceding, for the quadratic cost function with x as the only argument the level set is an ellipsoid. Now the level sets

$$L(\tau) = \{(x, y) | f(x, y) - x \circ f_x = \tau\}$$

are hyperboloids. Let

$$f(x, y) = \beta + x \circ a - y \circ b + (1/2) \langle x, y \rangle \circ C[x, y], \qquad (20)$$

where the scalar $\beta > 0$, the vectors a, $b > 0$, and C is a symmetric, positive definite matrix. Hence f is a convex function of x and y. Partition C into submatrices so that

$$C = \begin{bmatrix} C_{xx} & C_{xy} \\ C_{yx} & C_{yy} \end{bmatrix}.$$

Hence $f_x = a + C_{xx} \circ x + C_{xy} \circ y$ and $f_y = -b + C_{yx} \circ x + C_{yy} \circ y$. Routine calculations give

$$f(x, y) - x \circ f_x = \beta - y \circ b - (1/2)[x^T C_{xx} \circ x - y^T C_{yy} \circ y].$$

The level sets for this function can cover zero if both C_{xx} and C_{yy} have only positive elements.

$$f_x(x + \Delta x) - f_x(x) > 0 \quad \forall \Delta x > 0 \quad \text{and}$$

$$f_y(y + \Delta y) - f_y(y) > 0 \quad \forall \Delta y > 0.$$

The cost-reducing effect of y is maximal if the elements of C_{xy} are all negative so that the bigger the y-input, the lower is the marginal cost of x. Therefore, by symmetry the bigger the x-output, the lower is the marginal cost of y.

To study the shape of the level sets we may confine our attention to $L(0)$. Let $x = \xi x_0$ and $y = \eta y_0$ where x_0 is the extremal vector of C_{xx} so that $x_0 > 0$, $C_{xx} \circ x_0 = \rho_x x_0$ and similarly for y_0, the positive extremal vector of C_{yy}, so that $C_{yy} \circ y_0 = \rho_y y_0$. If $(\xi x_0, \eta y_0)$ belongs to $L(0)$ it must satisfy the following equation:

$$\beta - \eta b \circ y_0 - (1/2)\xi^2 x_0^T C_{xx} \circ x_0 + (1/2)\eta^2 y_0^T C_{yy} \circ y_0 = 0. \qquad (21)$$

In a more concise notation, with $\theta = y_0^T b$, $\alpha = (1/2)x_0^T C_{xx} \circ x_0$, and $\lambda = (1/2)y_0^T C_{yy} \circ y_0$, equation (21) can be compressed to become

$$\beta - \eta\theta - \alpha\xi^2 + \lambda\eta^2 = 0. \qquad (22)$$

Complete the square in η and obtain

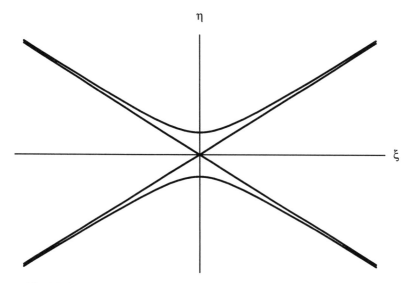

Fig. 32. Level sets for input and output for a quadratic cost function for which η is a minimum

$$\alpha\xi^2 = \lambda\left(\eta - \frac{\theta}{2\lambda}\right)^2 + \beta - \frac{\theta^2}{4\lambda}.$$ (23)

The graph of this equation is a hyperbola. Depending on the sign of $\beta - \theta^2/4\lambda$ there are two alternatives shown in figures 32 and 33. In figure 32, $\beta - \theta^2/4\lambda$ is negative. This sets a lower bound on η. In the relevant quadrant where both η and ξ are nonnegative, they move up or down together. In figure 33, $\beta - \theta^2/4\lambda$ is positive placing a positive lower bound on ξ. In this case as well ξ and η move up or down together in the positive quadrant. For the level set $L(\tau)$, the pertinent parameter is $\tau + \beta - \theta^2/4\lambda$. For big enough τ, figure 33 applies because $\tau + \beta - \theta^2/4\lambda$ is positive. The parameter $\theta = y_0^T b$, and b can become large as we shall see. For given τ, $\tau + \beta - \theta^2/4\lambda$ is negative and figure 32 applies. In either case the main result is the same, namely, the combinations of ξ and η determined by the condition that the firm operates on the locus where unit cost is a minimum, $L(0)$, by no means determine a unique optimal scale for a multiproduct firm. The shapes of the level set shown in the graphs in Figures 32 and 33 are also valid for an arbitrary pair of nonnegative x and y. It would add nothing new to elaborate on this.

3. Optimal Coalitions

Let a type i household be willing to pay up to an amount $w_i = B^i(x^i)$ for quantities of n goods given by the coordinates of the n-vector x^i, $i = 1, \ldots, m$. The

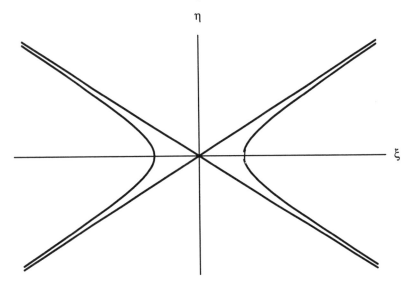

Fig. 33. Level sets for input and output for a quadratic cost function for which ξ is a minimum

function $B^i(.)$ denotes the valuation of x^i by household i. It shows the most that household i would be willing to pay for x^i so it is measured in terms of money (cf. chap. 1). The n goods are private as indicated by the superscript i. This means that household i can choose the quantities of each of the n goods on its own. Private goods differ from nonprivate goods. The latter are such that every member of a group must obtain the same quantities. Hence a vector of nonprivate goods has no superscript. Nonprivate goods are either semiprivate or public. Goods are semiprivate if the group can prevent outsiders from obtaining them. This does not hold for public goods. It is not possible to confine the effects of public goods solely to the members of that group which determines the quantities of public goods.

The total number of type i households is assumed to be a positive real number, t_i (see chap. 2, append.). The grand coalition of all the households is given by the m-vector $t = \langle t_1, t_2, \ldots, t_m \rangle$. The aggregate valuation of the n goods by all these households is defined to be the sum $\sum_{i=1}^{m} t_i B^i(x^i)$. The total quantity of goods going to coalition t is the n-vector $x(t)$ defined as follows:

$$x(t) \equiv \sum_i t_i x^i. \tag{1}$$

The presence of t as an argument of $x(t)$ shows the dependence of the total quantities on the size and composition of the coalition. A subcoalition of t corresponds to an m-vector s such that the ith coordinate of s, s_i, satisfies the inequalities $0 \leq s_i \leq t_i$. The total valuation for the coalition s is $\sum_{i=1}^m s_i B^i(x^i)$, and the total quantity is the vector $X(s) = \sum_i s_i x^i$. A type i household may obtain different n vectors in different coalitions.

The characteristic function of a coalition measures its maximal gain from the commodities directly chosen by the coalition's members and the inputs used to make these commodities. It is the total value of these commodities minus their total cost. Let $v(s)$ denote the characteristic function of the coalition s defined as follows:

$$v(s) = \max \sum_{i=1}^m s_i B(x^i) - C(x, y, z, \mu, \sigma) \tag{2}$$

with respect to x^i, x, y, z, μ, and σ. The number of plants in the coalition is the integer μ and the number of facilities that make z is the integer σ. The output per plant in the coalition s is $x(s)$ and the y-input per plant is $y(s)$. The inputs y and z are semiprivate because they are the same for all the households in the coalition and because the coalition can confine their use solely to its own membership. By definition,

$$X(s) \equiv x(s)\mu(s) \equiv \sum_{i=1}^m s_i x^i, \quad Y(s) \equiv y(s)\mu(s) \quad \text{and} \quad Z(s) \equiv z(s)\sigma(s).$$

This formulation allows the z-input to be made by different entities than those that make x and use y. These inputs z and y only affect the costs of the commodities produced by the firms in the coalition s. This definition of $v(s)$ says that the gain is the difference between the total valuation of the commodities going to the households in that coalition minus the costs of the inputs of the plants and other entities in the coalition. Note that households value directly the final goods x but do not value directly either the y-inputs or the z-inputs, that it is advantageous to use these inputs because they can lower the costs of making the things that households do value directly, that the y and z inputs are made within the coalition, and that all coalitions have unrestricted access to the stock of technological knowledge.

A coalition is defined as a set of households. While the integer number of firms and other producing entities in the coalition is chosen optimally according to the definition of v, the total number of households of each type is given. Any coalition $s \leq t$ is feasible, any household can join any coalition, and all coalitions can compete for any household to join them. Because the characteristic function of a coalition is defined as the maximum gain to its members taking into account the costs of furnishing them with the things they value, other kinds of organizations are implicitly present in the coalition. These are the firms that supply the households with the things they want and the other entities that supply the firms with the z-inputs used to make the goods and services that the households want. The y-inputs are intermediate things the firms make and use for themselves. This definition of the characteristic function implies the profits and losses of these firms and other entities stay within the coalition. Hence one may say that the households in the coalition own the producing entities by virtue of the fact that the households reap all the profits and bear all the losses of these entities. While a coalition is closed with respect to the production of the commodities and the inputs it uses to make them, coalitions are open with respect to households owing to competition among coalitions for households as members.

To show how this competition among coalitions enters the picture, begin with a household's gain. Let a_i denote the gain of household i and let $a = \langle a_1, \ldots, a_m \rangle$ denote the m-vector of gains for the coalition of all households, t. The sum of the gains to all the households in coalition t is $\Sigma_i a_i t_i$. Because this sum cannot exceed the maximum gain attainable by the coalition of everybody, namely, the coalition t, it must obey the following feasibility constraint:

$$a \circ t = \sum_i a_i t_i \leq v(t). \tag{3}$$

The sum of the gains going to the members of a subcoalition s of t is $a \circ s = \Sigma_{i=1}^m a_i s_i$. Using its own resources this coalition can guarantee itself a gain equal to $v(s)$. The sum $a \circ s$ would not be acceptable to s unless it were at least as large as $v(s)$. In this way competition among coalitions for households as members establishes lower bounds on the gains going to the households in the shape of the following inequality

$$a \circ s \geq v(s). \tag{4}$$

Any m-vector a that can satisfy inequalities (3) and (4) is in the core.

We now derive some implications of a nonempty core. If a can satisfy (3) and (4) then a_i cannot exceed the incremental contribution of household i to the coalition t. To prove this needs two lemmas.

LEMMA 1.   *Let $v(.)$ be positive and let a satisfy (3) and (4). Then $a > 0$.*

PROOF.   By hypothesis the core is not empty so that $a_i s_i \geq v(s^i) > 0$ where s^i is the m-vector whose ith coordinate is s_i and remaining $m - 1$ coordinates are zero.   QED

LEMMA 2.   *In addition to the hypotheses of Lemma 1, let $v(s)$ be continuous for all s such that $0 \leq s \leq t$. Then a must satisfy condition (3) with equality.*

PROOF.   Suppose not so that $a \circ t < v(t)$ and $v(t) - a \circ t = M > 0$. Since v is continuous by hypothesis, choose an arbitrary $\varepsilon > 0$.

$$\left| v(t) - v(t - \Delta t) \right| < \varepsilon \qquad \text{for all } \|\Delta t\| < \delta \qquad \Delta t \neq 0.$$

Hence $v(t) > v(t - \Delta t) - \varepsilon$ for a suitable choice of $\Delta t \neq 0$ and small enough $\|\Delta t\|$. By hypothesis a satisfies all the core constraints so that for $\Delta t \geq 0$,

$$a \circ (t - \Delta t) \geq v(t - \Delta t) > v(t) - \varepsilon \Rightarrow \varepsilon - a \circ \Delta t > v(t) - a \circ t = M > 0.$$

It would follow that for arbitrarily small positive ε, $-a \circ \Delta t > M - \varepsilon > 0$. By Lemma 1, $a > 0$ and since $\Delta t \geq 0$ it would follow that $-a \circ \Delta t < 0$, giving a contradiction.   QED

THEOREM 1.   *In addition to the hypotheses of Lemmas 1 and 2, let $v(t)$ be differentiable on an open set containing t. Then*

$$a_i \leq \frac{\partial v(t)}{\partial t_i} . \tag{5}$$

PROOF.   By Lemma 2, $a \circ t = v(t)$ and by the hypothesis of a nonempty core,

$$a \circ (t - \Delta t) \geq v(t - \Delta t) \quad \forall \Delta t \geq 0.$$

Therefore, $-a \circ \Delta t \geq v(t - \Delta t) - v(t)$. Since v is differentiable,

$$\varepsilon \|\Delta t\| > v(t) - v(t - \Delta t) - v_t(t) \circ \Delta t > - \varepsilon \|\Delta t\|,$$

which implies that

$$a \circ \Delta t < v(t) - v(t - \Delta t) < v_t(t) \circ \Delta t + \varepsilon \|\Delta t\|.$$

Consequently, $[v_t(t) - a] \circ \Delta t \geq 0$ for all $\Delta t \geq 0$ and $\|\Delta t\|$ small enough. Hence each coordinate of $v_t(t) - a$ is nonnegative.   QED

This result is valid in the present application for those t's in which the optimal number of plants and other producing entities is constant. Neither the first- nor the second-order partials of v with respect to t are defined where μ or σ changes.

Theorem 1 gives an upper bound on the gain any household can obtain from any coalition. Consider the coalition s. Using its own resources it can furnish its members a total return not above $v(s)$. Let the gain of household i in s be a_i and the total gain of the members of s be $a \circ s$. Confined to its own resources this coalition s can give its members a total gain of at most $v(s) = a \circ s$. This total would be acceptable to all subcoalitions of s if these subcoalitions could not give more to their members. That is, any coalition $r \leq s$ would accept a if $a \circ r \geq v(r)$. By the same reasoning as proves Theorem 1 we may conclude that

$$a_i \leq \frac{\partial v(s)}{\partial s_i} . \tag{6}$$

This upper bound on the individual gains can be attained only by coalitions s that can satisfy the following equation:

$$\sum_i s_i \frac{\partial v(s)}{\partial s_i} = v(s). \tag{7}$$

This result points the way toward optimal coalitions.

Level sets for coalitions consistent with equation (7), $V(\beta)$, are defined as follows:

$$V(\beta) = \{s | s \circ v_s - v(s) = \beta\}. \tag{8}$$

A level set contains many coalitions, but only one has special interest. It is given by the solution of the following maximum problem:

$$\max v(s)$$

with respect to $s \geq 0$ subject to $s \in V(\beta)$.
Define the function $\Gamma(s)$ as follows:

$$\Gamma(s) = s \circ v_s - v(s). \tag{9}$$

If $\Gamma(s)$ is continuous and the level set $V(\beta)$ is compact then a maximum exists by the Weierstrass extremum theorem. These conditions hold when the optimal number of plants and other producing entities do not change as s changes. For these s, v is twice continuously differentiable. The Lagrangian for the maximum problem is

$$v(s) + \lambda[\Gamma(s) - \beta], \tag{10}$$

where λ is a scalar. If a maximum exists, it must satisfy

$$v_s + \lambda s \circ v_{ss} \leq 0 \quad \text{and} \quad s^T(v_s + \lambda v_{ss} \circ s) = 0. \tag{11}$$

Therefore, the optimal coalition in $V(\beta)$ is the one that maximizes v. Moreover, the optimal coalition in s must be positive since a zero coordinate of the optimal s would mean that type is not present in the coalition. Hence the first condition in (11) holds with equality. The second condition in (11), the equation implied by complementary slackness and that the optimal coalition is in $V(\beta)$, implies

$$\beta + v(s) = -\lambda s^T v_{ss} \circ s. \tag{12}$$

If v is concave at the optimal coalition and in a neighborhood of it, which is necessary if v is differentiable and a maximum exists, then $s^T v_{ss} \circ s \leq 0$. Since $\lambda > 0$, equation (12) implies that

$$\beta + v(s) = -\lambda s^T v_{ss} \circ s \geq 0. \tag{13}$$

The next step is to find the optimal β. A coalition s can distribute its total gain among its members so that $a \circ s = v(s)$. Such a distribution would not be rejected by any subcoalition of s if and only if $a \leq v_s$. Hence

$$v(s) = a \circ s \leq v_s \circ s \Rightarrow 0 \leq \beta = v_s \circ s - v(s).$$

The latter inequality means that we may focus on level sets for which $\beta \geq 0$. For each $\beta \geq 0$, the optimal $s \in V(\beta)$ gives the maximum of v. The best choice of β is the subject of

THEOREM 2. *Let v be twice continuously differentiable and let v_s be positive. For each $\beta \geq 0$, let $s(\beta)$ denote the best coalition given by the solution of the maximum problem in the level set $V(\beta)$. Then v has a maximum at $\beta = 0$.*

PROOF. For the optimal $s \in v(\beta)$, $s \circ v_s - v = \beta$, $d\beta = v_s \circ ds + s^T v_{ss} \circ ds - v_s \circ ds$ so that

$$d\beta = \sum_j \sum_i s_i v_{ij} ds_j = s^T v_{ss} \circ ds. \tag{14}$$

Since $s(\beta) > 0$, the necessary condition for the maximum given by (11) must hold with equality so that $v_s = -\lambda s \circ v_{ss}$. By hypothesis $v_s > 0$ and $\lambda > 0$. Therefore, $0 < v_s = -\lambda s \circ v_{ss} \Rightarrow s \circ v_{ss} < 0$. Together with equation (14), it follows that

$$v_s \circ ds = -\lambda s^T v_{ss} \circ ds = -\lambda d\beta \quad \text{and} \quad dv = v_s \circ ds.$$

giving the implication that $dv = -\lambda d\beta$ so that $dv/d\beta = -\lambda < 0$. Hence it is optimal to make β as small as possible, namely, set $\beta = 0$. QED

There is another useful way to look at this. Let $v(s)$ be a strictly superhomogeneous function of s in a neighborhood of s so that $v(\lambda s) > \lambda v(s)$ for all λ such that $\lambda_0 > \lambda > 1$. The next two lemmas apply in this case.

LEMMA 3. *Let $v(.)$ be differentiable on an open set containing s.*

$$v(\lambda s) - \lambda v(s) > 0$$

$\forall \lambda$ *such that* $\lambda_0 > \lambda > 1 \Rightarrow s \circ v_s(s) - v(s) \geq 0$.

PROOF. First, define the function $f(\lambda) = v(\lambda s) - \lambda v(s)$ so that $f_\lambda(\lambda) = s \circ v_s(\lambda s) - v(s)$. Since v is differentiable by hypothesis so is f. Therefore,

$$|f(\lambda) - f(1) - f_\lambda(1)(\lambda - 1)| < \varepsilon |\lambda - 1|.$$

But $f(1) = 0$ so it follows from this inequality and the definition of f that

$$v(\lambda s) - \lambda v(s) \leq (\lambda - 1)(s \circ v_s - v + \varepsilon). \tag{15}$$

Inequality (15) and the hypothesis on v imply

$$0 < v(\lambda s) - \lambda v(s) \leq (\lambda - 1)(s \circ v_s - v + \varepsilon).$$

Since $\lambda - 1 > 0$,

$$0 < s \circ v_s - v + \varepsilon \Rightarrow s \circ v_s - v > -\varepsilon \Rightarrow s \circ v_s - v \geq 0. \qquad \text{QED}$$

The next result goes in the reverse direction.

LEMMA 4. *Let v be differentiable as in in Lemma 3.*

$$s \circ v_s - v \geq 0 \Rightarrow v(\lambda s) - \lambda v(s) > 0 \qquad \forall \lambda$$

such that $\lambda_0 > \lambda > 1$.

PROOF.   The differentiability hypothesis implies that

$$\varepsilon(\lambda - 1) \leq v(\lambda s) - v(s) - (\lambda - 1) s \circ v_s.$$

Therefore,

$$(\lambda - 1)(s \circ v_s - v + \varepsilon) \leq v(\lambda s) - \lambda v(s). \qquad (16)$$

By hypothesis, $s \circ v_s - v \geq 0$ so the desired conclusion follows from (16).

QED

The characteristic function defines the maximum gain for a given coalition, and coalitions compete for members. Therefore those coalitions survive that can offer their members the best terms. A coalition can also see whether a proportional expansion of its membership would be advantageous. Provided the gain to each of its present members does not decrease as a result of such an expansion, no current member would oppose it. Indeed they would welcome an expansion that would raise their individual gains. Consequently, the behavior of $v(\lambda s)/\lambda v(s)$ as a function of λ is relevant. If this ratio is a strongly concave function of λ then there is a unique λ giving the size of the coalition, s, at which this ratio attains its maximum. This optimal size must satisfy the following equation:

$$\lambda s \circ v_s(\lambda s) - v(\lambda s) = 0.$$

Theorem 2 says that the optimal β with respect to all $\beta \geq 0$ is $\beta = 0$. However, $v_s > 0$ in conjunction with $dv = v_s \circ ds$ implies that $dv > 0$ if $ds > 0$. Therefore, the maximum of v on the set of admissible coalitions is at the biggest possible coalition, namely, where $s = t$. However, according to Theorem 2, $v[s(\beta)] < v[s(0)]$ for all $s \in V(\beta)$ such that $\beta \geq 0$. Because v is an increasing function of s, it is also true that $v[s(\beta)]_{\beta=0} \leq v(t)$. There is equality if and only if $t \in V(0)$. This means if t does not belong to the level set $V(0)$, then $v_t(t) \circ t < v(t)$ and β would be negative. In addition, by Theorem 1, a nonempty core requires that any imputation a in the core must not exceed $v_t(t)$. Therefore, $v_t(t) \circ t < v(t)$ implies an empty core. Summarizing,

COROLLARY.   *If t does not belong to the level set $V(\beta|0 \leq \beta)$ then the core is empty.*

Figure 34, in section 4, illustrates these results. Under the hypothesis of the corollary the optimal coalition is not t. It is that coalition in $V(0)$ for which v is a maximum and that coalition is a proper subset of t. Therefore, the core is empty for the case shown in figure 34.

4. The Relation between the Characteristic Function and the Cost Function

The definition of $v(s)$ given in equation (3.2) implies that

$$\frac{\partial v(s)}{\partial s_i} = v_{s_i} = B^i(x^i) - h(Z)f_x(x, y) \circ x^i. \tag{1}$$

Therefore, recalling that $X(s) = \mu x(s) = \sum_i s_i x^i(s)$, it follows that

$$\sum_i v_{s_i}(s)s_i - v(s) = C(.) - h(Z)f_x \circ X(s)$$

$$= \sigma g(z) + \mu h(Z)[f(x, y) - f_x \circ x] + \mu \ell(y)k(Z). \tag{2}$$

It is understood that z, Y, x, y, σ, and μ are optimal for the coalition s so that these variables thereby become implicit functions of s. Thus s does not appear explicitly only for the sake of brevity and should cause no ambiguity. Likewise, let the function $G(.)$ stand for the right-hand side of equation (2) so that

$$G(x, y, z, \sigma, \mu) \equiv C(.) - h(Z)f_x \circ X(s). \tag{3}$$

By Theorem 3.2, the optimal coalition $s(0)$ belongs to the level set $V(0)$ so it must satisfy the equation

$$s \circ v_s - v = 0. \tag{4}$$

Consequently, for each σ and μ, the equation

$$G(x, y, z, \sigma, \mu) = 0 \tag{5}$$

must have roots for x, y, and z.

It is instructive to compare the situation given by equation (5) with the necessary conditions for minimizing the industry total cost function given by equations (2.18) and (2.19). If σ and μ were continuously divisible variables instead of being integers then the g-facilities would make quantities of z that satisfy the equation $z \circ g_z = g(z)$ according to equation (2.18). The f-facilities would make x using amount of y that would satisfy the equation

$$h(Z)[f(x, y) - f_x(x, y) \circ x] + \ell(y)k(Z) = 0.$$

Comparing this equation with the one for $G(.)$ given by equation (5), it appears that for the optimal coalition $s(0)$ the output per plant is bigger when σ and μ are integers than when they are continuously divisible. This is a plausible result. When the number of plants is an integer, each operates at a higher output rate in order to spread its fixed cost over a bigger output.

The optimal coalition in the level set $V(0)$ also satisfies inequality (3.11). Consequently, the function $\Gamma(s) = s \circ v_s - v$ must be decreasing at $s(0)$ as well as in a neighborhood of $s(0)$. To prove this we begin with

LEMMA 1.

$$\frac{d\Gamma(s)}{ds_j} < 0 \Leftrightarrow -x^T \frac{dh(Z, y)}{ds_j} \circ f_x < 0$$

PROOF.

$$\frac{d\Gamma(s)}{ds_j} = \sum_i s_i \frac{dv_{s_i}}{ds_j}.$$

Because $\Gamma(s) \equiv G(.)$ is an identity in s by virtue of equation (2), so that

$$\frac{d\Gamma(s)}{ds_j} \equiv \frac{dG(.)}{ds_j},$$

$$\frac{dG(.)}{ds_j} = \sigma g_z \frac{dz}{ds_j} + \mu h_Z \frac{dZ}{ds_j} [f - x \circ f_x] + \mu \ell(y) k_Z \circ \frac{dZ}{ds_j}$$

$$+ \mu [h(Z)f_y + k(Z)\ell_y] \circ \frac{dy}{ds_j} + \mu h(Z) \left[-x^T f_{xx} \circ \frac{dx}{ds_j} \right]. \tag{6}$$

Because a coalition chooses the optimal quantities of x, y, and z given the optimal integer values of σ and μ, equation (6) reduces to

$$\frac{dG(.)}{ds_j} = -\mu x^T \left[f_x h_Z \circ \frac{dZ}{ds_j} + h(Z)f_{xx} \circ \frac{dx}{ds_j} \right]$$

$$= -x^T \frac{d}{ds_j} [h(Z)f_x(x, y)]. \tag{7}$$

The desired conclusion follows from equation (7).   QED

The term on the right-hand side of equation (7) has an important economic meaning. It is the change in the marginal cost of producing the commodities that are valued by the households due to a change in the size of the coalition with respect to type j households multiplied by the initial bundle of all the household-valued commodities. If the prices of all the commodities desired by the households were equal to the marginal costs of these commodities then the right-hand side of equation (7) would be the change in these prices multiplied by the initial quantities of these commodities. When a change in the membership of the optimal coalition, $s(0)$, would raise marginal costs, then, since the expression in equation (7) is multiplied by a minus sign, it would lower the gain of the present members of $s(0)$. This explains why $s(0)$ is a locally but not a globally optimal coalition. For each type j household that does belong to $s(0)$, meaning that $s_j(0) > 0$, it is true that

$$v_j + \lambda \sum_i s_i v_{ij} = 0 \Leftrightarrow v_j = -\lambda \sum_j s_i v_{ij}.$$

Since $v_j = B^j(x^j) - h(Z)f_x \circ x^j$, equations (3.13) and (7) assert that for each $s_j(0) > 0$,

$$B^j(x^j) - h(y, Z)f_x \circ x^j = \lambda x^T \frac{d[h(Z)f_x(x, y)]}{ds_j}. \tag{8}$$

The optimal coalition is that $s(0)$ in the level set $V(0)$ which maximizes v. If $s(0) < t$ so that $s(0)$ is a subset of t, then by the corollary of Theorem 3.2, the core is empty. Suppose this is so, so that the core is empty. Since x, y, and z are roots of equation (5) and since $g(.)$, $h(.)$, $\ell(.)$, and $k(.)$ are all positive, it follows that

$$f(x, y) - x \circ f_x(x, y) < 0. \tag{9}$$

Hence if the optimal coalition $s(0)$ sets the prices of the commodities that households desire equal to the marginal costs of these commodities then the excess of the receipts over the direct costs, $x \circ f_x(x, y) - f(x, y)$, just suffices to cover the total costs of the inputs of y and z. Those who belong to the optimal coalition would not wish to have more members. The demands of the households excluded from $s(0)$ must remain content with membership in a nonoptimal coalition. The demand from households in this nonoptimal coalition, $t - s(0)$, could be satisfied only if they were numerous enough to support at least one producing entity. Households excluded from $s(0)$ would like to join it even if at higher prices for the x-commodities than those paid by the original members of $s(0)$. Although the original members may be tempted to accept these excluded households on these terms, it would destabilize the optimal coalition to admit them. This is just another way of describing an empty core.

Figure 34 illustrates the situation. The curve Q_0Q_3 shows the net gain for a coalition with one plant. The curve $Q_4Q_2Q_5$ shows their net gain with two plants ($\mu = 2$). The optimal coalition maximizes the gain per member. Because the ray OP_2 is above the ray OP_1, the optimal coalition in figure 34 would have two plants if t were big enough. The point Q_4 is where it would be best for the coalition t to switch from one to two plants. The optimal coalition for one plant is at the tangency Q_1. With two plants the gain per member is a maximum where the ray OP_2 is tangent to the arc $Q_4Q_2Q_5$. This is at the point Q_2 so the optimal coalition with two plants corresponds to Q_2. The core is empty for all t in the interval S_1 to S_2. Note that S_2 lies to the right of the point where it would be best to add a plant and that it corresponds to the point R where the ray OP_1 intersects the arc for two plants. The core is not empty in the interval S_2S_3. Accord-

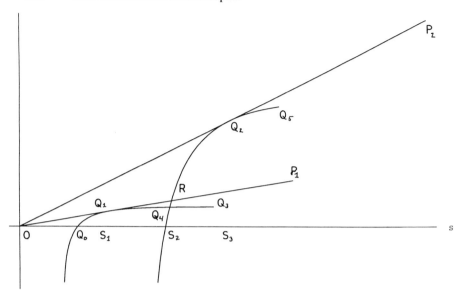

Fig. 34. Cost function for the best coalition

ing to the preceding analysis, the optimal coalition S_1 would not admit more members until t becomes so big it lies to the right of S_3.

This theory can explain several commonly observed phenomena. Optimal coalitions set prices equal to marginal cost and produce outputs that satisfy the demands of their members at these prices. Those who are outside the optimal coalitions can satisfy their demands, if at all, from smaller and higher cost firms. The members of the optimal coalition may correspond to regular customers who have long-term contracts with their suppliers, would be vertically integrated with their suppliers, or would have similar relations with their suppliers. When total demand becomes big enough as measured by the size of t, the optimal coalition is willing to admit more members. It would increase the number of facilities that make the three kinds of commodities, represented by the vectors x, y, and z. However, the response to bigger demand is discontinuous. Outputs go up only when the accumulated increment of demand is big enough.

This description of an optimal coalition seems to resemble a keiretsu of Japanese companies. Some upstream companies in a keiretsu make commodities they sell as inputs to downstream members. The members of a keiretsu are not legally integrated under a single control, but they do have implicit long-term relations with each other (Peck 1988). According to Badaracco (1988):

> In Japan, in fact, the blurring of corporate boundaries has reached its most ornate, almost rococo elaboration. Roughly a quarter of all Japanese

industrial assets belong to firms that are members of economic groups called keiretsu, the offspring of zaibatsu, the giant concerns that dominated the Japanese economy until after World War II. Each keiretsu comprises dozens of member firms—the largest, Mitsubishi, has 101—and each member may itself have hundreds of affiliates, which it may own completely or in part. Some affiliates make and sell the same products as others; some supply others with raw materials; some are sales companies that handle other affiliates' products. These firms may have joint ventures with each other; their boards of directors may interlock; their presidents meet regularly with each other in times of difficulty, they may aid each other through favorable credit terms or purchasing decisions. (70)

5. The Motion Picture Industry; An Application of the Model

The motion picture industry[1] illustrates optimal coalitions in the form of vertical integration between the producers and the exhibitors of films. Many details about this industry have become available thanks to the numerous antitrust suits and the investigations of its practices. TNEC Monograph 43 (Bertrand et al. 1941) is especially helpful owing to its useful and concise summary of some pertinent material.

The industry began around 1900, and movies rapidly became a popular form of entertainment. By 1914, when the first theater that specialized in exhibiting movies opened for business on Broadway, the producers and exhibitors of motion picture films had invented or found many of the business practices that could solve their peculiar problems. Many of these derive from a single basic fact. The popularity and profitability of motion pictures are highly unpredictable. Although a more costly film, one with a script written by better and presumably more expensive authors, more popular and thereby more highly paid actors, more lavish scenery, more intricate special effects, and more promotional outlays, is expected to garner a bigger audience and more revenue, experience demonstrates that the results are seldom close to the predictions. Film producers must incur the expense for all of these inputs well before any revenue flows into their coffers. If exhibitors wait to see which films are successful before deciding what to show in their theaters, then this would shift all the risk onto the producers. On the other hand, the producers might refuse to offer films to exhibitors on a spot basis and rely instead on longer-term contracts. In

---

1. For different views of the practices of this industry based on versions of discriminating monopoly, see Stigler 1963 and Kenney and Klein 1983. De Vany and Eckert (1991) give a useful survey with an extensive bibliography. Their emphasis on the effects of uncertainty and risk on the practices of the industry makes their analysis and conclusions congenial to mine. For a recent analysis emphasizing the effects of uncertainty on the industry see De Vany and Walls 1996.

this fashion exhibitors and producers would share the risks of their business. Initially, producers sold prints of films to the exhibitors, who consequently owned the films that were shown in their theaters. This method was no solution of the industry problems because it shifted them from the producers to the exhibitors, who had no better ways of solving them than did the producers themselves. Producers soon changed from outright sale to rental of the films. This allowed a producer to retain property rights in the films and control the terms and conditions under which exhibitors could show the films to the public. Longer-term arrangements between producers and exhibitors replaced spot transactions. The following description of industry practices applies to the period from 1920 to 1940. On the latter date the leading film producers accepted the government's terms of a consent decree.

By 1920, arrangements between producers and distributors had taken on the characteristic aspects that subsequently led to the antitrust complaints against the industry. The top 8 studios, 5 major firms, and 3 somewhat smaller companies each produced about 50 films per year. These were shown in movie theaters throughout the United States as well as in many foreign markets. By 1940 there were 17,000 theaters of which more than 2,800, owned or controlled by the major firms, had about 25 percent of the seating capacity and were situated in the largest cities. These theaters showed the feature films of the eight leading firms in the industry who controlled 80 percent of all first-run theaters in the largest metropolitan centers. Since the first-run theaters showed only one feature film, unlike the lower ranked theaters that showed two or even three films for the price of one admission, the annual output of a studio could satisfy the demand of a first-run theater affiliate that showed about one film per week. This means there was almost complete vertical integration in the biggest markets. From 1935 to 1940, about 70 percent of the total industry rental receipts went to the 5 major film producers, the next 3 producers got about 25 percent of the total, and the numerous remaining independent producers received about 5 percent. Since the top 8 producers made only about 60 percent of all the feature films, their films must have been the more popular and probably the more costly ones. Theaters were put into different classes from the first-run theaters on down. "Zoning" and "clearance" describes how a producer decides where and when to show a film. On a given date new films were shown in first-run theaters in central locations of the biggest cities. This is zoning. After the films appeared in the first-run theaters there was a delay, called clearance, before these films were allowed to appear in the second-run theaters. The first-run theaters showed the newest films, charged the highest admission prices, were the largest, most elaborate, and best situated outlets in the biggest cities. Most of these were either owned or controlled by a major studio. Eventually, depending on their popularity, all feature films were shown everywhere down to the smallest rural establishment. The later the run of the film, the lower was the minimum admission price. The longer the clearance, the higher were the minimum admission prices at the earlier run theaters.

Given how long a feature film ran and given that most non–first-run theaters showed at least two feature films, most theaters had to obtain films from more than one studio either directly or indirectly. At the beginning of each season studios offered nonaffiliated exhibitors a package of films at a price per film proportional to the exhibitors' gross box office receipts, a practice known as "block-booking." Films in the package were sorted into groups by grade, A, B, C, and so on. Grades did not measure artistic or aesthetic quality. The higher grades were for the films more costly to produce. The grades were supposed to measure expected receipts on the assumption that the more costly a film, the bigger are its expected box office receipts. The oldest films going to the smallest theaters were available for a lump sum payment per film. Because exhibitors did not see the films in advance, this arrangement became known as "blind selling." It should not escape attention that producers were also in the dark because they did not know in advance what films they would make. Their knowledge was often limited to the type of film, who would direct, write, and act in it, and how much would be spent promoting it. Producers might not even know the plot or title of the film. Therefore, neither the seller nor the buyer of the package knew in detail its contents. Producers set minimum ticket prices. They did so because movie theaters also sold soft drinks, candy, popcorn, and other items. Without a minimum ticket price, theater owners could charge a low admission price and set higher prices on these complementary products, thereby reducing the amount they paid to producers for the rental of their films. Producers took other precautions. Tickets were numbered, and producers could audit the box office receipts of the exhibitors. Studios hired inspectors who cruised the streets in the larger cities watching movie theaters to ensure that none was showing a film in ways that violated the arrangements with the studio. They also were on guard for theaters that had obtained films from a source other than one approved by the studio.

Revenue per film is like a random variable. If revenues per film were mutually independent identically distributed random variables then the expected return from a bundle of films would correspond to the mean of a random sample of independent random drawings from a population multiplied by the sample size. The standard deviation of the mean receipts would vary inversely with the square root of the sample size so the standard deviation of the sum would vary directly with the square root of the sample size. Therefore, the coefficient of variation of the expected receipts, namely, the ratio of the standard deviation to the expected total receipts, would vary inversely with the square root of the number of films. It follows that the film producers would have a profit incentive to put into a single package a sufficiently large number of films for which the returns would be independently distributed in order to derive benefits from this source of scale economies. Including films for which the revenues are likely to be negatively correlated would yield even more economies of scale. For instance, romance films and action westerns might be types with a negative correlation. At the extreme, if the correlation between pairs of films in a package of n films were $-1/(n-1)$, the standard deviation of the mean revenue per film would be zero and there would be no risk either to producer or to exhibitor, who could agree on terms for the whole package. It is likely that the cost to the producer is an increasing function of the variability of revenue. The producer must make commitments in advance while the film is in production. The more variable the receipts, the bigger are the reserves it is prudent for the producer to have in order to satisfy prior financial obligations. The larger the reserves, the higher are the costs to the producer. It is a consequence of the law of large numbers that the production of feature films is subject to economies of scale. This explains why a studio can offer a block of films on more favorable terms, the bigger is the number of films in the block. The optimal total number of feature films for a major studio also depends on vertical integration between the first-run theaters and the studio. Because first-run theaters show only one feature film at a time, depending on the average length of run for a feature film, a major producer would aim at supplying the first-run affiliated theater with a one year supply of these films. This explains the total number of films produced annually by major studios. The lower rung movie theaters need more films than any single studio can supply. In order to ensure an adequate number, these theaters must obtain films from several sources, not only from the top 8 studios but also from some of the smaller independent ones.

This argument claims that vertical integration in the motion picture industry between film studios and their affiliated first-run theaters may constitute an optimal coalition. It raises the question of whether prices of the commodities equal their marginal costs. Even more basic is how to define a commodity for this industry. Say it is the viewing of a feature film by one person. What is the marginal cost? In some sense it may seem that the marginal cost is virtually zero because the theater is there, it is open for business, an empty seat is available, ushers stand ready, the projection camera is running attended by a projectionist, the film print is available, and the planning, filming, and publicizing of the film by the studio all lie in the past. Stepping back and seeing all the things that had to be done to enable someone to see the movie, then, independently of whether or not that person does see it, apparently the marginal cost of an individual viewing is nearly zero. Moreover, everyone in the theater who sees the film obtains the same "quantity," so that with respect to the members of the audience, the movie is a semiprivate commodity, ignoring how the location of the viewer's seat may affect the quantity. For semiprivate commodities the optimal quantity is where a certain weighted sum of the marginal valuations equals the marginal cost. Although the ticket price is positive so it exceeds this narrow measure of marginal cost, of course it does not follow that the theory is wrong. Not only are movies a semiprivate good to the members of the theater audience but also in a more important sense the marginal cost is positive because it equals the incremental cost of all the inputs that were used to bring the film before the audience. At a price equal to marginal cost that covers the total industry cost, the theory of optimal coalitions says that firms in the industry would obtain a competitive return. Whether this is true, taking into account both the effects of the Great Depression and the effects on profits of a highly successful innovation, the motion picture industry, has yet to be demonstrated.

It is plausible to conclude that vertical integration between major film producers and most of the first-run theaters constitutes an optimal coalition as described in the preceding sections.

References

Aivazian, V. A., and J. L. Callen. 1981. The Coase Theorem and the Empty Core. *Journal of Law and Economics* 24 (April): 175–81.

Apostol, Tom M. 1957. *Mathematical Analysis.* Reading, MA: Addison-Wesley.

Arrow, Kenneth J. 1962. Optimal Capital Adjustment. In *Studies in Probability and Management Science,* edited by K. J. Arrow, S. Karlin, and H. Scarf, 1–17. Stanford, CA: Stanford University Press.

———. 1985. The Economics of Agency. In *Principals and Agents: The Structure of Business,* edited by John W. Pratt and Richard J. Zeckhauser. Boston, MA: Harvard Business School Press.

Atkinson, Thomas R. 1956. *The Pattern of Financial Asset Ownership: Wisconsin Individuals, 1949.* Princeton, NJ: Princeton University Press.

Aumann, Robert. 1964. Markets with a Continuum of Traders. *Econometrica* 32 (January–April): 39–50.

———. 1966. Existence of Competitive Equilibria in Markets with a Continuum of Traders. *Econometrica* 34 (January): 1–17.

———. 1989. *Lectures on Game Theory.* Boulder, CO: Westview Press.

Axelrod, Robert. 1984. *The Evolution of Cooperation.* New York: Basic Books.

Babbage, Charles. [1835] 1971. *On the Economy of Machinery and Manufactures.* Reprint, New York: Augustus M. Kelley.

Badaracco, Joseph L. Jr. 1988. Changing Forms of the Corporation. In *The U.S. Business Corporation: An Institution in Transition,* edited by John K. Meyer and James F. Gustafson. Cambridge, MA: Balinger Publishing.

Barro, Robert J. 1989. The Stock Market and the Macroeconomy: Implications of the October 1987 Crash. In *Black Monday and the Future of Financial Markets,* edited by Robert W. Kamphuis Jr., Roger C. Kormendi, and J. W. Henry Watson. Homewood, IL: Dow Jones-Irwin.

Bertrand, Daniel, W. Duane Evans, and E. L. Blanchard. 1941. *The Motion Picture Industry—A Pattern of Control.* U.S. Temporary National Economic Committee Monograph No. 43. Washington, DC: U.S. Government Printing Office.

Blume, Marshall E., Jean Crockett, and Irwin Friend. 1974. Stock Ownership in the United States: Characteristics and Trends. *Survey of Current Business* 54 (November): 16–40.

Board of Governors. 1943. *Banking and Monetary Statistics.* Washington, DC: Federal Reserve System.

Böhm-Bawerk, Eugene von. [1891] 1930. *The Positive Theory of Capital.* Translated by William A. Smart. New York: Stechert.

Bondareva, O. N. 1963. Some Applications of Linear Programming Methods to the Theory of Cooperative Games (in Russian). *Problemy Kibernetiki* 10:119–39.

Bradley, Michael, Anand Desai, and E. Han Kim. 1988. Synergistic Gains from Corporate Acquisitions and their Division between the Stockholders of Acquiring and Target Corporations. *Journal of Financial Economics* 21 (May): 3–40.

Coase, R. H. 1981. The Coase Theorem and the Empty Core. *Journal of Law and Economics* 24 (April): 183–87.

———. 1988. *The Firm, the Market and the Law.* Chicago: University of Chicago Press.

Cohn, Richard A., Wilbur G. Lewellen, Ronald C. Lease, and Gary G. Schlarbaum. 1975. Individual Investor Risk Aversion and Investment Portfolio Composition. *Journal of Finance* 30:605–20.

Collett, D., and G. K. Yarrow. 1976. The Size Distribution of Large Shareholdings in Some Leading British Companies. *Oxford Bulletin of Economics and Statistics* 38: (November): 249–64.

Crockett, Jean, and Irwin Friend. 1963. Characteristics of Stock Ownership. *Proceedings of the Business and Economics Section.* Washington, DC: American Statistical Association.

De Vany, Arthur, and Ross D. Eckert. 1991. Motion Picture Antitrust: The Paramount Cases Revisited. *Research in Law and Economics* 14:51–112.

De Vany, Arthur, and W. David Walls. 1996. Bose-Einstein Statistics and Adaptive Contracting in the Motion Picture Industry. *Economic Journal* 106 (November): 1493–1514.

Debreu, Gerard, and Israel N. Herstein. 1953. Nonnegative Square Matrices. *Econometrica* 21:597–607.

Debreu, G., and H. Scarf. 1963. A Limit Theorem on the Core of an Economy. *International Economic Review* 4:235–46.

Demsetz, Harold, and Kenneth Lehn. 1985. The Structure of Corporate Ownership: Causes and Consequences. *Journal of Political Economy* 93 (December): 1155–77.

Edgeworth, F. Y. 1881. *Mathematical Psychics.* London: C. Kegan Paul.

Federal Reserve Board. 1966. *Banking and Monetary Statistics.* Washington, DC: U.S. Government Printing Office.

Feller, William. 1966. *An Introduction to Probability Theory and Its Applications.* 2d ed. Vol. 2. New York: John Wiley.

Goldsmith, Raymond, and Rexford C. Parmelee. 1940. *The Distribution of Ownership in the 200 Largest Nonfinancial Corporations.* U.S. Temporary National Economic Committee. Monograph No. 29. Washington, DC: U.S. Government Printing Office.

Granby, Helen. 1941. *Survey of Shareholdings in 1,710 Corporations with Securities Listed on a National Securities Exchange.* U.S. Temporary National Economic Committee. Monograph No. 30. Washington, DC: U.S. Government Printing Office.

Graves, Lawrence M. 1946. *The Theory of Functions of a Real Variable.* New York: McGraw-Hill.

Grunfeld, Yehuda. 1960. The Determinants of Corporate Investments. In *Demand for Durable Goods,* edited by Arnold C. Harberger. Chicago: University of Chicago Press.

Hardy, G. H., Littlewood, J. E., and Polya, G. 1959. *Inequalities.* 2d ed. Cambridge: Cambridge University Press.

Hildenbrand, Werner. 1974. *Core and Equilibria of a Large Economy.* Princeton, NJ: Princeton University Press.

———. 1994. *Market Demand.* Princeton, NJ: Princeton University Press.

Holmstrom, B. 1979. Moral Hazard and Observability. *Bell Journal of Economics* 10 (spring): 74–91.

———. 1982. Moral Hazard in Teams. *Bell Journal of Economics* 13 (autumn): 324–40.

Hume, David. [1752] 1955. *Writings on Economics.* Edited by Eugene Rotwein. London: Nelson.

Kenney, Roy, and Benjamin Klein. 1983. The Economics of Block Booking. *Journal of Law and Economics* 26 (October): 497–540.

Knight, Frank H. [1921] 1933. *Risk, Uncertainty and Profit.* No. 16. Reprints of Scarce Tracts in Economics and Political Science. By the London School of Economics. Reprint, Boston: Houghton Mifflin Co.

———. 1956. The Common Sense of Political Economy (Wickstead Reprinted). In *On the History and Method of Economics* (Chicago: University of Chicago Press). First published in *Journal of Political Economy* 43 (1934): 660–73.

Lampman, Robert J. 1962. *The Share of Top Wealth-Holders in National Wealth, 1922–1956.* Princeton, NJ: Princeton University Press.

Lazear, Edward P., and Sherwin Rosen. 1981. Rank-Order Tournaments as Optimum Labor Contracts. *Journal of Political Economy* 89 (October): 841–64.

Lease, Ronald C., Wilbur G. Lewellen, and Gary G. Schlarbaum. 1974. The Individual Investor: Attributes and Attitudes. *Journal of Finance* 29 (May): 413–33.

Lewellen, Wilbur G., Ronald C. Lease, and Gary G. Schlarbaum. 1977. Patterns of Investment Strategy and Behavior among Individual Investors. *Journal of Business* 50 (July): 296–333.

Mas-Colell, Andreu. 1985. *The Theory of General Equilibrium: A Differentiable Approach.* Cambridge: Cambridge University Press.

Matsumoto, Koji. 1995. *The Rise of the Japanese Corporate System.* Translated by Thomas J. Elliott. New York: Columbia University Press.

Menger, Carl. [1871] 1994. *Principles of Economics.* Translated from German by James Dingwall and Bert F. Hoselitz. Grove City, PA: Libertarian Press.

Mirrlees, James A. 1976. The Optimal Structure of Incentives and Authority within an Organization. *Bell Journal of Economics* 7 (spring): 105–31.

Mises, Ludwig von. [1924] 1981. *The Theory of Money and Credit.* Translated by H. E. Batson in 1934 with additions by the author to English edition in 1953. Reprint, Indianapolis: Liberty Classics.

Modigliani, Franco M., and Merton H. Miller. 1958. The Cost of Capital, Corporation Finance and the Theory of Investment. *American Economic Review* 48 (June): 261–97.

Negishi, Takashi. 1985. *Economic Theories in a Non-Walrasian Tradition.* Cambridge: Cambridge University Press.

Neumann, John von, and Oskar Morgenstern. 1947. *Theory of Games and Economic Behavior.* 2d ed. Princeton, NJ: Princeton University Press.

Peck, Merton J. 1988. The Large Japanese Corporation. In *The U.S. Business Corpora-*

tion: An Institution in Transition, edited by John K. Meyer and James F. Gustafson. Cambridge, MA: Balinger Publishing.

Pirrong, S. C. 1992. An Application of Core Theory to the Analysis of Ocean Shipping Markets. *Journal of Law and Economics* 35 (April): 89–131.

Projector, Dorothy S., and Gertrude W. Weiss. 1966. Survey of Financial Characteristics of Consumers. *Federal Reserve Technical Papers.* Washington, DC: Board of Governors of the Federal Reserve System.

Rhodes, Richard. 1986. *The Making of the Atomic Bomb.* New York: Simon and Schuster.

Sargent, Thomas J. 1979. *Macroeconomic Theory.* Orlando, FL: Academic Press.

Savage, Leonard J. 1954. *The Foundations of Statistics.* New York: John Wiley.

Scarf, H. 1962. An Analysis of Markets with a Large Number of Participants. In *Recent Advances in Game Theory,* 127–55. Princeton, NJ: Princeton University Conference (private printing for members of the conference).

———. 1973. *The Computation of Economic Equilibria.* New Haven, CT: Yale University Press.

———. 1986. Notes on the Core of a Production Economy. In *Contributions to Mathematical Economics in Honor of Gerard Debreu,* edited by Werner Hildenbrand and Andreu Mas-Colell. Amsterdam: North-Holland.

Scarf, H., and G. Debreu. 1963. A Limit Theorem on the Core of an Economy. *International Economic Review* 4 (September): 235–46.

Scarf, H., and Lloyd Shapley. 1974. On Cores and Indivisibility. In *Studies in Optimization,* edited by G. B. Dantzig and B. C. Eaves. Vol. 10. Mathematical Association of America.

Schlarbaum, Gary G., Wilbur G. Lewellen, and Ronald C. Lease. 1976. Market Segmentation: Evidence on the Individual Investor. *Financial Analysts Journal* 32 (September–October): 53–60.

———. 1978. Realized Returns on Common Stock Investments: The Experience of Individual Investors. *Journal of Business* 51 (April): 299–325.

Shapley, Lloyd S. 1971. Cores of Convex Games. *International Journal of Game Theory* 1:12–26.

Sharkey, William W., and Telser, Lester G. 1978. Supportable Cost Functions for the Multiproduct Firm. *Journal of Economic Theory* 18 (June): 23–37.

Sjostrom, W. 1989. Collusion in Ocean Shipping. *Journal of Political Economy.* 97 (October): 1160–79.

Smith, Adam. [1776] 1981. *An Inquiry into the Nature and Causes of the Wealth of Nations.* Reprint, Indianapolis: Liberty Classics.

Smith, James D., and Stephen D. Franklin. 1974. The Concentration of Personal Wealth, 1922–1969. *American Economic Review* 64 (May): 162–67.

Stigler, George J. 1939. Production and Distribution in the Short Run. *Journal of Political Economy* 47 (June): 305–27.

———. 1963. United States v. Leow's, Inc.: A Note on Block Booking. In *Supreme Court Review,* edited by Philip B. Kurland. Chicago: University of Chicago Press.

———. [1951] 1968. The Division of Labor Is Limited by the Extent of the Market. In *The Organization of Industry* (Homewood, IL: Richard D. Irwin). First published in *Journal of Political Economy* 59 (June 1951): 305–27.

Stiglitz, Joseph E. 1974. On the Irrelevance of Corporate Financial Policy. *American Economic Review* 64 (December): 851–66.

Telser, Lester G. 1972. *Competition, Collusion and Game Theory.* Chicago: Aldine-Atherton.

———. 1978. *Economic Theory and the Core.* Chicago: University of Chicago Press.

———. 1980. A Theory of Self-Enforcing Agreements. *Journal of Business* 53 (January): 27–44.

———. 1987. *A Theory of Efficient Cooperation and Competition.* Cambridge: Cambridge University Press.

———. 1988. *Theories of Competition.* New York: North-Holland.

———. 1990. Why Should Manufacturers Want Fair Trade II? *Journal of Law and Economics* 33:409–17.

Telser, Lester G., and Robert L. Graves. 1972. *Functional Analysis in Mathematical Economics.* Chicago: University of Chicago Press.

Viner, Jacob. 1952. Cost Curves and Supply Curves. In *Readings in Price Theory,* edited by G. J. Stigler and K. Boulding American Economic Association Series of Reprinted Articles in Economics, vol. 6. (Chicago: Irwin). First published in *Zeitschrift fur Nationalökonomie* 3 (1931): 23–46.

White, Eugene N., ed. 1990. *Crashes and Panics: The Lessons from History.* Homewood, IL: Business One Irwin.

Name Index

Aivazian, V. A., 11n
Apostol, Tom M., 58, 90
Arrow, Kenneth J., 120, 194, 197n
Atkinson, Thomas R., 93–94
Aumann, Robert, 4n, 206n
Axelrod, Robert, 162

Babbage, Charles, 201
Badaracco, Joseph L., Jr., 260
Barro, Robert J., 85
Bertrand, Daniel, 261
Blanchard, Daniel, 261
Blume, Marshall E., 93
Böhm-Bawerk, Eugene von, 2n
Bondareva, O. N., 202
Bradley, Michael, 86

Callen, J. L., 11n
Coase, R. H., 11n
Cohn, Richard A., 93
Collet, D., 98
Crockett, Jean, 93

De Vany, Arthur, 261n
Debreu, Gerard, 4n, 30, 244
Demsetz, Harold, 98
Desai, Anand, 86

Eckert, Ross, 261n
Edgeworth, F. Y., 1, 103, 159
Evans, W. Duane, 261

Feller, William, 99
Franklin, Stephen D., 93
Friend, Irwin, 93

Goldsmith, Raymond, 98
Granby, Helen, 98
Graves, Lawrence M., 57, 58
Graves, Robert L., 120
Grunfeld, Yehuda, 85

Hardy, G. H., 221
Herstein, Israel N., 244
Hildenbrand, Werner, 4n, 23
Holmstrom, B., 189n
Hume, David, 41

Kenney, Roy, 261n
Kim, E. Han, 86
Klein, Benjamin, 261n
Knight, Frank H., 201

Lampman, Robert J., 93
Lazear, Edward P., 189n
Lease, Ronald C., 93
Lehn, Kenneth, 98
Lewellen, Wilbur G., 93
Littlewood, J. E., 221

Matsumoto, Koji, 155, 201n
Menger, Carl, 2n
Miller, Merton H., 125
Mirrlees, James A., 189n
Mises, Ludwig von, 44
Modigliani, Franco M., 125
Morgenstern, Oskar, 2n, 38, 106

Negishi, Takashi, 28
Neumann, John von, 2n, 38, 106

273

Parmelee, Rexford C., 98
Peck, Merton J., 155, 260
Pirrong, S. C., 10
Polya, G., 221
Projector, Dorothy S., 93–97

Rhodes, Richard, 187
Rosen, Sherwin, 189n

Sargent, Thomas J., 117
Savage, Leonard, 57
Scarf, Herbert, 4n, 23n, 30, 239, 240
Schlarbaum, Gary G., 93
Shapley, Lloyd, 30, 65–66
Sharkey, William W., 240
Sjostrom, W., 10

Smith, Adam, 201, 216
Smith, James D., 93
Stigler, George J., 201, 218, 261n
Stiglitz, Joseph E., 126n

Telser, Lester G., 4n, 7n, 8n, 23n, 36,
    36n, 67, 72, 105, 120, 175, 179, 239,
    240

Viner, Jacob, 8

Walls, W. David, 261n
Weiss, Gertrude W., 93–97
White, Eugene N., 154

Yarrow, G. K., 98

Subject Index